I0605551

The Periodic Table of Broadway Musicals

978-1-4549-5884-0

Union Square & Co. books may be purchased in bulk for business, educational, or promotional use. For more information, please contact your local bookseller or the Hachette Book Group's Special Markets department at special.markets@hbgusa.com.

Printed in China

APS

2 4 6 8 10 9 7 5 3

unionsquareandco.com

Cover and interior design by Erik Jacobsen
Illustrations by Tatiana Bischak and Nicholas Matej

The Periodic Table of
BROADWAY MUSICALS

AN ILLUSTRATED GUIDE TO 118 ESSENTIAL SHOWS

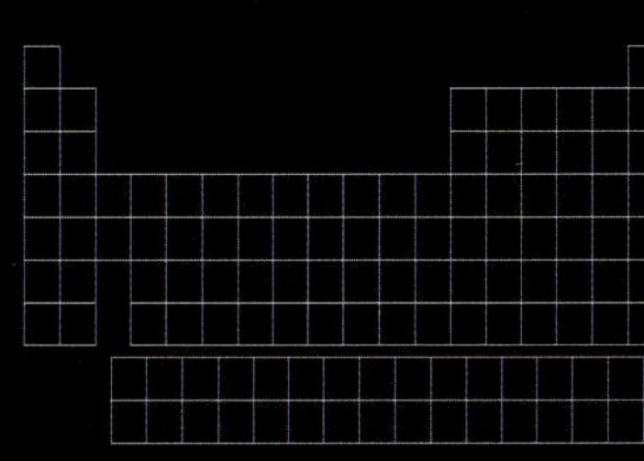

ANDREW GERLE & JOSEPH ZELLNIK

Illustrations by Tatiana Bischak & Nicholas Matej

Fela!
Bye Bye Birdie
Cats
Hairspray
Caroline, or Change
T | 2003
2534
Avenue Q
L
MPTR | 1975
6137
A Chorus Line
Ev
MT | 2016
1672
Dear Evan Hansen
My
MTR | 1956
2717
My Fair Lady
Ph
MT | 198
1398
The Phantom of the Opera
n
MR | 1946
1147
e Get Your Gun
Mu
MTR | 1957
1375
The Music Man
Hm
T | 2015
583
Fun Home
Ag
MR | 1934
420
Anything Goes
Si
MTR | 196
121
1776
z
MTR | 1987
6680
s Misérables
Td
MTR | 1979
557
Sweeney Todd
Bt
2014
2416
Beautiful
Fs
R | 1992
486
Falsettos
Lt
MTR | 197
60
A Little Night Musi
R | 1998
85
Parade
G
MR | 1959
702
Gypsy
Eh
2017
1669
Come From Away
Fd
MTR | 1964
3242
Fiddler on the Roof
Cz
T | 199
16
Crazy for You
d
R | 1963
330
Tm
R | 1993
899
Gr
MR | 1972
3388
Cd
R | 1956
73
R
MPT | 19
51

TABLE OF CONTENTS

INTRODUCTION AND KEY 6

The Classics ★ 12

The Hits ★ 28

The Broadway Operas ★ 42

The Canon ★ 56

Off-Broadway ★ 134

The Show Biz Series ★ 142

The Leading Ladies Series ★ 174

The Ensemble Pieces ★ 206

The Entertainers ★ 230

The True Stories ★ 246

The Groundbreakers ★ 260

ALPHABETICAL LIST OF SHOWS 276

INDEX 280

INTRODUCTION

You may be asking what the periodic table and Broadway musicals have to do with each other. It's a fair question, and the short answer is: *me*. Let me explain.

My love of musicals started at an early age, but when I was growing up in the 1980s, the Broadway musical was basically dead. There were a handful of megahits that sloshed their way across the Atlantic and ran for years (sometimes decades!), but that only made the sad state of Broadway even sadder—the quintessential American art form kept alive by *foreign imports*. For a while, Broadway was living up to the nickname "the fabulous invalid," in some seasons barely generating enough new musicals to fill out a Tony Award category.

So, if you were a fan, as I was, you looked backward to the Golden Age, listening to cast albums and learning the scores to the few dozen shows that made up the heart of the Broadway canon. You watched *The Sound of Music* on TV, your high school did *The Pajama Game* or *Man of La Mancha*, maybe your local community theatre got adventurous and put on a Sondheim show from the '70s. If you had a piano, you sang through musical theatre songbooks, learning the scores in your living room. By doing all this, you could get a fairly comprehensive overview of the most important shows, the songs that survived long after the final curtain of the show they originated in, and the recurring names of the major writers, directors, choreographers, and stars who made that prolific era so magical.

If you had told twelve-year-old me that the dawn of the 21st century would see Broadway roaring back to life, and that I would have a career writing musicals and teaching their craft in one of literally hundreds of flourishing undergraduate degree programs around the world, I would have said you were

as high as a flag on the Fourth of July. But to the delight of millions, that is exactly what has happened. The past two decades have seen a wide range of successful and hugely popular shows added to the Broadway canon, featuring a variety of musical and theatrical styles, from a diverse crop of writers, directors, and performers. And more shows come down the pike every year.

While all this new content is clearly a bonanza for current musical theatre fans, it does, however, make acquiring a comprehensive knowledge of the art form difficult to achieve. When I make a reference in one of my classes, I can see even die-hard young fans struggling to keep straight all the important shows, writers, and characters from nearly a century of Broadway history. I recently asked my students which show starred a character named Rosabella, and a hand quickly shot up: "*Cats*!" (If you don't get why that's funny, that's okay; by the end of this book, you will.)

At that moment, I thought, "There should be a simple resource somewhere with all the shows people ought to know," and I suspected I might be able to create one. I came up with an initial list, but it wasn't organized, and that bothered a little voice in my brain. Then I remembered that masterpiece of data organization, the periodic table of elements, from everyone's high school chemistry class. I looked it up to refresh my memory, and was once again impressed by its elegant structure: 118 elements, organized in an ascending numerical order, and grouped into 10 families. I realized I could use the same form to tame the sprawling list I had begun.

With that idea in place, I started compiling my list in earnest. At first, I worried I wouldn't be able to find enough shows of lasting importance to deserve being included, but that fear proved unfounded—instead, I had trouble *narrowing* the list to only 118 shows. In the end, I reached out to other Broadway professionals for their input and winnowed the list down to its final state.

With the addition of terrific, witty icon illustrations to each show's "tile" by artists Tatiana Bischak and Nicholas Matej, the finished poster launched in 2019. It turned out to be exactly the comprehensive overview of Broadway musicals that I'd hoped for, and happily, many theatre fans were excited enough by it to want to hang it on their walls (who knew so many people love both musicals and chemistry?).

This book provides a terrific opportunity to greatly expand on my original idea. Each show's entry begins with the wonderful artwork from the poster, now enlarged so you can enjoy all the details and hidden jokes. Next come the major credits—writers, directors, choreographers, and actors—plus a quick plot summary. After that comes the centerpiece, a mini article that explains the show's place in the Broadway canon, the reasons it was included on the poster in the first place. Best of all, and what makes this book unique among similar lists, the family structure illuminates connections between shows that opened years apart, spotlighting how certain themes and styles were interpreted by successive generations of musical theatre makers, and how the shows of one decade often influence and inspire the shows of the next.

Turning a poster with almost no text into a full-fledged book is no small thing. To pull it off, I've enlisted the help of my husband, Joseph Zellnik, who in addition to knowing more about musical theatre than anyone I know, is also a musical theatre composer and published author in his own right. Together, we've crafted each entry based on what we feel are that show's most important contributions—sometimes we focus on the score, the star, or the choreography; other times, it's the social impact the show had, or the theatrical innovations it introduced. We've also called out one of the show's song titles that we feel is particularly appropriate, and created a "Miscellaneous Matter" section for facts and historical tidbits too juicy to leave out.

I'm also extremely grateful to the theatre artists I've had the honor to work with over the years who shared with me personal stories and reflections from the shows they helped create. Huge thanks to Lynn Ahrens, Susan Birkenhead, Betty Buckley, Jeff Calhoun, John Carrafa, Kirsti Carnahan, Scott Frankel, Jordan Gelber, Jared Gertner, Randy Graff, Mark Hollmann, Tom Jones, Greg Kotis, Garth Kravits, Anika Larsen, Robert Lopez, Richard Maltby Jr., Howard McGillin, Brad Oscar, Lee Roy Reams, Michael Rupert, Rachel Sheinkin, and Maryrose Wood.

My hope is by the time you have perused these 118 entries, you will not only know your Rosabellas from your Grizabellas*, but you will have a deeper understanding of these essential shows and how they connect to one another. You'll understand the trends that have shaped the art form and

*Okay, I'll tell you now: Rosabella is the sublime leading lady of Frank Loesser's near-opera *The Most Happy Fella*; Grizabella is the glamour cat who sings the iconic "Memory" in *Cats*.

have a greater appreciation for the artists responsible both for Golden Age musicals and Broadway's present-day flourishing. And when you see a new show, or simply one that's new to you, you'll be able to see how it fits into the history of this extraordinary art form.

There's a lot of information crammed between these two covers, and no right or wrong way to enjoy it. Choose a show at random, read up on a whole family, or search the index for your favorite writers, directors, and performers; you're sure to find old friends and new connections. And when you're done, put on your favorite cast album and celebrate what makes musicals the beloved (and, yes, fabulous) works they are.

Enjoy!

ANDREW GERLE

KEY

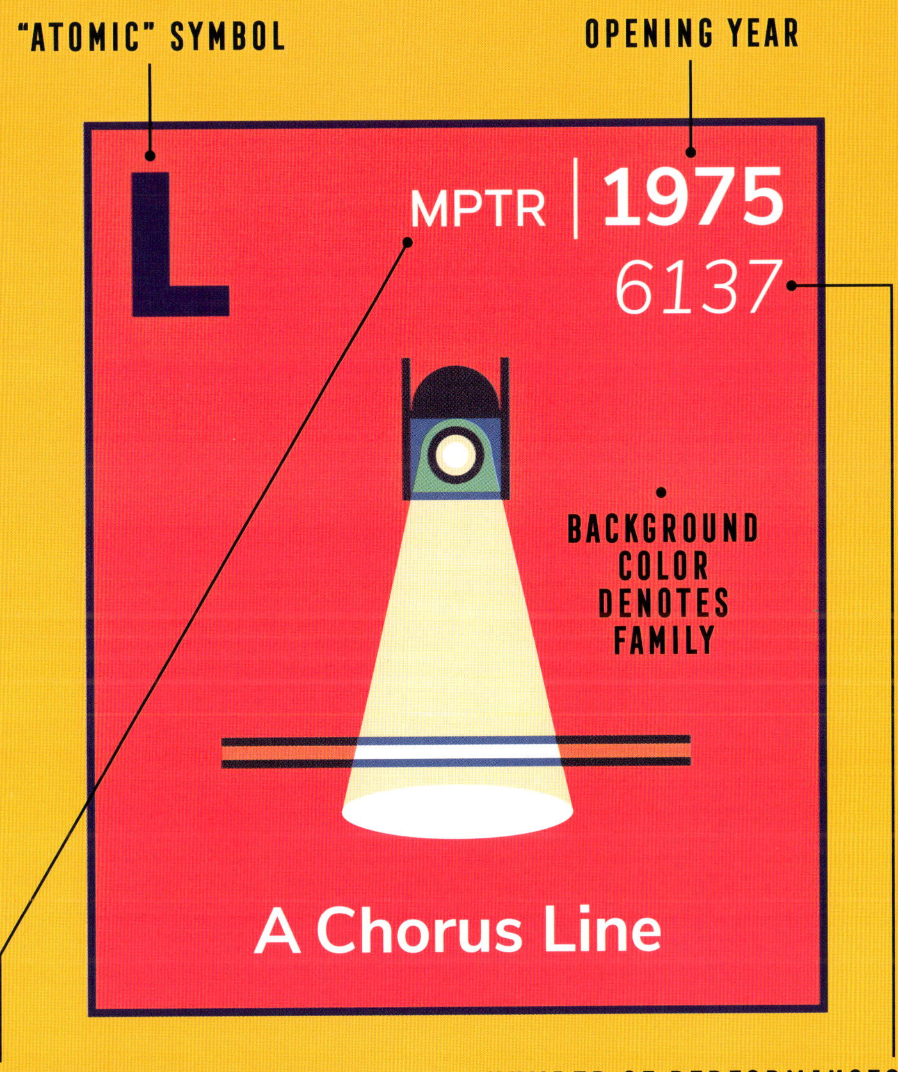

NOTABLE ACHIEVEMENTS

M: Adapted into a movie
P: Pulitzer Prize for Drama
T: Tony Award® for Best Musical
R: Has had a Broadway revival

NUMBER OF PERFORMANCES

An asterisk * denotes still running as of April 13, 2025

All data refer to the original Broadway production.

THE CLASSICS

ELEMENTAL BUILDING BLOCKS

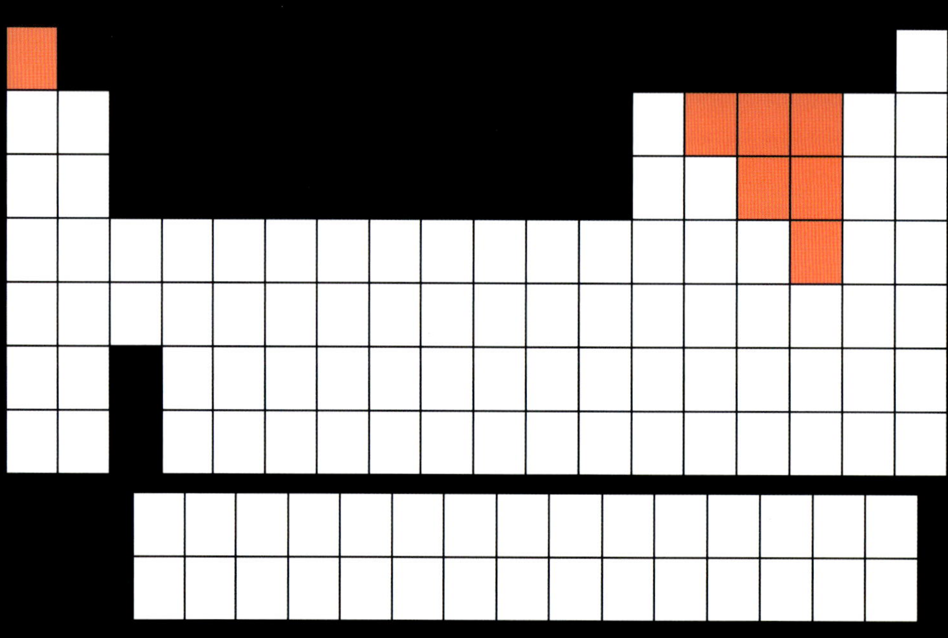

The most common question when people first hear about *The Periodic Table of Broadway Musicals* is "Which show is hydrogen?" For good reason—if nothing else, we all remember that hydrogen sits all by itself at the top of the table, given pride of place because it is the most basic element in the physical world (making up a whopping seventy-five percent of the *entire cosmos*!).

The answer to the question (drumroll, please) is the Ol' Man himself, *Show Boat,* from 1927. This was the show that taught audiences to expect more from musicals. It took bits and pieces from grand opera, operetta, musical comedy, and even vaudeville, and combined them into a fresh, new form that contained innovations that theatre creators would use for decades.

Just as hydrogen belongs to a family that contains five of the ten most common elements in the universe, the family headed by *Show Boat* includes some of the most frequently performed, and most emulated, musicals. The Classics represent the building blocks of the musical theatre as it evolved and matured over nearly a century, with a new one seeming to come along about once a decade. Hence, the *Oklahoma!* model that dominated in the 1940s—serious main plot and comic subplot, plus the use of extended ballets to further the story—eventually gives way to the biggest hit of the 1950s, *My Fair Lady*, with its subplot-free structure, more naturalistic song placement, and very little dance. *Cabaret* and *Hair* both broke new ground in the 1960s, the first using presentational songs as cultural commentary, the second bringing a rock sound into the theatre and essentially eliminating the need for plot altogether. The musical's evolution continues, as you'll read in the following pages.

Musical theatre survives because it constantly reinvents itself while maintaining the foundational elements that make it a captivating art form. It's notable that, in recent decades, even the Classics themselves have become subject to reinvention. The 2019 Broadway revival of *Oklahoma!* didn't change a word of the text, but drastically altered the tone, taking a hard look at the personal dynamics of the story and arranging the music for a greatly reduced country/bluegrass band. The 2023 revival of *Cabaret* was reworked to include an immersive-style preshow. What marks a true Classic is that it is rich enough to support and transcend reimaginings like these, while continuing to inspire new generations of audiences and writers alike.

Book and lyrics by Oscar Hammerstein II ★ Music by Jerome Kern
Based on the novel by Edna Ferber
Staged by Zeke Colvan and Oscar Hammerstein II

Ziegfeld Theatre, December 27, 1927–May 4, 1929

Helen Morgan.......Julie
Howard Marsh.......Gaylord Ravenal
Norma Terris.......Magnolia
Jules Bledsoe.......Joe

ART NOTE: The river boat *Cotton Blossom* sailing down the Mississippi, with an actual cotton blossom on her side.

The sprawling, episodic saga of the colorful characters tied to the floating theatre Cotton Blossom. *Starting in Natchez, Mississippi, in 1887 and ending in the Roaring '20s, the story follows their show business triumphs and personal hardships, including episodes of racial prejudice and revelations of personal secrets. A stormy romance between young Magnolia and a roving gambler named Gaylord leads first to heartbreak, then a heartfelt reunion 20 years later after their daughter has become a Broadway star.*

Ol' Man River

The first spot in the periodic table rightly belongs to *Show Boat,* widely considered the first work of modern musical theatre. Its use of songs to further the plot and illuminate character (rather than merely to entertain or savor a moment) were innovations that, like its Mississippi River setting, just keep rollin' along. But its biggest innovation was to expand what was possible in a "musical comedy" by tackling controversial societal and racial issues, with storylines that required a cast of Black and white actors to share the stage for the first time in Broadway history. Astonishingly, the producer with the courage to present this serious, ambitious work was none other than Florenz Ziegfeld Jr., who'd made his name and fortune presenting yearly *Follies*, lavish Parisian-style revues that showcased girls in extravagant costumes. Ziegfeld's history with the composer might have given him some courage: Kern's *Sally* had run for 570 performances and was one of the top moneymakers of the 1920s.

The breadth of the score's varied styles is dazzling. Lyrical love songs like "Make Believe" look backward to Kern's operetta history, but "Ol' Man River" is so convincing a spiritual that theatregoers then (and some today) thought it was an actual Black folk song. "Can't Help Lovin' Dat Man," used ingeniously in the story to reveal Julie's Black roots, has become a jazz standard. And interspersed throughout are numerous period-perfect comedy and charm songs, from show-within-a-show performance numbers to character-driven songs like Ellie's warning the Natchez fangirls against "Life Upon the Wicked Stage."

As might be expected, a show this old has had many incarnations as musical and dramatic tastes changed, all of them with different song lists. A 1936 movie remained mostly faithful to the original, even maintaining some original Broadway cast members and its music director, though Kern and Hammerstein did write some new numbers. A 1946 Kern biopic, *Till the Clouds Roll By,* included an extended medley from the show, featuring Black megastar Lena Horne as Julie. Sadly, the Technicolor MGM blockbuster version from 1951 cut much of the original's bold racial themes and uglier character complexities, even passing over Horne and casting a white movie star, Ava Gardner, as Julie. More recent productions, including Harold Prince's 1994 Broadway revival, have strived to address the show's powerful themes in ways that reflect America's changing understanding of its past.

MISCELLANEOUS MATTER

- ★ Hammerstein's uncle, Arthur, claimed he got the rights to produce the musical from his nephew; Ziegfeld said he had gotten them from Kern. A few weeks later, that claim was "amicably adjusted" and Ziegfeld retained the rights.
- ★ Helen Morgan was arrested twice during the first year of the production for singing in nightclubs serving alcohol. Though she denied any ownership, the second club was called "Helen Morgan's Summer Home."
- ★ Famed pilot Amelia Earhart attended a performance the night after her return from her first transatlantic flight on July 7, 1928.
- ★ Nearly two years into the run, Edna Ferber was denied admittance backstage, despite protesting that she was the author of the novel. She was required to get a pass from the company manager to enter.

Book and lyrics by Oscar Hammerstein II ★ Music by Richard Rodgers
Based on the play *Green Grow the Lilacs* by Lynn Riggs
Directed by Rouben Mamoulian ★ Choreographed by Agnes de Mille

St. James Theatre, March 31, 1943–May 29, 1948

Alfred Drake.......Curly
Joan Roberts.......Laurey
Celeste Holm.......Ado Annie
Howard Da Silva.......Jud Fry

ART NOTE: Stalks of "wavin' wheat" from the title song.

It's 1906 in the sunny Oklahoma Territory (soon to become the forty-sixth state). Stubborn cowboy Curly and spunky farm girl Laurey like each other, only neither wants to be the first to admit it. Meanwhile, Laurey's man-crazy friend Ado Annie somehow finds herself with two fiancés. Some narrative darkness is provided by Jud, a brooding farmhand whose thwarted love for Laurey leads to a dramatic climax, but this quickly gives way to a happy ending.

Many a New Day

Oklahoma! took the advances in integration of story, song, and dance pioneered in 1927's *Show Boat* even further (it's no accident both featured book and lyrics by Oscar Hammerstein II). It was a box office bonanza like nothing before it, running for a then-unprecedented five-plus years, and was hugely influential, laying the groundwork for what would become known as the Golden Age of musicals.

If some of *Show Boat*'s formal innovations were hidden under the familiar trappings of operetta, everything about *Oklahoma!* signaled its newness: instead of an opening scene-setting chorus number, a woman sat churning butter, and an offstage voice sang a lazy tune. Instead of an epic narrative covering four decades, action mostly centered on a single day. Instead of a dozen elaborate settings, there was simple, Folk Art–style scenery and a lot of similarly stylized, eye-searingly colorful costumes. And instead of weighty social issues, the plot mostly revolved around who will take a girl to a box social.

Everywhere that *Show Boat* was heavy, *Oklahoma!* was light. The original cast was young and sexy, bursting with energy and vitality as they leapt their way through Agnes de Mille's frisky dances—dances that drew on both classical and contemporary choreographic vocabularies. Audaciously, *Oklahoma!* even devoted the last fifteen minutes of the first act to a narrative ballet exploring Laurey's inner life. This innovation alone inspired a steady stream of "dream ballets" in Broadway musicals that stretched all the way to 1957's *West Side Story.*

What made *Oklahoma!* such a hit? Besides its freshness, it was the inherent and undeniable quality of every individual component: songs that immediately entered the hit parade, talented newcomers giving performances that would eventually become legendary, and a sensitive director who ensured all the elements of the show blended seamlessly. In *Oklahoma!*, as Rodgers put it, "the orchestrations sound the way the costumes look." (In this case, the lush, elegant orchestrations were by Robert Russell Bennett, who would go on to orchestrate nearly every subsequent Rodgers and Hammerstein show.) Another part was simply lucky timing. When the show opened, the United States had been in WWII for a little over a year, and immediately the show was hailed as the perfect example of what the country was fighting for: an energetic, forward-looking America where the power of community triumphs over outside threats.

MISCELLANEOUS MATTER

- ★ Even the writers didn't understand entirely what they'd created; Rodgers especially hated Mamoulian's naturalistic staging, with actors sometimes turning their backs to the audience. He thought Mamoulian was ruining his music and didn't invite him to the opening night party.
- ★ There was great skepticism about the show before it opened among Broadway professionals. Famously, when gossip columnist Walter Winchell sent his secretary Rose to report back on the show's first out-of-town preview, her telegram to him read, "NO LEGS NO JOKES NO CHANCE."
- ★ Set designer Lemuel Ayers went on to become a Broadway producer, most notably for *Kiss Me, Kate* (for which he also designed sets and costumes).

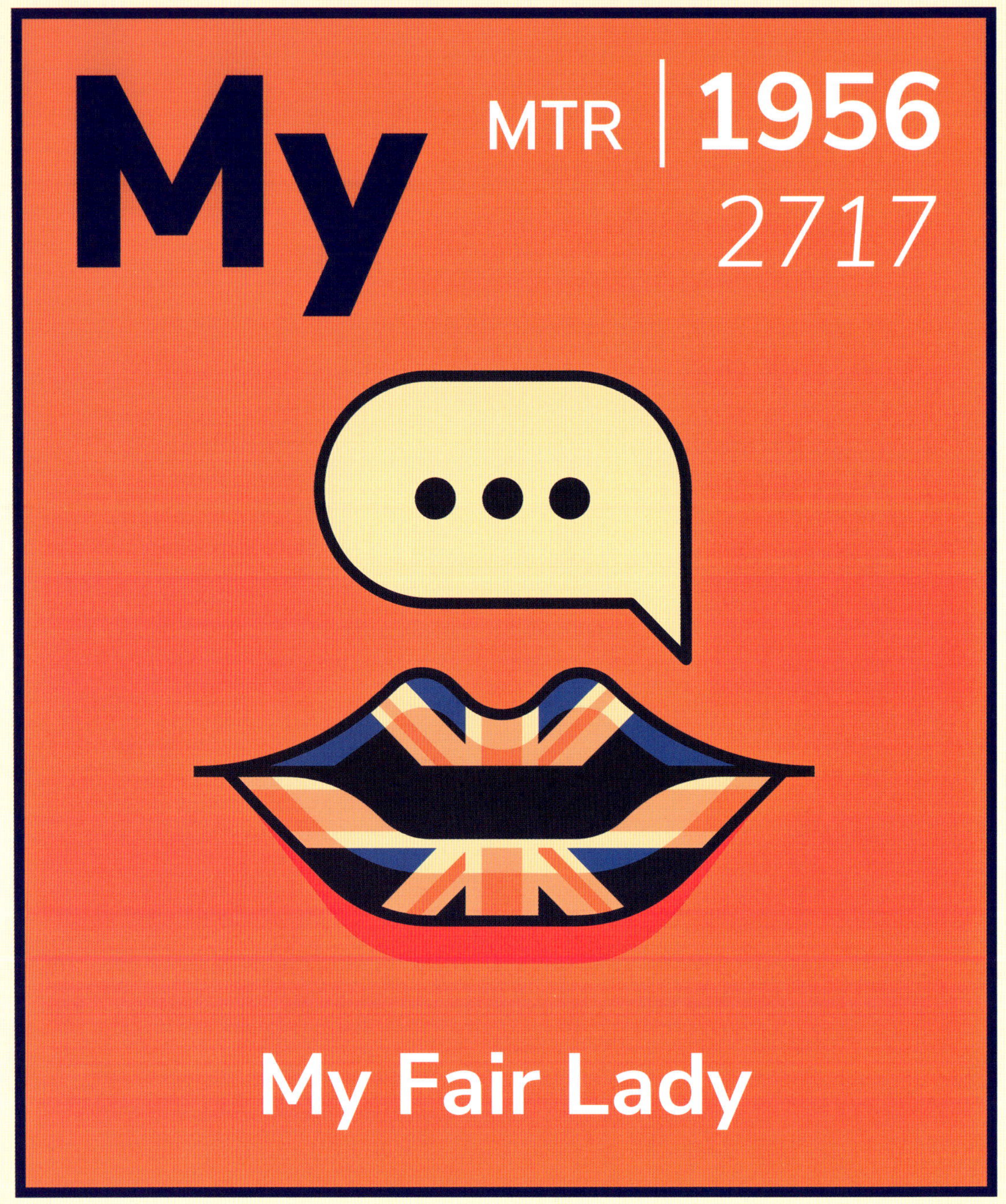

Book and lyrics by Alan Jay Lerner ★ Music by Frederick Loewe
Adapted from the play *Pygmalion* by George Bernard Shaw
Directed by Moss Hart

Mark Hellinger Theatre*, March 15, 1956–September 29, 1962

Julie Andrews.......Eliza Doolittle
Rex Harrison.......Henry Higgins
Robert Coote.......Colonel Pickering
Stanley Holloway.......Alfred P. Doolittle

ART NOTE: Eliza's mouth, made up with the British flag and starting to say something . . .

**First of three theatres*

Feeling that her lower-class Cockney accent is holding her back in life, London flower girl Eliza boldly approaches phonetics professor Henry Higgins for elocution lessons. Higgins turns her request into the subject of a wager with his friend Pickering: within six months he'll pass her off as an upper-class lady. Through (and despite) his condescending and abusive tutoring, she succeeds . . . and then leaves him, effectively schooling him in matters of the heart.

Wouldn't It Be Loverly?

British playwright, novelist, and critic George Bernard Shaw captured lightning in a bottle in his 1913 play *Pygmalion*, a mix of a classic Cinderella tale and the ancient Roman story of a sculptor who falls in love with one of his statues. Shaw went on to win an Academy Award for his 1938 screenplay adaptation, but a musical adaptation was not immediately in the cards. Rodgers and Hammerstein considered and rejected it as impossible to adapt. In the early '50s, Lerner and Loewe started work on it, but soon they, too, put it aside, finding no way to make up for its lack of a real love story, subplot, or opportunity for ensemble numbers. However, coming back to it a few years later, they finally realized that including events that happen offstage in the play, between the acts, could give the property the wings it needed and allow for the kind of spectacle audiences expected from a musical. Cecil Beaton's wildly inventive black-and-white costume designs for the Ascot races instantly became iconic; Oliver Smith's lavish sets required not one but two turntables and included five glittering chandeliers for the Embassy Ball. Lerner once wondered whether these were the real reason for the show's success.

Of course, he was jesting. The score was a treasure trove of inspired Loewe melodies—song after song became a hit, and the cast album was the best-selling record in the United States in 1956. In addition (rare for a musical but fitting for a story about language), the words are every bit the music's equal. Intelligent, fast-paced, witty, sometimes caustic, the virtuosity of the show's lyrics and book had audiences chuckling over potentially abstruse matters of English pronunciation (to give credit where it's due, many scenes come straight from Shaw). The chemistry between Julie Andrews and Rex Harrison must be given credit as well, though that took some time to jell. Just like her character, Eliza, Andrews underwent her own transformation at the hands of director Moss Hart, who, over the course of a weekend-long solo acting boot camp, honed her performance and gave the twenty-year-old the spine to stand up to the much older, more experienced, and sometimes badly behaved Harrison.

Though contemporary productions must find new ways to address Higgins's misogyny and cruelty to Eliza, the show's exceptional tunes and smart, smart words continue to win audiences' hearts.

MISCELLANEOUS MATTER

- ★ The play *Pygmalion* was first performed at the Hofburg Theatre in Vienna, Austria—in German!
- ★ Performing with an orchestra terrified Harrison; he became calmer only once the orchestration was reworked to include a clarinet doubling his melodies, to keep him from losing his place.
- ★ After the first preview, fifteen minutes were cut from the show's first act, including the songs "Come to the Ball," "Say A Prayer for Me Tonight" (later used in the film *Gigi*), and a ballet called "Decorating Eliza."

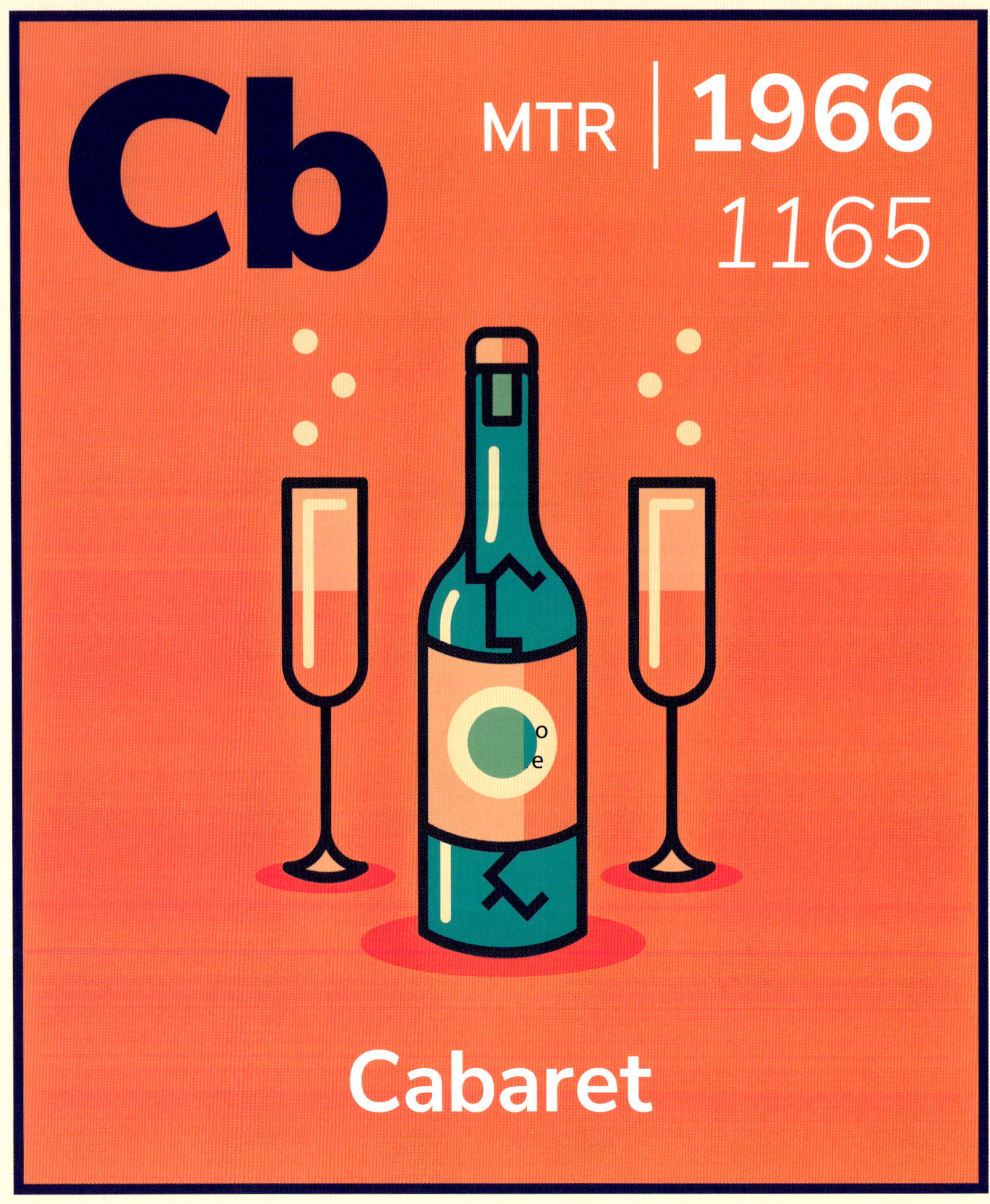

Book by Joe Masteroff ★ Lyrics by Fred Ebb ★ Music by John Kander
Based on the play *I Am a Camera* by John Van Druten
Based on stories by Christopher Isherwood
Directed by Harold Prince ★ Choreographed by Ronald Field

Broadhurst Theatre*, November 20, 1966–September 6, 1969

Joel Grey.......Master of Ceremonies
Jill Haworth.......Sally Bowles
Bert Convy.......Clifford Bradshaw
Lotte Lenya.......Fraulein Schneider

ART NOTE: Champagne flutes promise it's "time for a holiday," but the bottle is dangerously cracked.

*First of three theatres

In pre–WWII Berlin, American writer Cliff becomes the roommate (and soon, romantic partner) of Sally Bowles, an English singer at the bawdy Kit Kat Club. Performance numbers at the club, led by the sinister Emcee, echo a growing anti-Semitism in the city, and a romance between their landlady and a Jewish grocer brings this issue to the fore. Everyone must decide how much they can confront—or even acknowledge—the evil growing around them.

What Would You Do?

The play *I Am a Camera* provided some of the material for *Cabaret*, but the experience of watching the musical was more like looking into a not-so-funhouse mirror. In fact, designer Boris Aronson and director Harold Prince forced audiences to literally see themselves in the world of the show by hanging a giant mirror over the stage. During rehearsals, Prince made it clear to the company that the story, though set in the early years of Nazism, was meant to be a reflection on the growing civil unrest in America, where demonstrations and riots were becoming more frequent, and more violent.

Many of the songs, too, were distortions of what mid-century audiences expected—not sincere glimpses into a character's inner life, but twisted refrains of a morally adrift society desperate to entertain itself. Other musicals like *West Side Story, South Pacific,* and *Fiddler on the Roof* had dealt with societal issues of race and bigotry, but they did so from the inside, inviting us to empathize with naturalistically presented characters. *Cabaret* made it clear that we weren't meant to agree with or empathize with the denizens of the Kit Kat Club, we were meant to be appalled by them, and perhaps also by our own toes, tapping along involuntarily with the infectious tunes.

Audiences got the message, and the reactions were understandably mixed. The end of WWII was only just over twenty years in the past, and many New York theatregoers had actually survived the Holocaust or had family members who hadn't. For them, numbers like "If You Could See Her Through My Eyes," in which the Emcee goofily dances with a gorilla before finishing the title phrase with ". . . she wouldn't look Jewish at all," were simply too much to bear in a musical. (The line was eventually changed, but Joel Grey still whispered the original lyric at some performances, eliciting gasps.)

Grey himself was the unlikely meteor of the show. A friend of Prince's, he had been a successful nightclub singer but had only had a single one-week Broadway job in the past two and a half years. Given this chance, he made the most of it, turning a role with no dialogue into a grabbing, leering satyr, horrifying and thrilling in his clown-faced immorality. His characterization is even more remarkable considering his background: he is Jewish.

MISCELLANEOUS MATTER

★ Kander and Ebb initially hoped to have their friend Liza Minelli play Sally Bowles, but Harold Prince thought her too good a singer to be believable as the not-so-talented Sally. Famously, Minelli did play the role in the film adaptation, nabbing herself a Best Actress Oscar, too.

★ Isherwood's collection of stories was titled *Goodbye to Berlin*; Kander and Ebb's original title for the show was *Welcome to Berlin.* When a theatre party ticket seller told them her Jewish clients would never see a show with "Berlin" in the title, they took alphabetical inspiration from two recent hits, *Carnival* and *Camelot.*

★ The show originally was performed in three acts; when Prince (on mentor George Abbott's advice) told the writers it needed to be two, Ebb panicked that it would destroy the show.

Book and lyrics by Gerome Ragni and James Rado
Music by Galt MacDermot
Directed by Tom O'Horgan

Biltmore Theatre, April 29, 1968–July 1, 1972

James Rado.......Claude
Lynn Kellogg.......Sheila
Gerome Ragni.......Berger
Sally Eaton.......Jeanie

ART NOTE: The astrological symbol for Aquarius, plus the peace sign and three flower-power designs.

This celebration of late 1960s countercultural attitudes and movements features a "tribe" of performers who confront social, political, and cultural issues in songs, skits, visions, and LSD trips, centered loosely around Claude's decision whether or not to show up for induction when drafted for the Vietnam War.

Good Morning Starshine

The late 1960s, when *Hair* opened off-Broadway and then transferred to Broadway, were years of dramatic political and social changes in the United States. The Vietnam War was escalating, necessitating an increasingly unpopular draft, and the civil rights movement was gaining momentum, forcing the country to confront its legacy of racism. Countercultural musicians like The Who, the Grateful Dead, Jimi Hendrix, and Janis Joplin were making their first big impact on the American music scene, and 1967's Summer of Love and the Monterey Pop Festival drew hundreds of thousands to the San Francisco area to "turn on, tune in, and drop out." At the same time, hippies and other young people were increasingly exploring more open-minded and compassionate ways of coexisting and expanding their consciousness with the use of LSD and other psychedelic drugs.

Musical theatre had a lot of catching up to do. The public's idea of a successful Broadway show remained resolutely old-school: *Mame*, *Dolly*, and *Fiddler* were all still running strong, and 1968's Best Picture winner was the family-friendly *Oliver!* *Hair*'s combination of rock music with frank scenes and songs about free love and racial relations hit the stage like a tornado. Written by two actors, *Hair* was produced by Joseph Papp, who used the show to open his new off-Broadway Public Theater in the East Village and to pivot his Shakespeare company to the works of living authors. After a change of directors (O'Horgan had been unavailable for the off-Broadway run) and significant revisions to the score and storyline, *Hair* stormed Broadway, where it ran for years alongside its more traditional peers.

Critical reception was mixed. Was this the genuine expression of an urgent, youthful political movement, or a phony, crass exploitation of it? The public didn't care. For the first time, rock music was on a Broadway stage, and audiences around the world welcomed this "tribe" and its message with open arms. But its promise of ushering in a new era of rock musicals never really came to fruition. Some composers began to incorporate rock timbres and rhythms, but it wouldn't be until 1993's *The Who's Tommy* that rock purists would get to revel in this sound again. *Hair*'s loose, non-linear form would have more impact, with the 1970s becoming the decade of the "concept musical," where an overall theme, rather than a narrative, holds a show together.

MISCELLANEOUS MATTER

- ★ Oscar-winning actress Diane Keaton made her Broadway debut as Sheila; she refused to disrobe for the scene when much of the cast stands naked on stage. That nude scene, as well as ones depicting the desecration of the flag and the burning of draft cards, caused many tour stops to cancel performances.
- ★ In the original off-Broadway version, Claude was a space alien.
- ★ The song "Aquarius" reached number one on the Billboard Hot 100 and was inducted into the Grammy Hall of Fame in 2004. The "Age of Aquarius" refers to the current 2,150-year astrological era that most astrologers agree "dawned" in the 20th century.

Book by Claude-Michel Schönberg and Alain Boublil ★ Lyrics by Herbert Kretzmer
Music by Claude-Michel Schönberg ★ Based on the novel by Victor Hugo
Directed and adapted by Trevor Nunn and John Caird

Broadway Theatre and Imperial Theatre, March 12, 1987–May 18, 2003

Colm Wilkinson.......Jean Valjean
Terrence Mann.......Javert
Randy Graff.......Fantine
Frances Ruffelle.......Eponine

ART NOTE: The stolen loaf of bread that started it all.

A monumental tale centering on Jean Valjean, imprisoned for stealing a loaf of bread, and the ruthless police inspector Javert who vows to recapture him for breaking his parole. In his "second" life, Valjean turns over a new leaf, taking care of a young girl, Cosette, but Javert refuses to believe a criminal can change. As a student uprising tears Paris apart, both men meet their ends—Javert in a crisis of faith, Valjean at peace.

A Heart Full of Love

Although now virtually synonymous with "long-running megahit," *Les Misérables'* success took everyone by surprise. Initially a French concept album, staged in Paris for 100 performances, it was hard to envision how it could be put on stage anywhere other than in France, where the plot of the 1,200-page novel is so well-known that it could be told in shorthand, in a brisk two hours. Covering all that story for English audiences, however, required fleshing out the libretto and including a long prologue to explain character backstories. Even at its current length, the show remains a greatly condensed version of the novel, but it's still so long that the conductor must adhere to strict tempos throughout so as not to creep past three hours (when musicians' overtime pay kicks in).

When it finally did open in London, coproduced by British producer Cameron Mackintosh and the Royal Shakespeare Company, critics slammed the show as Victorian melodrama, with generic characters and overblown emotions. Even so, the day after opening, crowds were lining up to buy tickets. What was so irresistible about a sung-through 19th-century French epic set in the slums of Paris?

First came the richly melodic score, with numbers ranging from tender prayers to rousing battle cries to British music hall–style debauchery. The story, though lacking much of Hugo's nuance, still tugged at the heartstrings, with characters painted in the bold colors of Saint, Sinner, Oppressor, and Oppressed. And a civic uprising, though only vaguely sketched in (it's not the French Revolution, as many think), lent life-and-death stakes to a story of young love.

The other aspect of the show that audiences adore is the very thing that made it a challenge to condense: its massive scope. The size and gravitas of the story, combined with the literary source material, leaves audiences feeling they've experienced a rich banquet of Serious Art. And directors Trevor Nunn and John Caird smartly employed every theatrical device at their disposal, building on American theatrical innovations and adding cinematic lighting and staging effects of their own to create breathtaking stage images that quickly became the talk of the town. With the arrival of "*Les Miz*" in New York, America's long dominance of musical theatre was over, and the era of the "big sing" musicals had begun on Broadway, mostly imported from London.

MISCELLANEOUS MATTER

★ The iconic little girl on the poster is an etching of Cosette by Gustave Brion, based on an illustration by Émile Bayard for the very first edition of the book in 1862.

★ The show has been translated into over twenty languages, including Hungarian, Korean, and Catalan.

★ The role of Fantine was created in the West End production by Broadway diva Patti LuPone (the only American in the principal cast), yet when the show moved to New York, she chose not to remain with it. Two British cast members, Colm Wilkinson and Frances Ruffelle, did make the transfer.

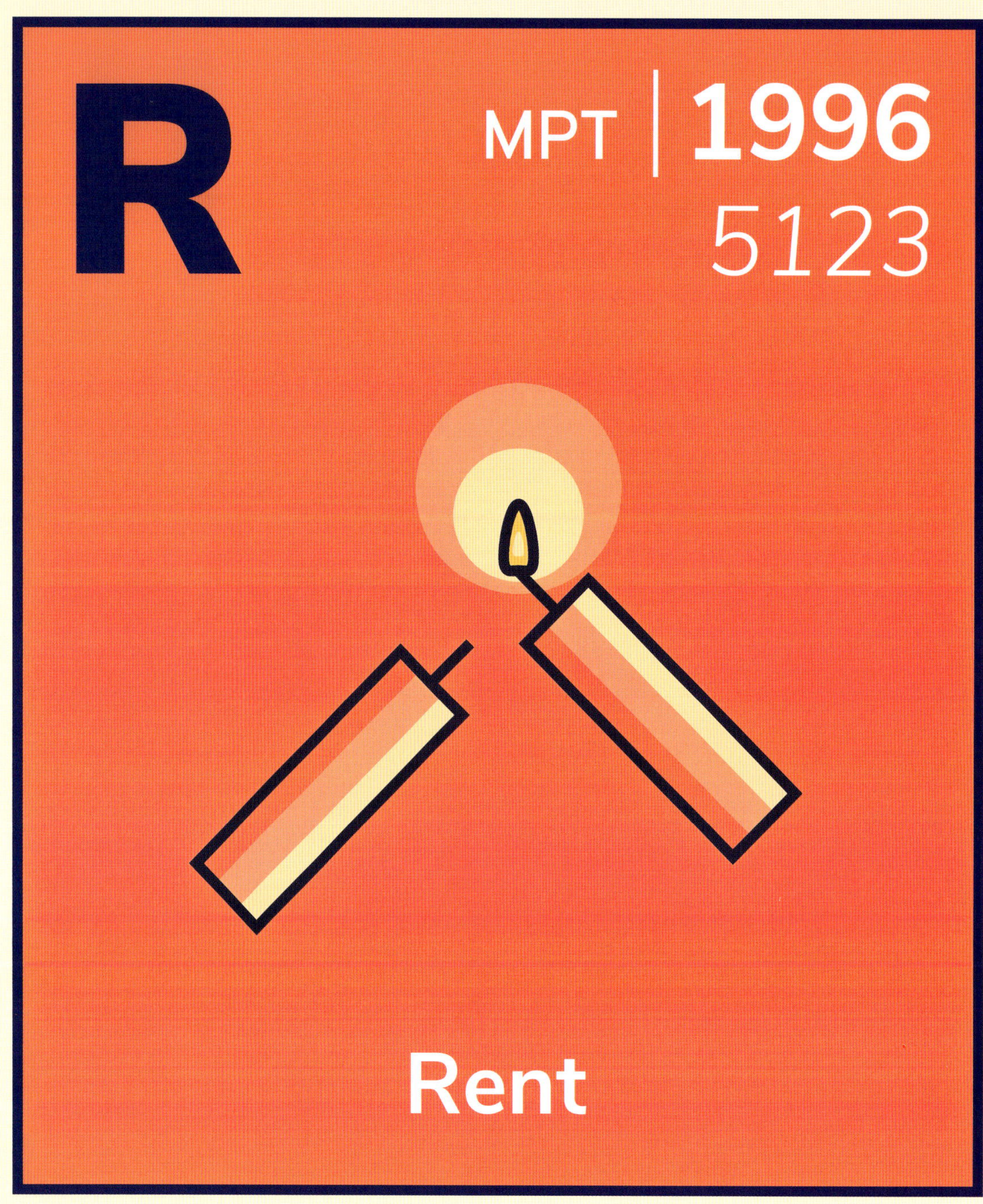

Book, music, and lyrics by Jonathan Larson
Original concept and additional lyrics by Billy Aronson
Directed by Michael Greif

Nederlander Theatre, April 29, 1996–September 7, 2008

Adam Pascal.......Roger Davis
Anthony Rapp.......Mark Cohen
Daphne Rubin-Vega.......Mimi Marquez
Idina Menzel.......Maureen Johnson

ART NOTE: Mimi asks Roger to help her "Light My Candle."

A group of aspiring artists in New York's East Village struggles to make ends meet and stay true to themselves and their artistic ambitions. Based on Puccini's opera La Bohème, *the show replaces the original tuberculosis plot line with the HIV/AIDS crisis, and multiple characters must confront and try to accept their diagnosis while finding love. One other major change: Mimi survives!*

One Song Glory

For a show in which the specter of death hovers over many of the characters, *Rent* is resolutely about life. What makes a good life, what can or should we leave behind, how do we make the most of whatever time we have? The power of this message, and of young Jonathan Larson's dazzling score, was already evident as the show moved toward its off-Broadway opening, mere blocks from the gritty streets where the show is set. But when Larson died of an aortic aneurysm after its final dress rehearsal, the show and its message took on a deeper sense of urgency.

Rent didn't need the resulting news coverage to work its magic. The cast was uniformly thrilling, with high-wattage performances from newcomers Adam Pascal, Anthony Rapp, Daphne Rubin-Vega, and Idina Menzel. And the songs combined a truly modern MTV sound with virtuoso rhymes overtly inspired by Sondheim (who is name-checked in the act one finale "La Vie Bohème"). Larson was able to blend formal experimentation, especially the use of conversational sections basically spoken on pitch (including film narration and even voicemails) with instantly memorable musical/lyrical hooks (title phrases). For the first time in many years, teenage and twenty-something audience members saw and heard themselves on a Broadway stage; the cast album felt like the voice of a generation. *Tommy* had brought rock back to Broadway three years earlier, but that score was based on an album from the 1960s and was missing the trademark irony, and yes, earnestness of more recent pop music. And, except for *Falsettos,* a musical had yet to truly look the AIDS crisis in the eye and raise a fist in defiance.

When *Rent* transferred to Broadway, already a phenomenon in the making, its choice of theatre surprised many. Bypassing more established and historic venues, the show chose the Nederlander, which was not only in disrepair and notoriously difficult to rent (Stacy Keach's one-man show in 1992 was the last production it had housed), but it was also on distinctly unglamorous 41st Street. That was the point: the producers wanted to indicate that *Rent* was eschewing the high gloss of Broadway, and they left much of the shabby atmosphere in place, transforming the exterior of the building to look like a downtown nightclub.

MISCELLANEOUS MATTER

- ★ *Rent* was the first show to offer a low-price ticket lottery for the first two rows of the orchestra; initially, patrons needed to line up early to buy tickets for that day, but when people began sleeping on the sidewalk to score these seats, they switched to the lottery system many productions have since employed.
- ★ The first road company opened in Boston, with Carol Burnett's daughter Carrie Hamilton playing Maureen and jazz/soul superstar Nina Simone's daughter, Lisa, playing Mimi.
- ★ In Boston, a line referring to the town of Hicksville (on Long Island) had to be changed to "Jersey," since audiences didn't understand that it was an actual town and not where hicks come from.

THE HITS

HIGHLY REACTIVE CROWD-PLEASERS

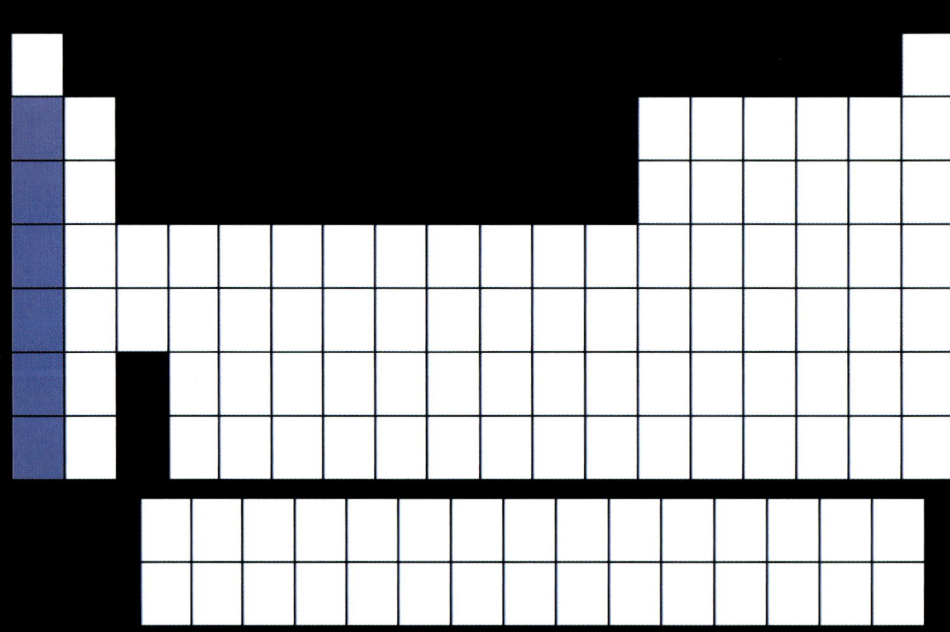

There's a long-simmering argument among Broadway mavens about when a musical can legitimately be called a hit. For many decades, the answer was a run of 500 performances or more. But then, somewhere in the 1970s, when it became possible to play 500 shows and still close at a loss, alternative answers began to be bandied about, like "did the show win a Best Musical Tony?" "Did it turn a profit?"

The argument lives on, but everyone agrees on one thing: you know a hit when you see it. And the musicals in this family all more than qualify. As it happens, each one did win the Tony and had a long and profitable run, but the reasons we've termed them "The Hits" goes far beyond these factors.

"The Hits" are musicals that audiences have taken to their hearts in a very special way. Ask any musical theatre fan what the very first show they ever saw was, or the very first show they performed in, and there's a decent chance you'll hear one of these titles in reply. You've likely seen most of them yourself . . . probably more than once. The first four are regularly revived in theatres large and small around the world, and the two feline entries have been seen by hundreds of millions, on stage and on screen; *Lion King Jr.* is one of the top ten most produced children's shows more than twenty-five years after its big brother opened on Broadway.

The scores of these musicals feature songs everyone knows and can probably sing from memory—tunes like "My Favorite Things," from *The Sound of Music*, "Guys and Dolls" from (of course) *Guys and Dolls* or, fittingly, "Memory" from *Cats*. Even sixty years after it was introduced to the world, "Sunrise, Sunset" from *Fiddler on the Roof* remains a mainstay of wedding singers everywhere, and the words "Hakuna Matata" are familiar to nearly every person on the planet. When a song from one of "The Hits" starts playing, the emotional reaction it elicits is most often a nostalgic smile and big "Awww." Why? Because the cast albums from these shows are the ones everyone grew up with. These are the musicals that made us love musicals; like the elements in this column, they never fail to generate huge reactions.

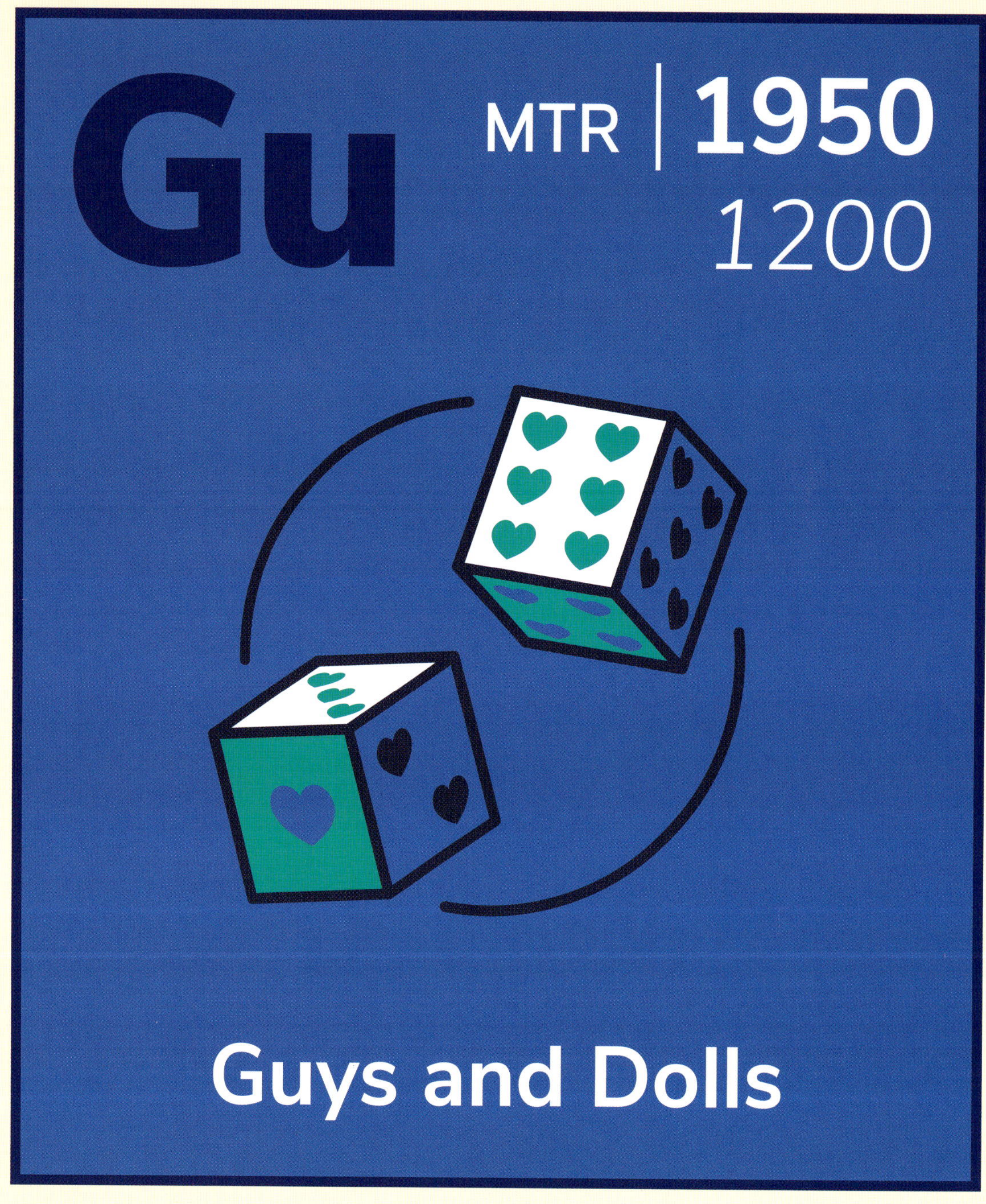

Book by Abe Burrows and Jo Swerling ★ Music and lyrics by Frank Loesser
Based on a story and characters by Damon Runyon
Staged by George S. Kaufman
Dances and musical numbers staged by Michael Kidd

46th Street Theatre, November 24, 1950–November 28, 1953

Robert Alda.......Sky Masterson
Isabel Bigley.......Sarah Brown
Vivian Blaine.......Miss Adelaide
Sam Levene.......Nathan Detroit

ART NOTE: A gambler's lucky dice, with hearts instead of pips; "Love is the thing that has licked 'em!"

Professional (but illegal) gamblers reject the moral instruction of the Save-a-Soul missionaries in this Broadway fable set in 1950s New York City. Sky courts the straitlaced missionary Sarah on a bet he can't take her to dinner in Havana, while Nathan's long-time fiancée, nightclub singer Adelaide, demands they finally tie the knot. The mission is saved from closing when Sky gets his gambler buddies to attend a meeting, and love wins when both women decide to reform their men after *they marry them.*

Luck Be a Lady

Guys and Dolls is one of a very few musicals often referred to as a "perfect show." This high praise has a lot to do with the meticulous attention paid to creating a unified tone, one of the trickiest tasks for creative teams. In Loesser, Burrows, and Swerling's hands, the lovable denizens of Damon Runyon's New York are all flawlessly brought to life: the hard-boiled but insecure professional gamblers, sincere but naive missionaries, and nightclub dancers who are somehow simultaneously risqué and innocent. Each type is portrayed with a wink and a chuckle, but also taken seriously as real human beings.

When producers Cy Feuer and Ernest Martin wanted to turn Runyon's street-smart short stories into a musical, Loesser was their first choice for songwriter. Though his only previous Broadway show was the operetta-tinged farce *Where's Charley?*, he'd made his name (and fortune) writing snappy hits for countless movies. His knack for combining sneakily sophisticated, jazzy tunes with fresh, colloquial lyrics made it possible for Runyon's colorful characters to believably open their mouths and start singing. Jo Swerling, screenwriter of *It's a Wonderful Life*, wrote the first draft of the book, but dissatisfied producers brought in veteran radio writer Abe Burrows to punch up the dialogue. He managed to work around Loesser's already completed score while incorporating Runyon's peculiar Noo Yawk-ese dialect, in which gamblers spoke in a semi-erudite style that famously did not use contractions.

This faux-elevated tone was matched by elements like an extended quasi-ballet to start the show, with Broadway street characters cleverly choreographed by Michael Kidd, followed immediately by the famous "Fugue for Tinhorns." To populate this world, much time was spent casting believable underworld toughs for the ensemble and supporting roles. Abe Burrows heard the voice of character actor Sam Levene in his head for Nathan Detroit, so when Levene also demanded to sing in the show, Loesser decided his vocal limitations were worth writing around and Nathan ended up with one song (albeit a duet).

Producer Martin told Burrows he didn't want a show that was just New York inside jokes "for the Lindy boys" (referring to the famous Broadway cheesecake restaurant). *Guys and Dolls* delivered, hitting the magical sweet spot and creating a world both highly specific and universal. It's a good bet to stay in the Hit column for a very long time.

MISCELLANEOUS MATTER

- ★ The show was awarded the Pulitzer Prize for Drama, but because Burrows had run afoul of the House Un-American Activities Committee (HUAC), the board of Columbia University vetoed the award, and none was given that year.
- ★ B. S. Pully, the notoriously "blue" comic cast as Chicago hood Big Jule, told Burrows "This is three-time loser material." He was then reportedly amazed he could get laughs with clean jokes. (He also brought his own dice to rehearsal.)
- ★ For the character of a beat cop, eventually cut, Loesser wrote a song "Ooh, My Feet;" he later recycled it (with new lyrics) as the plaint of a tired waitress in scene one of his next Broadway musical, *The Most Happy Fella*.

Book, music, and lyrics by Meredith Willson
Story by Meredith Willson and Franklin Lacey
Staged by Morton Da Costa ★ Choreographed by Onna White

Majestic Theatre and Broadway Theatre, December 19, 1957–April 15, 1961

Robert Preston.......Harold Hill
Barbara Cook.......Marian Paroo
David Burns.......Mayor Shinn
Pert Kelton.......Mrs. Paroo

ART NOTE: Three of the famous "76 Trombones."

Con man Harold Hill makes a living convincing small Midwest towns he'll start a boys' band for them; after they buy instruments and uniforms, he skips town without teaching the kids to play. Hill meets his match in the citizens of River City, Iowa—especially its shrewd and suspicious librarian, Marian. But his charm and infectious salesmanship end up bringing music and camaraderie to the town after all, and his phony flirting with Marian turns into true love.

Iowa Stubborn

Meredith Willson was a Hollywood composer, radio host, and musical director when he turned his attention to creating a musical based on his hometown of Mason City, Iowa. He attempted the trifecta—writing music, lyrics, *and* book—the first person since George M. Cohan in the 1920s. The story went through many major changes (with help from screenwriter Franklin Lacey), and more songs were cut than ended up on stage, but the final version was an instant hit when it finally opened on Broadway. Willson managed to marry his gift for melody (he wrote the infectious "It's Beginning to Look a Lot Like Christmas") with musical forms rare on Broadway, like barbershop quartet and semi-spoken rhythmic patter songs. *Music Man*'s opening number, "Rock Island," is performed by a train full of salesmen *a cappella*, entirely spoken, in rhythms that mimic the departure, journey, and arrival of a locomotive, while "Trouble," Hill's sales pitch to the town, is a spoken tour de force, one of the all-time classics of musical theatre.

"Trouble" directly led to the casting of Robert Preston, a freelance character actor from Hollywood tired of playing stock villains in B pictures, who thought he'd give musical theatre a try. For the audition, actors were given "Trouble," since it was thought its tricky rhythms would give actors the most, well, trouble, but for Preston it was a natural fit. And his somewhat conversational baritone was more than adequate for Harold Hill's sung material. His costar, the silver-throated soprano Barbara Cook, proved a feisty match, and the leading pair both took home Tonys, as did the show, somewhat controversially.

The 1958 Tonys was a face-off between *Music Man* and *West Side Story*, pitting traditional vs. contemporary, rural Americana vs. urban multicultural, and feel-good vs. tragedy. America's cities were changing at that time, and difficult conversations were starting to be had about their future. *West Side Story* felt, looked, and sounded like that future, but *The Music Man*'s fictional River City offered a glimpse back to a simpler time, one that many theatregoers remembered with great nostalgia. The show's heart was worn proudly on a braided marching band sleeve, and the original production's polish, humor, and sly-but-affectionate pokes at small-town America snagged the award. *West Side Story* may now loom larger in musical theatre fan's minds, but—even today—it's hard to resist seventy-six trombones.

MISCELLANEOUS MATTER

- ★ The show won the first Grammy Award for Best Original Cast Album (Broadway or TV).
- ★ Liza Redfield took over the position of musical director in May 1960, becoming the first woman to be the full-time conductor in a Broadway pit.
- ★ The opening number, "Rock Island," originally had a normal orchestral accompaniment and it fizzled. When Willson took away the orchestra and turned the actors and their text into the sound of the train, it was a smash.
- ★ A Broadway revival led by Hugh Jackman and Sutton Foster was delayed for over eighteen months by Broadway's Covid-19 shutdown. Despite this, it still went on to break box office records.

Book by Howard Lindsay and Russel Crouse
Music by Richard Rodgers ★ Lyrics by Oscar Hammerstein II
Suggested by *The Story of the Trapp Family Singers* by Maria Augusta Trapp
Directed by Vincent J. Donehue ★ Musical staging by Joe Layton

Lunt-Fontanne Theatre and Mark Hellinger Theatre, November 16, 1959–June 15, 1963

Mary Martin.......Maria Rainer *Theodore Bikel.......Captain Georg von Trapp*

ART NOTE: An edelweiss blossom from the show's famous faux folk song, in front of the majestic Alps.

In pre–WWII Austria, spunky postulant Maria struggles to behave properly (she sings without permission!), so the Mother Abbess appoints her temporary governess to seven motherless kids while she decides if she really wants to become a nun. The children love her for bringing music into their household, and (eventually) the father does, too. After they marry, they form a family singing group, and the nuns help them escape the Nazis by climbing over the Alps from the abbey garden.

No Way to Stop It

The Sound of Music was the final collaboration between Richard Rodgers and Oscar Hammerstein II; at the time of the show's 1959 premiere, the lyricist was already suffering from the stomach cancer he'd die of nine months later. While the show is now beloved, at the time it was received by critics as a lesser work, overly sugary and sentimental, and somewhat old-fashioned, though with an outstanding score.

In the years since, the stage musical has been completely overshadowed by the Oscar-winning movie, which is substantially different. Screenwriter Ernest Lehman reassigned some songs to different characters at different moments in the story—for example, on stage, "My Favorite Things" is an early duet for the Mother Abbess and Maria, while "The Lonely Goatherd" is what Maria and the kids sing to keep their spirits up. In addition, Rodgers wrote his own lyrics for two new songs for the film (Hammerstein had died by then), "I Have Confidence" and "Something Good." In the wake of the movie's success, stage productions now often choose to incorporate these changes.

One of the reasons Lehman was able to shift songs around the way he did is that the score for *The Sound of Music* is unusual among classic musicals: the majority of its musical numbers don't reveal characters' inner thoughts and emotions, they are merely preexisting songs (in the world of the show, that is). In other words, "Edelweiss" is a traditional Austrian folk song, "Do-Re-Mi" is a song Maria uses to teach the kids the fundamentals of music theory, etc. This choice makes sense for a story that is all about a family embracing the joy of making music together, but is part of the reason why reviewers felt the show was a step backward for Rodgers and Hammerstein, who had pioneered the sophisticated use of songs to add dimension and subtext to their characters and to advance the plot.

Regardless of critical opinion, it's worth noting that audiences loved *The Sound of Music* from the start, both on stage and on screen. In the end, the final Rodgers and Hammerstein musical would prove to be their most culturally enduring—and financially successful.

MISCELLANEOUS MATTER

★ The show was the first Broadway musical to use surround sound. Rodgers wanted the audience to feel like they were inside a giant European cathedral hearing the nuns' choral music, an effect achieved by speakers placed throughout the theatre.

★ Mary Martin was forty-four when she first played the young postulant. To producers (and audiences), what mattered more than her age was that she was a Broadway superstar who'd created the roles of Nellie Forbush in *South Pacific* and Peter in *Peter Pan*.

★ In the original production, no swastikas or Nazi soldiers appeared on stage; the creators feared audiences only fifteen years removed from WWII might be upset and distracted from the story.

Book by Joseph Stein ★ Music by Jerry Bock ★ Lyrics by Sheldon Harnick
Based on the stories by Sholom Aleichem
Directed and choreographed by Jerome Robbins

Imperial Theatre*, September 22, 1964–July 2, 1972

Zero Mostel.......Tevye
Maria Karnilova.......Golde
Beatrice Arthur.......Yente
Bert Convy.......Perchik

ART NOTE: A "sunrise/sunset" from the beloved song, over a village rooftop.

*First of three theatres

Tevye, a poor milkman who lives with his wife and five daughters in the Russian shtetl Anatevka, just wants to continue living life according to Jewish tradition, but events force him to grapple with a changing world. First, his three daughters all marry men he doesn't choose, then an edict from the tsar forces all Jews to leave Anatevka. Tevye and family depart for America, where life will hopefully be easier (if no less a challenge to their traditions).

Miracle of Miracles

It can truly be said that *Fiddler on the Roof* was a labor of love. No one expected it to be a smash—not the writers, not the director, not the producer—and yet it was the longest-running hit of the 1960s (and briefly the longest-running show in Broadway history). The subject matter was considered by all to be too niche, too Jewish, to appeal to a large mainstream audience. That said, the Tevye stories by writer Sholom Aleichem, the source material for the piece, were hardly unknown; dramatizations had appeared off-Broadway in 1953 and 1957, and in a one-night TV special in 1959.

The genius who found a way to universalize this material was director/choreographer Jerome Robbins (originally Rabinowitz). He came on to the project after the authors had already completed a draft, but at his insistence they created a new opening number, "Tradition," that would crystallize the show's central theme: that time-tested ways of life and strict family roles will inevitably shift and crumble as a new generation matures and outside societal pressures come to bear. This wide-lens focus has allowed *Fiddler* to resonate in every country, for viewers of every culture. When it played Japan, for example, a patron even approached book writer Stein to ask, "Do they understand this show in America? It's so Japanese!"

Of course, many other aspects of *Fiddler* contributed to its success: a titanic lead performance by Zero Mostel, an actor primarily associated with comedy who here showed his dramatic chops; a stunning, folk art–style scenic design by Boris Aronson (channeling the modernist Jewish painter Marc Chagall); and a memorable score, marrying simple, heartfelt, witty lyrics with modal Jewish harmonies and thumping, muscular dance music.

The overwhelming success of the show now makes it hard to believe its creators hoped merely for a run of a year or so. It has been (as of this writing) revived five times on Broadway and embraced around the world. And, in a strange twist, some of Robbins's theatrical inventions have now become traditions themselves: his famous bottle dance at the end of act one, for example, is now a frequent sight at orthodox Jewish weddings.

MISCELLANEOUS MATTER

- ★ Zero Mostel was famous for improvising during performances, a habit that frustrated authors, director, and costars but tickled audiences. It was one reason Mostel's contract was not renewed, and he left the megahit, the biggest triumph of his career, after only nine months.
- ★ Two original cast members would later be better known for their TV work: Bert Convy became a popular game show host in the 1970s and '80s, and Bea Arthur went on to star as Maude in *Maude* and Dorothy on *The Golden Girls.*
- ★ The slow, mournful "Anatevka" at the end of the show was originally part of an up-tempo number early in act two (with slightly different lyrics) that was cut in Detroit. It went back in after the deletion of a wry comic song called "When Messiah Comes" left a gap in the show's penultimate scene.

Music by Andrew Lloyd Webber ★ Lyrics by T. S. Eliot
Based on *Old Possum's Book of Practical Cats* by T. S. Eliot
Directed by Trevor Nunn ★ Choreographed by Gillian Lynne

Winter Garden Theatre, October 7, 1982–September 10, 2000

Betty Buckley.......Grizabella
Ken Page.......Old Deuteronomy
Terrence V. Mann.......Rum Tum Tugger
Harry Groener.....Munkustrap

ART NOTE: A cat's tail disappearing behind a London streetlamp from the song "Memory."

On the night of the fabled Jellicle Ball, a group of cats with outlandish names gather to see which one of them Old Deuteronomy will choose to be reborn into a new life. Though the ensemble includes many charming, charismatic, and funny feline contenders, it's the faded glamour cat Grizabella, with her plaintive song "Memory," that eventually wins a trip up to the "Heaviside Layer" on a giant tire.

The Jellicle Ball

By the time *Cats* opened on Broadway in 1982, it was a presold hit from the United Kingdom, but when it premiered in London the year before, it was in no way a sure thing. Given its eventual worldwide triumph, it's worth remembering that at first it seemed like a risky, not to say bizarre, idea: a musical with no scenes, no plot, and no human characters. Raising money for the show was so difficult that composer Andrew Lloyd Webber had to get a mortgage on his country house in order to fully capitalize the production.

The source material is a 1939 book of poems for children by the esteemed poet/playwright T. S. Eliot, which Lloyd Webber had loved as a kid. Eliot's widow became a fan of the evolving piece early in its development process and gave the composer some unpublished material that included "Grizabella, the Glamour Cat" and some poetic fragments that ended up in the lyric for the hit song "Memory." She also passed along a letter in which the poet had written about how his cat poems might be strung together for theatrical presentation. With this structure in hand, Lloyd Webber was finally able to conceive *Cats* as a full-fledged musical.

The creative team that was assembled was top-notch: director Trevor Nunn from the Royal Shakespeare Company, choreographer Gillian Lynne, and innovative designer John Napier, whose junkyard set included oversized pieces designed to make the actors seem cat-size. Napier also installed massive machinery for the show's final special effect and cut a hole into the theatre's ceiling, just so Grizabella could disappear into the Heaviside Layer after rising on a levitating tire. *Cats* also marked Lloyd Webber's first collaboration with young producer Cameron Mackintosh, who went on to produce many of the mega-musicals that dominated Broadway for the remainder of the 1980s, such as *Les Misérables* and *The Phantom of the Opera.*

In its later years, tourists were the main ticket buyers, partly because of *Cats*' winning combination of dance, costumes, and spectacle. In addition, the minimal spoken dialogue meant it was fun even for people whose English wasn't great. For that reason, its Tony Award for Best Book of a Musical (awarded to long-deceased T. S. Eliot) was something of a head-scratcher, but there's never any point in arguing with a cat.

MISCELLANEOUS MATTER

- ★ Judi Dench was hired to create the role of Grizabella in the London premiere, but she tore her Achilles tendon; Dame Judi eventually had her chance as a cat, though, playing Old Deuteronomy in the 2019 film version of the musical.
- ★ When the show finally closed in New York after nearly 18 years, Andrew Lloyd Webber quipped, "Obviously I am sad, but . . . 18 is a great age for a cat!"
- ★ Despite its whimsical-sounding name, the Heaviside Layer is a real phenomenon (a layer of gas in Earth's ionosphere) named after scientist Oliver Heaviside.

Book by Roger Allers and Irene Mecchi
Music by Elton John ★ Lyrics by Tim Rice
Directed by Julie Taymor ★ Choreographed by Garth Fagan

New Amsterdam and Minskoff Theatres, November 13, 1997–publication

Jason Raize.......Simba
Heather Headley.......Nala
Samuel E. Wright.......Mufasa
John Vickery.......Scar

ART NOTE: Two lions with traditional Kenyan-style patterns create the "Circle of Life."

On the plains of Africa, newborn cub Simba grows up under the watchful eye of his father, King Mufasa, and the resentment of his uncle Scar who covets the throne. Scar schemes with the hyenas to cause a stampede that kills Mufasa, but Simba escapes. He conquers his fears with the help of some animal pals, and returns to vanquish Scar, taking his place as the new king. The Circle of Life continues with his and Nala's newborn cub.

Can You Feel the Love Tonight?

Disney's first foray onto a Broadway stage came in 1994 with *Beauty and the Beast*, which was a sturdy enough success to encourage the entertainment giant to give another recent animated musical the Broadway treatment. *The Lion King* was a movie box office smash, but could it be translated to the stage, with human actors? A kind of big *Cats*? Luckily, as Disney Theatricals was trying to decide these questions, its director, Thomas Schumacher, asked an artist whose work he admired, Julie Taymor, to propose how she might address the show's challenges. Taymor, who had studied puppetry and dance in Indonesia and Japan and had directed several major Shakespeare productions, described a technique where the actors would use animal puppets while still being very visible in costumes of their own, blending character and actor into a visually poetic whole, greater than both.

Taymor got the job, and the effect was ravishing. The opening number, "Circle of Life," had the cast of animal/actors parading down the aisles of the theatre so the audience could get a good look at the puppets; once on stage, they simply transformed in the audience's minds into the beloved characters from the film. The score of the stage show was significantly altered, too; only five movie songs were used, and ten more added, emphasizing South African musical styles and performed by an ensemble of South African singers and those trained in its traditions. Taymor would win the Tony for her direction (the first woman to do so) as well as her costume design. The show has since been performed around the world in many countries and languages, and it is still running on Broadway as of this book's publication, long since having become the highest grossing musical of all time.

The Lion King marked the first musical to play the New Amsterdam Theatre in decades. After years of neglect, Disney partnered with New York City to revamp the ornate theatre, once home to the Ziegfeld *Follies* but in the '90s a seedy, dilapidated, and abandoned movie theatre. Along with a new movie theatre and a Madame Tussaud's wax museum, the stunningly refurbished New Amsterdam became the backbone for the revitalization of 42nd Street. While some New Yorkers bemoaned the "Disneyfication" of Times Square, most got used to the new shopping mall/theme park atmosphere and all welcomed the tourist dollars it brought in, a kind of commercial circle of life.

MISCELLANEOUS MATTER

★ For the original Broadway production, artisans, puppeteers, and sculptors spent approximately 1,700 hours handcrafting Julie Taymor's designs for masks and puppets. Among the materials used was carbon fiber, the same material used to craft airplanes to ensure their durability and longevity. The tallest of these puppet creatures (the giraffes) top out at eighteen feet tall.

★ *The Lion King* has had productions on six continents. For April Fool's Day 2019, Disney sent out an announcement that the show would soon make this a perfect seven by premiering in Antarctica.

★ Six different indigenous African languages—Swahili, Zulu, Xhosa, Sotho, Tswana, and Congolese—are sung and/or spoken during the show.

THE BROADWAY OPERAS

LUSTROUS VOCAL SHOWPIECES

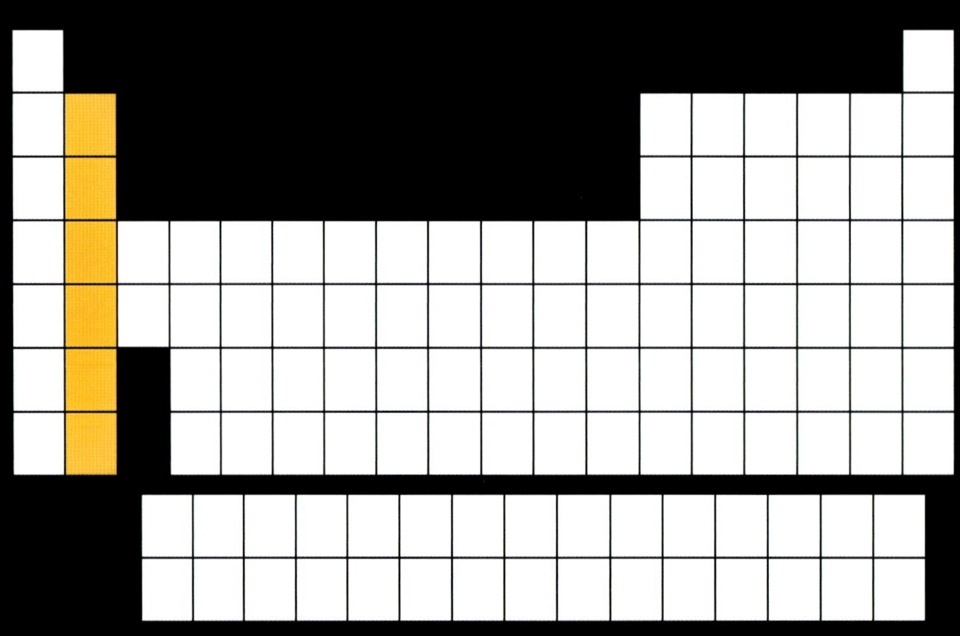

What makes something an opera? The answer usually includes compositional ambition, text that is mostly or completely sung, and vocal writing for big and/or classically trained voices, with their larger sound and wider ranges. *Porgy and Bess*, the first in the family, was what Gershwin called a "folk opera," and except for Broadway revivals, it is mostly presented by opera companies due to its musical demands. It paved the way for Broadway productions of other operatic works by classically trained composers like Kurt Weill, Gian Carlo Menotti, and Leonard Bernstein.

The high ratio of music to spoken dialogue typical of operas helps composers create a seamless world. Traditional musical theatre and pop/rock singing is often very close to the actors' spoken register and slipping in and out of song feels exciting but not too unnatural. But when a show's vocal writing requires larger ranges and longer notes, songs sound increasingly different from speech, and switching back and forth between them becomes more and more distracting. It can feel more natural to stay in a sung world and just accept that that is how people express themselves all the time.

In their own ways, the shows in this category all looked backward to the 19th-century traditions that gave birth to the musical. Like the silvery chemical elements in this column, they have a luster that emanates from their vocal writing. *Porgy and Bess*'s "Summertime," *Candide*'s "Glitter and Be Gay," Rosabella and Tony's lush duets from *Most Happy Fella*, *Sweeney Todd*'s "Epiphany," the operatic pastiches and Victorian art songs of *The Phantom of the Opera*, and the bilingual arias and ensembles of *The Light in the Piazza* give singers a chance to shine and audiences the joy of basking in their light.

Classical operas gave much more importance to the music than the text, and are credited to their composers, with the librettists often unknown—we talk about "Verdi's *Aida*," not "Verdi and Ghislanzoni's *Aida*." It is a testament to the musicals in this family that not only did the music reach for greatness, but the libretti did, too, creating rich characters and unforgettable lyrics whose stories fly as high as their voices.

Libretto by DuBose Heyward ★ Music by George Gershwin
Lyrics by DuBose Heyward and Ira Gershwin
Based on the play *Porgy* by DuBose Heyward and Dorothy Heyward
Staged by Rouben Mamoulian

Alvin Theatre, October 10, 1935–January 25, 1936

Todd Duncan.......Porgy
Anne Wiggins Brown.......Bess
Warren Coleman.......Crown
John W. Bubbles.......Sportin' Life

ART NOTE: From the song "Summertime," where "fish are jumpin' and the cotton is high."

It's summer in Catfish Row, a Black neighborhood in Charleston, South Carolina. Porgy, a disabled beggar, defends Bess when the other women shun her for her forward demeanor and drug habit. The two fall in love, and Porgy kills Bess's violent boyfriend, Crown. He briefly goes to prison; when he gets out, Bess has left for New York with her dealer Sportin' Life, who convinced her Porgy would be in jail for years. Porgy vows to go after her.

They Pass By Singin'

By 1935, not only had George Gershwin created dozens of hit songs and fourteen Broadway musicals (one of which won the Pulitzer), he had also helped bring jazz and blues into the concert hall with works like *Rhapsody in Blue* and *An American in Paris*. When he read DuBose Heyward's popular novel and subsequent play adaptation, *Porgy*, he saw the perfect material to fulfill a larger ambition: to write a grand opera. Set in Heyward's native Charleston, *Porgy and Bess* featured high-stakes drama and a cast of characters for whom music was an integral part of community life. Heyward and Gershwin both studied the local Gullah speech and music, and Gershwin combined folk-like songs with symphonic writing (plus a dash of Tin Pan Alley, thanks to some lyrics by his brother Ira) to create a new kind of operatic hybrid.

Broadway was the ideal venue for this new work, not only because Gershwin's goal was always to reach a wide audience, but for practical reasons: New York opera houses were at least ten years away from allowing Black performers on their stages. The Gershwins' stipulation that the show be performed by Black actors (to avoid blackface performers) launched the careers of many classical Black singers and forced the integration of theatres where it toured, introducing much of the country to the depth of Black vocal talent. And the score quickly jumped into the mainstream, with songs like "Summertime," "I Got Plenty o' Nuttin'" and "It Ain't Necessarily So" frequently heard in jazz clubs and on hit records by Black and white stars.

The opera's influence extended beyond the borders of the United States. European productions began in the late '40s; one major tour, in 1952, starring Leontyne Price, William Warfield, Cab Calloway, and Maya Angelou went on to play all across Europe and Latin America, funded by the U.S. State Department. *Porgy and Bess* was the first American opera to be presented at the famed La Scala opera house in Milan, and its historic productions in Russia during the heart of the Cold War were a kind of "good will" tour, the first American theatrical troupe to play Russia since the Bolshevik Revolution. Though some look at the original's all-white creative team and describe the show as a "white man's idea" of a Black opera, the strength of its score and its indisputable longevity and smashing of racial and artistic barriers enshrine it in Broadway history.

MISCELLANEOUS MATTER

- ★ Armenian director Rouben Mamoulian helmed the original play production of *Porgy* and went on to direct Rodgers and Hammerstein's first two watershed musicals, *Oklahoma!* and *Carousel*.
- ★ In the novel, Bess was a secondary character. Anne Brown, the first Black vocalist admitted to Juilliard, wrote to Gershwin asking to audition; when he heard her, he was so enthusiastic he expanded the part and even changed the name of the show from *Porgy* to *Porgy and Bess*.
- ★ Ira Gershwin was originally going to write all the lyrics, but Heyward asked to contribute, and ended up helping create, as Sondheim put it, "the finest set of lyrics in the history of the American musical theatre."

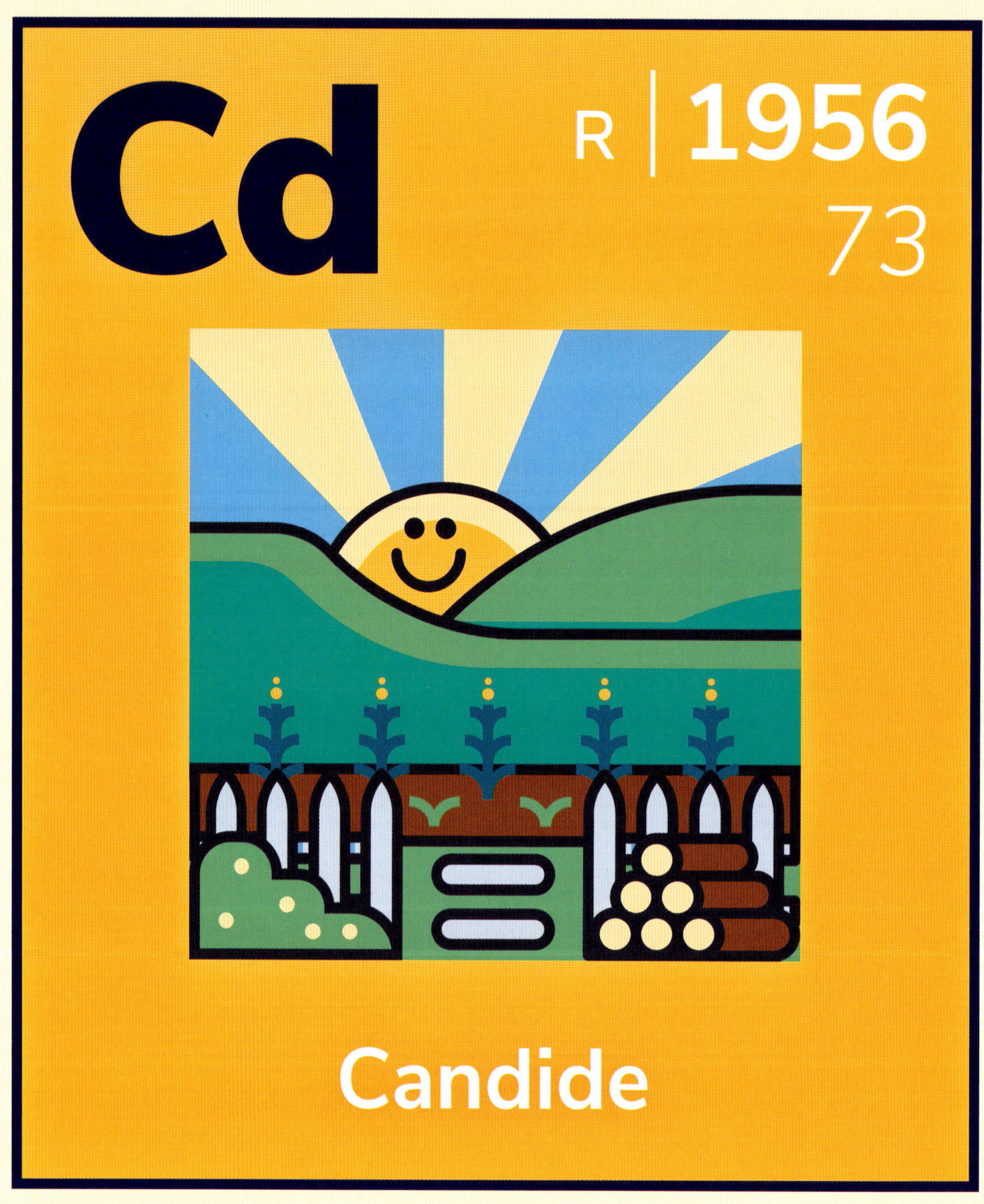

Book by Lillian Hellman ★ Music by Leonard Bernstein
Lyrics by Richard Wilbur, John Latouche, and Dorothy Parker
Based on the novel by Voltaire ★ Directed by Tyrone Guthrie
Choreographed by Wallace Seibert and Anna Sokolow

Martin Beck Theatre, December 1, 1956–February 2, 1957

Robert Rounseville.......Candide
Max Adrian.......Dr. Pangloss
Barbara Cook.......Cunegonde
Irra Petina.......Old Lady

ART NOTE: An overly happy sun, helping to "Make Our Garden Grow," the final song in the show.

In a series of fantastical adventures that span the globe, wide-eyed Candide and the object of his affections, the cunning Cunegonde, are confronted with the cruelty and injustice of the world, which challenges their tutor Dr. Pangloss's assertion that everything is for the best in this "best of all possible worlds." By the time they return to their hometown, their blind optimism has been replaced with a more practical philosophy: to tend their lives as they would a garden.

You Were Dead, You Know

Between 1953 and 1957, in addition to his busy career as America's preeminent classical conductor, Leonard Bernstein somehow found time to compose three musicals. The first was the traditional musical comedy *Wonderful Town*, and the third was the Latin-infused urban explosion *West Side Story*. In between came *Candide,* a picaresque adventure based on 18th-century French philosopher Voltaire's controversial political satire. The idea to musicalize this work was suggested to Bernstein by Lillian Hellman, who'd written numerous successful Broadway plays. She saw in Voltaire's attacks on the Spanish Inquisition an opportunity to skewer the actions of HUAC, which, along with the FBI, had been persecuting left-leaning artists like her and Bernstein for years. Hellman's most direct attacks on HUAC were nixed at the last minute by gun-shy director Tyrone Guthrie. Lyricist John Latouche had written the lyrics for the Broadway musical *The Golden Apple* and one of the most popular American operas, *The Ballad of Baby Doe*, so he was a natural choice for this hybrid show. Tragically, he died while working on it at the age of forty-one and was replaced by the young but decorated poet Richard Wilbur.

Despite the show's brief original run, its superlative score guaranteed its longevity. Bernstein's music was partly an homage to the show's European origin and partly a demonstration and celebration of his own eclecticism. He borrowed from operetta, Baroque dance forms, jazz, tango, and even Stravinsky. "I Am Easily Assimilated" could be straight out of a Jewish vaudeville sketch, "Bon Voyage" is pure Gilbert and Sullivan operetta, "What's the Use" resembles a French music hall waltz, and the coloratura showpiece "Glitter and Be Gay" was a pitch-perfect reimagining of the famous "Jewel Song" from Gounod's opera *Faust.* In short, it's a score that could only have been written by someone with Bernstein's vast musical experience and training.

Unlike most shows in this book, *Candide* has undergone many versions over the years. In 1973, Harold Prince staged a version in a radically altered theatre with the audience in the center of multiple playing areas and actors sometimes sailing above them on pulleys. This version had a rewritten book by Hugh Wheeler, and new and rewritten lyrics by Stephen Sondheim. A final opera house version was put together by Bernstein and English satirist and actor John Wells in the late '80s.

MISCELLANEOUS MATTER

- ★ Its short run belies the many rave reviews *Candide* received, and box office was on the upswing when it closed, possibly because of a screaming match between the volatile Hellman and producer Ethel Reiner.
- ★ Edie Adams, costar of the Bernstein musical *Wonderful Town*, claimed the composer had written the role of Cunegonde, and specifically the bravura aria "Glitter and Be Gay," with her in mind. She turned down the role to play Daisy Mae in that same season's *Li'l Abner.*
- ★ One of the songs Sondheim wrote lyrics for includes a pair of bleating sheep. It's called "Sheep Song."

Book, music, and lyrics by Frank Loesser
Based on the play *They Knew What They Wanted* by Sidney Howard
Staged by Joseph Anthony ★ Choreographed by Dania Krupska

Imperial Theatre and Broadway Theatre, May 3, 1956–December 14, 1957

Jo Sullivan.......Rosabella
Robert Weede.......Tony
Art Lund.......Joe
Susan Johnson.......Cleo

ART NOTE: Grapes from Tony's farm, and the letter that kicked off his romance with Rosabella (complete with an Italian flag stamp).

Waitress Rosabella arrives in Napa to marry vineyard owner Tony after a whirlwind romance conducted by mail. She's under the impression Tony is a young man, but the photo that middle-aged Tony sent was actually that of his handsome farmhand, Joe. Embarrassed to admit she was duped, Rosabella marries Tony anyway (but sleeps with Joe). When this one-night fling results in a pregnancy, Rosabella and Tony (by now in love for real) must find a way to forgive each other and start again.

Abbondanza

For those who mostly know Frank Loesser as the urbane, witty songwriter of *Guys and Dolls* or his hit songs for Hollywood, the lush, nearly sung-through, three-act *Most Happy Fella* seems a glorious anomaly. In fact, it's the fullest representation of all of his wide-ranging musical voices. The swinging tunes and colloquial fizz of *Guys and Dolls* are easily identifiable in comic couple Cleo and Herman's numbers like "Ooh! My Feet!," "Standing on the Corner," and "I Like Everybody." For the main love story's musically complex writing for big, classically trained voices, we can find the germs in Loesser's first Broadway show, the operetta-inspired *Where's Charley?*

This musical "split personality" may partly have been a result of Loesser's upbringing. His parents were Jewish intellectuals—his father a pianist, his mother a literary scholar—and he was raised on a diet of the highest of high art. His older brother Arthur became a well-known classical pianist, but Frank was drawn to Tin Pan Alley and the rhythms of New York City. Throughout his life, despite his great success and popularity, his mother and brother continued to look down on Broadway and popular music as unserious and disposable. Frank played into his black sheep role, even claiming not to read music when he did (though he did rely on musical assistants when it came time to compile *The Most Happy Fella*'s full 268-page piano score).

The score is extremely sophisticated on every level. The music is harmonically complex, unpredictable, shifting keys and tonal centers without warning, interpolating unusual chords that come from the jazz world but are deployed in more surprising contexts. He uses operatic techniques like extended counterpoint (two or more people singing different lines at the same time) and *recitative*, speech-like sections on pitch but delivered conversationally. Incorporate these techniques into over forty separate musical numbers and the result is what *New York Times* theatre critic Brooks Atkinson called "about as close to opera as the rules of Broadway permit."

Some critics felt the two halves of the score didn't mesh, as if Loesser were trying to write a serious music drama but couldn't help adding some crass Broadway razzle-dazzle. But Loesser himself loved mixing languages, as he called it: "I'm kind of hipped on the idea that there aren't any rules."

MISCELLANEOUS MATTER

- ★ A film version was floated in 1962, to be produced by Warner Bros., with Shirley Jones and Fred Astaire set to star. However, Jones was busy making the film of *The Music Man* and Astaire ended up refusing the offer, so the project fizzled.
- ★ Since the show was nearly wall-to-wall songs, record producer Goddard Lieberson opted to record the entire show (even dialogue) and release it as a three-LP set, something almost unheard-of in the 1950s. (In the '70s and '80s, with sung-through shows, it became more common.) A single LP of score highlights was also sold.
- ★ Maxene Andrews of the popular '40s singing group the Andrews Sisters worked with Frank on early versions; Cleo was partly written for her, but she decided the part was too vocally demanding.

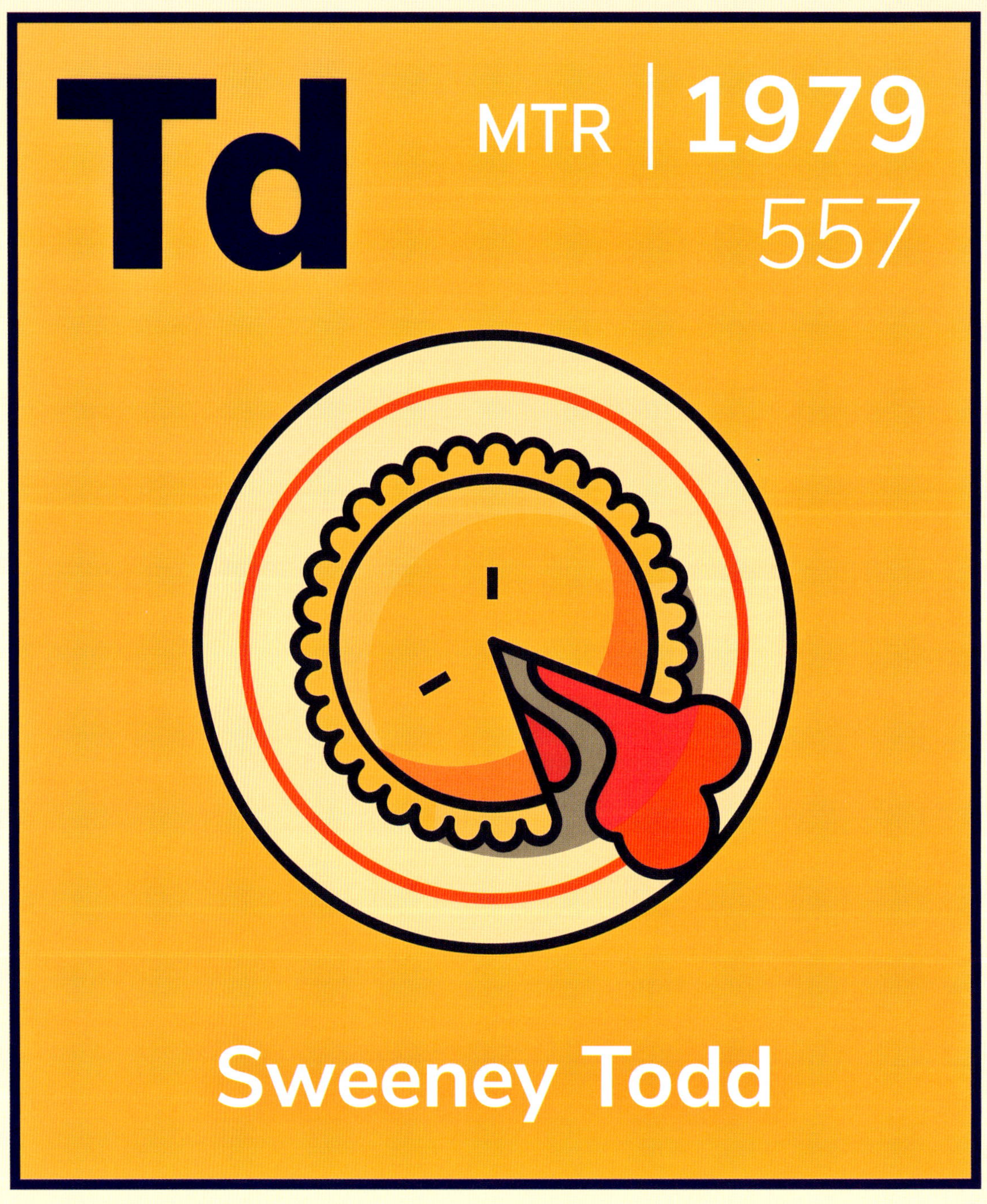

Book by Hugh Wheeler ★ Music and lyrics by Stephen Sondheim
Based on a version of *Sweeney Todd* by Christopher Bond
Directed by Harold Prince ★ Dance and movement by Larry Fuller

Uris Theatre, March 1, 1979–June 29, 1980

Len Cariou.......Sweeney Todd
Angela Lansbury.......Mrs. Lovett
Victor Garber.......Anthony Hope
Sarah Rice.......Johanna

ART NOTE: An "eater's eye view" of a bloody pie, putting a different kind of "graphic" in graphic design.

In 19th-century London, bloodthirsty barber Sweeney Todd returns home to seek revenge on the judge who unjustly shipped him off to prison. He reconnects with Nellie Lovett, a cheerfully amoral, down-at-the-heels pie maker who has long carried a torch for him, and together the two repurpose the victims of Sweeney's razor into savory offerings for her shop. Like most revenge stories, by the time the show ends, many of the leading characters have met unsavory ends as well.

God, That's Good!

With shows like *Company*, *Follies*, and *Pacific Overtures*, the team of composer/lyricist Stephen Sondheim and director/producer Harold Prince won acclaim for taking risks and pushing the boundaries of what a musical could be. With this, their fifth and most ambitious offering, they tackled perhaps the most outrageous themes of their collaboration: serial murder and cannibalism.

The idea for the show originated with Sondheim, who saw a play version of the story in London. Originally, he toyed with the idea of writing the book in addition to the music and lyrics but finding that he needed assistance cutting the play down to size in order to make room for songs, he turned to Hugh Wheeler (with whom he had written *A Little Night Music*) so he could better focus on writing the score.

And what a score! Blurring the line between musical theatre and grand opera, the rhapsodic, almost through-composed score (even spoken sections are usually underscored with music) features a web of musical motifs tied to each character. It also weaves in references to the *Dies irae* from the Catholic mass for the dead and includes a large amount of complex choral writing. Jonathan Tunick's lush, symphonic orchestrations add further colors and richness to the music. *Sweeney Todd* is a great example of the role an orchestrator can play in heightening mood, as some of the scariest and most heart-stopping moments in the show rely as much on the sounds emanating from the orchestra pit as they do on what's happening on stage.

If audiences worried the show might be too dark, the creators surprised them with a blend of horror and humor. For every grisly murder, there's a lighter moment like Sweeney and Mrs. Lovett imagining how different human "fillings" might taste in "A Little Priest," or ecstatic customers clamoring for "More Hot Pies," not knowing why they're so delicious. The top-notch cast was led by a haunted-looking Len Cariou and a chillingly gleeful Angela Lansbury (it was her third Sondheim show and won her a fourth Best Actress Tony Award). Still, the gruesome subject matter scared some audiences away, and the show closed at a financial loss, after only sixteen months. Only in the years since has *Sweeney Todd* been embraced by mainstream audiences and acclaimed as the masterpiece it is.

MISCELLANEOUS MATTER

- ★ There are three completely different songs in the show that carry the same simple title: "Johanna."
- ★ The original production's cavernous, factory-like setting was a reproduction of a Rhode Island iron foundry (Prince wanted to emphasize the dehumanizing aspects of industrialization, a theme Sondheim was indifferent to).
- ★ A 1989 revival that transferred from off-Broadway's York Theatre was nicknamed "Teeny Todd" by Broadway wags, because the cast was reduced from 27 to 14 and the large orchestra replaced by three synthesizers. Little did anyone guess that by the 2005 revival, directed by John Doyle, the show would have gotten even smaller, with a cast of ten who also played instruments, eliminating the need for any orchestra at all.

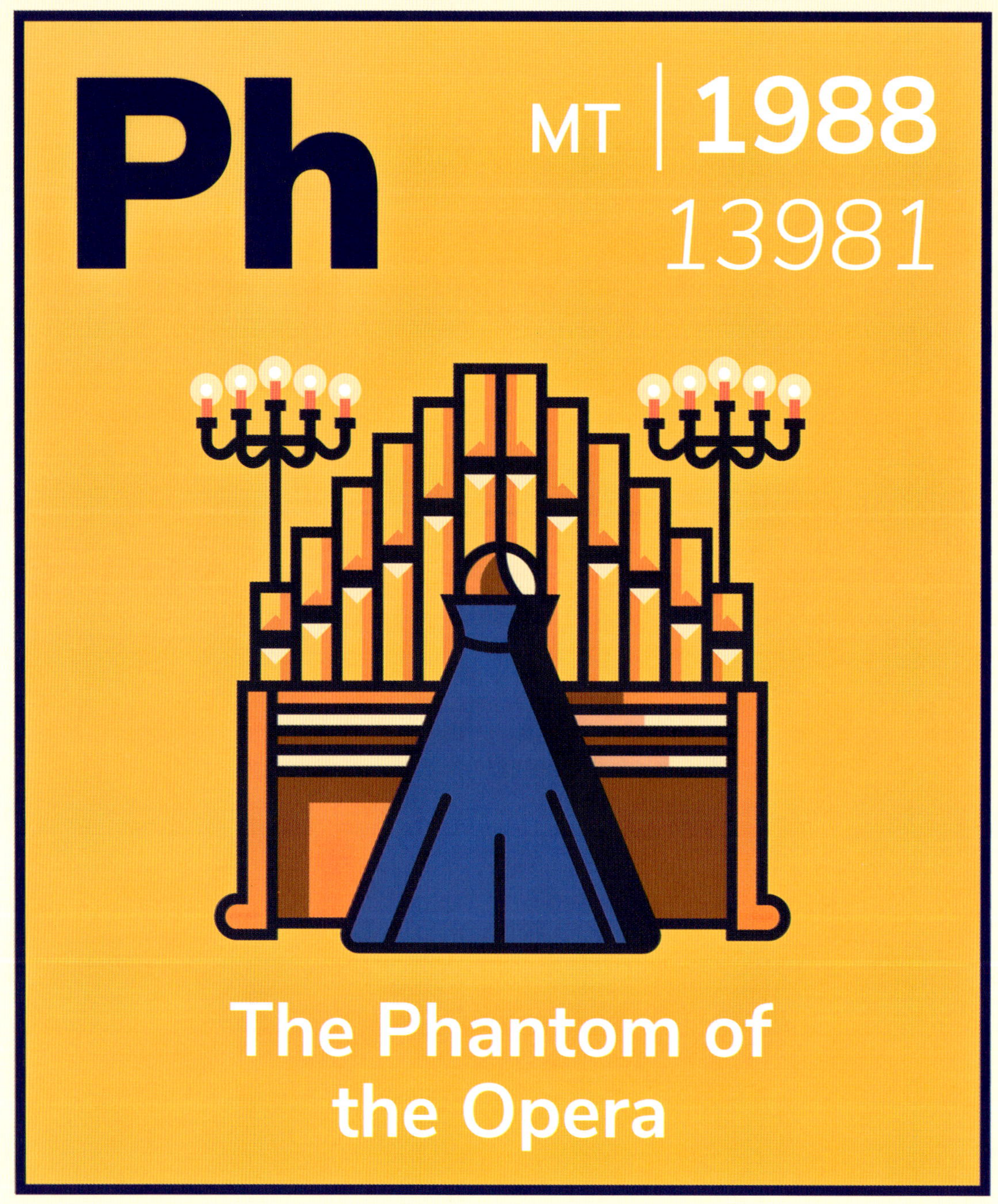

Book by Richard Stilgoe and Andrew Lloyd Webber
Music by Andrew Lloyd Webber ★ Lyrics by Charles Hart
From the novel by Gaston Leroux ★ Directed by Harold Prince
Musical staging and choreography by Gillian Lynne

Majestic Theatre, January 26, 1988–April 16, 2023

Michael Crawford.......The Phantom of the Opera
Sarah Brightman.......Christine Daaé
Steve Barton.......Raoul
Judy Kaye.......Carlotta Guidicelli

ART NOTE: The Phantom himself, playing his organ in his subterranean lair.

Performers in the Paris Opera must accommodate the whims of a mysterious, murderous Phantom who haunts the building. He demands that a young singer he has secretly trained, Christine, star in an opera he wrote. On its opening night, he spirits her off to his underground lair, where her fiancé, Raoul, tries and fails to rescue her. Christine saves Raoul's life by agreeing to stay with the Phantom, finally teaching the tortured soul what kindness feels like, and he releases them both.

The Music of the Night

Like producer Cameron Mackintosh's earlier show, *Les Misérables, The Phantom of the Opera* started in London, but unlike the French import, *Phantom* was an immediate hit, riding the 1980s wave of successful West End musicals. This was a time when American writers and producers seemed to have lost touch with what audiences thought was fresh and exciting, and there was much hand-wringing about Britain taking over Broadway. When it opened, Andrew Lloyd Webber was the undisputed king of musical theatre both in the West End and on Broadway; Mackintosh was likewise the star producer on both sides of the Atlantic, so New York theatres were clamoring to land *Phantom*, a drama that played out in the major newspapers. After having their bid initially rejected, the Shuberts agreed to spend a million dollars to renovate their Majestic Theatre, reinforcing its roof to support the giant chandelier and raising the proscenium arch so the audience could see the Phantom as he stalked the catwalks.

But even the Shuberts couldn't have predicted just what kind of megahit it would become, running for a staggering thirty-five years and far outpacing every other musical in the history of Broadway. What gave it such magical and enduring allure? A big part of Mackintosh's recipe, first with *Cats* and then *Les Miz* and now *Phantom*, was visual spectacle. After a string of expensive flops, Hal Prince and his genius for staging were again on full display, and the astonishing sets of Maria Björnson delivered thrilling stage pictures one after the other: the lavish Paris Opera, the Phantom's boat gliding through the catacombs, and, of course, the crashing chandelier. Lloyd Webber created an equally spectacular score that took full advantage of the Opera setting, a symphonic tapestry (for a huge 28-piece orchestra) that included arias and multi-person ensembles requiring singers with real classical chops. And of course, his trademark soaring melodies were perfectly suited for these larger-than-life characters. Though better known for using pop music in his shows, Lloyd Webber was no stranger to classical music; in fact, his Grammy Award–winning symphonic *Requiem* had premiered just a year before *The Phantom of the Opera* opened in the West End. The combination of these large-scale creative elements and a macabre tale of obsession and love in a grand theatre seemed, in the end, to become something more than merely a musical—it was a lavish love letter to the possibilities of theatre itself.

MISCELLANEOUS MATTER

- ★ The American actors' union originally banned Sarah Brightman (Lloyd Webber's wife at the time) from playing Christine on Broadway unless a role of similar size could be guaranteed to an American actor in London. In response, Lloyd Webber threatened to pull the show, and, for a while, producers couldn't sell advance tickets.
- ★ Over the course of the show's 35-year Broadway run, only 16 actors starred as the title character, but they played opposite 36 different actresses in the role of Christine Daaé.
- ★ Two different Phantoms (Michael Crawford and Hugh Panaro) had the same costume mishap, getting their lip prosthetics stuck to their Christines during the kiss scene.

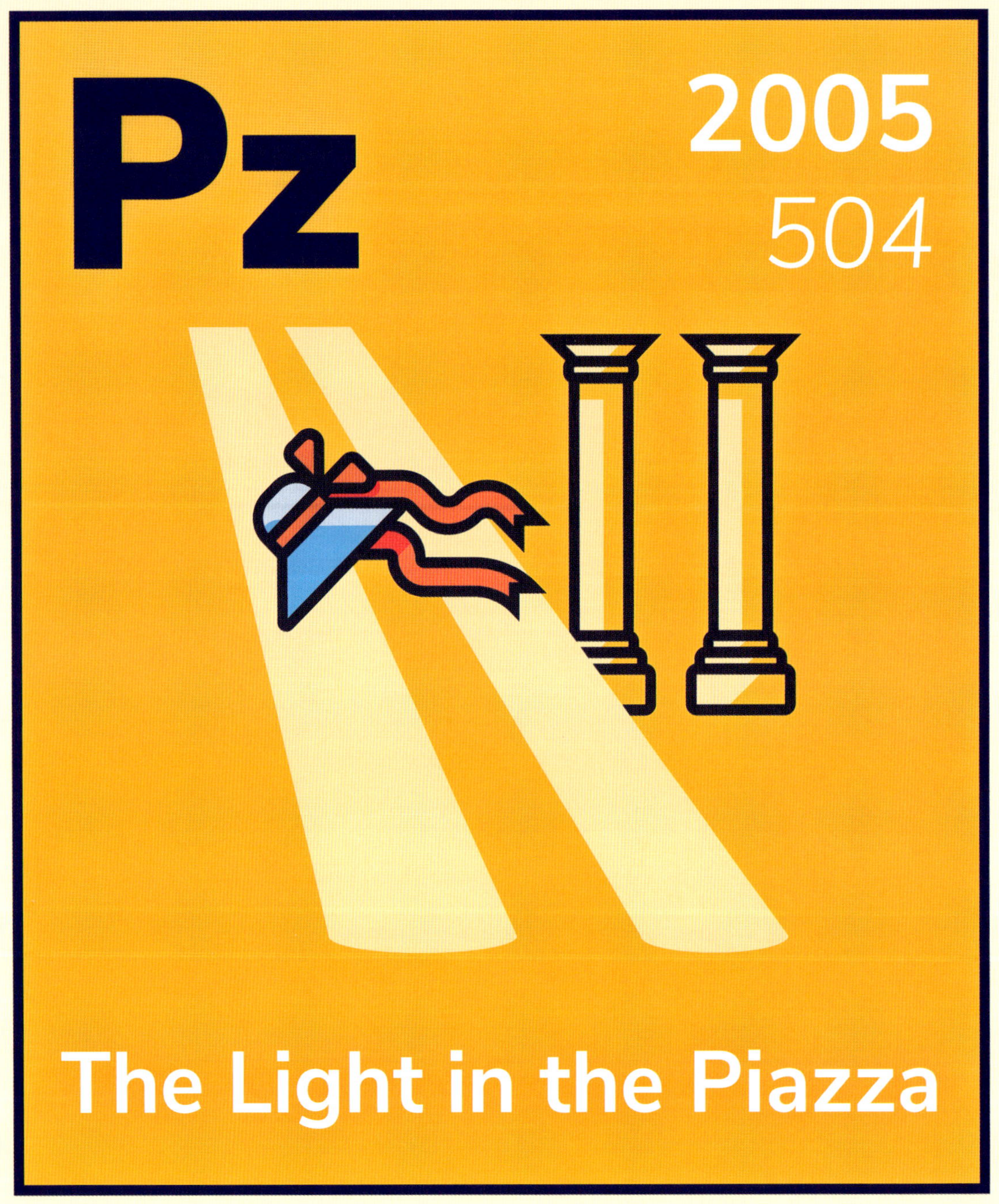

Book by Craig Lucas ★ Music and lyrics by Adam Guettel
Based on the novella by Elizabeth Spencer
Directed by Bartlett Sher ★ Musical staging by Jonathan Butterell

Vivian Beaumont Theater, April 18, 2005–July 2, 2006

Victoria Clark.......Margaret Johnson
Kelli O'Hara.......Clara Johnson
Matthew Morrison.......Fabrizio Naccarelli
Patti Cohenour.......Signora Naccarelli

ART NOTE: Clara's hat, blowing across a Florence piazza just so Fabrizio could see her chase it.

In the 1960s, Margaret and her daughter, Clara, visit Florence, where Clara falls in love with an Italian boy. Margaret tries to separate them, and her reason becomes clear when Clara has a strangely childish meltdown (Clara's development was stunted by a head injury). But, in the end, moved by Clara's pleading and realizing her daughter has a chance for the happiness her own marriage has lost, Margaret relents; the possibility of true love, she decides, is worth any risk.

Love to Me

When your grandfather is Richard Rodgers, composer of the most beloved American musicals, and your mother is Mary Rodgers, a Broadway composer in her own right and hugely successful author of YA fiction, it takes courage and true talent to stake out your own path as a writer. Adam Guettel did just that, first with a cycle of what can only be described as contemporary art songs called *Saturn Returns* (the album was titled *Myths and Hymns*), and then with an off-Broadway chamber musical, *Floyd Collins*, that featured a dense and sophisticated bluegrass sound new to musical theatre.

In *The Light in the Piazza*, Guettel again imbued his score with a unique sound. It's inspired by the romanticism of Italian song, with lush harmonies and soaring melodies, but also contains pointillistic, conversational vocal writing reminiscent of Stravinsky or the British composer Benjamin Britten (both of whom Guettel cites as influences). Much like Tony in *The Most Happy Fella*, *The Light in the Piazza*'s hero Fabrizio speaks only stilted English, and many of his lyrics are completely in Italian. His family speaks Italian, as well, and the writers made the bold choice not to translate their dialogue (except for one delightful moment when the mother, who speaks no English, talks to the audience in English to explain what's going on). Fabrizio's courting of the American girl, Clara, is accomplished despite this language barrier; in fact, large parts of their duets are *vocalise*, melodies sung simply on "ah" or "oh." With music alone, they tell us—and each other—everything about what they're feeling.

The original production was a triumph for its two leading ladies. Victoria Clark, long a respected character actress, won her first Tony Award for her deeply emotional portrayal of the conflicted Margaret (she won a second Tony for *Kimberly Akimbo* in 2023). Likewise, Kelli O'Hara, who'd only had major roles in minor Broadway shows before this, showcased her classical training and quiet, joyful fortitude as Clara, and the show became her springboard to a major career; over the next fifteen years, she starred in no fewer than six major Broadway revivals and two new shows, one of which was Guettel's and Lucas's second collaboration, 2023's *Days of Wine and Roses*.

MISCELLANEOUS MATTER

- ★ In July 1960, Oscar Hammerstein suggested to Richard Rodgers that they might want to musicalize Elizabeth Spencer's *The Light in the Piazza*; Hammerstein died before the idea went any further.
- ★ Victoria Clark originally wanted to be a director but fell into acting almost by accident. Eventually, she did make her way to the other side of the table, and one of her first major directing gigs was a 2014 production of *The Light in the Piazza* at Pace University.
- ★ Book writer Craig Lucas was in the original production of another Broadway opera, *Sweeney Todd*; on that show, he met Stephen Sondheim, who set Lucas on the road to becoming a full-time writer by allowing Lucas to use some of his trunk songs to create the revue *Marry Me a Little.*

THE CANON

FUNDAMENTALS OF ANY SEASON

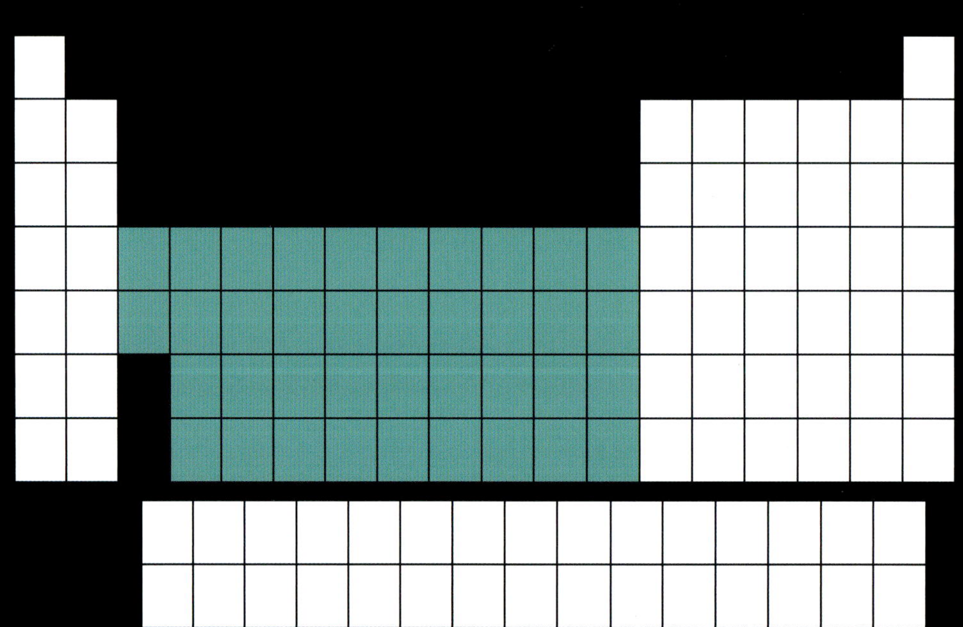

Some shows just work. Every time, in any production, from a high school gym to a 3,000-seat auditorium, in English, Japanese, German, or Hungarian. Creating a show like that takes a huge amount of craft, trial and error, and seemingly endless refining. When a piece hums like a finely tuned engine, it becomes a part of the Canon.

Each show in this family, the largest by far in the Table, had a unique journey to Broadway. Many followed the model of the blockbuster *Oklahoma!*, whose compelling structural formula was so successful that artists riffed on it for decades. Some were the first shows of writers who went on to later break records and push the form: Leonard Bernstein (*On the Town*), Lerner and Loewe (*Brigadoon*), Andrew Lloyd Webber and Tim Rice (*Jesus Christ Superstar*), Lin-Manuel Miranda (*In the Heights*). Some were second shows by teams anxiously trying to re-create the magic of their first: Rodgers and Hammerstein with *Carousel* (their follow-up to *Oklahoma!)* Jones and Schmidt with *110 in the Shade* (after *The Fantasticks* had made such a splash off-Broadway), or Boublil and Schönberg with *Miss Saigon* (younger sibling to the blockbuster *Les Misérables*). Some were immediate hits, touching something in the zeitgeist and running for years, like *Man of La Mancha*, *Mamma Mia!*, or *The Book of Mormon*, while others snuck in under the radar as cult hits, like *She Loves Me* or *Merrily We Roll Along*.

But regardless of their journey, each show in the Canon accomplishes what all great musicals do: introduce us to characters we care about and create a unique, vibrant world. While the settings may vary—Siam, a South American prison cell, even Hell itself—each one feels truthful and real. The music can hearken back to the 19th century or point the way into the 21st, and may call upon bagpipes, harmonicas, or electric guitars, but the goal is the same: to lift our spirits and/or break our hearts. Some of these shows are so familiar, so much a part of general culture, they feel like they've been around forever. But the next time you see any musical, take time to appreciate the spectacular effort that went into creating two and a half hours of music, dance, story, and song.

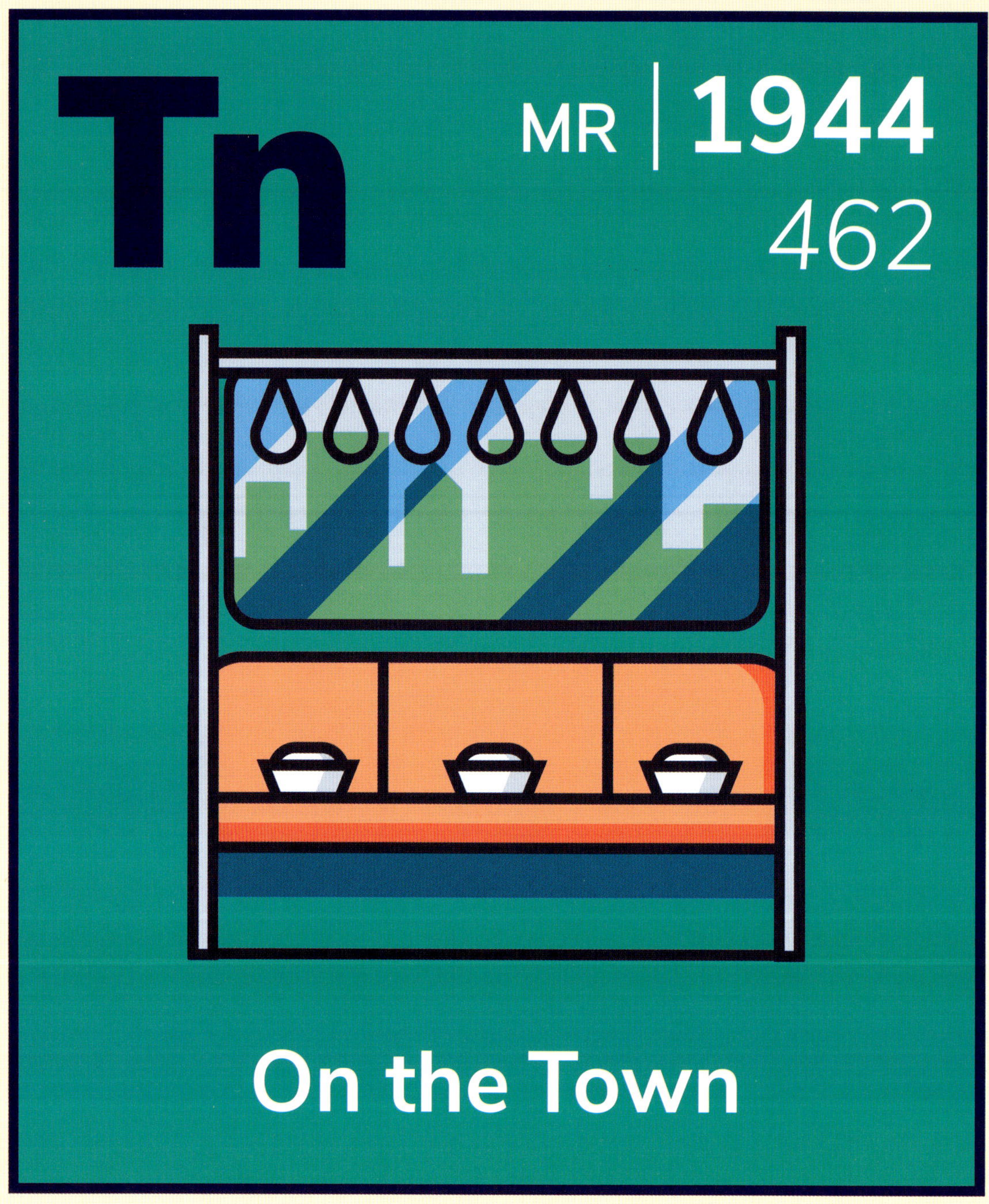

Book and lyrics by Betty Comden and Adolph Green
Music by Leonard Bernstein ★ Based on an idea by Jerome Robbins
Directed by George Abbott ★ Choreographed by Jerome Robbins

Adelphi Theatre*, December 28, 1944–February 2, 1946

John Battles.......Gabey
Cris Alexander.......Chip
Adolph Green.......Ozzie
Betty Comden.......Claire DeLoone

ART NOTE: Three sailors' hats taking a ride on a New York subway train.

First of three theatres

During WWII, three sailors have just twenty-four hours' shore leave in New York City to find love and adventure. Chip and Gabey search for "Miss Turnstiles," a beauty they see on a poster. Gabey finds her and asks her out, while Chip gets sidetracked by an amorous taxi driver. Ozzie ends up with a paleontologist, Claire. After a wild day traversing the city and a brush with the law, all part ways fondly, vowing to catch up again "Some Other Time."

Carried Away

Rarely has one show marked the Broadway debuts of so many artists who would become theatre legends. In 1943, a twenty-five-year-old dancer/choreographer with the prestigious American Ballet Theatre named Jerome Robbins was looking for a composer to collaborate with on a new ballet. Several people recommended Leonard Bernstein, a young classical pianist/composer who had feet in both the symphonic and pop music worlds. Together, they created *Fancy Free*, a twenty-five-minute ballet about three sailors on shore leave in New York. The piece's urban rhythms and dynamic movement made it an immediate hit, and the ballet's set designer Oliver Smith told them he'd produce it if they adapted it into a full musical. So Bernstein asked his friends Betty Comden and Adolph Green, currently performing in an original revue in downtown Manhattan, to write the book and lyrics (the two ended up writing themselves into the show) and set to work.

In turning the ballet into a musical, all but the premise of *Fancy Free* was jettisoned, leaving the young team with a blank slate. Comden and Green decided that whatever the plot ended up being, it should take the characters on a dizzying romp all over New York City, and their book and lyrics dazzled with the satirical wit they'd honed as sketch comics. Bernstein pulled from his love of jazz and experience as a pop vocal arranger for his completely new score, melding swing and boogie-woogie with the more sophisticated harmonic vocabulary of his classical background. And Robbins, determined to make ballets that represented contemporary America, drew on his training at the Actors Studio to create nearly thirty minutes of character- and story-forwarding dance. With dance and music both operating on a heightened artistic level, the show became a blast of fresh theatrical air, an urban counterpoint to *Oklahoma!*'s rural Americana.

Another milestone was the casting of Black and Asian American performers, not just in the extraordinary dance ensemble (many from ABT), but in major roles. The original company's Ivy Smith, "Miss Turnstiles," was played by half-Japanese Sono Osato, an ABT alum who'd made a splash the year before in *One Touch of Venus*. Even she was astonished that audiences, in the middle of WWII, accepted her as an All-American poster girl. "Only in the theatre," she said, and truthfully, given the very real discrimination the cast suffered on tour, perhaps only in "New York, New York."

MISCELLANEOUS MATTER

★ Green and Bernstein coincidentally ended up in the hospital at the same time and requested the same room so they could work on the show, an endeavor that proved not very restful for neighboring patients.

★ Oliver Smith went on to design dozens of the biggest Broadway shows, including *My Fair Lady*, *West Side Story*, and *The Sound of Music*.

★ MGM was the production's largest investor, purchasing the film rights for $250,000 before the show opened, a very unusual move.

★ The musical director of the original production was Everett Lee, the first Black person to hold that position on Broadway.

Book and lyrics by Oscar Hammerstein II ★ Music by Richard Rodgers
Based on the play *Liliom* by Ferenc Molnár
Directed by Rouben Mamoulian ★Choreographed by Agnes de Mille

Majestic Theatre, April 19, 1945–May 24, 1947

Jan Clayton.......Julie Jordan
John Raitt.......Billy Bigelow
Jean Darling.......Carrie Pipperidge
Murvyn Vye.......Jigger Craigin

ART NOTE: One of the horses from the opening sequence's carousel.

In a Maine fishing village, millworker Julie and carnival barker Billy's mutual attraction compels them to defy their employers, and they both lose their jobs. Their marriage is clouded by Billy's darkness, and he eventually turns to crime to make money when Julie announces she's pregnant. During a botched robbery, Billy kills himself and learns admission to heaven depends on returning to Earth for a single day to try and improve the lives of his wife and daughter.

What's the Use of Wond'rin'

How in the world could Rodgers and Hammerstein follow up the unprecedented, historic success of *Oklahoma!*? Legendary film producer Samuel Goldwyn's advice was succinct: "Shoot yourself." Happily, after a brief detour to Hollywood to compose the film *State Fair*, they returned to Broadway with a musical much darker and richer: an adaptation of the popular play *Liliom* by Hungarian playwright Ferenc Molnár. *Liliom*'s depiction of criminal compulsion, domestic violence, and a main character who commits suicide halfway through (a first for a musical) would require Rodgers and Hammerstein to further extend the musical and dramatic techniques they employed in *Oklahoma!*

Luckily, the play was beautifully written, and Hammerstein could make use of much of its structure, and even entire scenes, some of which became *Carousel*'s most innovative moments. Just as *Liliom* began with a silent carnival pantomime introducing its main characters, *Carousel* did the same, but it was set to an eight-minute suite of waltzes. With no overture (Rodgers disliked them), the audience was dropped directly into the world of the play, and shortly thereafter into what Sondheim called "the most important moment in the evolution of contemporary musicals." This twelve-minute section known as "the bench scene" weaves a series of sung musical sections, underscored dialogue, and *recitative*-like moments of speaking on pitch into an organic whole. As Julie and Billy flirt and banter, the number illuminates Julie's quiet courage and Billy's surprising philosophical depths. By scene's end, these two characters are more fully drawn than many musical's characters are at curtain call.

It's Billy, the deeply flawed misfit, who gets the show's eight-minute tour de force solo, "Soliloquy." John Raitt, a Curly in a road company of *Oklahoma!*, remembered being handed this number on accordion-folded manuscript paper that stretched most of the way across the stage. Perfectly suited to his powerful baritone, this near-aria reveals Billy's soft side as he reacts to his imminent fatherhood and reflects on how he'd raise a son compared to a daughter.

All these musical riches plus more innovative narrative ballets from *Oklahoma!*'s Agnes de Mille combined to create a show that was Rodgers's favorite. When people commented on the huge amount of music, he'd say, "It isn't opera. It's just *Carousel*."

MISCELLANEOUS MATTER

- ★ In 1999, *TIME* magazine named *Carousel* the best musical of the 20th century.
- ★ A huge amount of material was cut in a hotel room meeting immediately after the first out-of-town preview, including whole scenes, sections of songs, and a big chunk of the ballet. "Now I see why these people have hits," said stage manager John Fearnley. "I never saw anything so brisk and brave in my life."
- ★ The show also marked the Broadway debut of German composer and arranger Trude Rittman, who composed *Carousel*'s dance music and went on to be invaluable on most Rodgers and Hammerstein and Lerner and Loewe shows.

Book by E. Y. Harburg and Fred Saidy
Music by Burton Lane ★ Lyrics by E. Y. Harburg
Directed by Bretaigne Windust ★ Choreographed by Michael Kidd

46th Street Theatre, January 10, 1947–October 2, 1948

Ella Logan.......Sharon McLonergan
Donald Richards.......Woody Mahoney
David Wayne.......Og
Anita Alvarez.......Susan Mahoney

ART NOTE: Finian's pot of gold, making sure we "Look to the Rainbow."

In this whimsical, politically minded fantasy, a leprechaun, Og, tracks his pot of gold from Ireland to the American South, where the man who stole it, Finian, has reburied it. As Finian, his daughter, Sharon, and Og become entangled in the lives of the locals, the magical pot creates societal mayhem by granting any wish made while standing over it. Some characters find racial enlightenment, some find love, and Finian, after losing the gold, heads off in search of a new rainbow.

Something Sort of Grandish

The songs for the 1939 film *The Wizard of Oz* (written with composer Harold Arlen) mark E. Y. "Yip" Harburg's most enduring contributions to American culture. But those delightful, childlike lyrics aren't representative of his progressive politics, which were a major part of his three Broadway shows. A firm believer in socialist ideals and racial equality, Harburg had previously written lyrics for a 1944 show, *Bloomer Girl* (also with Arlen), which told the story of a fictional Civil War–era women's rights pioneer who aids escaping enslaved people on the Underground Railroad.

Harburg's next Broadway outing outdoes both the fantastical and political ambitions of these earlier works, with its leprechaun-chases-pot-of-gold story and its satirical depiction of the fictional "Missitucky," where villainous Senator Billboard Rawlins makes life difficult for local sharecroppers. The leprechaun's pot grants wishes, like all fantasy pots do, but in *Finian's Rainbow*, the first wish (sort of an accident) turns Rawlins Black. This shocking twist immediately upends his life and starts him on a path toward empathy for the very people he'd had so little regard for. Harburg initially wanted to include scenes where Rawlins was turned away at a restaurant or on a bus, but he was convinced to keep things lighter for the sake of musical comedy.

The absurdities of the plot went down easy in part because of Burton Lane's exceptional score. The composer had been writing music for New York revues and Hollywood musicals since he was a teenager, and for *Finian's Rainbow*, he conjured lilting Irish tunes and rousing love songs, the melodies of which leapt about as much as Michael Kidd's dancers. The underlying joy in his music was a perfect match for Harburg's inventive, expression-coining wordplay (love is "something sort of grandish" that makes your heart feel "sugar candish" "You're under my skinnish / So please be give-innish."). Lane even wrote a blues stomp called "The Begat" fit for a Harlem nightclub.

Audiences of the day were surprisingly ready for this strong social commentary and bizarre and adventurous story. Though some of *Finian's* messaging is a bit dated today, recent revivals continue to show that its huge heart is still decidedly in the right place.

MISCELLANEOUS MATTER

- ★ Fittingly, directly below the *New York Times* review of opening night, the actors' union announced a four-point program to strongly encourage the end of segregation in Washington, DC, theaters. Next to it, in a less progressive vein, ran an ad for Disney's controversial (even then) plantation story *Song of the South.*
- ★ Michael Kidd went on to become a four-time Tony Award winner and one of the only true director/choreographers of the day. He was also a dancer in the original cast of *Fancy Free*, the Jerome Robbins ballet that inspired *On the Town.*
- ★ In 1968, at the heart of the civil rights movement, Francis Ford Coppola (*Singin' in the Rain, The Godfather*) made a film adaptation of the musical, starring Fred Astaire as Finian.

Book and lyrics by Alan Jay Lerner ★ Music by Frederick Loewe
Staged by Robert Lewis ★ Choreographed by Agnes de Mille

Ziegfeld Theatre, March 13, 1947–July 31, 1948

Marion Bell.......Fiona MacLaren
David Brooks.......Tommy Albright
Lee Sullivan.......Charlie Dalrymple
Pamela Britton.......Meg Brockie

ART NOTE: The town, half disappearing into the mists of the Scottish Highlands.

Two New York tourists in Scotland, Tommy and Jeff, stumble upon a town that's strangely not on the map: Brigadoon. Only after Tommy falls for a local, Fiona, does he learn the reason—Brigadoon is under a spell and only appears once every hundred years. Though Fiona begs him to stay, Tommy reluctantly returns home; however, the siren call of Brigadoon eventually lures him back to the highlands where, through the power of love, he's magically reunited with his bonny lass.

Once in the Highlands

Brigadoon is best known as Lerner and Loewe's first bona fide hit, which earned the team the respect of critics and the hearts of audiences transported by its romance and atmospheric Scottish setting. But this triumph only came after three somewhat unconventional (and unsuccessful) little shows. Their unlikely pairing—European cosmopolitan Frederick "Fritz" Loewe and Harvard-educated Alan Jay Lerner, seventeen years his junior—was the result of a chance meeting at a theatrical hangout, the Lambs Club, but their artistic tastes aligned. With their fourth musical, the duo fully embraced the emerging Rodgers and Hammerstein model (serious central love story, comic side plot, big romantic ballads for the principals, and plenty of up-tempo ensemble numbers) and this proved the magic formula.

But *Brigadoon* was far more than an imitation, a Scottish *Oklahoma!* For one thing, the show was not an adaptation; it had an original story whose underlying conceit—lovers potentially separated by time (and therefore death) itself—was preloaded with heightened emotion. Its time-traveling story allowed for wry humor in the clash between antique and modern cultures, brought charmingly to life by a stellar cast. Choreographer Agnes de Mille expanded on her favorite themes (some of which she had also explored in *Oklahoma!*) like the power of community, especially among women. She also brought in new colors through traditional Scottish forms like highland flings and a showstopping "sword dance" in the wedding scene, played in front of Oliver Smith's lush, painterly scenery.

Loewe's music was a match for it all. Trained as a classical pianist in prewar Berlin, Loewe brought a romantic musical vocabulary of significant breadth and the ability to adapt it to whatever period or country a story required. A latecomer to Broadway, he had spent fifteen years in a wide variety of jobs across the United States, from cattle punching to prizefighting to improvising piano accompaniments for silent films, where he learned much of his musical ventriloquism. His melodies are unparalleled in the Broadway canon, often landing unexpectedly on dissonant notes that create a sense of yearning. His classical training shines through in his meticulous inner voices and harmonic progressions, inverted chords, and added tones that create lush textures that evaporate like Brigadoon itself.

MISCELLANEOUS MATTER

- ★ The show became a New York favorite, revived six times at City Center over the next twenty years.
- ★ In pushing musical comedy toward the "musical play," the creators opted to interrupt, rather than put a button on some production numbers so the flow of the story wouldn't be halted by a big round of applause.
- ★ The show's long-lasting cultural impact was reinforced in 2021 on Apple TV's *Schmigadoon!*, a series in which a backpacking couple stumble into a magical town trapped inside a Golden Age musical.

Book and lyrics by Oscar Hammerstein II ★ Music by Richard Rodgers
Based on the novel *Anna and the King of Siam* by Margaret Landon
Directed by John Van Druten ★ Choreographed by Jerome Robbins

St. James Theatre, March 29, 1951–March 20, 1954

Gertrude Lawrence.......Anna Leonowens
Yul Brynner.......The King
Doretta Morrow.......Tuptim
Dorothy Sarnoff.......Lady Thiang

ART NOTE: Anna in her gown, silhouetted inside a traditional Thai house.

Anna, a British widow, travels to Siam in the early 1860s to teach the numerous offspring of the Siamese king. Anna and the monarch immediately clash, but they ultimately develop a wary friendship underlaid with a hint of romantic attraction. Though Anna's Western know-how proves instrumental in helping the kingdom retain its sovereignty against the British, her Western social attitudes undermine the king's authority. Only on his deathbed do the two make peace.

Something Wonderful

Arguably the richest and most varied score Richard Rodgers composed with Oscar Hammerstein, *The King and I* was also the only one that garnered some lukewarm reviews for the music. Possibly, critics felt they had to find *something* to critique so they wouldn't appear to be rubber-stamping a new R&H hit. The writers had worried that anything new they wrote would be unfavorably compared with *South Pacific*, a megahit then less than two years old—so they consciously chose to create a very different, more stately type of musical.

While the credits for *The King and I* list Landon's novel as its source material, the show owes more (its plot arc, and the king's style of article-free speech) to a 1946 movie version of the book. The idea to musicalize this stranger-in-a-strange-land story was suggested to R&H by its original leading lady, legendary British star Gertrude Lawrence, so her participation was a given. The opposite was true when casting a King. Only late in the process, after a number of famous actors declined the role, including Rex Harrison (who'd played the role in the movie), Noël Coward (Gertrude Lawrence's partner in plays like *Private Lives*), and Alfred Drake (the original Curly in *Oklahoma!*) was the little-known Yul Brynner chosen. Now it's impossible to imagine anyone else creating the role.

The original production was opulent, the most expensive R&H show to that point. A big portion of the outsize budget went to Irene Sharaff's sumptuous costumes, many made with actual imported Thai silks. Jerome Robbins was responsible for the choreography, which was minimal except for a much-lauded ballet in the second act, "The Small House of Uncle Thomas." This retelling of *Uncle Tom's Cabin* was rich in both humor and pathos and, unlike most ballets in the R&H canon, was not primarily based on songs in the score, but was instead an original composition of Trude Rittman, Rodgers's longtime dance arranger. Out of town, the show was deemed too long and too somber, so a number of songs were cut, while two were added: a cheery number for Anna and the kids ("Getting to Know You") and an additional ballad for the secondary lovers ("I Have Dreamed").

Mixed reviews aside, the show was another triumph for Rodgers and Hammerstein, winning the Tony for Best Musical, and later revived a whopping four times on Broadway.

MISCELLANEOUS MATTER

- ★ Though not known in 1951, Anna Leonowens, author of the original memoir, had falsified her identity. She was of Anglo-Indian heritage and only claimed to be Welsh to explain her darker complexion. She never set foot in the United Kingdom before arriving in Siam.
- ★ While the show was conceived as a star vehicle for the actress playing Anna, in the numerous tours and revivals that Brynner led, he (and therefore the King) attained solo star status. Now most productions give the two characters equal billing.
- ★ Gertrude Lawrence, never a particularly strong singer, began having severe problems singing in tune shortly after the show opened. Only after her death would it be discovered she'd been suffering from cancer. She was buried in her ball gown from *The King and I.*

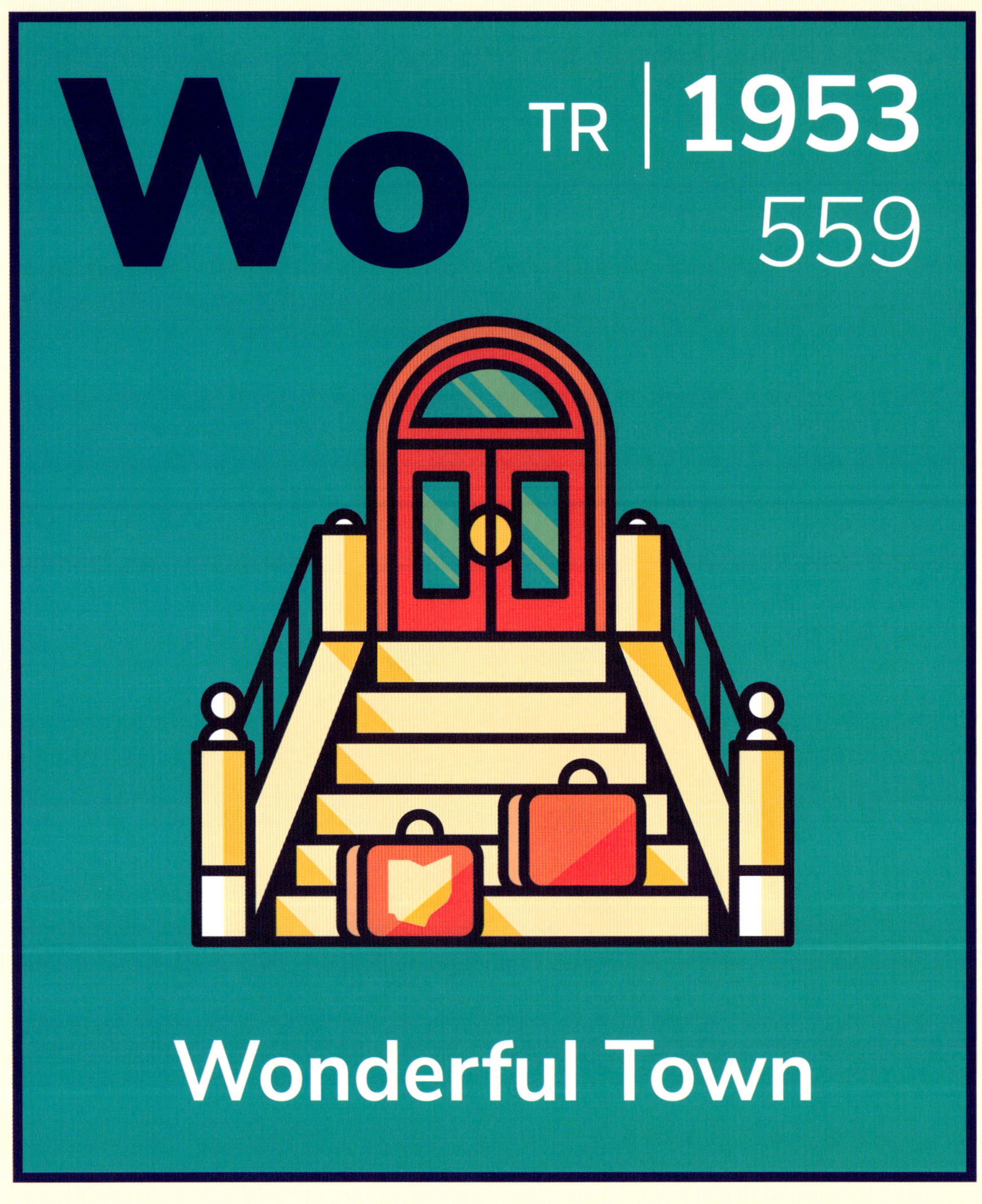

Book by Joseph A. Fields and Jerome Chodorov
Lyrics by Betty Comden and Adolph Green ★ Music by Leonard Bernstein
Based on the play *My Sister Eileen* by Joseph A. Fields and Jerome Chodorov
Directed by George Abbott ★ Musical numbers staged by Donald Saddler

Winter Garden Theatre, February 25, 1953–July 3, 1954

Rosalind Russell.......Ruth Sherwood
Edith Adams.......Eileen Sherwood
George Gaynes.......Robert Baker
Jordan Bentley.......Wreck

ART NOTE: Eileen's and Ruth's suitcases on the steps of a Greenwich Village brownstone, one decorated with an Ohio sticker.

Two sisters from Ohio, Ruth and Eileen, move to New York's Greenwich Village in the 1930s. In their quest to conquer the big city (Ruth aspires to be a writer, Eileen an actress) they must cope with a noisy basement apartment, wacky neighbors, a cynical newspaperman, a shy soda jerk, jazz hipsters, and a cadre of Brazilian Navy cadets (who just want to conga!). It takes until the finale for them to finally feel at home in this wonderful town.

Conquering New York

In late 1952, first-time lead producer Robert Fryer had a problem. He had a hot property under option: *My Sister Eileen*, a long-running play and later a successful film, based on a series of autobiographical short stories in *The New Yorker.* He even had a movie star signed to play the lead: Rosalind Russell (who had played the character of Ruth in the film). Unfortunately, he didn't have an acceptable score. And the clock was ticking: if Fryer's production failed to go into rehearsal in just over a month, Russell would back out.

In a panic, the producer had his director, George Abbott, reach out to Betty Comden and Adolph Green about supplying lyrics for a new score. They said, "Why not?" and suggested Leonard Bernstein as composer (all four had previously collaborated on *On the Town*). Despite the fact he was now the conductor of the New York Philharmonic, Bernstein also said, "Why not?" The race to write a musical in five weeks was on.

Though there was discussion about whether to update the story to the 1950s, the songwriters rejected this idea. They had great fondness for the pop culture of their youth and bet contemporary audiences would, too (peddling nostalgia is nothing new on Broadway). Musical and verbal references to the '30s abound—the vamp after the curtain goes up is a nod to big band leader Eddy Duchin, there are echoes of Gershwin in the ballets, and the lyrics to "Conga" and "Swing" contain a virtual compendium of '30s arcana. The writers also wisely tailored Rosalind Russell's material to the star's minimal vocal range; theatre historian Steven Suskin later described her voice as sounding "somewhat like a lovable barking seal."

Although (according to Abbott) the show's rehearsal and out-of-town tryout was the most acrimonious and contentious of any production he ever worked on (and he directed well over seventy!), none of it mattered. On stage, *Wonderful Town* was sweet, funny, and ebullient. Audiences immediately loved it, and so did critics. It won all five Tonys for which it was nominated, and the wacky, bohemian Greenwich Village it conjured is still where people with any artistic leanings at all dream of living.

MISCELLANEOUS MATTER

★ Rosalind Russell's first and only Broadway replacement, near the end of the run, was Carol Channing.

★ Edie Adams was a classically trained Juilliard grad and 1950's "Miss U.S. Television" who went on to frequent TV appearances.

★ A decade later, when Rosalind Russell was cast as Rose in the movie of *Gypsy*, her singing voice would be almost entirely dubbed by Lisa Kirk (*Kiss Me, Kate*).

★ George Gaynes, who originated the role of Robert Baker (his only major role in a musical), is now mostly remembered for his comic turn as veteran soap opera actor John Van Horn in the movie *Tootsie*.

Book by George Abbott and Richard Bissell
Music and lyrics by Richard Adler and Jerry Ross
Based on the novel *7½ Cents* by Richard Bissell
Directed by George Abbott and Jerome Robbins ★ Choreographed by Bob Fosse

St. James Theatre and Shubert Theatre, May 13, 1954–November 24, 1956

John Raitt.......Sid Sorokin
Janis Paige.......Babe Williams
Eddie Foy Jr.......Hines
Carol Haney.......Gladys

ART NOTE: A pair of pajamas literally "Racing with the Clock," the show's opening number.

On his first day at work as the new superintendent at the Sleep-Tite pajama factory, Sid immediately gets a call from the union for a 7½-cent-an-hour raise. Things get awkward when romantic sparks start to fly between him and Babe, one of the union's top brass. When she sabotages the factory, he fires her, but then discovers the company president is cooking the books. Sid forces him to authorize the raise and wins Babe's love in the bargain.

Steam Heat

There are different kinds of Broadway hits. Some are expected, created by major names with winning track records (think *South Pacific, Mame, The Phantom of the Opera*). And then there are come-from-nowhere surprises that delight critics and audiences because little is expected of them; foremost among these is *The Pajama Game*. When it opened at the end of a busy season, there was little advance sale—if the reviews hadn't been good, it would have closed immediately. Happily, Brooks Atkinson in the *New York Times* proclaimed, "The last new musical of the season is the best," thus launching many a legendary Broadway career. Among the many first-timers involved: producers Robert E. Griffith and Harold Prince (previously a stage manager), young pop songwriters Richard Adler and Jerry Ross, and choreographer Bob Fosse, whose only claim to fame at this point was a brief but red-hot section in "From This Moment On" in the film of *Kiss Me, Kate.* To say all would find further musical theatre success is an understatement.

These newcomers brought a freshness that made *Pajama Game* stand out from its competition, grander, more operatic shows like *Kismet* or *The Golden Apple*. The score was a top-to-bottom delight, with several innovative numbers. The opening, set on the bustling factory floor, uses rapid-fire lines from the chorus to simulate the frantic pace of machinery. Its big ballad, "Hey There," was a theatrical knockout in which John Raitt (*Carousel*'s original Billy Bigelow) recorded a song into his dictaphone, then played it back to sing a counterpoint duet *with himself.* And Fosse's act two trio, "Steam Heat," featuring his signature angular shapes and effortless "cool," stopped the show at every performance.

Presiding over the youngsters was Broadway legend George Abbott. Between 1926 and 1994, he directed and/or wrote the book for nearly fifty Broadway shows, and assisted as a "show doctor" on countless others. He also mentored more young writers, actors, and producers than anyone else. His discipline as both writer and director was legendary, as was his devotion to cutting anything extraneous. His brilliance at keeping both storylines and actors in motion created what came to be thought of as simply the Broadway style. And at his side (partly to supervise young Fosse) was the experienced Robbins, who took charge of the larger production numbers. With mentors like Abbott and Robbins, it's no surprise the heights everyone on this dream team reached.

MISCELLANEOUS MATTER

- ★ Composer/lyricist Frank Loesser (*Guys and Dolls*) was also a respected mentor—Adler and Ross were on contract to his publishing company when they were hired, and Loesser ghost wrote two of the show's songs.
- ★ In Broadway's most famous "understudy-to-star" story, a Hollywood producer was in the audience when Haney was out with a hurt ankle and saw her replacement: Shirley MacLaine.
- ★ Adler and Ross had a knack for writing radio-friendly tunes that caught the country's ear. "Hernando's Hideaway" and "Hey There" were numbers one and two on the Billboard charts.
- ★ When asked what the biggest change was in theatre in his lifetime, Abbott replied, "Electricity."

Book by Douglass Wallop and George Abbott
Music and lyrics by Richard Adler and Jerry Ross
Based on the novel *The Year the Yankees Lost the Pennant* by Douglass Wallop
Directed by George Abbott ★ Dances and musical numbers staged by Bob Fosse

46th Street Theatre and Adelphi Theatre, May 5, 1955–October 12, 1957

Gwen Verdon.......Lola
Ray Walston.......Applegate
Stephen Douglass.......Joe Hardy
Shannon Bolin.......Meg

ART NOTE: A baseball bat crossed with the devil's pitchfork and a hellish flaming ball.

This riff on the legend of Faust sees Joe Boyd, passionate fan of the bottom-ranked Washington Senators baseball team, trade his soul to the Devil (here in the guise of the suave Mr. Applegate) to become Joe Hardy, the long-ball hitter the team sorely needs. However, by insisting on an escape clause that allows him to return to his wife, Joe forces Applegate to use every trick (mostly the seductive Lola) to capture his soul for eternity. The Devil fails, love wins.

A Little Brains, A Little Talent

In most ways, *Damn Yankees* was a direct follow-up to the previous year's smash hit *The Pajama Game*, reassembling the same producers, director, choreographer, and songwriters. But to audiences, these artists mattered less than the redhead playing the Devil's secret weapon, the temptress Lola. This part was Gwen Verdon's first lead on Broadway, after having stolen 1953's *Can-Can* in a featured dance role; in fact, the creators hadn't originally envisioned Lola as a major character, but when audiences adored her, they kept adding new material. Verdon's numbers showcased both her sensuality and her terrific sense of humor—"Gwen danced with her face," recalled Lee Roy Reams, who danced with her in *Sweet Charity*. "That was the difference."

It's hard to overstate how big Verdon became in 1955. She appeared on the cover of *TIME* magazine a month after the show opened, at about the same time the producers retooled the posters to put her name alone above the title. This is also when they began to use the now-familiar photo of Verdon, attired only in the scanty leotard she strips down to in her sultry showstopper "Whatever Lola Wants," in all the production's advertising.

Not only was *Damn Yankees* the show that made Verdon a star, it also made Broadway history by introducing her to Bob Fosse, who would become her long-time collaborator and eventual husband. Highly trained in everything from ballet to Latin to the East Indian vocabulary of pioneering jazz choreographer Jack Cole, Verdon's breadth of knowledge pushed Fosse further in the direction he was beginning to stake out artistically, and his movement fit her body perfectly. The two would do four more musicals together, including *Sweet Charity* and *Chicago*.

Of course, *Damn Yankees* did have other things going for it besides Verdon and Fosse. The theatre was decked out like a baseball stadium, with stadium lights, hot dogs on sale at intermission, and an entire curtain made of baseballs (donated by Spaulding). It had a tuneful, wide-ranging score that included joyful odes to athletic showmanship and camaraderie, alongside poignant love songs. And mention should be made of Ray Walston, who turned in a delightfully hammy performance as Applegate that was so singular he was asked to repeat it in the 1958 film version.

MISCELLANEOUS MATTER

★ The number "Two Lost Souls" originally had a rock-and-roll beat and would've been the first rock song in a Broadway show. But rock was still controversial, and Abbott refused to have anything that might offend a family audience, so Adler and Ross revised it as a bluesy swing.

★ When *Damn Yankees* reached the screen in 1958 with most of its Broadway cast intact, Fosse stepped in to dance the mambo "Who's Got the Pain" with his wife; it was the only time they would dance together in a film.

★ Radio play for the show's songs hit a snag because federal regulations prohibited using the *D* word. DJs had to change the title to "Dum Yankees" or the Bronx-style "Dem Yankees."

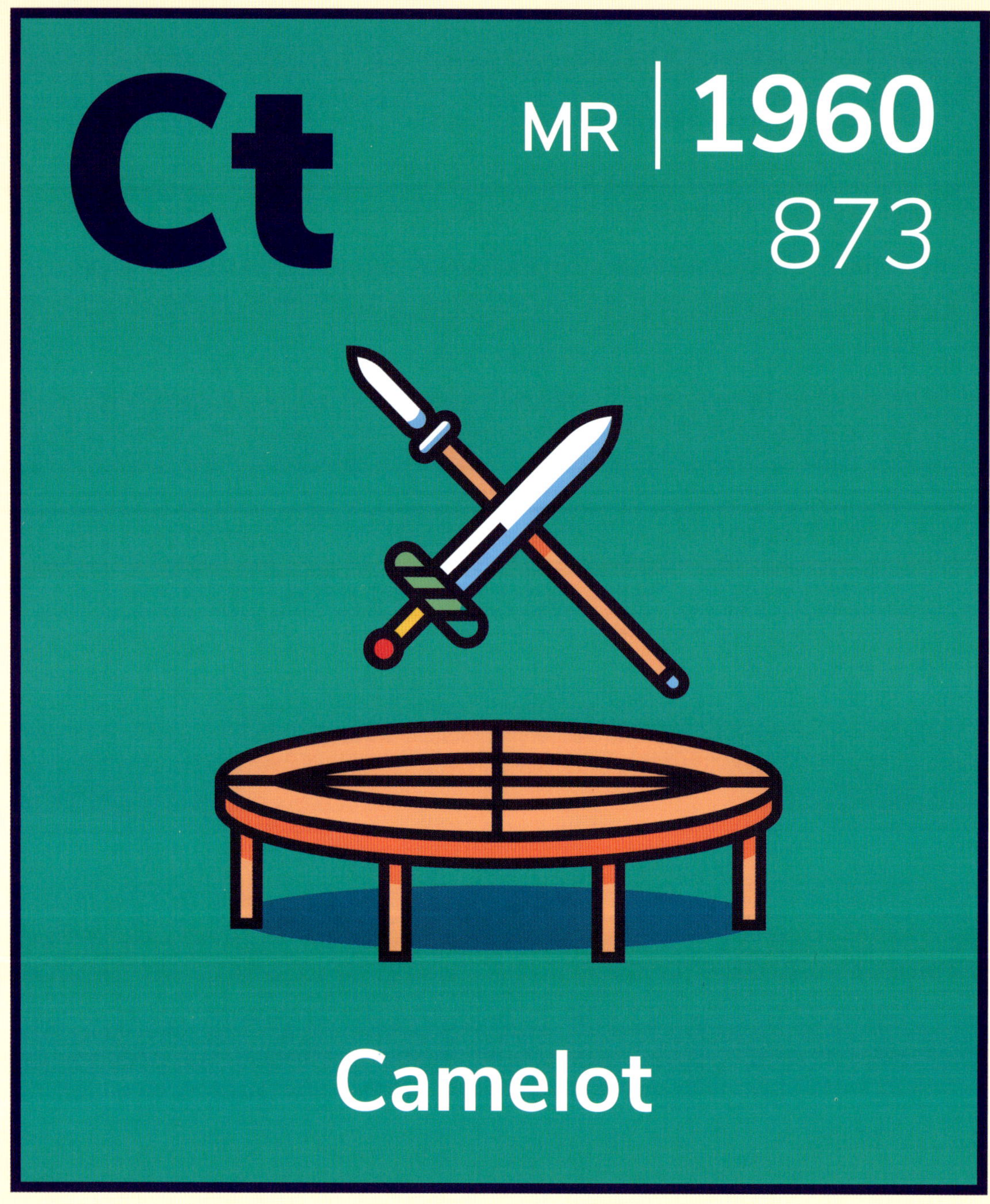

Book and lyrics by Alan Jay Lerner ★ Music by Frederick Loewe
Based on the novel *The Once and Future King* by T. H. White
Staged by Moss Hart ★ Choreographed by Hanya Holm

Majestic Theatre, December 3, 1960–January 5, 1963

Julie Andrews.......Guenevere
Richard Burton.......Arthur
Robert Goulet.......Lancelot
Roddy McDowall.......Mordred

ART NOTE: King Arthur's sword crossed with a lance (for Lancelot), suspended over the Round Table.

Arthur and Guenevere meet-cute and fall in love. Inspired by his new marital bliss, Arthur dreams up the Round Table, an idea that draws a French knight, Lancelot, to Camelot. But trouble arrives with Lancelot; he and Guenevere fall helplessly in love, and their passionate, if chaste, affair eventually leads to civil war. In the end, all that's left are the ideals Camelot represents, waiting to be revived by a new generation.

Follow Me

Camelot is a show that was shaping up to be a disaster, but which somehow emerged as a musical theatre warhorse. From the start, there were problems. Lerner was excited about adapting T. H. White's novel into a serious musical (or at least adapting the later parts—Disney had optioned the first section, about young Arthur, for their animated film, *The Sword in the Stone*), but Loewe, with his central European sensibility, felt the tale of a cuckold was subject matter fit only for a comedy. Additionally, there was added pressure because *Camelot*'s development was taking place in the shadow of *My Fair Lady*, the team's 1956 blockbuster; all Broadway was waiting (some with sharpened knives) to see if they could equal that triumph. The new show seemed to court this comparison, since it reassembled much of the team from the earlier hit: director Moss Hart, choreographer Hanya Holm, supporting player Robert Coote, leading lady Julie Andrews, and, last but not least, designer Oliver Smith (who, perhaps attempting to outdo *My Fair Lady*'s lavish sets, generated "more scenery than Switzerland," as Lerner later quipped).

The show's out-of-town tryout was especially fraught, and its inordinate length (over three and a half hours!) was only one issue. The primary drama was offstage. First, Lerner collapsed with a bleeding ulcer, then Hart had a massive heart attack. Lerner took over direction, a decision that angered Loewe and is primarily what led to the dissolution of their collaboration. The Broadway reviews, when they finally came, were mixed to negative. And while the show's large advance meant it wouldn't close immediately, ticket sales were abysmal.

A pair of near-simultaneous events three months later led to the show's miraculous turnaround. Ed Sullivan gave *Camelot* an extended slot on his top-rated TV show to perform a series of numbers; the next day, and for the first time, there were lines at the box office. Earlier that same week, a now recovered Moss Hart had arrived back in New York, re-rehearsed the cast, and trimmed an additional fifteen minutes. This meant the new crowds clamoring to see *Camelot* encountered a tighter, more satisfying show, boosting word of mouth.

One thing everyone agreed on, all along, was that Lerner and Loewe's final theatre score is one of their best. As much as anything, *Camelot*'s witty lyrics and lush melodies are why musical theatre lovers will "never let it be forgot."

MISCELLANEOUS MATTER

- ★ The original cast album was enormously successful, the best-selling LP in America for sixty weeks.
- ★ When it upset preview audiences to see "fair lady" Julie Andrews as a wanton adulteress, the script was changed to make Lancelot and Guenevere's affair chaste—they love each other but barely share a kiss.
- ★ For the 2023 revival at Lincoln Center, acclaimed playwright and screenwriter Aaron Sorkin (*The West Wing*) devised a completely new script to accompany Lerner and Loewe's songs. The result? Same as in 1960: critics loved the score and slammed the book.

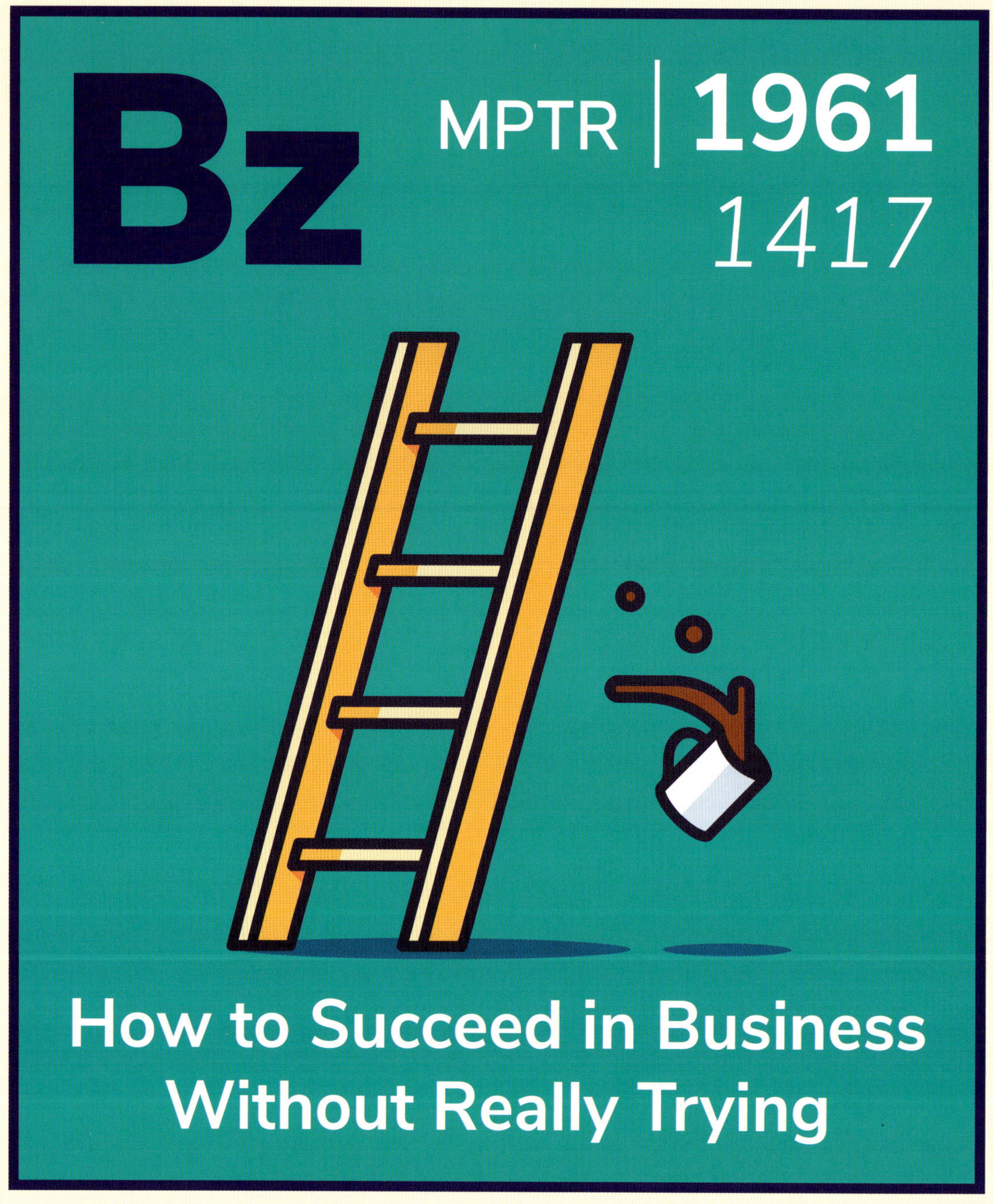

Book by Abe Burrows, Jack Weinstock, and Willie Gilbert ★ Music and lyrics by Frank Loesser ★ Based on the book by Shepherd Mead ★ Directed by Abe Burrows ★ Musical staging by Bob Fosse ★ Choreographed by Hugh Lambert

46th Street Theatre, October 14, 1961–March 6, 1965

Robert Morse.......J. Pierrepont Finch
Bonnie Scott.......Rosemary Pilkington
Rudy Vallee.......J. B. Biggley
Claudette Sutherland.......Smitty

ART NOTE: A corporate ladder and a mug from the number "Coffee Break" that's about to cause a mess.

An ambitious window-washer follows the instructions of a self-help book to advance up the corporate ladder, starting in the mailroom. With the help and encouragement of a marriage-minded secretary, he ingratiates himself with the president, manipulates competitors into getting fired, causes a national TV debacle, almost gets fired himself, then inspires everyone with a rousing anthem to mediocrity and ends up chairman of the board.

I Believe in You

The *tone* of a show—romantic, dark, broadly comic, sincere, etc.—is often said to be the most important thing for a creative team to get right, and one of the easiest to get wrong. Perhaps the hardest tone for a musical to pin down is that of a satire, that stiletto-bladed art of exaggerating a topic until it lies bleeding on the sidewalk while everyone laughs. Music is inherently sincere—it's nearly impossible for a character to sing sarcastically—and in a great satire, the characters must believe every word they say; in fact, authors use their characters' sincerity to expose just how ridiculous they are.

Satirical revues were once quite common, but full satirical musicals are rare; keeping that delicate balloon in the air for one song, mocking a single topic of the day, is one thing, but sustaining it over two hours takes a bit of genius. The Gershwin brothers had managed it with *Of Thee I Sing* way back in 1931, skewering American political campaigns, and Betty Comden and Adolph Green, with their sketch comedy background, could generally be counted on to poke gentle fun at some trend or character type in their shows. But in *How to Succeed*, the creators lined up every aspect of corporate life and gunned them down one by one. The consistency of tone was breathtaking, both breezy and vicious, with characters (always sincerely) praising the inanity of office dating, women who dream of nothing more than housework, and fatuous C-suite Ivy League alums. Everything that *Mad Men*–era society outwardly lauded was skewered and exposed, and audiences ate it up.

Loesser and Burrows had worked magic together eleven years earlier with their smash hit, *Guys and Dolls*, and just as before, Loesser kept the beats lively and the lyrics clever. But unusually for a musical, this time there wasn't a hint of sentimentality or even a real emotion that wasn't sent up in some way. Also a rarity: an actual leading *man* show! Boyish Robert Morse almost never left the stage, and he somehow was able to expertly walk the line between naive and devious, insecure and brazen, with a constant, scheming glint in his eye. He managed to keep an audience rooting for him to succeed, while still being appalled at his tactics. The fact that everyone else was just as shallow, venal, and/or stupid made the entire evening a ridiculous delight.

MISCELLANEOUS MATTER

★ Just like its satirical forerunner *Of Thee I Sing*, the show won the Pulitzer Prize for Best Musical, in a near-unanimous vote.

★ In the ultimate "promotion," Morse appeared in *Mad Men* as the ad company's eccentric founding partner Bertram Cooper for eight years. His final appearance was a song-and-dance routine from beyond the grave.

★ Rudy Vallee sold millions of records in the 1930s and 1940s with a small "crooner" voice perfect for the radio. But he had trouble projecting in live concerts and used a megaphone, so this prop was added to numbers for Biggley's character.

Book, music, and lyrics by Lionel Bart
Freely adapted from the novel *Oliver Twist* by Charles Dickens
Directed by Peter Coe

Imperial Theatre and Shubert Theatre, January 6, 1963–November 14, 1964

Georgia Brown.......Nancy
Clive Revill.......Fagin
Bruce Prochnik.......Oliver Twist
David Jones.......The Artful Dodger

ART NOTE: Oliver's empty bowl from the orphanage; no wonder he asked for more.

An adorable, pure-of-heart orphan, Oliver, leads an eventful, adventurous life in early Victorian London: first he's a workhouse boy, next an undertaker's apprentice, and finally a thief when he falls in with a band of underage pickpockets led by the conniving Fagin. After being arrested for a botched theft, he somehow ends up quasi-adopted by kind, rich Mr. Brownlow, who (after Oliver is briefly abducted, then rescued by the selfless serving-wench Nancy) is revealed to be his genuine grandfather. Whew.

It's a Fine Life

The Golden Age Broadway musical, in its mature, unified synthesis of song, dialogue, and dance, was an entirely American invention. Although Great Britain had a centuries-long history of extraordinary plays and operettas, it wasn't until the early 1960s, when triple-threat Lionel Bart created *Oliver!* that there was a truly classic British musical.

Bart came squarely from the British music hall tradition, similar to American vaudeville. He had a natural gift for rousing, catchy melodies (which he dictated to a musical arranger, as he couldn't read or write music) as well as a knack for smart rhymes and colloquial phrases. He embraced the "let's all sing a song now!" exuberance of a music hall production, while crafting solos that plumbed unexpected psychological depths. "As Long as He Needs Me," for example, is not only a complex admission from a woman about why she stays with an abusive lover, its indestructible melody gave British pop diva Shirley Bassey a hit that stayed on the British charts for six months.

Bart lightened and modernized the tone of the original novel, but if its lovable urchins are not entirely Dickensian, the murderous Bill Sikes still terrifies. More important was how he transformed the role of Fagin, historically depicted as a grasping Jewish stereotype. He and Ron Moody, who originated the role, were both Jewish, and together they made the character more of a charmingly amoral trickster. Though Moody didn't accompany *Oliver!* to Broadway because of his own projects, his masterful performance (especially in the tour de force soliloquy "Reviewing the Situation") was thankfully captured in the movie version, one of the few musicals to win an Oscar for Best Picture.

Credit for bringing the show across the Atlantic in the first place goes to producer David Merrick, an early proponent of transferring established West End hits (both plays and musicals) to New York. Since he was uncertain if the very British *Oliver!* would succeed on Broadway, he hedged his bets by first running the show in Los Angeles and San Francisco, and releasing a cast album, to put cash in the bank before it got to the Great White Way. In the end, *Oliver!* became a true crowd-pleaser in both countries and was the longest-running West End show until it was overtaken by the next revolutionary British musical, Andrew Lloyd Webber's *Jesus Christ Superstar.*

MISCELLANEOUS MATTER

★ *My Fair Lady*'s Rex Harrison, *Peter Pan*'s Cyril Ritchard, and *The Wizard of Oz*'s Ray Bolger all expressed interest in playing Fagin when it transferred to Broadway. Barry Humphries (of Dame Edna fame) originated the role of Mr. Sowerberry, the undertaker, in the West End, then played Fagin in a 1980s revival.

★ British authorities prosecuted London-born Prochnik's father under child exploitation laws for allowing him to work in the United States. He was fined £5.

★ David Jones, who played the Artful Dodger in the West End and on Broadway, became Davy Jones of the hit pop group the Monkees. Appearing on the *Ed Sullivan Show* in an *Oliver!* segment the same night the Beatles drove the crowd into a frenzy, he decided he wanted that kind of fame.

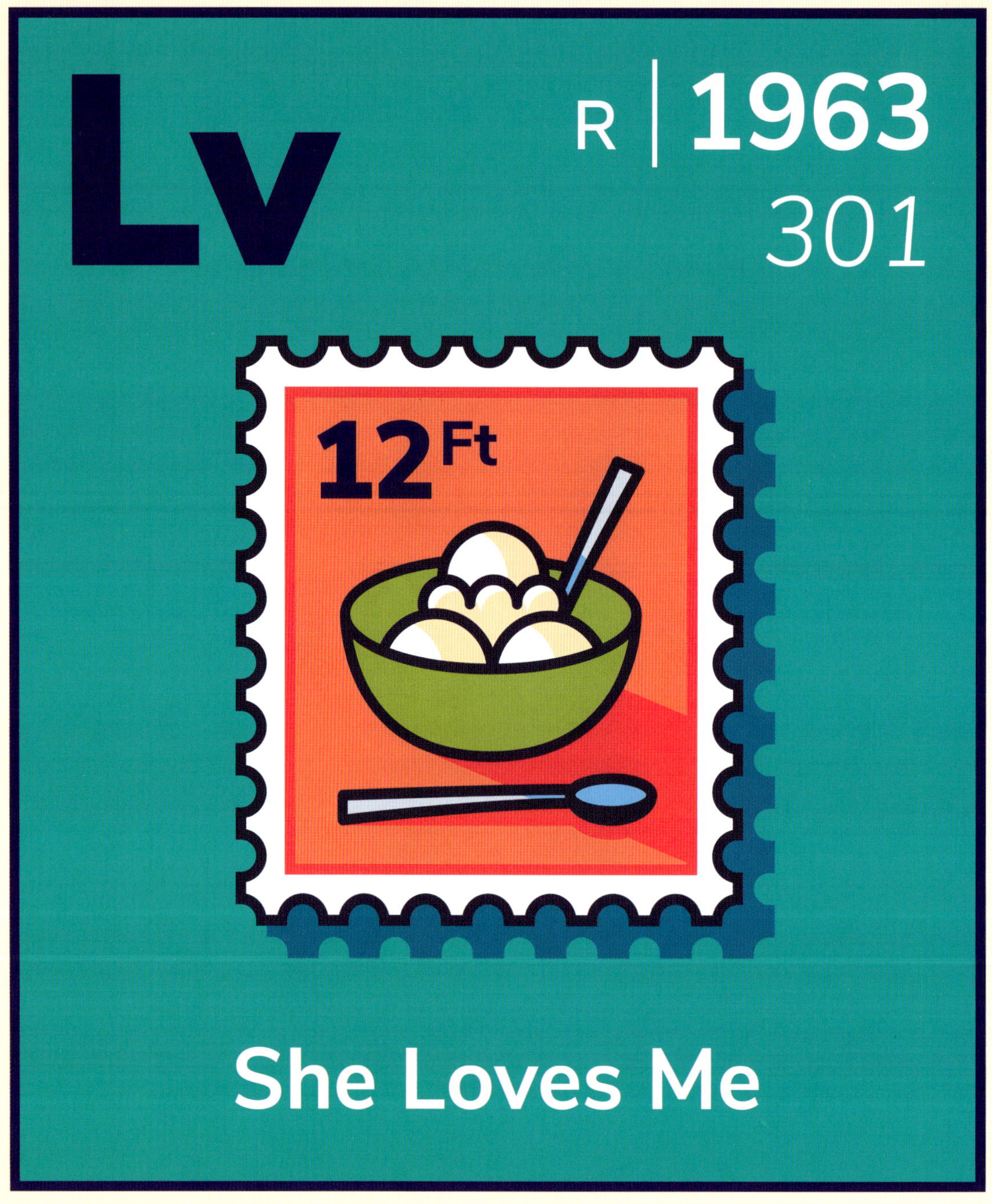

Book by Joe Masteroff ★ Music by Jerry Bock ★ Lyrics by Sheldon Harnick
Based on the play *Parfumerie* by Miklós László
Directed by Harold Prince ★ Musical staging by Carol Haney

Eugene O'Neill Theatre, April 23, 1963–January 11, 1964

Barbara Cook.......Amalia Balash
Daniel Massey.......Georg Nowack
Barbara Baxley.......Ilona Ritter
Jack Cassidy.......Steven Kodaly

ART NOTE: A Hungarian 12-forint stamp (the number of days till Christmas) showing a bowl of "Vanilla Ice Cream," one of the show's hits.

At a bustling parfumerie in 1934 Budapest, Amalia shows up looking for a job, impresses the owner into hiring her, but immediately starts quarreling with the head salesman, Georg. As the tension between them continues, he can at least take comfort in the romantic letters he's been exchanging with an anonymous "Dear Friend." When he discovers it is none other than Amalia before she does, he gently woos her in real life before revealing his identity.

A Romantic Atmosphere

In the first scene of *She Loves Me*, quick-thinking Amalia grabs an item to sell to a customer to impress the owner of the parfumerie into hiring her. Just one problem—she doesn't know what it is, exactly. It's a box that plays music when you open it, so she decides it's a candy dish whose music warns you not to eat too much, and deftly persuades the woman to purchase one. (It turns out to be a cigarette case.) *She Loves Me* was a similar delicate musical treat that people couldn't easily identify. It was a hugely romantic show, but with a love story that centers around anonymous letters between two "dear friends" more likely to disclose opinions regarding Dumas and Debussy than their feelings; their first kiss only happens just before the final curtain comes down. There are few big production numbers, barely any dancing (though Carol Haney's staging of the pre-Christmas rush was a sublime sort of shopping ballet).

It's no wonder this little show got drowned out by the noisy shenanigans over at *How to Succeed in Business Without Really Trying* and *A Funny Thing Happened on the Way to the Forum* and closed in less than eight months.

But *She Loves Me*'s quiet charms slowly turned it into a cult favorite, one of the rare shows that only became beloved long after its initial run (*Chicago* is another), a success that can be attributed to its impeccable craft at every level. The story of the underlying play is irresistible, and although Joe Masteroff was a first-time book writer (his next show would be *Cabaret*), it demonstrated intelligence and a deft hand at setting up songs and getting out of their way. And the songs seemingly never stopped—seventeen in the first act alone! Elegant, sweet but never cloying, the show swept audiences along in a cloud of perfumed nostalgia, with top notes of blithe waltzes, polkas, and tangos, and a base of more grown-up yearnings.

Moreover, *She Loves Me* was a physically beautiful show. Husband-and-wife team William and Jean Eckart (*Damn Yankees, Fiorello!*) again created innovative sets, here perfectly in tune with the show's intimate feel. The centerpiece was the shop itself, which was composed of opulent Art Nouveau curves and opened up like a Fabergé egg, thanks to three revolving wagons, an impressive feat given that the Eugene O'Neill Theatre has one of Broadway's smallest stages.

MISCELLANEOUS MATTER

- ★ *Parfumerie* also inspired three film versions: 1940's *The Shop Around the Corner* starring Jimmy Stewart and Margaret Sullavan, 1949's musical *In the Good Old Summertime* with Judy Garland and Van Johnson, and the 1998 Tom Hanks/Meg Ryan blockbuster *You've Got Mail.*
- ★ Although the show won only a single Tony Award (for Jack Cassidy), its two-record cast album snagged a Grammy.
- ★ After winning the Oscar for playing Anita in the movie of *West Side Story*, Rita Moreno had a surprising seven-year film drought, during which she played Ilona in the show's 1964 West End premiere.

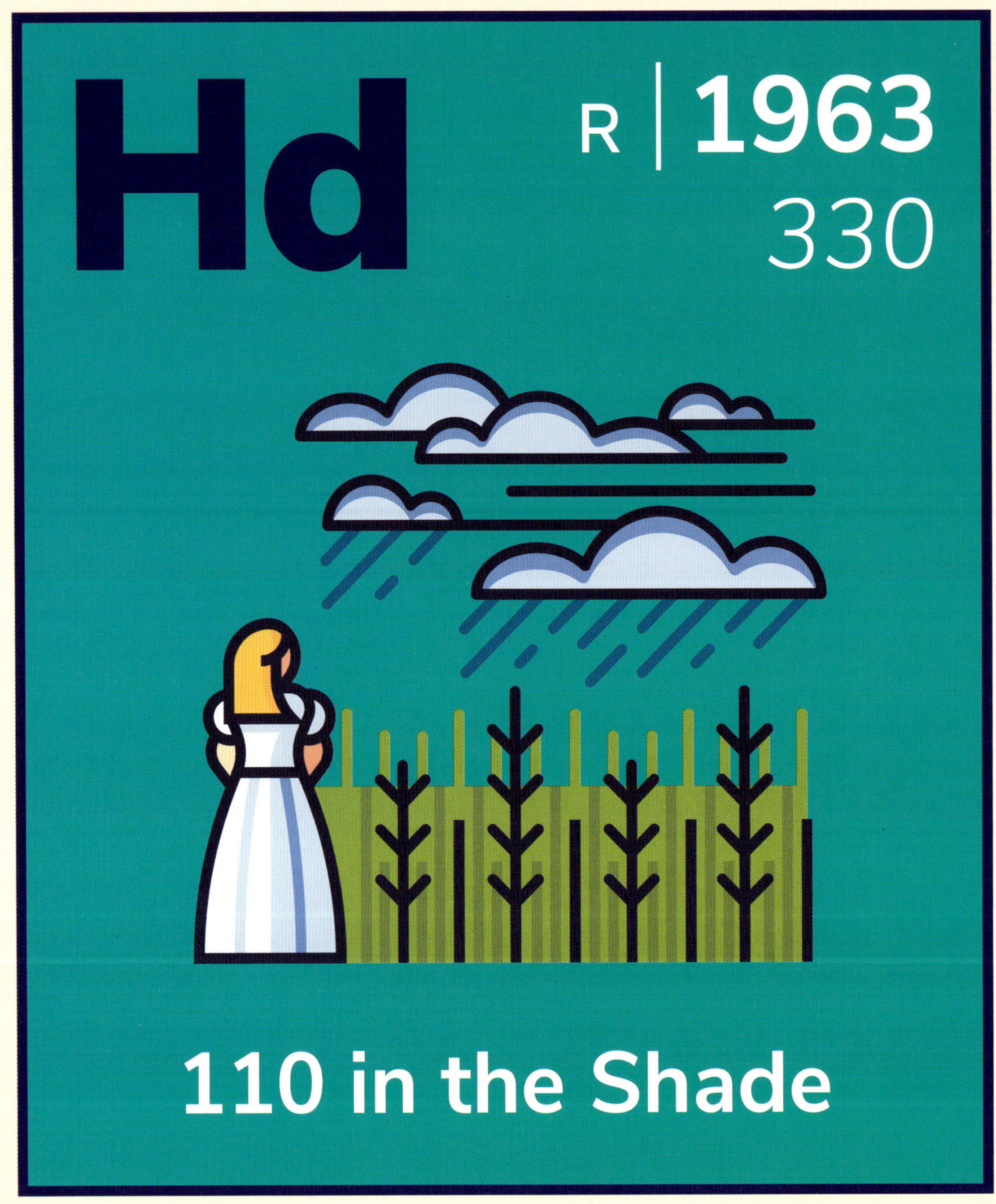

Book by N. Richard Nash ★ Music by Harvey Schmidt
Lyrics by Tom Jones ★ Based on the play *The Rainmaker* by N. Richard Nash
Directed by Joseph Anthony ★ Choreographed by Agnes de Mille

Broadhurst Theatre, October 24, 1963–August 8, 1964

Inga Swenson.......Lizzie Curry
Stephen Douglass.......File
Robert Horton.......Bill Starbuck
Lesley Ann Warren.......Snookie

ART NOTE: Lizzie in her "nice white dress all buttoned up tight," gazing longingly toward distant rain clouds.

In a drought-stricken southwestern town, Lizzie's father and brothers try to get her to soften her sharp tongue and disguise her intellect long enough to catch a husband. She dreams of love, but reflexively pushes men away, even salt-of-the-earth sheriff File. When a traveling huckster comes to town promising he can make it rain, he opens up Lizzie's dreams; then, as rain actually does begin to fall, he rides away, leaving her and File to start a new life together.

Simple Little Things

The play *The Rainmaker* had a modest Broadway run in 1954–55, then became a movie starring Katharine Hepburn and Burt Lancaster. But it wasn't until playwright N. Richard Nash saw *The Fantasticks* (then in the third year of its incredible 42-year run off-Broadway) that he found the writers he'd been looking for to make it sing. Tom Jones and Harvey Schmidt had met at college in Texas and had honed their skills writing songs for revues in Manhattan nightclubs. *110 in the Shade* would be their first Broadway show, and its combination of a setting they both knew intimately, a town of plain-spoken people with thoughtful depths, and a wildly theatrical charlatan was a natural match for their talents.

Schmidt was not a formally trained musician; like Richard Adler (*Pajama Game, Damn Yankees*), he needed an assistant to transcribe the music that poured from him. But unlike Adler, Schmidt was a terrific pianist, and his ear was excellent—growing up, he internalized anything he heard on the radio, from pop and country songs to the Texaco Metropolitan Opera broadcasts his mother would listen to every Saturday. The score for *110 in the Shade* reflects that diversity. Wide-open fourths and fifths reminiscent of Aaron Copland's American ballets would slide into honky-tonk piano with a Western bass. And like the *Fantasticks* score, a surprising dissonance with a jazzy kick often sneaks in when things get too sentimental. Jones was a theatrical scholar, well-versed in the theatrical traditions of many countries and eras. His simple lyrics get right to the heart of a character's situation, in words both poetic and colloquial. He could channel Lizzie's dreams of "simple little things," and then just as easily conjure the pseudo-Shakespearean swashbuckling fantasies of con man Starbuck.

Together, they created an affectionate portrait of a hardscrabble town and a huckster whom you both distrust and root for—his heart is simultaneously in the right and wrong place as he cons the town but brings out a new confidence in Lizzie. Some of the score's lyrics actually started life in the play; Jones thought Nash's words were already heightened, and he simply had to nudge them into a form Schmidt could set. *110 in the Shade*'s rural American charms and finely-wrought characters touched people's hearts, and Jones and Schmidt's score was nominated for a Tony, making the show a quieter—and simpler—alternative to the big-city brass over at *Hello, Dolly!* and *Funny Girl*.

MISCELLANEOUS MATTER

- ★ Horton was famous from the hit TV Western *Wagon Train*, and Douglass was the original Joe Hardy in *Damn Yankees*. But it was little-known Inga Swenson, a standby Guinevere in *Camelot*, who received the show's only acting Tony nomination.
- ★ Producer David Merrick behaved badly throughout (see *42nd Street*). First, he forced the writers to change the two-act structure back to three, like the play, then threatened to close the show when it didn't work.
- ★ Unique among composers, Schmidt was also a very successful commercial artist and would first paint characters and scenes to get the notes flowing.

Book by Dale Wasserman ★ Music by Mitch Leigh
Lyrics by Joe Darion ★ Suggested by the life and works of Miguel de Cervantes
Directed by Albert Marre ★ Choreographed by Jack Cole

ANTA Washington Square Theatre*, November 22, 1965–June 26, 1971

Richard Kiley.......Cervantes/Don Quixote
Joan Diener.......Aldonza/Dulcinea
Irving Jacobson.......Sancho Panza
Robert Rounseville.......The Padre

ART NOTE: The bucket Quixote uses for a helmet, and the "Little Bird" from the song of the same name.

*First of four theatres

The poet Cervantes lands in a dungeon during the Spanish Inquisition. Other prisoners grab his belongings, including a manuscript, Don Quixote, *but then agree to hold a mock trial before deciding whether to confiscate them. As his defense, Cervantes and the prisoners enact scenes from the book, about an idealistic but deluded man who thinks he's a heroic knight. This convinces some, especially the prostitute Aldonza, that there are times when blind idealism can change the world, and they let him keep his manuscript.*

The Impossible Dream

By 1965, Greenwich Village had for decades been the epicenter of the off- and off-off-Broadway scene, the home of adventurous artists longing to escape what they considered the creatively stifling pressures of Broadway. So it is only fitting that *Man of La Mancha*, which borrowed extensively from the experimental theatre movement, opened at the ANTA in the Village (despite its downtown location, it was considered a Broadway house because of its seating capacity).

Like *The Fantasticks,* the off-Broadway megahit that became the longest running musical of all time, *La Mancha* embraced elements of the emerging poor theatre aesthetic, which rejected expensive sets and costumes in favor of asking audiences to use their imaginations. It had a spare unit set (a dungeon that could only be entered from above, via a rickety staircase lowered on chains), and the actors transformed into different characters in view of the audience. The only props were everyday items that, with imagination, became the trappings of a knight and his entire world. And, because the ANTA had a thrust stage, its playing area extended out into the audience, bridging the gap between performers and viewers, story and reality.

Man of La Mancha actually started as a television play by writer Dale Wasserman, which was broadcast live in 1959 to an estimated audience of twenty million viewers. Wasserman then brought in Mitch Leigh, a Yale-educated composer who had moved into jazz and TV jingles (and who was especially appealing since he had the money to finance much of the production) to adapt the piece as a musical. Leigh employed Spanish rhythms, meters, and instrumentation to conjure a fantastical world of heroism and idealism; unusually, he decided on an orchestration with no strings other than two guitars and a bass. Originally, poet W. H. Auden was going to write the lyrics, but his early efforts were considered too dark and biting, so the creative team replaced him with Joe Darion.

There was no such second-guessing about their star—no one could have asked for a more perfect Don Quixote than Richard Kiley. His majestic baritone and classical diction gave the confused knight a powerful sound and a quiet dignity. And his performance of the character's signature anthem, "The Impossible Dream," helped make it a huge hit—to this day, it remains one of the great, inspiring songs of musical theatre.

MISCELLANEOUS MATTER

- ★ Mitch Leigh had a TV jingle production company and wrote the music for the advertising earworm "Nobody Doesn't Like Sara Lee."
- ★ *La Mancha* was the last Broadway show choreographed by "The Father of Jazz Dance," Jack Cole; it capped a long career with his biggest hit.
- ★ Albert Marre's previous success had been directing 1954's *Kismet*, also starring Kiley and Diener (whom he married in 1956). He also directed Jerry Herman's first musical, *Milk and Honey*, in 1961.

Book by Neil Simon ★ Music by Burt Bacharach ★ Lyrics by Hal David
Based on the film *The Apartment* by Billy Wilder and I. A. L. Diamond
Directed by Robert Moore ★ Musical numbers staged by Michael Bennett

Shubert Theatre, December 1, 1968–January 1, 1972

Jerry Orbach.......Chuck Baxter *Jill O'Hara.......Fran Kubelik*

ART NOTE: The door to the apartment with the key in the lock.

Chuck Baxter loans his bachelor pad to various superiors at his life insurance company for romantic trysts in return for positive evaluations. The personnel director catches on and starts using it as well; unfortunately, he's sleeping with Fran, the girl Chuck has a crush on. When Fran learns she's not the director's only fling and he won't leave his wife, she overdoses on sleeping pills. Chuck nurses her back to health, making her finally realize how much he loves her.

Where Can You Take a Girl?

From the 1930s through the early '60s, Broadway was a big part of popular music. Hits by Berlin, Kern, Gershwin, Porter, Rodgers and Hart, and Rodgers and Hammerstein topped the charts and received extensive radio play. But with the advent of rock and roll, Broadway and pop music went separate ways. So when producer David Merrick signed the king of Broadway comedies, Neil Simon, to adapt the Academy Award–winning film *The Apartment,* and the playwright suggested bringing in two of the top pop hit-makers of the late '60s, he was intrigued. True, Bacharach and David had never written a musical, but Merrick hoped they could be the answer to reuniting Broadway and the hit parade, and his gamble paid off. Bacharach had his number one star, Dionne Warwick, record three songs from *Promises, Promises* before the show opened, and one more during the run; two became number one hits.

Bacharach brought a sophisticated background in jazz as well as classical composition, writing songs with dropped beats and meter changes that gave periodic rhythmic "kicks." In the studio, he was meticulous about getting the sound he wanted, and he brought this discipline to Broadway. He introduced "pit singers" who'd guarantee a great vocal sound even when onstage performers were dancing, and he separated groups of orchestra musicians with acoustic dividers to achieve the perfect aural balance. These techniques created "the record sound" on Broadway, and though Merrick worried the audience would think they were hearing a recording, people loved it.

To balance his neophyte theatre songwriters and first-time director, Merrick assembled a roster of Broadway regulars. In addition to book writer Simon, the team included scenic designer Robin Wagner (*Hair*), modish costumer Donald Brooks, and wunderkind choreographer Michael Bennett, who, after two flops, would finally get his first Broadway hit. His use of dance moves you might see at a club matched Bacharach's contemporary style, and his choreographed scene changes were praised by critics in *Promises'* raves.

Despite the show's big success, Bacharach never wrote another. He couldn't stomach the uncontrollable variables involved in live theatre and went back to recording studios, where once you finish a song, it sounds the same every time it's played.

MISCELLANEOUS MATTER

- ★ When the show was out of town, Merrick demanded a new song even though Bacharach was in the hospital with pneumonia. So Hal David supplied a lyric, and Bacharach added music post-recovery. The tune was "I'll Never Fall in Love Again," the last song from a musical to hit number one on the Billboard charts. David even snuck in a reference to pneumonia, rhyming it with "he'll never phone ya."
- ★ *Promises, Promises* was Michael Bennett's first time working with the dancer who would become his muse, Donna McKechnie; he put her front and center in the standout number "Turkey Lurkey Time."
- ★ The role of Marge MacDougall, drunk bar patron, is small but such a showstopper that both actresses who played it on Broadway—Marian Mercer, and Katie Finneran in the 2010 revival—won the Tony Award for Best Featured Actress in a Musical.

Music by Andrew Lloyd Webber ★ Lyrics by Tim Rice
Directed by Tom O'Horgan

Mark Hellinger Theatre, October 12, 1971–July 1, 1973

Jeff Fenholt.......Jesus of Nazareth
Ben Vereen.......Judas Iscariot
Yvonne Elliman.......Mary Magdalene
Paul Ainsley.......King Herod

ART NOTE: An electric guitar and a microphone creating a cross, lit with heavenly rays.

In this modern rock opera retelling of the story of the last seven days of Jesus's life, he quarrels with his disciples and questions God's plan, while the traditional "villains" of the story, Judas, Caiaphas, and Pontius Pilate, are shown to have more complex and not entirely unsympathetic motives.

Heaven on Their Minds

Andrew Lloyd Webber was just seventeen when he met Tim Rice, and the two quickly started writing together, bonding over their love for both musical theatre and pop music. Rice at the time was drawn to stories about historical figures who had short and dramatic lives, and the new pair's first produced work in this vein was the well-received "pop cantata" *Joseph and the Amazing Technicolor Dreamcoat,* written for a London school choir. They next turned their attention to Judas Iscariot (Rice was also fascinated by Eva Perón, but her musical was still a few years off). After writing and releasing one single, "Superstar," they decided to create a two-disc album of the entire opera in order to attract investors for a full production. The finished piece was sung-through, the default style for the team. And the boldness of the storytelling—humanizing Judas and showing the all-too-human frustrations of Jesus—was matched by the big style swings of the eclectic score, which embraced traditional musical theatre and jazzy pop as well as hard rock. Some songs featured wailing guitars backing a screaming Jesus, while others had more symphonic orchestrations, giving *Jesus Christ Superstar* a unique sound that was both lush and electric (literally and figuratively), rough and sentimental, highbrow and low.

Though the 1970 double album flopped in Britain, it quickly became a bestseller in the United States. Its popularity led to hundreds of concert performances—mostly unlicensed and illegal—and spurred producer Robert Stigwood to option the piece for Broadway. Only after signing a contract with Stigwood did Lloyd Webber, much to his chagrin, learn that Hal Prince had wanted to produce and direct the show (Prince's telegram expressing interest had gone astray to Lloyd Webber's parents). Instead, Stigwood hired *Hair* director Tom O'Horgan, and both writers hated the campy, over-the-top phantasmagoria he made of *Jesus Christ Superstar*'s Broadway premiere. Lloyd Webber later lamented the piece was "turned into a mountain of kitsch that looked like a monument to a demented pastry chef."

Despite very mixed reviews, the Broadway production ran for almost two years. A revised version, directed by Jim Sharman, opened a year later on the West End, and that ran for eight years. *Jesus Christ Superstar* set Lloyd Webber up, financially and in the public's eye, as musical theatre's next big thing, and its success gave him the freedom and confidence to continue to experiment; without it, there's no *Evita,* no *Cats*, no *Phantom of the Opera*.

MISCELLANEOUS MATTER

★ The hit "I Don't Know How to Love Him" began life as a pop song, "I Love a Kansas Morning." Rice thought songs with U.S. place names were more likely to become hits, but it was never recorded. Rice himself said the words were "a bit stupid."

★ Pope Paul VI was treated to a special screening of the film, after which he predicted it would bring more converts to the church than anything before.

★ A 1972 Swedish production played to 74,000 people and starred Agnetha Fältskog, one of the two "A"s in ABBA.

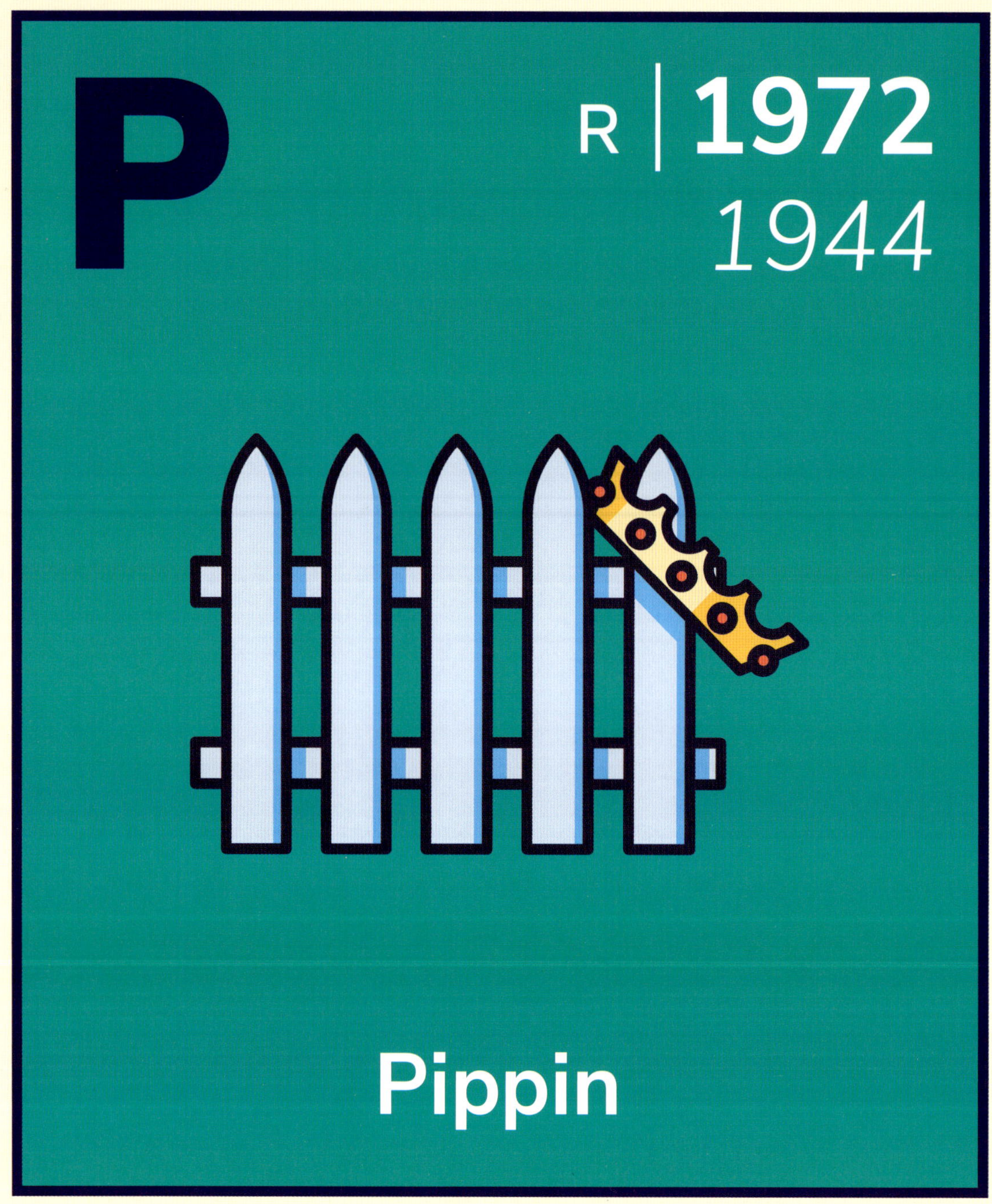

Book by Roger O. Hirson ★ Music and lyrics by Stephen Schwartz
Directed and choreographed by Bob Fosse

Imperial Theatre and Minskoff Theatre, October 23, 1972–June 12, 1977

John Rubinstein.......Pippin
Ben Vereen.......Leading Player
Jill Clayburgh.......Catherine
Irene Ryan.......Berthe

ART NOTE: Charlemagne's crown hanging on the modest fence of Catherine's farm.

A troupe of traveling players present the story of Pippin, son of Charlemagne, and his somewhat aimless search for a meaningful life. He goes to battle, looks for love (a little too much), assassinates his father and seizes the crown, then gives back the crown and has the Leading Player bring Charlemagne back to life. Eventually, he meets Catherine, a rural single mother, and abandons the "magical" story of the show (and the other actors) to settle down with her.

Extraordinary

1972 was the year of Bob Fosse: in February, his film adaptation of *Cabaret* opened to raves (he'd later win the Oscar for Best Director), and he filmed a TV special, *Liza with a Z*, in September, for which he'd win an Emmy for Best Director. So it's fair to say he went into *Pippin* at the top of his game.

Fosse was iffy on the material and felt the musical's story was slight. (*Pippin* started life as a student musical at Carnegie Mellon University, though Stephen Schwartz claims not a single line or note from that collegiate version still exists.) So Fosse set about remaking the show to match his own tastes, pushing to make it actively question society's mores, and giving it a dark and overtly sexual show biz razzle-dazzle that curdles even as you watch it.

Much of this style was created by his self-consciously theatrical ensemble of "players," commenting on the material. He also built up the role of "Leading Player" for the charismatic Ben Vereen, turning what had been a glorified narrator into a malevolent presiding spirit, a killer in the guise of a song-and-dance man.

Listening to the score of *Pippin* today, what stands out is its kaleidoscopic collection of musical styles; it's the sound of a young songwriter grabbing every influence that interested him. Fosse, working with arranger John Berkman and veteran orchestrator Ralph Burns (*Sweet Charity, Funny Girl*) pushed this stylistic diversity even further; the number "With You" starts as a lyrical French(ish) *chanson,* but the dance section segues from '70s mod-African-carnival to brassy, funked-up bossa nova, accelerating to a bedlam of screaming electric guitar riffs.

Fosse's directorial hand was breathtaking but ended up overpowering the writing. Schwartz was furious with many of Fosse's choices, and at how he was treated; though he was only twenty-four, his *Godspell* was a huge success, and he had a lot of opinions, most of which were ignored (Fosse even banned him from rehearsals at one point). Even today, there is a sense of two shows: there's *Pippin*, and then there's Bob Fosse's *Pippin.* And, oh yes, Fosse went on to win Best Director at that year's Tony Awards, too, completing his (as yet unmatched) triple crown: an Oscar, an Emmy, and a Tony for direction, all in the same year.

MISCELLANEOUS MATTER

★ Ben Vereen won the Tony Award for Best Actor in a Musical as the Leading Player in the original Broadway production; forty-one years later, Patina Miller played the same part and won Best Actress—the first time two performers won in different Tony categories for the same role.

★ *Pippin* was the first Broadway show to run a TV commercial that showed bits of footage from the production. "You can see the other 119 minutes live at the Imperial Theatre," it said, and sales quickly picked up.

★ The petite Irene Ryan became a TV star in her sixties playing Granny Clampett on *The Beverly Hillbillies.* Her number "No Time at All," about refusing to get old, was one of the show's standout hits; sadly, she suffered a stroke during a performance and never recovered.

Book by Hugh Wheeler ★ Music and lyrics by Stephen Sondheim
Directed by Harold Prince ★ Choreographed by Patricia Birch

Shubert Theatre and Majestic Theatre, February 25, 1973–August 3, 1974

Len Cariou.......Fredrik Egerman
Glynis Johns.......Desiree Armfeldt
Hermione Gingold.......Madame Armfeldt
Laurence Guittard.....Count Carl-Magnus

ART NOTE: "The sun won't set" from the "Night Waltz" through the window of a weekend country house.

During the unsettling, sunlit white nights of a Swedish summer, circa 1900, a group of unhappily partnered (or discontentedly single) people pursue, rebuff, and otherwise engage with each other before sorting themselves into appropriate romantic pairings. Mismatched lovers include an actress of a certain age, an indecisive lawyer, his still-virginal teenage wife and pious, sexually frustrated son, a hedonistic maid, and a hotheaded hussar with a dryly cynical wife. In act two, everyone shares an unusual, eventful weekend in the country.

Liaisons

After *Company* and *Follies*—contemporary pieces with a dark view of interpersonal relationships—both Sondheim and Prince were looking to work on something lighter and overtly romantic. (Prince, wearing his producer hat, was also hoping for something commercially successful, since *Follies* had lost money, and his cash cow, *Fiddler on the Roof*, had recently closed after an eight-year run.) After failing to secure the rights to Jean Anouilh's play *Ring Round the Moon*, Ingmar Bergman's film *Smiles of a Summer Night* was selected for adaptation instead.

Sondheim composed his entire score in variations of triple time: not just swirling waltzes, mazurkas, and polonaises in 3/4, but songs in compound meters, too (6/8, 9/8, 12/8, etc., where beats are composed of three-note patterns). This emphasis on "threes" echoes the plot of *A Little Night Music*, with its series of interlocking romantic triangles: Anne/Henrik/Fredrik, Fredrik/Anne/Desiree, Desiree/Fredrik/Carl-Magnus, etc. Harmonically, Sondheim drew inspiration from the lush chords of 19th and early 20th century European composers such as Ravel and Richard Strauss.

The score contains his best-known song, "Send in the Clowns," a late addition written the week before the show went out of town. Originally, Sondheim intended to write a number for Fredrik in the scene where it occurs, but on a rare visit to the theatre (he was home busy composing; they'd gone into rehearsal with only ten of sixteen songs completed!), he saw Glynis Johns as Desiree playing the moment in a new way, giving him a fresh idea. He wrote most of the new song in a single night, tailoring it to match the limitations of Johns's voice; since she couldn't sustain notes, he wrote shorter musical phrases and used words with clipped endings (like "rich" and "bliss"). Glynis immediately loved the song so much she insisted on performing it at an invited dress rehearsal the day she heard it, holding the music in her hand since she hadn't had time to memorize it.

In the end, Hal Prince got the commercial hit he hoped for. Clive Barnes, the *New York Times* critic (who'd disliked the earlier Sondheim-Prince collaborations), raved about *A Little Night Music,* calling it "civilized, sophisticated and enchanting." And for the third year in a row, Sondheim nabbed the Tony for Best Score.

MISCELLANEOUS MATTER

- ★ The title is the translation of "Eine Kleine Nachtmusik," a popular Mozart work. This presents a problem for German-language productions; they use *Das Lächeln einer Sommernacht*, a near direct translation of the Bergman movie's title.
- ★ Designer Boris Aronson wanted enormous translucent panels to create a birch forest that "sparkled"; only a polymer called Lexan, used for bulletproof windows, proved strong enough.
- ★ To date, "Send in the Clowns" has been recorded by over 900 singers, among them Frank Sinatra, Sarah Vaughan, and Barbra Streisand (for whom Sondheim added a second bridge to the song, with new lyrics).

Book by William F. Brown ★ Music and lyrics by Charlie Smalls
Based on the novel *The Wonderful Wizard of Oz* by L. Frank Baum
Directed by Geoffrey Holder ★ Choreographed by George Faison

Majestic Theatre and Broadway Theatre, January 5, 1975–January 28, 1979

Stephanie Mills.......Dorothy
André De Shields.......The Wiz
Clarice Taylor.......Addaperle
Ted Ross.......Lion

ART NOTE: Dorothy's silver (yes, silver!) slippers ready to "Ease on Down" the yellow brick road.

Dorothy's Kansas farmhouse is uprooted in a tornado and ends up in Oz, falling on the witch Evamean and killing her. The good witch Addaperle has Dorothy take Evamean's silver shoes as protection as she travels to Emerald City, where the Wiz says he can send her home if she kills Evamean's sister, Evilene. When the Wiz is revealed to be a hoax, Dorothy learns she can click her heels together and get home all by herself.

No Bad News

Take the perennial favorite *The Wizard of Oz*, give it a "sophisticated funk" score (as composer Charlie Smalls described it) and an extravagant visual style, and you get one of the most joyous hits of the 1970s. This all-Black retelling of Dorothy and her journey to meet the "Wiz" was part of a rising tide of Black culture and Black stories making their way to the mainstream in the early '70s. In the wake of the civil rights movement of the '60s, there were increasingly prominent and popular Black theatre companies and hit Black sitcoms like *Good Times* and *The Jeffersons,* and many of the most popular songs on the radio were from Motown artists or other Black performers. It's in this context that ex-DJ turned producer Ken Harper was determined to make his Black *Oz* dream come true, even though it took several years of pitching to make it happen.

Director and costume designer Geoffrey Holder recalled seeing the show unfold in his mind as soon as he heard Smalls's score. His costumes were both fantastical and urban—the Tin Man was made of items like a trash can and a tin pitcher, and the Wiz himself was decked out in a blinding white jumpsuit with an emerald-lined cape and sunglasses. The Emerald City was more Harlem than fairy tale, and some saw Dorothy's journey from her family's farm to the big city, chased by the slave-driving wicked witch Evilene, as a parallel for the flight of Blacks from the South to northern cities. But though there were darker undertones to find if you went looking, the overall experience for audiences was a celebration of Black music and culture.

Leading the party was little fifteen-year-old Stephanie Mills. She'd been singing gospel in her Brooklyn church since age three, and her crystal-clear voice and surprisingly adult mastery of R&B and gospel styles brought down the house in numbers like the finale, "Home." In a heartfelt ode to the love and peace one finds with one's family, she rejects the fantasy of the city, clicks her heels together, and returns to Kansas with Toto. Black music had also seemingly come "home" on Broadway; *The Wiz* was far and away the biggest Tony Award winner of the year, taking home a total of seven trophies.

MISCELLANEOUS MATTER

- ★ Of all the hit Black book musicals of this era—*Purlie*, *Raisin*, *The Wiz*, and *Dreamgirls*—only *The Wiz* was composed by a Black composer. Juilliard-trained Smalls was working on his next show when he unexpectedly died of complications from appendicitis while on tour. He was forty-three.
- ★ Oddly, though Holder had been the first director the producers approached, they ultimately hired someone else. When they eventually let that director go, Holder was brought in during out-of-town tryouts to bring his original vision to life.
- ★ In a delightful casting coincidence, Stephanie Mills joined the cast of *Hadestown* in 2024, playing Hermes, a role originated by André De Shields.

Book by George Furth ★ Music and lyrics by Stephen Sondheim
From the play by George S. Kaufman and Moss Hart
Directed by Harold Prince ★ Choreographed by Larry Fuller

Alvin Theatre, November 16, 1981–November 28, 1981

Jim Walton.......Franklin Shepard
Lonny Price.......Charley Kringas
Ann Morrison.......Mary Flynn
Jason Alexander.......Joe Josephson

ART NOTE: A desk calendar with its pages flipping backward.

A story bookended by two high school commencements, one in 1980, where a successful middle-aged Hollywood producer Franklin Shepard is a guest speaker, and an earlier one, in 1955, when Shepard is graduating as valedictorian. In between, the events of his life play out in reverse, and we see how his close friendships with writer Mary and songwriting collaborator Charley disintegrated over the intervening years. Curtain down on their youthful graduation picture, full of hope and promise.

It's a Hit!

Sixteen. By far the smallest performance count on the table, this catastrophically brief run has come to define Sondheim's biggest flop, a story of "How could these brilliant artists make so many bad decisions?" But let's start with what went right: the score. From the first notes of the overture—one of Broadway's greatest—the songs are first-rate Sondheim. Swinging big band jazz, blistering patter songs, and aching, bittersweet ballads turned the cast album (for a long time, the only way fans could hear the score) into a cult hit.

It was everything else that caused the problems, starting with the story. Prince's initial inspiration: he saw his daughter, Daisy, in a school play and was charmed. When his wife suggested he create a show about young people, he remembered a little-known play from the 1930s about how life doesn't always pan out the way idealistic youngsters expect. The play's gimmick? The story is told in reverse, with the disappointments and compromises of a lifetime coming early in the show, which then "progresses" to the hopes of youth. Even in the '30s, audiences struggled with this very dark structure, and the play *Merrily We Roll Along* was a rare Kaufman and Hart flop.

Another challenge: the creators decided to cast young actors so that they'd be the correct ages at the end of the show. This was effective, but it meant that the first, more difficult scenes for their older selves had to be played by these same inexperienced performers. The roughness of craft that had charmed Prince at his daughter's school play was not enough to endear these characters to audiences; in fact, the nastiness of those first scenes drove many people out of the theatre.

The design choices were also sadly misguided. Prince felt Judith Dolan's whimsical period costumes made the cast look too old, so he replaced them with simple T-shirts printed with character names. What he thought looked raw and appealingly youthful simply looked cheap (and unreadable from many seats in the house). Sets were similarly bare-bones, glorified bleachers really, not what ticket buyers expected from a Broadway show. Though the team worked tirelessly during their long preview period and the show improved dramatically, reviews were dreadful. Thankfully, Sondheim and Furth continued to rewrite the show for years, and its cult status helped elevate the 2023 revival to the unlikeliest of smash hits.

MISCELLANEOUS MATTER

- ★ One scenic fiasco cut during previews was a swimming pool made of construction paper that an actress had to fall "into" (through). Happily, the stage manager only sustained a minor head wound while demonstrating how "safe" the contraption was.
- ★ The cast album was recorded the day after the show closed, in what must have been the most bittersweet recording session in Broadway history.
- ★ The many rewrites and subsequent versions mean that the show has changed over the years, and songs have come and gone, notably the original opening, "Rich and Happy," and the bookending high school graduations. This article describes the original Broadway version.

Book by James Lapine ★ Music and lyrics by Stephen Sondheim
Directed by James Lapine

Booth Theatre, May 2, 1984–October 13, 1985

Mandy Patinkin.......George

Bernadette Peters.......Dot/Marie

ART NOTE: One of the ladies from Seurat's painting, with her pet monkey. Behind her are some of the painter's signature dots.

In act one, impressionist painter George Seurat sketches people and dogs in a park by the Seine. His mistress, Dot, tolerates modeling for the work-obsessed George but longs for a deeper romantic connection; she eventually leaves him. His only consolation is the finished masterpiece that comes to life on stage. In act two, George's great-grandson, also an artist, searches for inspiration, finding it when Dot comes to life and encourages him to cherish his unique voice.

Putting It Together

After the disastrous failure of *Merrily We Roll Along*, Sondheim was deeply depressed, questioning his future. He worried he was a dinosaur, claiming no one over fifty had ever written a good musical. The economic model of Broadway was changing, too, and it was harder and harder to raise the funds to produce risky artistic experiments in a commercial setting. *Merrily We Roll Along* had also caused a rift between Sondheim and longtime collaborator Harold Prince, and someone suggested that Sondheim meet with the thirty-year-old writer and director James Lapine, who had just staged William Finn's *March of the Falsettos* at off-Broadway's Playwrights Horizons. Lapine had a background in visual arts and, in their discussions, the two agreed that something could be made from Georges Seurat's painting *A Sunday Afternoon on the Island of La Grande Jatte.* Its statue-like profiles of various people in a park piqued their curiosity, and when Lapine pointed out that the principal character—the artist himself—was not in the painting, they realized they had the beginnings of a story.

Sunday in the Park with George's first act was presented at Playwrights Horizons as a public workshop while they were still working on the second, a new model for creating a musical. Producers came forward to move it to Broadway, even while not entirely sure what they'd be producing; well into its Broadway rehearsals, there was little music written for act two. At the last minute, Sondheim began bringing in new songs, including the monumental "Putting It Together" sequence, which, appropriately, details the self-promotion and hustling that goes into getting a work of art made. In his music, Sondheim mirrored Seurat's painting style, pointillism, which consists of placing different-colored dots next to each other so the canvas shimmers. The score likewise contains motifs made of staccato, sometimes dissonant points of sound that finally come together into beautiful, rich harmonies.

Sunday in the Park with George marked the first collaboration between Sondheim and his two leads, Mandy Patinkin and Bernadette Peters, both of whom would continue to sing his songs for decades to come. He and Lapine also hit it off, and wrote two more shows together, *Into the Woods* and *Passion,* as well as a revue, *Sondheim on Sondheim.* Although *Sunday* didn't make its money back, it was a critical darling and received ten Tony nominations, convincing Sondheim not to give up on his one-of-a-kind career after all.

MISCELLANEOUS MATTER

- ★ Though it received ten Tony nominations, it won only two for design, losing Best Score and Best Musical to Golden Age throwback *La Cage aux Folles.* In composer Jerry Herman's acceptance speech, he quipped that, rumors to the contrary, the "hummable show tune" was still alive on Broadway, which he denied was a dig at Sondheim's more challenging score.
- ★ The show was a very personal one for Sondheim, delving into the psychological processes of being a creative artist, and people immediately drew parallels between Sondheim and Seurat, both of whose art had been criticized as being "cold," with too much head and not enough heart.
- ★ Sondheim titled the two-volume collection of his lyrics after the stand-out song in the show, "Finishing the Hat," a title that refers to the miraculous, god-like act of an artist creating something from nothing.

Book by William Hauptman ★ Music and lyrics by Roger Miller
Adapted from the novel *Adventures of Huckleberry Finn* by Mark Twain
Staged by Des McAnuff ★ Choreographed by Janet Watson

Eugene O'Neill Theatre, April 25, 1985–September 20, 1987

Daniel H. Jenkins.......Huckleberry Finn
Ron Richardson.......Jim
Patti Cohenour.......Mary Jane Wilkes
René Auberjonois.......The Duke

ART NOTE: Huck and Jim's raft, floating down the "River in the Rain."

Teenaged Huck Finn, escaping his abusive father, meets up with Jim, who's escaping his enslavement by Huck's adoptive aunt Miss Watson. Huck decides to help Jim reach the North (though he worries it's a sin), and they develop a deep friendship. When a couple of devious con men sell Jim back into slavery, Huck and his pal Tom Sawyer come to his rescue. Miss Watson dies and frees Jim in her will, and he and Huck part, each off to new adventures.

Crossing Over

In the 1960s and '70s, Roger Miller was a hit country songwriter and performer, with songs like "Dang Me" and "King of the Road" topping the pop and country charts. He also found success as a TV actor, and he wrote and performed songs for Disney's 1973 *Robin Hood*, but by the early '80s, he hadn't recorded in years. Enter Rocco Landesman, a Yale School of Drama graduate and huge Miller fan who approached Roger and suggested he should create a musical adaptation of *The Adventures of Huckleberry Finn*. Miller originally resisted writing a musical, saying he couldn't write "seventeen songs about the same thing"—when he first met with Hauptman, he half-jokingly claimed he'd only ever seen two musicals, and one was "*George in the Park with Sunday.*" But in the end, he was persuaded, and after several workshops, the show and Miller's country/bluegrass score came into foot-stomping, hand-clapping shape.

Adapting what many consider the Great American Novel into a musical was not an easy task—far more experienced writers had tried and failed, including Alan Jay Lerner and Burton Lane, and Kurt Weill and Maxwell Anderson. The structure, a picaresque story made up of many small adventures, is difficult to fit on a stage (*Big River*'s twenty actors would eventually play a total of sixty-five characters in forty-five scenes). And Huck's internal journey strikes at the heart of America's primal shame, slavery—challenging waters to navigate in a novel, let alone a musical. Updating dialect, as well as larger questions of characterization for both Huck and Jim, would also require a careful touch. In Jenkins and Richardson, the writers found the perfect pair to portray the two friends and opposites with depth and dignity, as young men society had abandoned and who were searching for lives they could call their own.

Big River had other big assets. The set design by Landesman's wife, Heidi, created a world of luminous landscapes, and young director Des McAnuff kept the action (and the raft) moving in innovative ways. In a year with few musicals (none that ran more than a couple months), the show was a homespun hit, with music from the heart of America and a story about bringing the country together. Seeing Huck and Jim afloat in the rain, sharing a cigar, one could imagine the rest of their fractured society was very far away.

MISCELLANEOUS MATTER

- ★ Three of the four Tony Award nominations for Best Featured Actor in a Musical went to *Big River*; Richardson won out over Jenkins and Auberjonois.
- ★ In a decade defined by British imports, *Big River* was one of only four 1980s American musicals to run over 1,000 performances.
- ★ The show had a unique and stunning revival in 2003, when a production by the Deaf West Theatre Company transferred to Broadway; featuring a cast equally made up of hearing and deaf actors, and completely signed as well as sung, it won a special Tony Honor for Excellence in Theatre.

Book by Alain Boublil and Claude-Michel Schönberg
Music by Claude-Michel Schönberg ★ Lyrics by Alain Boublil and Richard Maltby Jr.
Directed by Nicholas Hytner ★ Musical staging by Bob Avian

Broadway Theatre, April 11, 1991–January 28, 2001

Lea Salonga.......Kim
Willy Falk.......Chris
Hinton Battle.......John
Jonathan Pryce.......The Engineer

ART NOTE: From the song "Sun and Moon," Kim's moon "floats on high" above her bed, which is adorned with the Vietnamese flag.

Chris, an American soldier in Vietnam, falls in love with a young Vietnamese sex worker, Kim. When he is evacuated, he must leave her behind, and she raises their son alone. Three years later, Chris returns with his American wife, Ellen, to try and find Kim and his son. Kim doesn't know he's married and thinks he's there to take them back to America. When she meets Ellen, she realizes Chris will never take her back and commits suicide.

The Heat Is on in Saigon

When *Miss Saigon* opened at the Drury Lane Theatre in London in 1989, the buzz was deafening, with people desperate to see what the creators of the international smash *Les Misérables* had come up with for their second outing. A retelling of Puccini's opera *Madama Butterfly* set during the Vietnam war (instead of 1904 Japan), the show nearly guaranteed the British public romantic melodies, rousing ensemble numbers, and, if recent hits like *The Phantom of the Opera* were any guide, no small amount of spectacle. *Miss Saigon* delivered, and the show went on to run for over ten years.

Getting to Broadway proved a more complicated journey. When shows transfer from the U.K. to the U.S., the actors' union, Actors' Equity Association, must approve the actors being brought over. In this case, AEA refused to allow Jonathan Pryce to reprise his role as the sleazy French/Vietnamese nightclub owner called The Engineer, because Pryce was not even part Asian; his makeup, including eye prosthetics and bronzing cream, was offensive to many Asian Americans and was compared to the blackface of early American minstrel shows. AEA likewise was reluctant to allow Filipina Lea Salonga to reprise her role, instead wanting to replace her with an Asian American actress. After battles in both the courts and the press, and heavyweight producer Cameron Mackintosh (*Cats, Phantom, Les Misérables*) threatening to cancel the show despite a record-breaking $39 million advance, AEA backed down and both actors were allowed to open *Miss Saigon* on Broadway.

The show was just as big a hit in New York as it was in London, thanks to those star performances, its emotional story and score, and its lavish production values. Budgeted at $10 million, it was the most expensive and technologically advanced show ever produced on Broadway, with 375 costumes, an eighteen-foot fiberglass statue of Ho Chi Minh, double the automation of the dazzling *Phantom,* and of course, the 1,700-pound helicopter that landed on stage every night. It was so lavish, in fact, that it caused some backlash, with critics resenting the big-budget British hits that had colonized Broadway and bemoaning the theme-park aesthetic they said was cheapening musicals. But like it or not, no one could deny that, as lyricist Richard Maltby Jr. said about the British, "They're reinventing the form. Soon enough, America will do something else." And in the next five years, America did.

MISCELLANEOUS MATTER

★ The show also featured a real 1959 Cadillac that had to be cut in half to fit in the wings.

★ The 2013 West End revival set box office records as well, selling an unheard-of £4.4 million worth of tickets *in one day.*

★ Despite its popularity, *Miss Saigon* continues to be a controversial show, with some seeing the depiction of all Vietnamese and Thai women as sex workers and all Asian men as corrupt bullies merely a continuation of old stereotypes. For the 2014 West End and 2017 Broadway revivals, the authors made changes to flesh out the Vietnamese perspective, including adding more authentic Vietnamese lyrics.

Book and lyrics by Marsha Norman ★ Music by Lucy Simon
Based on the novel by Frances Hodgson Burnett
Directed by Susan H. Schulman ★ Choreographed by Michael Lichtefeld

St. James Theatre, April 25, 1991–January 03, 1993

Daisy Eagan.......Mary Lennox
Mandy Patinkin.......Archibald Craven
Rebecca Luker.......Lily Craven
Alison Fraser.......Martha Sowerby

ART NOTE: The gate and overgrown walls of the garden itself.

Mary, an orphan, comes to live with her reclusive uncle Archibald in his English manor, the house and grounds of which have been neglected since his wife, Lily, died. Mary's resemblance to Lily causes Archibald to keep her at a distance; he also avoids his sickly son, Colin. When a friendly housekeeper, Martha, tells Mary about a hidden garden, Mary shows it to Colin and he recovers. Lily's spirit appears to Archibald, helping him to let her go and embrace Mary and Colin.

A Bit of Earth

What is it about orphans and musicals? First came *Oliver!,* then fourteen years later, *Annie,* and then fourteen years after that, *The Secret Garden*'s Mary Lennox. Perhaps it's because musicals are often about a central character learning where they belong, and no one questions their place in the world more than an orphan.

The Secret Garden was a more grown-up show than its predecessors, and its story and sensibility resonated with the mothers (and grandmothers) in the audience as much as with the girls seated beside them. It's not incidental the show was based on a beloved book written by a woman, had a book, music, and lyrics by women, and was directed, produced, and designed by women—a first for a Broadway musical. Marsha Norman, previously known for her extremely dark Pulitzer Prize–winning play *'night, Mother*, was the perfect choice to adapt the novel and avoid any potential sentimentality—she said she saw herself in the ill-tempered Mary, out of place and looking for a sanctuary. Norman also spent a lot of scenes and lyrics on fleshing out the adult characters, so the show felt richer than the usual children's entertainment.

The score was a stand-out, a mixture of Victorian lushness, northern English dances, and haunting ballads created by Lucy Simon, supported by a musical team that included Jeanine Tesori, who would go on to compose shows like *Fun Home* and *Shrek*. The score called for a wide variety of vocal types and gave the crooning Mandy Patinkin and sublime soprano Rebecca Luker opportunities to soar. "Hold On," which Fraser's Martha sang to little Mary, was an inspirational anthem of tough love with a driving beat capable of inspiring every girl in the audience (and many grown women, too).

Producer Heidi Landesman also designed the beautiful set, as she had for *Big River* and *'night, Mother.* Rigged with nested, elaborately painted proscenium arches, it resembled a Victorian toy theatre, ringed by an oversize animal topiary and an enormous girl's face superimposed on a three-story doll's house. Though this was a darker *Secret* than some expected, for those whose tastes ran toward *Jane Eyre*–style moodiness, the show was a *Garden* of delights.

MISCELLANEOUS MATTER

★ Eleven-year-old Daisy Eagan made Broadway history, becoming the youngest actress to win a Tony for her old-soul performance; she was just slightly older than Frankie Michaels, who won in 1966 playing young Patrick in *Mame*.

★ Audra McDonald made her Broadway debut as the character Ayah. Norman and Simon wanted her to play it on the tour, and understudy Lily, but she was cast as Carrie Pipperidge in the 1994 Broadway revival of *Carousel*, for which she won the first of her six Tony Awards (so far).

★ The next musical created by an all-female team was *Waitress* . . . 25 years later!

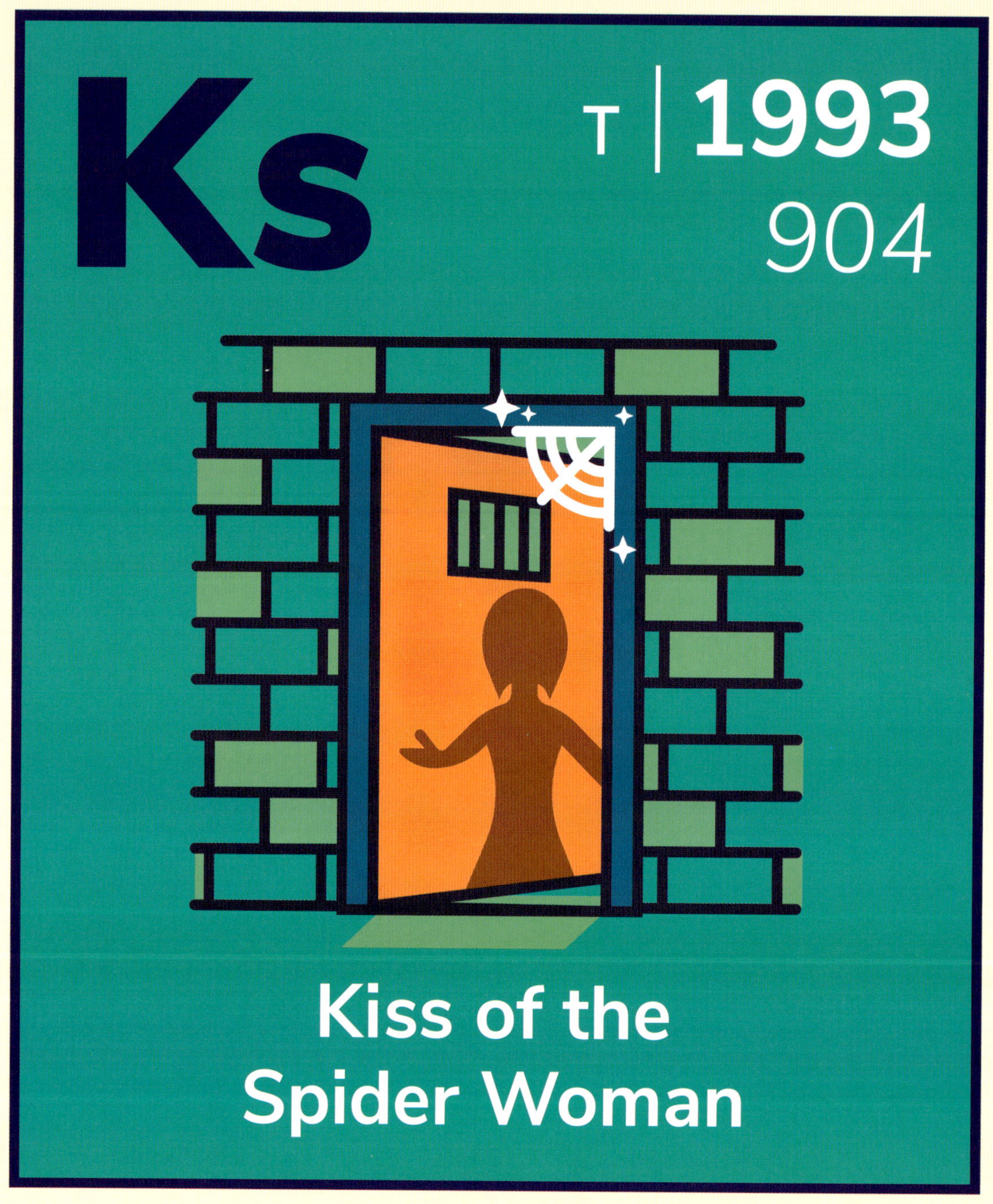

Book by Terrence McNally ★ Music by John Kander
Lyrics by Fred Ebb ★ Based on the novel by Manuel Puig
Directed by Harold Prince ★ Choreographed by Vincent Paterson

Broadhurst Theatre, May 3, 1993–July 1, 1995

Brent Carver.......Molina
Anthony Crivello.......Valentin
Chita Rivera.......Spider Woman/Aurora
Kirsti Carnahan......Marta

ART NOTE: Aurora's shadow beckons you to leave the prison cell, while her web glistens overhead.

In a Latin American prison, gay window dresser Molina shares a cell with Marxist rebel Valentin. As they struggle to survive, Molina develops feelings for Valentin, protecting him from guards and recounting movies starring his favorite actress to block out the horrors of their reality. Molina is released, then recaptured after making a phone call as a favor for Valentin. Out of love for Valentin, he refuses to tell the guards who he called and is shot and killed.

I Do Miracles

What role should art play in the world? For Luis Molina, a shy window dresser, it is an escape, a way to drown out the misery of daily life and to live instead in any fantastical world you choose. Valentin Paz, revolutionary firebrand, is disgusted by his cellmate's unwillingness to engage with reality, to look injustice in the eye and fight against it.

As in *Cabaret*, Kander, Ebb, and Prince seemed to be asking the audience, "What would you do?" This time, the setting was Latin America, not Berlin, and the story was adapted from a novel and an Oscar-winning film. It was challenging material, and given the changing economic realities of Broadway, a new developmental path was devised: put on a full production thirty miles north of Broadway on the campus of SUNY Purchase instead of a big city tryout. The creators thought they could work in a more private setting, without reviews, but it turned out an hour's drive was not enough to keep major critics away. The production and actors were panned, with the *New York Times* even suggesting a replacement for the actress playing Spider Woman, which the creatives happily took: theatre legend Chita Rivera.

At age sixty, Rivera hadn't been in a Broadway show since a terrible car accident had broken her leg in twelve places, but she worked to get back into top form, and her star charisma and electrifying dancing pulled audiences into her web every night. Brent Carver's tender yearning for her, and to live in her perfumed world even while tending Valentin's wounds, was heartbreaking. The team implemented major rewrites as they retooled for Broadway, and Prince managed again to combine show-biz razzle-dazzle with a societal message. For example, as Molina imagines Aurora's fantasy number "Where You Are," the prison transforms into the scene of a high stepping extravaganza with one simple trick—the prisoners grab pieces of their cell bars to use as dancing canes, a visual gesture that neatly summarizes Molina's philosophy. Terrence McNally, in only his second musical, skillfully wove together the fantastical and horrifying realities, and Kander and Ebb alternated Latin-inflected movie musical showstoppers with intimate ballads of longing, winning them their third pair of Tonys. In fact, *Spider Woman* nearly swept the awards, beating out *The Who's Tommy* for Best Musical and all performance awards in a triumph of old school over new.

MISCELLANEOUS MATTER

★ Rob Marshall was brought in to stage "Where You Are," his first Broadway choreography credit; he choreographed many more shows, and won an Oscar for directing and choreographing the film *Chicago*.

★ Rivera kept a bowl of candy inside her dressing room for the dancers to grab as they passed by. Incredibly, her dressing room was also a hangout for the Pinball boys from *The Who's Tommy*, performing across the street; they would pop over during performances and have a few laughs with the legend.

★ The original choreographer, Vincent Paterson, had had a successful career in music videos, working with Madonna and dancing with Michael Jackson in "Bad."

Book by Linda Woolverton, based on her screenplay
Music by Alan Menken ★ Lyrics by Howard Ashman and Tim Rice
Directed by Robert Jess Roth ★ Choreographed by Matt West

Palace Theatre and Lunt-Fontanne Theatre, April 18, 1994–July 29, 2007

Susan Egan.......Belle
Terrence Mann.......Beast
Burke Moses.......Gaston
Tom Bosley.......Maurice

ART NOTE: The Beast's rose, slowly losing its petals.

Belle, the local bookworm, is tired of her provincial hometown and constantly deflecting the advances of egotistical hunter Gaston. When she learns her father has been captured by a ferocious beast, she trades places with him. Imprisoned in the beast's castle, she discovers he and his staff are under a spell—only if the beast can find love before a magic rose loses its petals will they all be released. Over time, Belle warms to her host and, in the end, love triumphs.

A Change in Me

Alan Menken and Howard Ashman had a huge success off-Broadway with 1982's *Little Shop of Horrors*, but their subsequent New York projects (together and with others) flopped. So when new Disney CEO Michael Eisner approached the pair to write the score for an animated feature, they jumped, creating *The Little Mermaid*, a smash hit that transformed animated movies into musicals that happened to be animated.

The team won their first Oscars for that film, and with their second, *Beauty and the Beast*, they won again. Critics immediately commented that it would make an excellent stage musical, and despite being reluctant to branch out into live theatre in the past, Disney decided to give it a try. Woolverton was asked to adapt her screenplay, fleshing out some minor characters, adding places for new songs, and making adjustments to account for the limitations of live actors; Tim Rice (*Jesus Christ Superstar, Evita*) was brought in to write new songs with Menken since, sadly, Ashman had died just before the movie's release.

The show tried out in Houston to ecstatic reviews, but there was great suspicion awaiting it in New York. Disney's decision to produce it themselves rather than relying on the handful of producing families/companies that had run Broadway for decades did not make them popular. And despite the success of *The Little Mermaid* and *Beauty and the Beast* as films, Disney was still thought of as a theme park company, so when the show opened many critics went looking for any reason to dismiss their first endeavor on the "legitimate" stage. Though the affection for the original Ashman and Menken songs remained, the production itself was sharply criticized for being too fixated on (admittedly spectacular) special effects while not leaving enough room for the magic of theatre and, most important, an audience's imagination.

But faithfulness to the animated movie was exactly what Disney was aiming for, and it paid off—families were grateful to have something to see besides *Cats*. Children loved seeing their favorite movie characters come to life on stage, and Egan, Mann, and Moses stepped into those roles with style. Mann, especially, somehow managed to find intimate moments of real humanity even while trapped in a cumbersome costume. Disney went on to adapt seven more of its movies (as of 2025), creating a new theatrical dynasty on Broadway and changing much of how Broadway does business.

MISCELLANEOUS MATTER

★ Tony Award–winner Tom Bosley (*Fiorello!*) returned to Broadway after over twenty-five years to play Belle's father, Maurice, and had a new song written for him.

★ When pop star Toni Braxton went into the show as Belle, she demanded a new song also be written just for her. That song, "A Change in Me," was so successful that it has been included in all subsequent productions.

★ Completing the industry's overall snubbing, the show won only one of the nine Tonys for which it was nominated, for the truly magical costume designs of Ann Hould-Ward.

Book by Terrence McNally ★ Music by Stephen Flaherty ★ Lyrics by Lynn Ahrens
Based on the novel by E. L. Doctorow
Directed by Frank Galati ★ Musical staging by Graciela Daniele

Ford Center for the Performing Arts, January 18, 1998–January 16, 2000

Marin Mazzie.......Mother
Audra McDonald.......Sarah
Brian Stokes Mitchell......Coalhouse Walker Jr.
Peter Friedman.......Tateh

ART NOTE: The U.S. flag seemingly growing out of a piano keyboard, like ragtime becoming the "New Music" of the nation.

The lives of three families in early 20th-century New York intersect with each other and real public figures of the day. A married upper-class white woman yearning to make her own life choices connects with an immigrant whose creativity knows no bounds, while a successful Black ragtime pianist starts off on the road to prosperity with his girlfriend, only to be crushed by racial injustice. As the wheels of America roll on, not all survive to pursue their dreams.

New Music

The mid-nineties were a time when Broadway was figuring out what it wanted to be, and its future was still very much in doubt (at the 1995 Tonys there were only two nominees for best musical, and one was a revue). Revivals were hot tickets, notably the successful 1994 revival of *Show Boat,* a lavish production mounted by Canadian impresario Garth Drabinsky.

Drabinsky was interested in more than just revivals—he wanted to remake the Broadway producing model into something closer to a film studio, with everything created in-house and extensive crowd testing. Above all, he wanted his shows to dazzle, bringing the competition to Disney's theatrical entertainment machine that was just getting going. After deciding to create a musical adaptation of Doctorow's seminal novel about an America figuring out what *its* future would be, he requested sample songs from different teams, eventually selecting *Once on This Island* songwriters Ahrens and Flaherty. A tryout in Toronto was a critical success, and in a typically unusual Drabinsky move, he released a "concept album" with that cast, which was nominated for a Grammy in 1996.

Ragtime's ambitions were enormous: tell the stories of three families from different cultures and classes, weave in over half a dozen major historical figures like J. P. Morgan and Harry Houdini, and delve deeply into America's checkered history of women's rights, racial oppression, xenophobia, and economic injustice. The three segments of society—Blacks, whites, and immigrants—were deftly individualized by Santo Loquasto's costumes that gave each its own palette. And Graciela Daniele's choreography swirled the distinctive movements of each group together and apart again in a world-defining opening number.

Terrence McNally's Tony Award–winning book wrestled these subjects into a coherent whole, echoing the novel's cool tone, with characters narrating their stories in the third person. Flaherty's music countered with the heat of Coalhouse's ragtime piano and the soulful melodies of Tateh's Jewish culture, and the warmth of an extraordinary cast kept this melting pot simmering. Songs like Audra McDonald's searing "Your Daddy's Son," muscular anthems like "Make Them Hear You," and surprising, tender moments of connection like "Our Children" helped win Ahrens and Flaherty a Tony. Though the show lost for Best Musical to *The Lion King*, it demonstrated that Broadway's American dream, at least, was still very much alive.

MISCELLANEOUS MATTER

- ★ Mother's numbers in act one don't "button" (end neatly), they elide into the next, a mirror of how her character is evolving and looking toward the future.
- ★ Drabinsky took Broadway by storm with *Show Boat* and *Ragtime,* even creating a new 42nd Street Theatre for *Ragtime* out of two smaller ones. But after being charged with fraud and embezzlement, his company went bankrupt; he was exiled to Canada, where he was also charged and imprisoned. The theatre (now the Lyric) remains.
- ★ Not all historical figures from the novel made it into the musical—Sigmund Freud was one who didn't make the cut.

Book by Greg Kotis ★ Music by Mark Hollmann
Lyrics by Mark Hollmann and Greg Kotis
Directed by John Rando ★ Musical staging by John Carrafa

Henry Miller's Theatre, September 20, 2001–January 18, 2004

Jeff McCarthy.......Officer Lockstock
Jennifer Laura Thompson.......Hope Cladwell
John Cullum.......Caldwell B. Cladwell
Hunter Foster.......Bobby Strong

ART NOTE: Please don't make us explain.

During a terrible drought, water is strictly regulated, and everyone must pay to pee in public toilets controlled by a giant corporation. Bobby, a low-level employee, starts a rebellion after his father is sent to the mysterious "Urinetown" as punishment for not paying. He also romances the daughter of the corporation president, and she takes over the rebellion when Bobby is killed. The rebellion succeeds and water rationing is lifted! Unfortunately, the now "free" people quickly die of thirst.

It's a Privilege to Pee

Urinetown's ad campaign, with the title in heavy black ink and "Is this really the title?" scribbled in red above, was like the show itself: self-consciously mocking, unsavory, and very funny. Greg Kotis had the idea for the show while traveling Europe on a tight budget, when he literally had to choose between lunch and using one of the continent's common pay toilets. Taking that dilemma to its extreme (or beyond), he and Mark Hollmann conceived a dark satire of modern consumerism, where Mother Nature has turned on humans and a greedy, oppressive corporation is the only thing holding society together—and keeping people down.

Both writers were alums of Chicago's famed experimental theatre and improv comedy scene, and Kotis's political science background and Hollmann's musical training positioned them perfectly to take on the difficult task of a full-length musical satire, rarely attempted and even less often successful (1961's *How to Succeed in Business Without Really Trying* was the last example).

Urinetown not only skewered capitalism, environmentalism, and other institutions, but frequently parodied the presentational style used in Kurt Weill and Bertolt Brecht's brutal *The Threepenny Opera*; like that 1928 classic, the characters spoke directly to the audience of injustice and stalked the stage accompanied by percussive vamps. But *Urinetown's* score is more varied than that; when the rebels needed rousing, for example, out came the faux gospel "Run Freedom Run." In addition, characters winkingly referred to the musical they were in throughout, discussing and analyzing its structure even while telling its story.

The show's original opening date, September 13, 2001, was postponed after historical events interceded. And when it opened a week later, no one knew how New York audiences, still shell-shocked, would react. Happily, *Urinetown* suited the moment, striking a perfect balance between a hilarious good time and a sober look at how we treat each other on this planet we share. Even the show's bleak ending, where the downtrodden poor learn that the oppressive regime they toppled was the only thing keeping them alive, couldn't dampen (ahem) the good spirits or the gratitude audiences felt for being able to sit side-by-side and experience the magic of theatre.

MISCELLANEOUS MATTER

★ During its original New York Fringe Festival run, there was an actual water shortage in New York.

★ Henry Miller's Theatre hadn't been used as a theatrical house in decades—in the 1980s and '90s it had operated as a nightclub and then fallen into disrepair. When the production moved in, the producers played up its dilapidated reputation, nailing plywood over the façade as if revolutionaries had taken over the building.

★ Just as the score included references to other musicals, Carrafa included choreographic "quotes" from other choreographers' work, mostly for his own amusement. He was amazed when people actually recognized them.

★ The show's scrappy five-piece band is one of the smallest in Broadway history.

Book by Catherine Johnson
Music and lyrics by Benny Andersson and Björn Ulvaeus
Directed by Phyllida Lloyd ★ Choreographed by Anthony Van Laast

Winter Garden Theatre and Broadhurst Theatre, October 18, 2001–September 12, 2015

Louise Pitre.......Donna Sheridan
Judy Kaye.......Rosie
Tina Maddigan.......Sophie Sheridan
Karen Mason.......Tanya

ART NOTE: The "Dancing Queen" herself.

Sophie is getting married and wants her father to walk her down the aisle, but he could be any of three men. Sophie invites them all to the wedding without telling her mother, Donna, who is shocked to see them arrive. Though no final answer on paternity is reached, old relationships are rekindled and new ones formed. At the last minute, Sophie calls off her wedding and Donna receives a marriage proposal instead.

Thank You for the Music

In 1972, four Swedish musicians got together and formed the pop group ABBA, deciding to write their songs in English to achieve maximum popularity worldwide. This plan won them the 1974 Eurovision contest and led to hit after hit throughout the '70s across Europe and Australia, where songs like "Fernando," "Money Money Money," and "Dancing Queen" were on constant rotation. In the United States (where ABBA had toured less frequently), they had more of a cult following, but it turned out those infectious English-language songs had more fans than anyone knew.

One of those fans was lyricist Tim Rice (*Jesus Christ Superstar, Evita*), who teamed up with Andersson and Ulvaeus in 1988 to create the musical *Chess*. This dark, Cold War tale was ambitious, and its score of brand-new songs made for a much-loved and lauded concept album, but it never found its theatrical audience. After its failure, *Chess*'s executive producer Judy Craymer believed there was dramatic potential in ABBA's catalogue, but it took her years to get the group to grant her the rights. With respected British director Phyllida Lloyd on board, they agreed to take another chance on musical theatre.

The daunting task of weaving over twenty beloved hits into a coherent storyline fell to playwright Catherine Johnson, and as with so many successful shows, striking the perfect tone was the key. She centered the story around three middle-aged women—the age of much of the predicted audience—and made them members of a girl group in their youth, thus allowing them to slip into songs at the drop of a hat. There was a charming and artful clumsiness in the way the hit songs would pop up in the middle of scenes; it was obvious that everyone on stage was just there to have a great time.

Opening just five weeks after the devastation of 9/11, this was a feeling that was desperately needed in New York, but the astonishing fourteen-year run was not just the result of one historical moment. In the early 2000s, '70s nostalgia was cresting (*That '70s Show* was a top TV hit for five of those years), and audiences who had grown up during that decade loved hearing the delicious ear-candy songs they remembered, being performed by actors who looked a lot like them. *Mamma Mia!* was like attending a reunion of the best friends you never had, which made the show a worldwide Super Trouper.

MISCELLANEOUS MATTER

- ★ It ran so long that the Winter Garden changed its name to the Cadillac Winter Garden Theatre and then *back again* during the run.
- ★ The show was known as "the Lourdes of musicals" for inspiring elderly and infirm audience members to dance in the aisles.
- ★ The plot of *Mamma Mia!* bears an uncanny resemblance to a 1968 film *Buona Sera, Mrs. Campbell* that had already been the source material for a now-forgotten musical, 1979's *Carmelina*, written by musical theatre heavyweights Alan Jay Lerner and Burton Lane. It was slightly less successful, running 5,741 fewer performances than *Mamma Mia.*

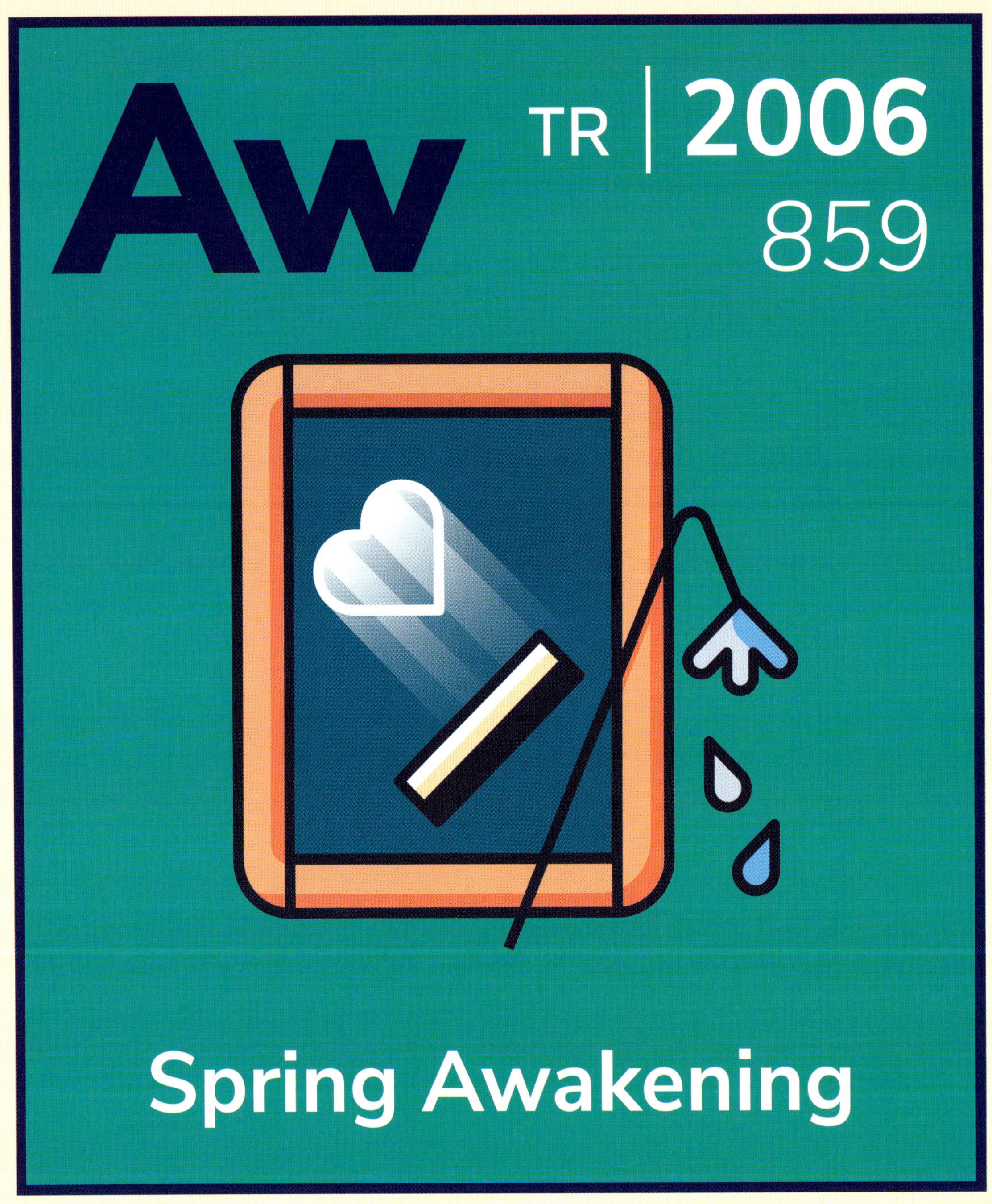

Book and lyrics by Steven Sater ★ Music by Duncan Sheik
Based on the play by Frank Wedekind
Directed by Michael Mayer ★ Choreographed by Bill T. Jones

Eugene O'Neill Theatre, December 10, 2006–January 18, 2009

Lea Michele.......Wendla
Jonathan Groff.......Melchior
John Gallagher Jr.......Moritz
Lauren Pritchard.......Ilse

ART NOTE: A 19th-century student's chalkboard with a heart partially erased and one of the "fading flowers of spring."

A group of teenage students in 19th-century Germany struggle to learn the facts about sex and sexuality. Their parents are too prudish to offer any help—some are even abusive—and the kids are left to fend for themselves. As they try to negotiate their changing minds and bodies, they make furtive connections, some of which end in tragedy. Those who are left can only grieve, and hope for a more open and informed future for the next generation.

The Dark I Know Well

Even after the huge success of *Rent*, contemporary rock musicals were still rare on Broadway in 2006. The responsibilities of a musical theatre song, to tell a story and illuminate character through easily understood lyrics, differ from rock, which normally prioritizes volume and energy. So when moody singer/songwriter Duncan Sheik and frequent collaborator Steven Sater decided to write a musical, their score brought a fresh new color to the stage. The two writers had surprising backgrounds—Sater was a classics scholar with a master's degree from Princeton, Sheik a semiotics major from Brown—and the source material wasn't typical Broadway.

German-born Frank Wedekind wrote his play in 1891, but it was so controversial it was quickly banned and didn't receive its first performance until fifteen years later. One of the earliest modernist plays, *Spring Awakening* tackles social taboos head-on, while indicting "proper" society for failing to educate its children, with tragic results (the play's subtitle is "a children's tragedy"). The darkness of the play's subject matter, and the emotional rawness of its young characters desperately searching for guidance in their sexual awakenings, lent itself perfectly to Sater's poetry and Sheik's angsty textures. Both writers were wary of musical comedy phoniness, so they settled on a format where characters would sing mostly interior monologues, using music as a way of stopping the action to heighten moments of frustration and longing.

Spring Awakening brought another newcomer to Broadway, acclaimed experimental choreographer and self-proclaimed "rule-breaker" Bill T. Jones, who adapted his physical vocabulary and method of working for this unusual piece. For example, to discover how young people would express themselves physically, he had actors scream lyrics in his face to see what their bodies did naturally. Director Michael Mayer was the Broadway veteran given the task of unifying these artists' visions. He was an apt choice; when Slater approached him with the project, he was surprised to learn Mayer had been hoping someone would bring him Wedekind's play for years! Mayer embraced the album/rock concert aesthetic of the piece, giving the actors handheld microphones to pull out of their 1890s school uniforms whenever a song started. This clash of old with new was electrifying, bringing home the idea that people today are exactly the same as they were 100 years ago.

MISCELLANEOUS MATTER

- ★ During the show's off-Broadway run at the Atlantic Theater Company, Sheik himself would play in the band for some shows.
- ★ Tickets were sold for 26 onstage seats, a constant visual reminder Mayer had used in the original off-Broadway production that this was a play people were watching.
- ★ Sheik and Sater are both Buddhists and struck up a friendship during chanting sessions. Sheik says that *Spring Awakening* deals with all ten Buddhist life states.
- ★ Like *Big River*, it had a successful revival by Deaf West with a mix of hearing and deaf actors; it was directed by Michael Arden, who had played Tom Sawyer in the Deaf West *Big River*.

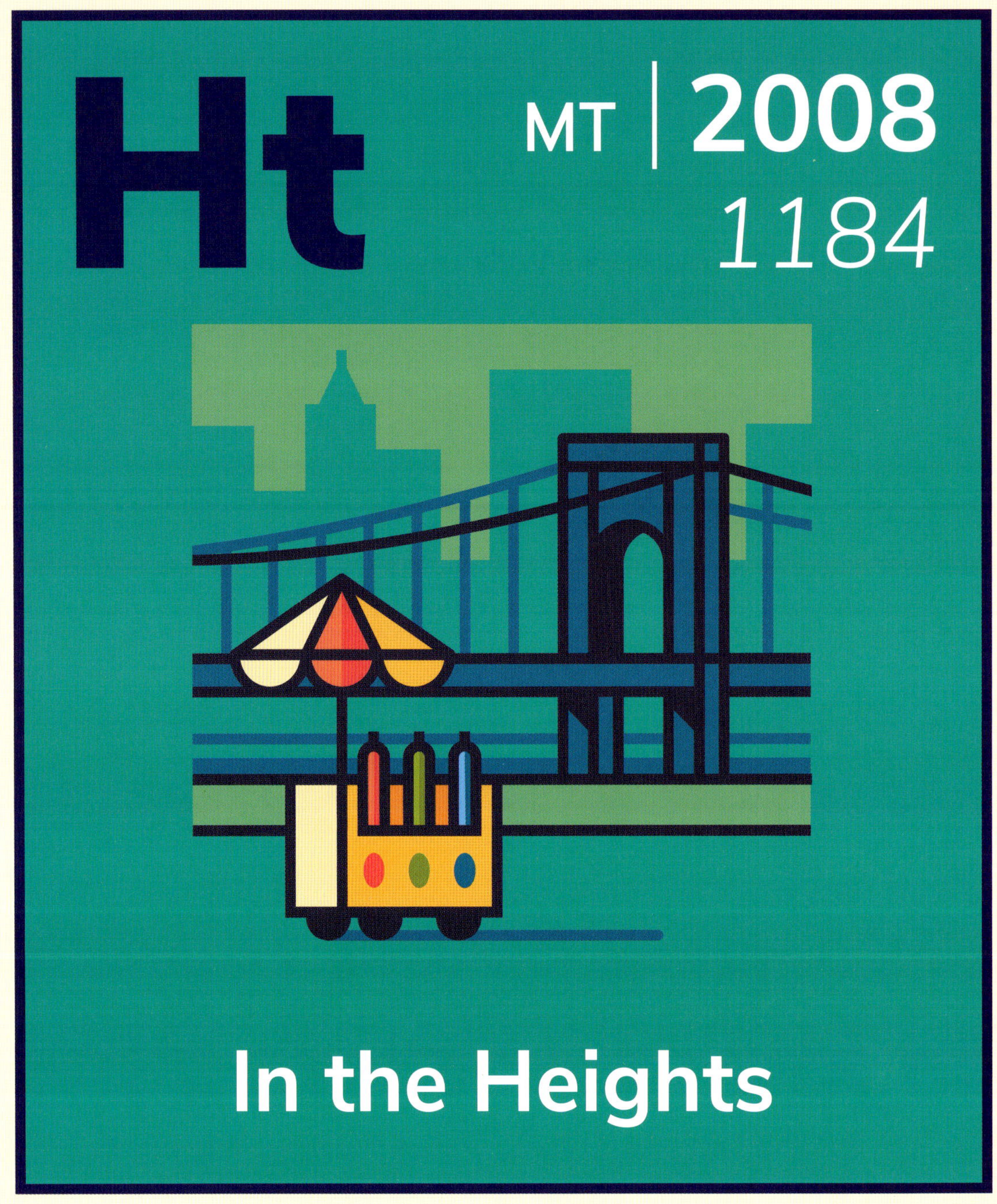

Book by Quiara Alegría Hudes ★ Music and lyrics by Lin-Manuel Miranda
Directed by Thomas Kail ★ Choreographed by Andy Blankenbuehler

Richard Rodgers Theatre, March 9, 2008–January 9, 2011

Lin-Manuel Miranda.......Usnavi
Mandy Gonzalez.......Nina
Karen Olivo.......Vanessa
Christopher Jackson.......Benny

ART NOTE: The Piragua Man's cart in front of the George Washington Bridge.

Over three summer days, the residents of the Dominican and Puerto Rican neighborhood of Washington Heights in Upper Manhattan explore the bonds of love and family. Bodega owner Usnavi narrates the story as he decides whether to move back to the Dominican Republic. Ultimately, he discovers his role in the neighborhood as others reaffirm their love for each other.

Hundreds of Stories

In the 2000s, Broadway seemed to be climbing out of the creative doldrums of the 1990s (an era when sometimes there were not enough new musicals in a season to warrant a full slate of five Tony nominations), but not all voices were being lifted by this rising tide. Even as late as 2014, less than a quarter of Broadway roles were characters of color, and less than three percent of characters were from South or Latin America or the Caribbean.

When Lin-Manuel Miranda started writing musicals at Wesleyan University, he wanted to include and celebrate his Puerto Rican heritage and present characters that represented the northern Manhattan neighborhood where he grew up. Avoiding the Latino clichés of gang members and drug dealers, his story centered around hardworking business owners, their daily lives, and family connections. A student of many genres—from traditional musical theatre to Latin forms to hip-hop—Miranda was able to call on a dizzying range of references, dropping them in both for humorous effect, and to show audiences of all backgrounds that this was their story, too.

His use of spoken rhythmic text combined the perfect rhymes of classic theatre lyricists with the slant and near rhymes of hip-hop artists to create a style new to Broadway musicals. Miranda's characters are equally comfortable describing a "mom-and-pop stop-and-shop," rhyming "exacerbated" with "exaggerated," "*Abuela*" with "*escuela*" or quoting from Cole Porter's *Kiss Me, Kate.* With the exception of the 1996 dance revue *Bring in 'da Noise, Bring in 'da Funk,* Broadway had stayed away from hip-hop, both because there simply weren't any characters writers could see naturally expressing themselves with that vernacular, and there weren't many writers with the skills to create them. But when Usnavi/Miranda addresses the audience in the opening number, his witty, intricately rhymed patter situates the audience in Washington Heights not only by its content but by its very form and vocabulary. It is the perfect representation of America's melting pot, and it felt both fresh and long past due.

Miranda's collaborators Thomas Kail, Andy Blankenbuehler, and orchestrator/arrangers Alex Lacamoire and Bill Sherman all shared this wide-ranging cultural knowledge and expertise, and together they created an authentic, vibrant world that significantly changed the look and sound of Broadway.

MISCELLANEOUS MATTER

★ Miranda actually grew up in Inwood, a few subway stops north of Washington Heights, but didn't set the show there because the word "Inwood" doesn't sing well.

★ Quiara Alegría Hudes went on to win the 2012 Pulitzer Prize for her play, *Water by the Spoonful.*

★ The show reinvented the overture by having a sound cue of a radio scanning through stations playing versions of songs from the show, perfectly conjuring the sonic world of the neighborhood.

★ Anthony Ramos, who played Usnavi in the 2021 movie adaptation, made his Broadway debut in *Hamilton* playing Hamilton's (Miranda's) eldest child, Philip.

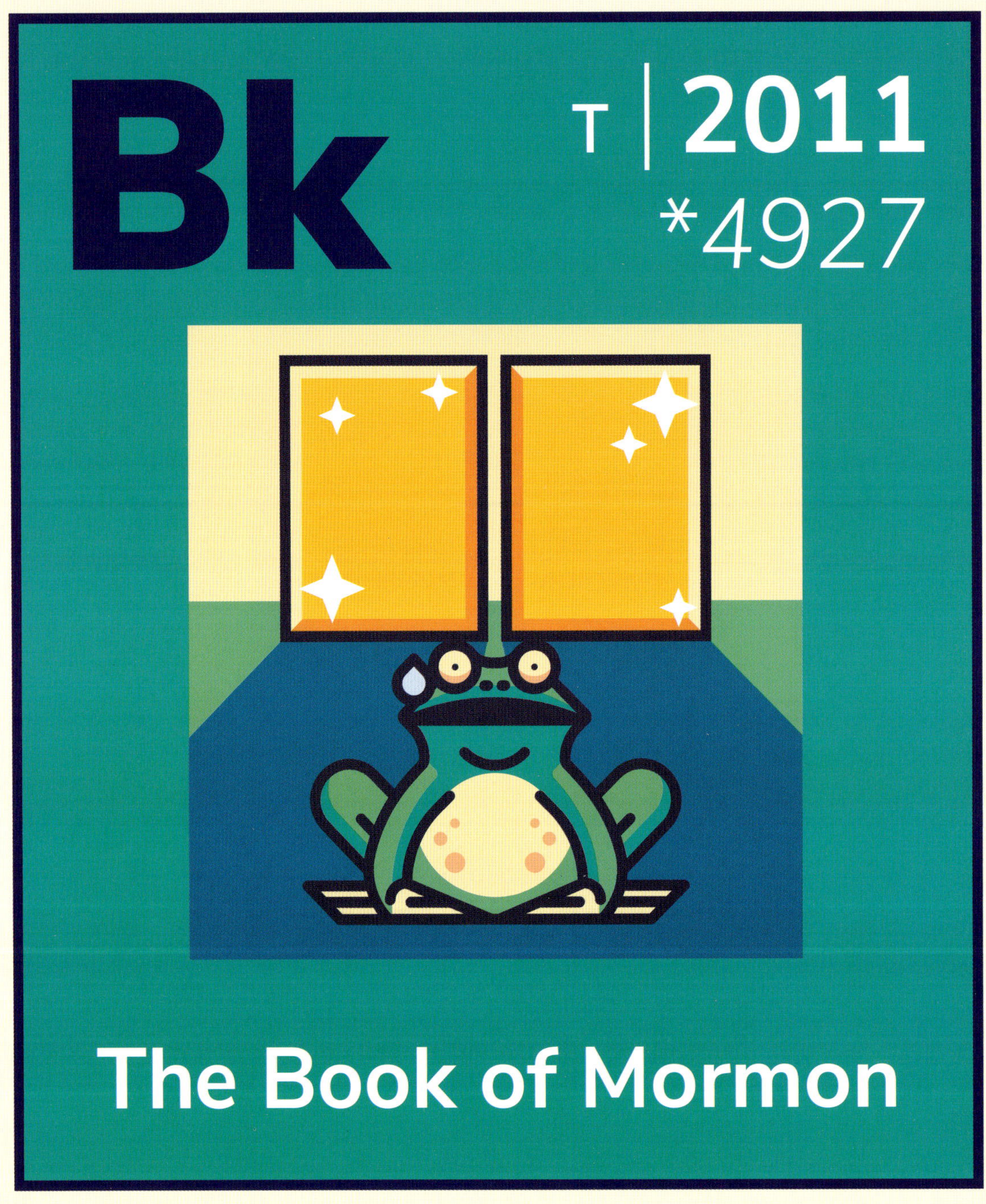

Book, music, and lyrics by Trey Parker, Robert Lopez, and Matt Stone
Directed by Casey Nicholaw and Trey Parker ★ Choreographed by Casey Nicholaw

Eugene O'Neill Theatre, March 24, 2011–publication

Josh Gad.......Elder Cunningham
Andrew Rannells.......Elder Price
Nikki M. James.......Nabulungi
Rory O'Malley.......Elder McKinley

ART NOTE: Two golden plates from Mormon scripture, and a frog who seems alarmed at what he's heard they contain . . .

Two Mormon missionaries are teamed for a two-year mission in Uganda. But the pair is not well-matched, and self-confident overachiever Elder Price initially dominates the slovenly Elder Cunningham. In Uganda, however, as they face challenges (a violent warlord among them), Elder Price gradually learns to value his mission partner, since it turns out that only Elder Cunningham's improvisational, factually challenged sermons succeed in winning Ugandan converts . . . if not to Mormonism, exactly, then to something close.

Two by Two

On many levels, *The Book of Mormon* is about divergent forces coming together to create something positive. In the story, polar opposites Price and Cunningham forge a friendship, and Mormon and Ugandan cultures blend in a whacked-out version of scripture. But the sentiment is equally true in terms of how the show was created: *The Book of Mormon* represents the triumph of writers from two different mediums joining to make a Broadway hit.

Trey Parker and Matt Stone were the creators of the irreverent, scabrous TV show *South Park*, and its tie-in movie *South Park: Bigger, Longer & Uncut* (which was, not incidentally, a musical). Robert Lopez and Jeff Marx were the songwriters of *Avenue Q*, and very much creatures of the theatre. When they met in 2003, it emerged that both teams were intrigued by the idea of writing about Joseph Smith, founder of Mormonism. Though Marx dropped out of the new project early on, the remaining three labored for another eight years before emerging with a finished show. Along the way, Lopez introduced the TV writers to the idea of workshopping, an iterative development process used on most modern musicals that allows creative teams to assess and revise material without the pressure of an impending opening night. In all, there would be over a half dozen workshops for *The Book of Mormon*, involving various directors, choreographers, and performers, but by the final one in summer 2010, choreographer/codirector Casey Nicholaw and stars Andrew Rannells and Josh Gad were all on board.

When the show finally opened on Broadway, everyone expected (given Parker and Stone's reputations) it would be funny and, probably, borderline offensive. It definitely was, and it skewered everything it touched. But what surprised critics was that it was also kind of sweet and charming, and oddly nonjudgmental. In the words of Ben Brantley in the *New York Times*, "its heart is as pure as a Rodgers and Hammerstein show." Once the raves landed, it became near impossible to score tickets. But while *The Book of Mormon* was, in structural terms, old-fashioned, it chose a box office pricing strategy that was innovative. Inspired by the ever-shifting model that airlines use to sell seats, the show boosted the cost of tickets for in-demand performances to stratospheric levels. A reminder that, though musical comedy may be something analogous to religion for some, show business is, first and foremost, a business.

MISCELLANEOUS MATTER

- ★ Elder Cunningham originally appeared in the "Spooky Mormon Hell Dream" in an enormous papier-mâché head—that looked exactly like his real head. It was cut.
- ★ Producer Scott Rudin originally planned to open the show off-Broadway first but, deciding that Parker and Stone "work best when the stakes are highest," instead went straight to Broadway without a tryout.
- ★ In the wake of George Floyd's 2020 murder, and the protests it engendered, the script was altered to center the viewpoint of the Ugandans and give the Black characters more agency.

Book by Enda Walsh ★ Music and lyrics by Glen Hansard and Markéta Irglová
Based on the film by John Carney
Directed by John Tiffany ★ Movement by Steven Hoggett

Bernard B. Jacobs Theatre, March 18, 2012–January 4, 2015

Steve Kazee.......Guy *Cristin Milioti.......Girl*

ART NOTE: The piano that Guy gives Girl, and her broken Hoover.

Girl meets Guy on a Dublin street, where he's busking. He says he's going to give up music and work as a vacuum cleaner repairman; she says she needs her vacuum fixed and can pay with one of her own songs. Thus begins a creative and almost romantic relationship, leading to a record contract. But when Girl's estranged husband reenters the picture, Guy heads to New York City, where the woman who broke his heart is waiting for a second chance.

Gold

In 2005, filmmaker John Carney had the idea for a small indie film about a singer/songwriter who meets a woman on the street busking. It was to star then up-and-coming Irish actor Cillian Murphy, with songwriter Glen Hansard as musical advisor. Hansard ended up introducing Carney to fellow musician (and on-again, off-again girlfriend) Markéta Irglová, and when Carney watched them on stage together, he made the decision to feature them instead. Their undeniable chemistry made the tiny film into an art house hit that grew into a worldwide sensation, mostly on the strength of the duo's quirky, intimate songs. When "Falling Slowly" won the 2007 Oscar for best song, it was the culmination of a very unexpected Cinderella story.

Initially resistant to turning their small, acoustic movie into what they feared would be a potentially embarrassing Broadway vehicle, the songwriters finally granted the rights to two newcomers to musicals, John Tiffany of the National Theatre of Scotland and Irish playwright Enda Walsh. They decided to set the show mostly in a pub, with chairs around the stage for actors to sit and play instruments when they weren't acting in scenes. It made the story and the songs the precious center of the evening and kept the movie's energy of a tale being told among friends. Walsh did inject more humor into the dialogue and made the Girl character a bit fiercer and spunkier to lift the energy of the show, and help it fill a theatre; for many viewers, these changes made the musical even stronger than the film.

Once was the happy beneficiary of an enlarged pool of actors who played one or more instruments, mainly due to the influence of English director John Doyle, who had made a name for himself directing revivals of traditional musicals like *Sweeney Todd* (2005) and *Company* (2006) where the cast doubled as the orchestra. Having found their remarkably versatile cast, the gentle show about a Czech pianist and an Irish guitarist went on to sell out at off-Broadway's New York Theatre Workshop. While it took a few months to catch on when it moved to Broadway, it eventually found its audience through word of mouth, and then ran for years.

MISCELLANEOUS MATTER

- ★ Hansard was very involved with the musical aspect of the show, putting together open mic nights at pubs to give Kazee opportunities to learn how to wow the crowds in small venues where the audience is mere feet away.
- ★ Kazee had been playing guitar since adolescence, but Milioti had to learn to play the piano for the show, working seven hours a day for the ten days before her audition to master a couple songs.
- ★ In 2013, Milioti was revealed as the mother on the hit TV show *How I Met Your Mother.*

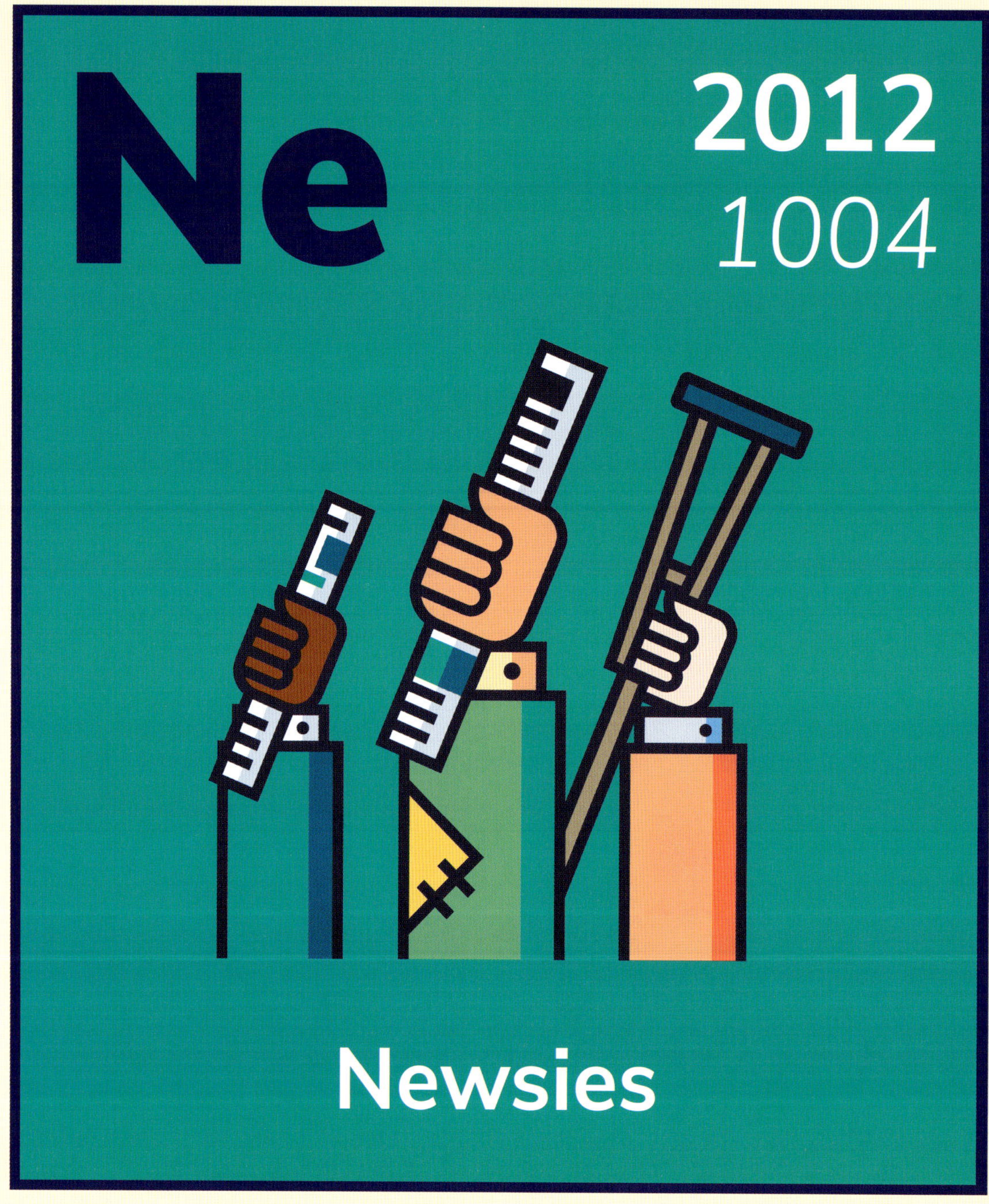

Book by Harvey Fierstein ★ Music by Alan Menken ★ Lyrics by Jack Feldman
Directed by Jeff Calhoun ★ Choreographed by Christopher Gattelli

Nederlander Theatre, March 29, 2012–August 24, 2014

Jeremy Jordan.......Jack Kelly
Kara Lindsay.......Katherine
Ben Fankhauser.......Davey
John Dossett.......Joseph Pulitzer

ART NOTE: Three upraised arms of protesting newsies, one clearly belonging to Crutchie.

It's 1899, and newspaper magnate Joseph Pulitzer has just raised the price newsboys must pay for their bundles of papers. In protest, an older boy, Jack, organizes the newsies into a strike, and a young reporter, Katherine, covers it. Defying Pulitzer and the cops, they start their own paper with Katherine's articles and Jack's illustrations, catching the eye of New York Governor Theodore Roosevelt, who supports the strike. Impressed with Jack's talent, Pulitzer offers him a job as a political cartoonist.

Something to Believe In

After the thrilling reboot of their animated musical film department with 1989's *The Little Mermaid* and 1991's *Beauty and the Beast*, Disney rolled the dice on the live-action musical film *Newsies*, which also featured music by Alan Menken. But reviews were poor ("disturbingly cold," "cliché," "Snoozies"), and the opening week box office was so disappointing that they actually pulled the film from many theatres. But they still released it on VHS, and with so many '90s families rushing to Blockbuster every weekend to stock up on movies, *Newsies* found a cult following. Over the years, it charmed a whole generation of fans who fell in love with the plucky energy of the score and, let's face it, the cute newsies themselves, led by Christian Bale.

In 2011, cautiously inspired by this existing fan base, Disney went ahead with a limited plan for a theatrical *Newsies.* Though their screen-to-stage *Beauty and the Beast* and *The Lion King* were Broadway hits, *The Little Mermaid* and *Tarzan* had been disappointments, and Disney was, as always, very aware of the bottom line. So they greenlit *Newsies* only for regional productions (like they'd done with *High School Musical*) and opened it at the Paper Mill Playhouse in New Jersey. When it received terrific reviews, they tiptoed across the Hudson and announced a limited run at the Nederlander, where the love only grew. The high-energy score, solid, traditional story, kinetic staging, and acrobatic choreography made for a polished package, and it turned out audiences were hungry for a Disney show about human beings for a change.

The humans at the center of this particular show were a formidable pair. When casting Katherine, actresses were given her big song, "Watch What Happens," which was so challenging that almost no one could do it justice. Happily, Kara Lindsay (previously a Glinda replacement in *Wicked*) showed up and knocked it out of the park. And her leading man was Jeremy Jordan, who was very busy during the Paper Mill run, playing Jack at night while rehearsing for his major Broadway debut as Clyde in *Bonnie and Clyde* during the day. When *Newsies* transferred to Broadway, it was still unclear if Jordan would be available to go with it; as it turned out, *Bonnie and Clyde* ran only a month, and Jordan could rejoin his newsie pals in March, on his way to a Tony nomination.

MISCELLANEOUS MATTER

★ Jack Feldman wrote the lyrics to the huge Barry Manilow hit song "Copacabana."

★ Fierstein smartly combined two separate characters from the movie into the musical's Katherine, creating a genuine female leading role in this boy-heavy piece.

★ The show's original sets stayed very true to the look and feel of the original movie; Calhoun and designer Tobin Ost were surprised when they were told "it looks like a revival" and encouraged to be bolder. They came up with three enormous, rotating towers that the boys scaled, reaching higher as they became more successful, like Davids conquering giant Goliaths.

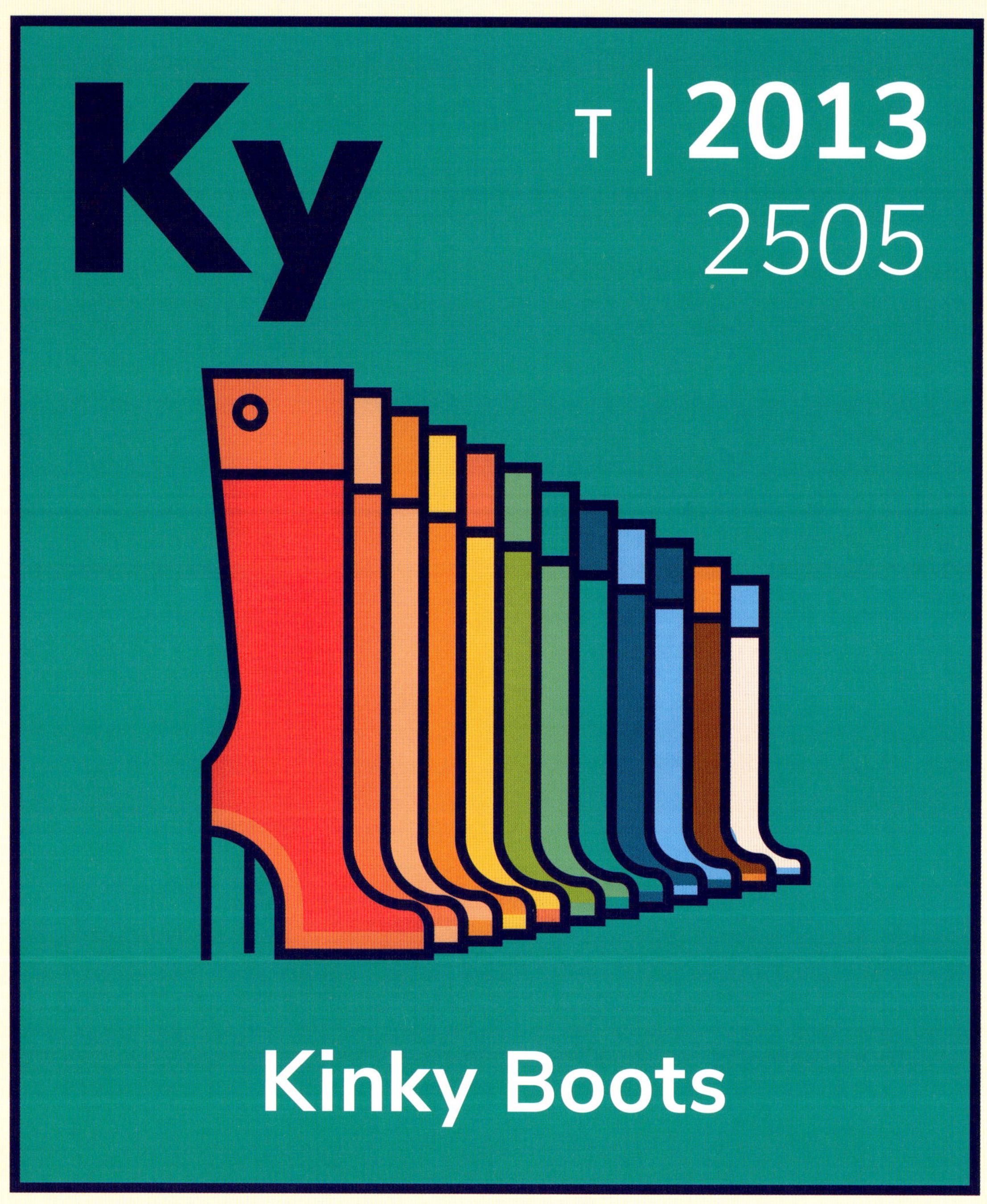

Book by Harvey Fierstein ★ Music and lyrics by Cyndi Lauper
Based on the film by Geoff Deane and Tim Firth
Directed and choreographed by Jerry Mitchell

Al Hirschfeld Theatre, April 4, 2013–April 7, 2019

Billy Porter.......Lola
Stark Sands.......Charlie Price
Annaleigh Ashford.......Lauren

ART NOTE: Stiletto-heeled boots coming off the line in every color of the rainbow.

Charlie inherits the family shoe business and discovers that it is near bankruptcy. He happens to meet a drag queen named Lola and, noticing her shoes are not constructed to hold a man's weight, engages her as consultant and retrofits the factory to produce high-heeled boots for men. As the two bond over their difficult relationships with their fathers, they must withstand hostility from some of the workers. Together, they change minds and hearts and save the factory, along with the workers' jobs.

I'm Not My Father's Son

In the act one finale, "Everybody Say Yeah," the drag queens and factory workers celebrate the first pair of boots off the factory line by dancing on four working conveyor belts that are wheeled around the stage. It's a good metaphor for the creation of any musical, with dozens of people coordinating hundreds of moving parts, all chasing an elusive target: a captivating work of art that delights the senses while telling a meaningful story to a live audience.

In 2012, pop singer/songwriter Cyndi Lauper was one of the hardest working people in show business—she had a new album, a tour, an autobiography, and a reality show all happening at the same time she was composing *Kinky Boots*, her first musical. A natural songwriter, she nonetheless immediately studied Rodgers and Hammerstein and *West Side Story* to create lyrics that could shoulder the responsibilities of a musical theatre song. She leaned on book writer Harvey Fierstein for guidance on how to build songs that gave characters and actors what they needed at different points in the story, and quickly learned how to judge from an audience's response what changes needed to be made. And she drew inspiration from the actors themselves; for example, when she was writing a particularly difficult number for Stark Sands's character, she asked him what music he listened to (his answer: Weezer). Once that effort and inspiration had worked its magic, her talented orchestrator and arranger Stephen Oremus (*Avenue Q, Wicked*) would take her musical ideas, sometimes recorded on her phone, and flesh them out into polished numbers for synths, brass, and strings, or expand them into full chorus production numbers.

Broadway veteran Fierstein was clear from the start that he didn't just want to repeat his success from *La Cage aux Folles*, the last major Broadway show about drag performers, so he centered the story on two men who both needed to get out from under their fathers' shadows. Drag, too, had changed since *La Cage aux Folles*. In 2013, *RuPaul's Drag Race* was in its fifth season, and it had turned drag from something niche and taboo into mainstream pop culture. In his second Broadway show as director/choreographer, Jerry Mitchell organized all these eclectic parts into a seamless whole where every sequin was in place and told the same story: we can do anything together.

MISCELLANEOUS MATTER

- ★ Cyndi Lauper was the first woman to win the Tony for Best Score (both music and lyrics).
- ★ Prior to *Kinky Boots*, Lauper had starred in the 2006 Broadway revival of *The Threepenny Opera* opposite Alan Cumming and fellow singer/songwriter Nellie McKay.
- ★ Gregg Barnes's design for the iconic 6½-inch high-heeled boots required steel reinforcements to support the weight of dancing men.
- ★ Movies were very ripe properties for adaptation that year, with *Bring It On, A Christmas Story, Hands on a Hardbody, Big Fish,* and the off-Broadway show *Dogfight* all premiering in 2012–13.

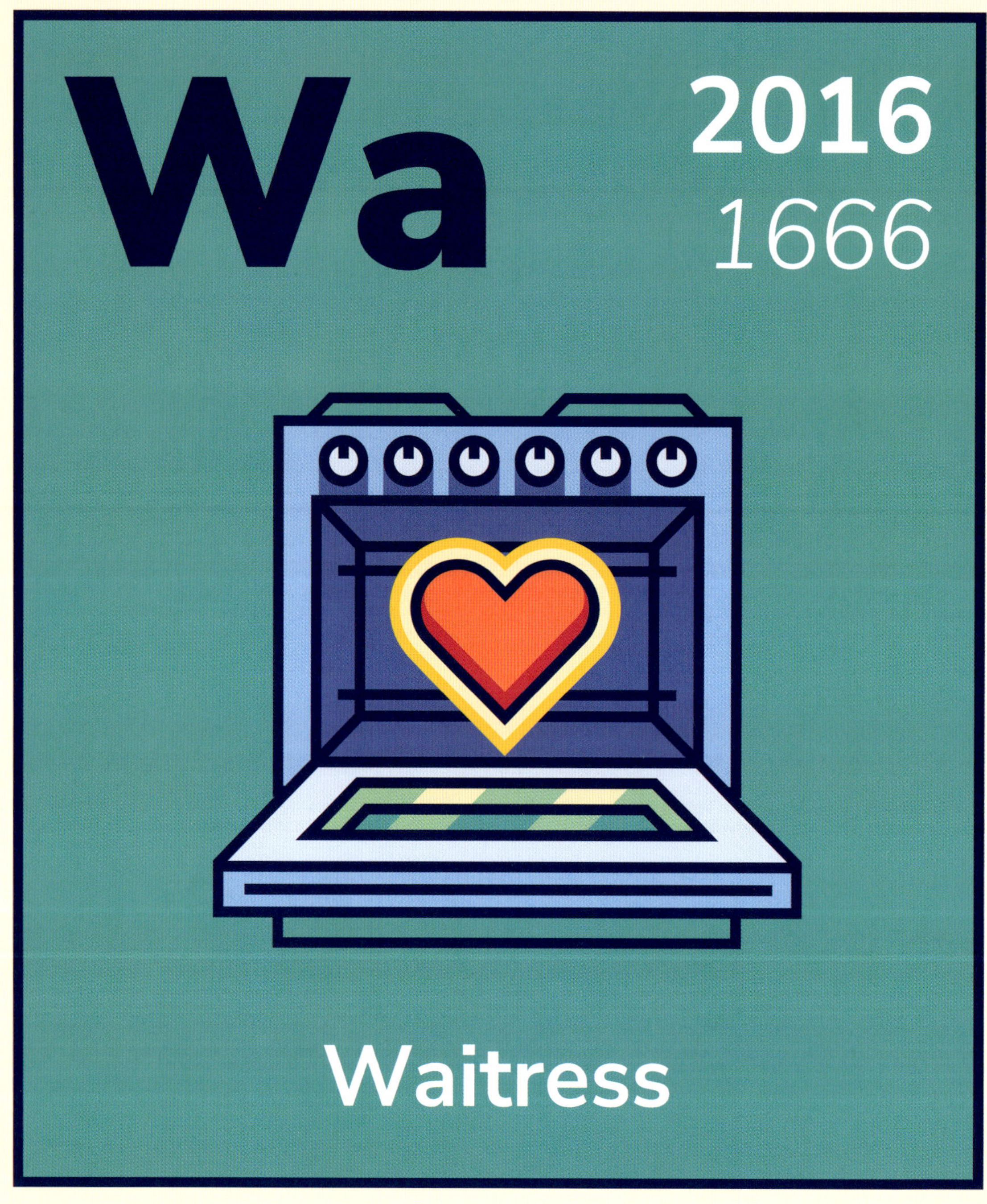

Book by Jessie Nelson ★ Music and lyrics by Sara Bareilles
Based on the motion picture written by Adrienne Shelly
Directed by Diane Paulus ★ Choreographed by Lorin Latarro

Brooks Atkinson Theatre, April 24, 2016–January 5, 2020

Jessie Mueller.......Jenna
Kimiko Glenn.......Dawn
Christopher Fitzgerald.......Ogie
Drew Gehling.......Dr. Pomatter

ART NOTE: "What's Inside"? Jenna baking from the heart (with a little something special in the oven . . .).

Jenna, a waitress at Joe's Diner, discovers she's pregnant. She plans to enter a contest with one of her famous pies to win enough money to leave her abusive husband, Earl. An affair with her married OB/GYN shows her sometimes a "Bad Idea" can be fun, for a while. Earl takes the money she'd been saving, and when the baby is born she says she's divorcing him. Joe leaves her the diner, which she names after her daughter, Lulu.

It Only Takes a Taste

It says a lot about how far musical theatre had come from its late 1980s and '90s doldrums that, starting in the late 2000s, a string of pop, country, and indie singer/songwriters all aspired to have a show on Broadway. *Spring Awakening* (Duncan Sheik), *9 to 5* (Dolly Parton), *American Idiot* (Green Day), *Passing Strange* (Stew), *Spider-Man: Turn off the Dark* (Bono and The Edge), *Ghost* (Dave Stewart), *Here Lies Love* (David Byrne, Fatboy Slim), *Bright Star* (Edie Brickell), *Kinky Boots* (Cyndi Lauper), and *The Last Ship* (Sting) are just some of the projects that made it to major productions in New York during this time, as the new popularity of Broadway lured even the biggest stars to Times Square.

When director Diane Paulus began thinking about turning Adrienne Shelly's indie film *Waitress* into a musical, singer/songwriter and pianist Sara Bareilles was already on her radar. She'd been impressed with Bareilles's smart 2007 hit "Love Song," and believed her thoughtful, character-driven lyrics might be a perfect fit for this show's intimate small-town relationships. Paulus also wanted to find a female writer to tell this female-centered story; in the end, the entire creative team for the show would be women, a Broadway first (*The Secret Garden* had been close, but that show's choreographer was male).

The women in *Waitress* were all refreshingly flawed, nervous about love and life, prone to lapses in judgement and to over- and under-thinking relationships in all-too-familiar ways. But if the characters felt lived-in and naturalistic, the staging was full of theatrical delights. The large diner set was brightly lit, and Paulus and Latarro filled it with constant movement, such as synchronized towel flicks and pie slides that emphasized the performative nature of being a waitress. Even quasi-love songs like "Bad Idea" had imaginative, kinetic staging, elevating and enlarging small moments so they filled a theatre. Every actor had their turn to shine, and two garnered Tony nominations: Christopher Fitzgerald (his third), for his love-struck, hyperkinetic Ogie, and Jessie Mueller in the conflicted and nuanced leading role. And having the band onstage in the middle of the diner kept the "show-ness" of the show always present, with each ingredient showcased even as they all added up to one delicious whole.

MISCELLANEOUS MATTER

★ Originally nervous about acting, in June 2016, Bareilles performed the part of Ariel in a two-night live presentation of Disney's *The Little Mermaid* at the Hollywood Bowl. In 2017, she replaced Jessie Mueller as Jenna in *Waitress*, then went on to TV roles including *Girls5eva*. She then earned a Tony nomination herself as Best Actress in the second Broadway revival of *Into the Woods*.

★ Though the show closed shortly before the COVID pandemic, the producers decided to reopen it when Broadway started up again. It and *Hadestown* were the first to welcome (fully vaccinated, masked) audiences back to the theatre.

★ Fitzgerald's most recent Tony nod had been for playing the similarly named Og in the 2009 *Finian's Rainbow*.

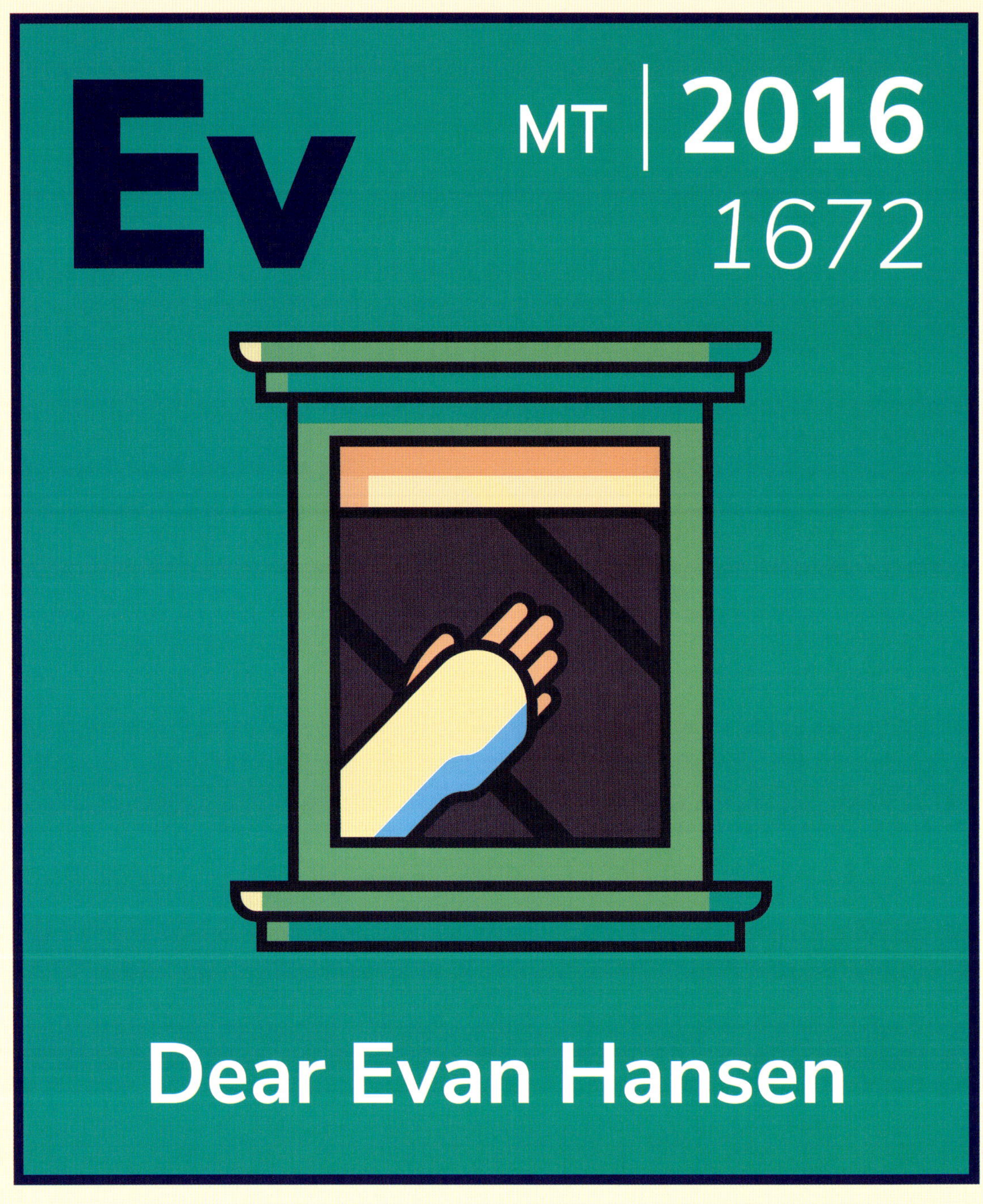

Book by Steven Levenson ★ Music and lyrics by Benj Pasek and Justin Paul
Directed by Michael Greif ★ Choreographed by Danny Mefford

Music Box Theatre, December 4, 2016–September 18, 2022

Ben Platt.......Evan Hansen
Laura Dreyfuss.......Zoe Murphy
Mike Faist.......Connor Murphy
Rachel Bay Jones.......Heidi Hansen

ART NOTE: Evan's arm in a cast, "Waving Through a Window."

Evan, a socially awkward teen, writes himself a letter as a therapy assignment, and it's stolen by school bully, Connor. When Connor commits suicide, the letter is discovered in his pocket, and everyone thinks he wrote it to Evan as a friend. Evan plays along with the misunderstanding, fabricating a history of emails and starting an online campaign to raise money for Connor's supposedly beloved apple orchard. When he admits the lies, the two families can begin to move on.

Anybody Have a Map?

Since the dawn of musical theatre, writers have looked to books and plays for stories to adapt. There were occasional film adaptations (*Sweet Charity, 42nd Street, Sunset Boulevard*), but it wasn't till the 21st century that movies became the go-to source material, starting with *The Producers, The Full Monty,* and *Hairspray.* By the 2010s, this reliance on movies was seen either as a joke or a cause for concern—were there no original stories anymore?

Dear Evan Hansen answered with a resounding "yes." In this thought-provoking original story by thirty-one-year-old playwright Steven Levenson, teens and parents grapple with the uses and abuses of social media. Director Michael Greif was no stranger to urgent, contemporary stories, having directed *Rent* and *Next to Normal*, and he once again managed to maintain the intimate heart of a tragic story while enlarging it to Broadway proportions. Scenic designer David Korins (*Hamilton*), aided by projections by Peter Nigrini (*Fela!*), drew inspiration from the high school world of omnipresent screens and filled the entire stage in pulsing images and text.

Songwriters Pasek and Paul's previous shows had both been movie adaptations: the off-Broadway *Dogfight* and the Broadway holiday run of *A Christmas Story*. Their character-driven lyrics had always been inspired by the best traditional musical theatre writing; with *Dear Evan Hansen*, they amped up the music with stronger pop-rock beats, made even more exciting by expert orchestrator/arranger Alex Lacamoire (*Wicked, Hamilton*). Young leading man Ben Platt made a huge splash as the title character, awkwardly soulful with an effortless, wide-ranging voice that easily handled the demanding score. And, as his mother, Rachel Bay Jones gave a heartbreaking performance every mother could identify with.

Interestingly, it was when this original stage production became a movie that it ran into trouble. Though it had been a Broadway smash, most of the country (including film critics) didn't know the plot, and they saw it with fresh eyes. For many, the lack of consequences for Evan's manipulative actions left a bad taste, even though the film devoted more time to the moral aftershocks. By the time it was made, Platt was also twenty-seven, and though everyone involved wanted to immortalize his terrific performance, audiences had trouble believing he was seventeen. The relationship between film and theatre continues to evolve, no matter which way the adaptation engine runs.

MISCELLANEOUS MATTER

- ★ The character of Evan has trouble with romance, but for actors who've played him, the role has been a ticket to love. In fact, original "Evan" Ben Platt ended up marrying the performer who replaced him in the Broadway company, Noah Galvin.
- ★ Each actor playing Evan on Broadway got a real fiberglass cast custom-molded to his arm; a new one is applied and wrapped like a real medical cast before each performance and sawed off during each intermission.
- ★ Reversing decades of Broadway adaptations, the musical was adapted into a novel in 2018.

Book, music, and lyrics by Anaïs Mitchell
Directed by Rachel Chavkin ★ Choreographed by David Neumann

Walter Kerr Theatre, April 17, 2019–publication

Reeve Carney.......Orpheus
André De Shields.......Hermes
Eva Noblezada ....Eurydice
Amber Gray.......Persephone

ART NOTE: The road to Hadestown's factory.

Orpheus and Eurydice are poor but in love. Orpheus is writing a song that will bring eternal spring, but until then, Eurydice suffers in the cold. She accepts Hades's invitation to come to Hadestown, where she works in a factory, secure but trapped. Orpheus plays Hades a song to win her release, and he agrees they can leave if Orpheus walks in front and never looks back. But Orpheus can't help himself and turns around, dooming Eurydice to live in Hadestown forever.

Our Lady of the Underground

The road to Broadway keeps changing length, but it's almost always paved with the same intention: to make money. Even when a producer falls in love with a show's artistic vision, they owe it to their investors to open the best possible version, which means the version most likely to recoup its capitalization. The most common model by which creators hone a show into its best possible condition has been the out-of-town tryout ever since Florenz Ziegfeld demanded major changes in 1927's *Show Boat* during a month-long pre-Broadway tour. But as Broadway has gotten more and more expensive, extra stops have been added on many shows' journeys.

Hadestown began as a kind of DIY theatre production that toured Anaïs Mitchell's home state of Vermont in a "magical" silver school bus in 2006. Wary of turning it over to mainstream producers who might "cheese it up," she recorded a concept album. Then, in 2012, she saw director Rachel Chavkin's production of *Natasha, Pierre & the Great Comet of 1812* and was impressed with her edgy staging. The two worked for several years filling in holes in *Hadestown*'s story and clarifying its themes, finally arriving off-Broadway in 2016 at the New York Theatre Workshop to glowing reviews.

Why, then, did the stylish, spare production take three more years to travel twenty minutes uptown? A Broadway opening, like the devil, is in the details, and to the creators' credit, they felt more work was needed. So they opted for two out-of-town productions between their New York openings. The set and the setting were reimagined; originally staged in a mini-Greek amphitheatre, the team experimented with a more literal set for an Edmonton, Alberta, production before settling on the now famous multilevel New Orleans jazz club/factory for a London run, complete with enormous hanging industrial lights that swing out over the audience. Thematic resonances with workers' rights and the fight against climate change were strengthened, while motives were clarified and relationships between characters emphasized.

But throughout, the score retained its unique sound. Nearly entirely sung through, *Hadestown* maintains a consistently seductive jazz/folk sound through solos, duets, the tight harmony Fates trio, and full-throated production numbers. The virtuoso onstage band makes it feel like the hottest concert on Broadway, and as of publication, it's still cooking . . . and not looking back.

MISCELLANEOUS MATTER

★ *Hadestown* was only the fifth show to win the Tony Award for Best Musical with book, music, and lyrics written by the same person, and the first by a woman. Three years later, *A Strange Loop* would become the sixth.

★ The original title of the show was *Crack in the Wall.*

★ Both Mitchell and Chavkin have *Hadestown*-inspired tattoos; Chavkin a lyre, and Mitchell Eurydice herself.

★ Unlike in the show, Noblezada and Carney's real-life love story had a happy ending: they became engaged in March 2025.

OFF-BROADWAY

CRUCIBLE FOR INNOVATION

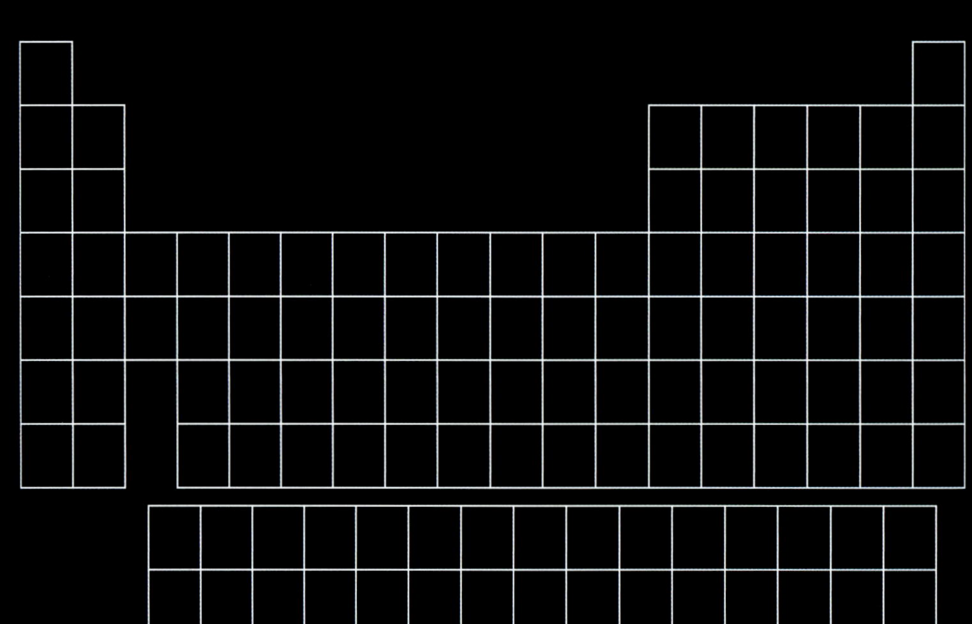

In 1954, esteemed theatre critic for the *New York Times* Brooks Atkinson bemoaned the current Broadway season as "tasteless, hackneyed, and dull . . . a gaudy wardrobe of old hats." His directions to find the smart, inventive shows? Hop a train 30 blocks downtown where the musicals *The Golden Apple* and *The Threepenny Opera* were playing in small theatres in the East and West Village. While *Golden Apple* transferred immediately to Broadway, *Threepenny* stayed put and ran for years, effectively inaugurating the off-Broadway musical.

The definition of what constitutes an off-Broadway theatre versus a Broadway one has changed over the decades, but for many years it simply referred to the size of the venue. Theatres with 100 to 499 seats are classified as off-Broadway and have different pay scales and other union requirements than the larger Broadway houses. Many of these smaller theatres sprang up in the 1950s, and producers embraced them because their lower overhead costs meant they could present shows that were more adventurous, with a potentially more limited appeal. Most productions in these smaller houses were not eligible for Tony Awards (though early on there was some wiggle room).

Starting in the late 1960s and led by Joseph Papp and his Public Theater, certain off-Broadway companies followed the model set by *The Golden Apple* and 1959's *Once Upon a Mattress* and took successful productions, with their good press and established buzz, and tried their luck with a Broadway transfer. Today, the Public Theater still follows this model, along with the Atlantic, the Vineyard, Second Stage, and Playwrights Horizons; all regularly produce shows with an eye on eventual Broadway transfers. The shows in this section of the book are the ones that never made a transfer, but which otherwise might have been considered for the table. (Okay, we acknowledge some of our favorite off-Broadway shows mentioned below have had Broadway *revivals*, but only long after their initial runs ended; in our eyes they remain, at heart, off-Broadway shows.)

Off-Broadway musicals often mark the first big breaks for major writers who go on to pen Broadway hits. Among these, to name just a few, are Schmidt and Jones (*The Fantasticks*), Ashman and Menken (*Little Shop of Horrors*), Jeanine Tesori (*Violet*), Andrew Lippa (*john & jen*), and Adam Guettel (*Floyd Collins*). For this reason, and because no account of musical theatre history would be complete without these beloved and important shows, we want to take a moment to pay tribute to our Top Ten little giants.

The Threepenny Opera

Book and lyrics by Bertolt Brecht ★ Music by Kurt Weill

Theatre de Lys, March 10, 1954–May 30, 1954; reopened September 20, 1955–December 17, 1961

Originally produced in Germany in 1928, this groundbreaking musical set Berlin on fire with its angular, modern jazz sound, rough language, and biting social commentary. As conceived by revolutionary playwright Bertolt Brecht, the songs served as breaks in the story, with the actors singing directly to the audience; viewers were invited not to identify with the characters but to criticize them (and, hopefully, themselves). *The Threepenny Opera* was the first time the young classical composer Kurt Weill crossed over into musical theatre, and his knack for melody and a unique slant on popular styles proved irresistible. He went on to a successful Broadway career, collaborating with the best of the best: Moss Hart, Ira Gershwin, Maxwell Anderson, Langston Hughes, and many others. The off-Broadway production marked the first big breaks for Bea Arthur (*Mame, Fiddler on the Roof*) and Jo Sullivan (*The Most Happy Fella*), and had Austrian actress (and Weill's widow) Lotte Lenya reprise her original role as Jenny, winning her a unique off-Broadway Tony Award. The show has had several Broadway revivals over the years, starring Raul Julia, Sting, Cyndi Lauper, Maureen McGovern, and Alan Cumming.

The Fantasticks

Book and lyrics by Tom Jones ★ Music by Harvey Schmidt

Sullivan Street Playhouse, May 3, 1960–January 13, 2002

For forty-two years and over 17,000 performances, *The Fantasticks* delighted audiences with its whimsical story of neighboring fathers who pretend to hate each other but are secretly scheming to pair off their naively adventurous children. The homemade feel of the set—some curtains, a trunk of props, and a cardboard sun/moon hung from a nail—reflected the authors' belief that what audience members' imaginations could conjure up would be more interesting than even the glitziest designs. The show's astonishing longevity (likely to forever remain the longest-running musical of all time) and broad appeal (it's been staged in at least sixty-seven countries) rests in part on its lighthearted, sometimes absurd story, grounded in universal truths about children and parents. Over the years, countless performers came and went through the stage door of the Sullivan Street Playhouse: Jerry Orbach (straight out of *The Threepenny Opera*), Liza Minelli, Glenn Close, Kristin Chenoweth, and many more. (Barbra Streisand auditioned and famously was not cast; nevertheless, she happily recorded several of the songs.) The show continues to be reimagined—a recent German opera company staged it with enormous futuristic projections, and Jones himself rewrote it for a production that wanted to feature a love story between two sons.

You're a Good Man, Charlie Brown

Book by Clark Gesner and ensemble ★ Music and lyrics by Clark Gesner

Theatre 80, March 7, 1967–February 14, 1971
(John Golden Theatre, June 1, 1971–June 27, 1971)

Okay, so this is a little bit of a cheat. As you can see above, this long-running off-Broadway hit based on the beloved Charles Schulz comic strip characters *did* transfer to Broadway's Golden Theatre . . . and immediately closed. It was such a successful off-Broadway show, running nearly four years, that we're willing to forget its Broadway bellyflop and pay tribute to its youthful spark, and the perfect way it translated comic strip favorites Charlie Brown, Lucy, Linus, and Snoopy to the stage. Based on a concept album of songs Gesner wrote, with a book assembled by him and the cast, it's a feel-good trip through some of the characters' most well-known scenarios and issues. In 1999, a revised and updated version was produced specifically for Broadway, featuring three new songs by Andrew Lippa; one of them, "My New Philosophy," written for Kristin Chenoweth as Sally, helped win her a Tony.

I'm Getting My Act Together and Taking It on the Road

Book and lyrics by Gretchen Cryer ★ Music by Nancy Ford

The Public Theater and Circle in the Square Theatre (downtown), June 14, 1978–March 15, 1981

Cryer and Ford were the first female songwriting team working both off-Broadway (1970's award-winning *The Last Sweet Days of Isaac*) and on (1973's short-lived *Shelter*). They then began focusing on songs that dealt with the evolving role of women in society and turned them into a new show. In *Getting My Act Together and Taking It on the Road*, a singer/songwriter (played by Cryer) surprises her misogynist manager with a new show of pro-women songs. His reaction is ugly (Cryer based many of his comments on ones she'd gotten in real life), but her character refuses to go back to her old material. Though the show received mixed reviews, it struck a chord with female audiences, and word-of-mouth made it a major success. A talk-back session after every Wednesday night show provoked both positive and negative reactions, highlighting the show's importance in the cultural discourse.

Little Shop of Horrors

Book and lyrics by Howard Ashman ★ Music by Alan Menken

Orpheum Theatre, July 27, 1982–November 1, 1987

The story of a bloodthirsty, homicidal plant (played by a puppet) that takes over the world, abetted by a lovestruck florist's assistant and commented on by a 1960s girl group—what could be more off-Broadway? Ashman and Menken's first megahit was bizarre, hilarious, heartbreaking, campy, and addictive. The high-energy score combined sweetly satirical songs like "Suddenly Seymour" and "Somewhere That's Green" with outrageous and now iconic numbers like "Feed Me" and "Dentist" (fun fact: Menken's father was a dentist). It won all the major awards for best off-Broadway musical, but when a Broadway transfer was suggested, Ashman declined, afraid that it might lose its subversive charms. It finally reached Broadway in 2003, where it played for less than a year, proving Ashman right. The 2019 off-Broadway revival, on the other hand, is still running as of publication.

Nunsense

Book, lyrics, and music by Dan Goggin

Cherry Lane Theatre and Douglas Fairbanks Theatre
December 12, 1985–February 26, 1995

Dan Goggin was a musical theatre performer, songwriter, and ex-seminarian who had started a line of greeting cards that quickly became popular, featuring a gaggle of salty nuns. He capitalized on their success by creating a little cabaret show for his characters, then expanded it into a full-length show for an off-Broadway run. The silly but endearing story of nuns with show biz aspirations trying to raise money to bury four of their deceased sisters had legs that no one could have imagined. It became a $500 million international industry, spawning six sequels, three spin-offs (including a drag version, *Nunsense A-Men!*), and two TV specials. Over the years, the five-woman show has provided countless opportunities for seasoned pros like Kaye Ballard, Phyllis Diller, and Rue McClanahan (as well as countless amateur and regional performers) to strut their holy stuff.

I Love You, You're Perfect, Now Change

Book and lyrics by Joe DiPietro ★ Music by Jimmy Roberts

Westside Theatre, August 1, 1996–July 27, 2008

This sparkling revue is a collection of vignettes and original songs about dating, love, and marriage, and it was an off-Broadway staple for an incredible twelve years and 5,000 performances. Over the course of the evening, the four-person cast rotated through dozens of characters, playing everything from familiar stereotypes recast with modern wit to more surprising scenarios, guaranteeing that every audience member could recognize themselves in at least a couple moments. The show has been translated and produced around the world from Japan to Hungary to Brazil, proving that love truly is universal.

Hedwig and the Angry Inch

Book by John Cameron Mitchell ★ Music and lyrics by Stephen Trask

Jane Street Theatre, February 14, 1998–April 9, 2000

New York had never seen anything like *Hedwig and the Angry Inch*. Staged as a bona fide rock concert by the titular genderqueer aspiring rock star as they follow their ex and ex-songwriting partner Tommy Gnosis on his much more successful concert tour around the country, the show was a celebration/deconstruction of gender nonconformity, drag, and, ultimately, love. This was in-your-face rock, a sonic blast with screaming, distorted guitars and pounding drums. Somehow, it also managed to be a witty satire of East German counterculture and the underbelly of show business, as well as an exploration of the main character's deeply messy inner life. The show was a tour de force for Mitchell, who also played Hedwig, and costar Miriam Shor, who played Hedwig's Serbian assistant and former drag queen Yitzhak; happily, both their performances were captured in the 2001 film version. The year 2014 saw Neil Patrick Harris bring Hedwig to Broadway; other stars who have stepped into Hedwig's boots include Anthony Rapp (*Rent*), Andrew Rannells (*The Book of Mormon*), and Jinkx Monsoon (*Little Shop of Horrors*).

The Last Five Years

Music and lyrics by Jason Robert Brown

Minetta Lane Theatre, March 2, 2002–May 5, 2002

After his Broadway debut won him a Tony but closed after a few months, Jason Robert Brown nearly quit musical theatre. Luckily, someone convinced him to write something small, so he came up with "the anti-*Parade*," a song cycle for two people that became his biggest hit. *The Last Five Years* audaciously tells the story of a couple's meeting, courtship, wedding, and breakup from two perspectives: Jamie's, moving forward in time, and Cathy's, moving backward, meeting only briefly in the middle, at their wedding. The alternating takes on the same relationship kept audiences searching for the "truth"; the smart lyrics and fresh, jazz-infused piano pop sound kept them on the edge of their seats. The original cast album, starring Norbert Leo Butz and Sherie Rene Scott, became a musical theatre favorite, and a movie starring Anna Kendrick and Jeremy Jordan premiered in 2014.

Altar Boyz

Book by Kevin Del Aguila
Music and lyrics by Gary Adler and Michael Patrick Walker

Dodger Stages, March 1, 2005–January 10, 2010

Like *Hedwig and the Angry Inch, Altar Boyz* is presented as a rock concert. Beyond that, no two shows could possibly be more different . . . except they both found their audiences. In *Altar Boyz*, four good Christian pop singers (Matthew, Mark, Luke, and John, of course) plus their Jewish songwriter (Abraham) perform the last concert of their latest tour, during which they must save ninety-nine souls, as monitored by an onstage machine. The early 2000s boy-band pop sound, which occasionally veered into Latin or rap, was lovingly sent up and a very funny contrast to the religious and inspirational lyrics. Though they were just a spoof group, the Boyz inspired real fans who dubbed themselves the "Altarholics," and this core audience, plus some smart producing, kept the show running for over 2,000 performances even as the off-Broadway economic model became more and more impossible. Which, in itself, was a small miracle.

Four Revues

Our Top Ten all featured terrific original scores, but there are four more off-Broadway shows we wanted to spotlight that were revues of preexisting songs, two of pop favorites and two of great theatre writers.

- ***Jacques Brel Is Alive and Well and Living in Paris (1968):*** A celebration of the hugely popular Belgian singer/songwriter Jacques Brel, its winning combination of world-weary songs of love and death plus unexpected silliness helped it run for four years. It pointed the way for many single-composer revues like *Ain't Misbehavin', Eubie!, Sophisticated Ladies, Marry Me a Little,* and more.

- ***Closer Than Ever (1989):*** No one writes smarter theatre songs than Richard Maltby Jr. and David Shire (*Baby, Big*), and this revue brought together some of their best—grown-up takes on relationships, loss, and living up to the pressures of modern society. The original cast album was seemingly on constant rotation in every college musical theatre dorm room for a decade.

- ***Forever Plaid (1989):*** One of the shows that inspired *Altar Boyz*, this charmer features a male quartet from the 1950s in one last show, performing the hits of the day before they join the afterlife (they were killed when they collided with a bus full of Catholic schoolgirls). Virtuoso vocal arrangements and lovably goofy gags made it an international hit, and even inspired a Christmas sequel, *Plaid Tidings.*

- ***And the World Goes 'Round (1991):*** Musical joys overflowed in this award-winning revue that featured thirty songs, both hits and obscurities, by John Kander and Fred Ebb (*Cabaret, Chicago, Kiss of the Spider Woman*). Sophisticated musical arrangements by David Loud and dizzying choreography by Susan Stroman (before her first Broadway success, *Crazy for You*) showcased the huge range of the beloved songwriters, performed by a stellar cast.

THE SHOW BIZ SERIES

STORIES THAT GLOW IN A SPOTLIGHT

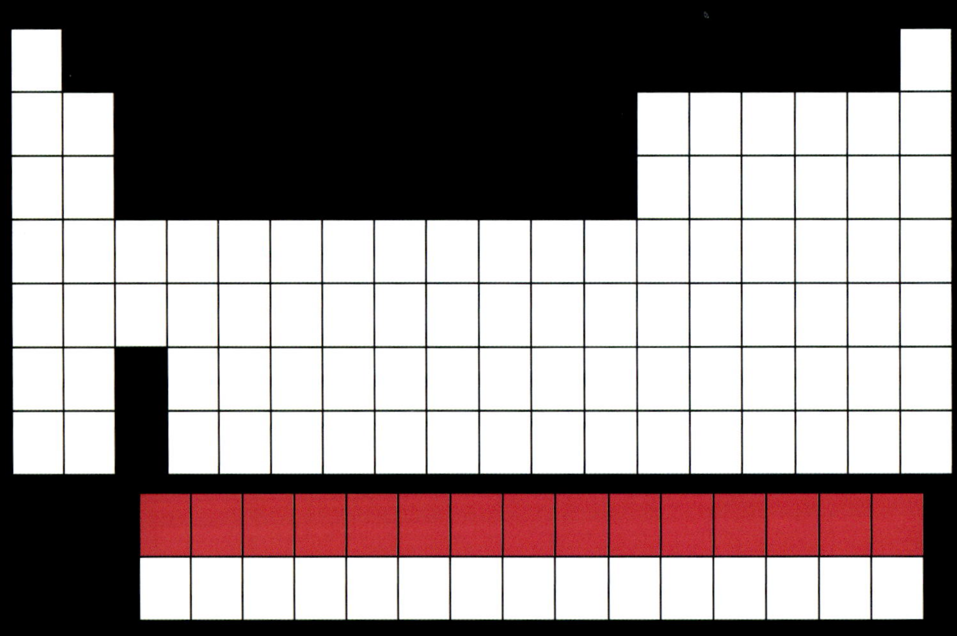

What better type of story to tell a bunch of people sitting in a theatre than one that takes place in a theatre? Audiences have always been fascinated by what happens backstage or behind the camera. Many ticket buyers have themselves performed in a school or community production, and many more have dreamed of making it on the Great White Way. Musicals about the colorful people who put on shows, or make movies, write songs, or start bands allow these aspiring stars in the audience to live vicariously, to imagine what having that sort of life might feel like. Show biz stories are also a great way to feature hit songs from the past, either in a nostalgia piece like *42nd Street* or bio-musicals like *Jersey Boys*, *Jelly's Last Jam*, or *Beautiful*. Many others feature new songs that *sound* like hit songs from the past (we call these pastiches); scores in this vein include *Follies, Dreamgirls,* and *City of Angels*.

Another reason show biz stories are popular is that characters who are performers seem more likely to burst into song than your average "civilian." The most common question that people (especially non-fans) ask about musicals is, "Why does everyone just start singing out of the blue?" When you think about it, it *is* weird. Where's the music suddenly coming from? Do the people around them not notice? (This has been the premise of many spoof shows.) Show biz stories offer a built-in answer by providing a context where the presence of music makes sense: they sing because they're performers. And even when a character who isn't a performer sings, it doesn't seem as jarring because we're accustomed to the alternation of speaking and singing by then.

It's notable that the very first show in the table, the musical that defined what musicals could be, is a show biz story. *Show Boat* made good use of its setting to include performers strutting their stuff in song and dance, and larger-than-life characters delivering "real" performance numbers that echo their inner lives. It even interpolated existing golden oldies to help an audience slip into a past decade. From these fictional performers floating up and down the Mississippi all the way to modern jukebox bio-musicals, stories of "life upon the wicked stage" have always been a great recipe for real-life theatrical success.

Book by John O'Hara ★ Music by Richard Rodgers ★ Lyrics by Lorenz Hart
Staged by George Abbott ★ Choreographed by Robert Alton

Ethel Barrymore Theatre*, December 25, 1940–November 29, 1941

Gene Kelly.......Joey Evans
Vivienne Segal.......Vera Simpson
Leila Ernst.......Linda English
June Havoc.......Gladys Bumps

ART NOTE: An elegant 1940s handbag "hung up on" a singer's microphone.

**First of three theatres*

Joey Evans is a singer, dancer, wannabe club owner, and overall sleaze. He'll lie to anyone if it'll get him ahead—and it does, for a while, with a naive stenographer and a rich older woman who helps him open his own place, Chez Joey. But when his dirty friends and deeds spill into his romantic life, both women wash their hands of him, sending him off without a dime to start his schemes over again from scratch.

Do It the Hard Way

In the late 1930s, Rodgers and Hart created a string of the most varied musical comedies in Broadway history: a Shakespearean farce (*The Boys from Syracuse*), a romantic comedy starring a literal angel (*I Married an Angel*), another with several full ballets (*On Your Toes*), and a circus extravaganza that featured Jimmy Durante and a live elephant (*Jumbo*). But while audiences cheered for seemingly anything the duo threw at them, nothing prepared them for the strangest leading character they'd ever seen on a Broadway stage: a jerk. Joey Evans has been described as "a heel," "a cad," "a punk," and even less-flattering names, and to have such an unlikeable guy as the center of a show was unheard of. That challenge, as it happens, was exactly what drew Rodgers and Hart to the material when O'Hara brought them a series of short stories he'd published in *The New Yorker* magazine.

Today, Rodgers's reputation mostly rests on his later work with Oscar Hammerstein II—lyrical, sentimental, with a waltz seemingly around every corner. But his work with Hart is the opposite: the up-tempo numbers swing hard, and even the love songs are always ready to slip you a dose of reality with an unexpected dissonance. This street-smart style came straight from Hart's view on life. A struggling alcoholic and a five-foot-nothing closeted gay man, his unhappy lot (at least as he saw it) couldn't help but color his work, leading to bittersweet love songs full of yearning and resignation that break your heart even while you marvel at their inspired wordplay.

Pal Joey's songs, depicting cheap nightclub acts and ill-fated love affairs between flawed adults who ought to know better, were a dozen years ahead of their time. Still, many embraced this surprisingly grown-up show, and welcomed it as a glimpse of the future of theater. Even when music licensing organization ASCAP banned radio stations from playing the score, one self-knowing sigh of a love song called "Bewitched, Bothered and Bewildered" found its way into many singers' albums and onto the pop music charts. The whole show eventually got a cast album in 1952 after a Broadway revival garnered raves and ran longer than the original production. Unfortunately, Hart was not around to see it; his troubled life was tragically cut short in 1943.

MISCELLANEOUS MATTER

- ★ The 1952 revival was produced by composer Jule Styne (*Gypsy, Funny Girl).* He got the idea for a revival when he saw a summer stock production at the Sea Cliff Summer Theatre on Long Island, starring the then-unknown Bob Fosse and Carol Bruce. Fosse would understudy Harold Lang (*Kiss Me, Kate*) in the Broadway production, and Bruce would open the West End revival in 1954.
- ★ The 1957 movie starring Frank Sinatra, Rita Hayworth, and Kim Novak altered the original's story and added some Rodgers and Hart standards. It was one of the top ten grossing films of the year and earned Sinatra a Golden Globe.
- ★ Gene Kelly left New York soon after *Pal Joey,* finding lasting fame in Hollywood; he never performed on Broadway again.

Book by Bella and Samuel Spewack ★ Music and lyrics by Cole Porter
Based on the play *The Taming of the Shrew* by William Shakespeare
Directed by John C. Wilson ★ Choreographed by Hanya Holm

New Century Theatre and Shubert Theatre, December 30, 1948–July 28, 1951

Alfred Drake.......Fred Graham/Petruchio
Patricia Morison.......Lilli Vanessi/Katharine
Harold Lang.......Bill Calhoun/Lucentio
Lisa Kirk.......Lois Lane/Bianca

ART NOTE: A bust of Shakespeare wearing a clown's propeller beanie.

A musical version of Shakespeare's Taming of the Shrew *is about to open, but there's more drama offstage than on. The two leads, movie star Lilli and her ex-husband, Fred, hate each other (at least on the surface); song-and-dance man Bill has forged Fred's name on an IOU to a gangster, who has sent his top two leg breakers to collect; and Bill's girlfriend, Lois, flirts with every guy in town. Eventually, crossed stars uncross and deliver happy endings in both realities.*

Brush Up Your Shakespeare

With *Kiss Me, Kate*, Cole Porter faced the same conundrum as Irving Berlin had with *Annie Get Your Gun*, namely: Rodgers and Hammerstein. "Those two made it harder for everybody else," he complained, after *Oklahoma!* and *Carousel* whetted the public's appetite for shows with songs that were deeply character-based and consistently furthered the story. Like Berlin (and Rodgers and Hart, and the Gershwins), Porter's string of Broadway hits in the 1930s were triumphs of pop songwriting loosely paired with featherweight stories and cardboard characters. He famously approached songwriting more like a puzzle to be solved than as a way to excavate and illuminate character.

So it wouldn't seem like a quasi-Shakespeare adaptation would be the right project for Porter, who in 1948 was considered distinctly old-fashioned and hadn't produced a musical on Broadway for two years (and that had been a flop). But the onstage/offstage structure devised by husband-and-wife team Bella and Samuel Spewack fit him like a glove: the "show-within-a-show" allowed him to create a virtuoso series of numbers in faux-Renaissance and classical styles, while the backstage plot provided for songs loosely tied to character in a dazzling variety of contemporary styles, from bluesy torch songs to waltzes (both Viennese and Bowery) to a near aria, "So in Love."

Always a fan of including pop culture references, here Porter could use them to double the delight: when Kate compares men to Lassie, we laugh at the reference and even more that a Shakespearean leading lady made it. And the two gangsters, it turns out, spent their jail time in the prison library, and can therefore rattle off puns on more than a dozen Shakespearean titles (including some of the very naughty sort that Porter was famous for).

As *Kiss Me, Kate* progresses, the action between the "real world" plot and the *Taming of the Shrew* musical inside it become more intertwined, so that what happens onstage in *Shrew* is easily understood as happening in the backstage story as well. When Kate finally surrenders to Petruchio's will in the last scene, we know it is also Lilli reconciling with Fred, a smart device that delivers two resolutions for the price of one. (This seemingly very anti-feminist ending has been dealt with in various ways in recent revivals; generally, Kate/Lilli delivers the lines with a wink, or even a spank, as if to ask, "Who really tamed who?")

MISCELLANEOUS MATTER

- ★ Bella Spewack worked for the Girl Scouts and came up with the idea for them to sell cookies.
- ★ Harold Lang played Joey for the 1952 album and revival of *Pal Joey.*
- ★ After inspiring Porter with their theatrical innovations, Rodgers and Hammerstein turned around and tried their hands at Porter's trick of combining an onstage and offstage musical into one evening. Unfortunately for them, their 1953 *Me and Juliet* was only a modest success and has rarely been done since.
- ★ The 1953 movie version was made during the height of the 3D movie craze and shot entirely in 3D!

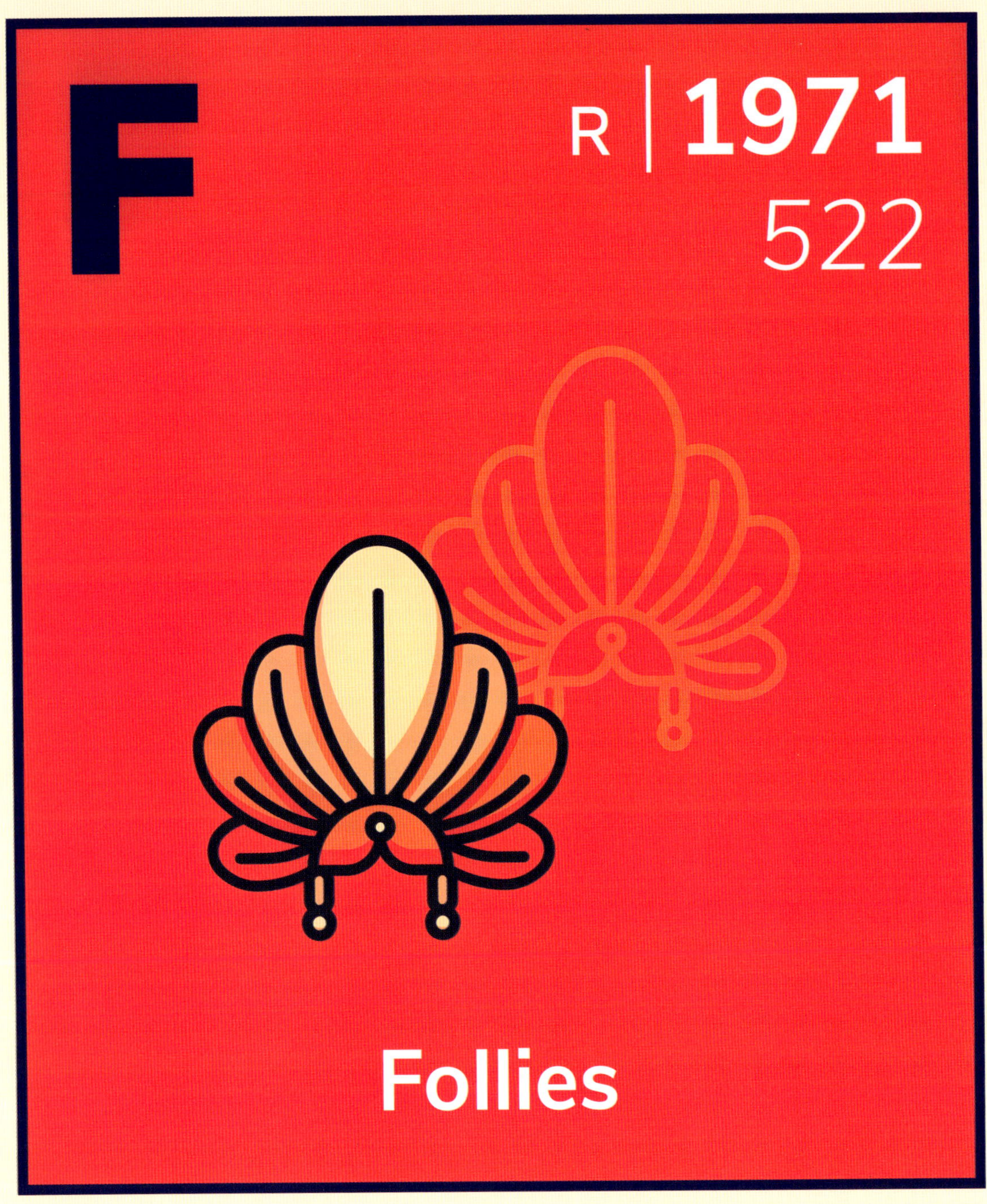

Book by James Goldman ★ Music and lyrics by Stephen Sondheim
Directed by Harold Prince and Michael Bennett
Choreographed by Michael Bennett

Winter Garden Theatre, April 4, 1971–July 1, 1972

Alexis Smith.......Phyllis Rogers Stone
John McMartin.......Benjamin Stone
Dorothy Collins.......Sally Durant Plummer
Gene Nelson.......Buddy Plummer

ART NOTE: A Follies-style headpiece and its ghostly echo.

Showgirls from the famed "Weissmann Follies" of the 1920s and '30s attend a reunion at their old theatre, which is slated for the wrecking ball. Shadowed by ghosts of themselves, the now middle-aged and older women re-create their vintage numbers, while two of them, once best friends, confront each other, their husbands, and the truth about their rocky relationships. Past and present blur in an elaborate vaudeville-style fever dream.

Beautiful Girls

If one could go back in time to experience one moment in Broadway history, many theatre fans would choose Michael Bennett's opening of *Follies*. A cavernous, dilapidated theatre slowly begins to fill with eight-foot showgirls in spectacular black-and-white gowns and towering headdresses, gliding to an ominous, sad waltz through flickering shafts of light. Is this a memory? Are these ghosts? Is there a difference? As older, present-day women arrive for a reunion, they're shadowed by their former selves without comment, even in their scenes, a wan reminder of their past glamour. The casting of the show added to this poignant effect. Many of the older actresses were former stars of stage and screen who hadn't been in the public eye for years, so the actors themselves embodied the passage of time—the audience's memories of them as they'd been superimposed over how they looked now.

The brilliant score reflected this constant, sometimes cruel blurring of past and present. Sondheim set out to write his first real pastiche show, channeling a specific Golden Age songwriter for each song and creating one charming specialty number after another. Goldman and Prince then wove these numbers between bitter fights and breakdowns among the two central couples. The extended "Loveland" sequence capped the evening with characters singing show tunes that questioned their very sanity within the frame of what was essentially a 25-foot-tall Valentine's card.

And if this already feels like a very heady trip down a dark lane, there was even another layer to *Follies*. In the early 1970s, America was fracturing just like the poster's iconic stone showgirl. The stories we had told of America in the '50s as a country of prosperity, of heroes who had literally saved the world, looked threadbare and ridiculous in the context of the '60s civil rights movement, multiple assassinations, and an unwinnable war in Vietnam. Just as America at this time was casting a critical eye inward, *Follies* deconstructed the very type of entertainment people came to the theatre to enjoy, surrounding old-fashioned love songs with crumbling marriages in a crumbling theatre. Predictably, it received mixed reviews. *Follies* was a chocolate lava cake of a show: decadent, dark as night, and ready to erupt, and for those whose tastes ran that direction, it was, and remains, the epitome of every delicious thrill Broadway can provide.

MISCELLANEOUS MATTER

★ The opening went through many versions before Bennett was happy. The secret? To make the ghosts seem otherworldly, performers were instructed to dance not to the music coming from the orchestra, but to a song in their heads they danced to later in the show.

★ Sondheim's original concept for "Who's That Woman?" was a chorus line number where one dancer has died, leaving a hole. Bennett replaced it with a "mirror" theme, with the ladies' ghost counterparts dancing behind, then eventually with them. According to Sondheim, the showstopping result was "one of the best numbers I ever saw in my life."

★ In "Buddy's Blues," Margie and Sally were initially played by male performers in drag before being replaced by women.

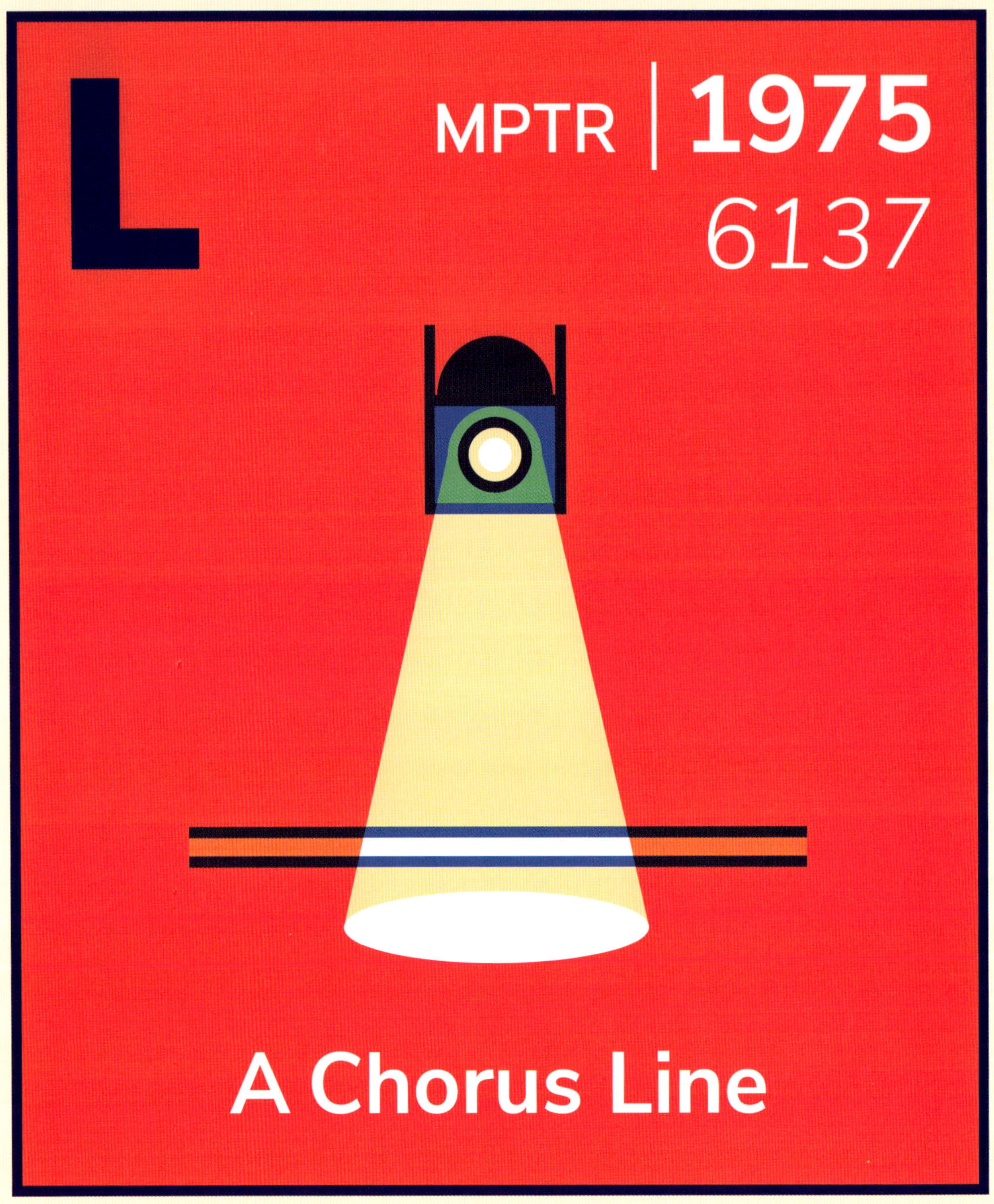

Book by James Kirkwood and Nicholas Dante ★ Music by Marvin Hamlisch
Lyrics by Edward Kleban ★ Conceived and directed by Michael Bennett
Choreographed by Michael Bennett and Bob Avian

Shubert Theatre, July 25, 1975–April 28, 1990

Donna McKechnie.......Cassie
Sammy Williams.......Paul
Carole "Kelly" Bishop.......Sheila
Priscilla Lopez.......Diana

ART NOTE: A theatrical light waiting for someone from the line to step into it.

Twenty-four dancers audition for spots in the chorus of a new Broadway show, including an out-of-work former star, Cassie. After an initial cut, Zach, the director, asks the remaining actors to talk about themselves. As they reveal their personal histories, they bond over the precarious nature of a dancer's life, something made tangible when Paul injures his knee and is carried off. Ironically, in the spectacular finale, the dancers' individuality is erased as they perform identical steps in matching costumes.

What I Did for Love

In 1974, two dancers, Michon Peacock and Tony Stevens, had an idea for a new dance troupe, and they invited their star choreographer friend Michael Bennett to attend an initial meeting (Bennett, only thirty-one, had already won four Tonys for *Follies* and *Seesaw*). Over the course of two evenings, they and a group of dancers recorded themselves speaking about their intimate personal histories, the ups and downs of their careers, and what dance meant to them. Bennett immediately thought there might be a show in these stories, and brought the tapes to young producer Joe Papp, who'd made a name for his Public Theater six years before by producing *Hair*. Although he had to take out a loan to do it, Papp gave Bennett an extraordinary amount of time to workshop this unusual idea. Bennett assembled a top-notch team to craft a musical out of the hours of recorded discussion, including playwrights Kirkwood and Dante, star Hollywood tunesmith Marvin Hamlisch, and lesser-known lyricist Ed Kleban.

Most backstage stories center around the stars—glamorous, larger-than-life performers who hit it big. Bennett wanted to focus on the majority of working performers, those who fill out ensembles, whose stories are every bit as gripping. (In his *Playbill* bio for the show, he chose to list only his own dancer credits, not his director/choreographer ones.) Many people thought Papp was crazy to risk so much on a big, expensive show with no sets, almost no costumes, no stars, and basically no story. But Bennett saw that an empty stage could easily morph from a bland workplace to the inside of a character's mind, or act as a shared dream space where the group could come together in choreographed memories of how dance shaped their lives. Hamlisch masterfully alternated '70s pop grooves with a classic Broadway sound, and Kleban performed a lyrical magic trick, turning the specific details of the original interviews into focused and electrifying character portraits, equally hilarious and heartbreaking.

The result was what original cast member Baayork Lee called "the first reality show," and it was an immediate hit. It has been credited with almost single-handedly turning around an alarming Broadway box office slump—by the fifth year of its record-smashing fifteen-year run, Broadway audiences overall had doubled from an all-time low. Papp's gamble had paid off big time, funding the Public Theater for years.

MISCELLANEOUS MATTER

★ The original dancers from the interview sessions had to audition to play themselves in the show.

★ Ed Kleban died very young, and his story was itself turned into a Broadway show, *A Class Act*. The royalties from *A Chorus Line* fund the generous Ed Kleban Award, given to lyricists and librettists "of extraordinary promise."

★ Nicholas Dante was the first Latino to win the Pulitzer Prize for Drama.

★ The show again reunited Bennett and his muse, McKechnie, with whom he'd worked on *Promises, Promises* and *Company*.

Book by Michael Stewart and Mark Bramble ★ Music by Harry Warren
Lyrics by Al Dubin ★ Additional lyrics by Johnny Mercer and Mort Dixon
Based on the novel by Bradford Ropes
Directed and choreographed by Gower Champion

Winter Garden Theatre*, August 25, 1980–January 8, 1989

Tammy Grimes.......Dorothy Brock
Jerry Orbach.......Julian Marsh
Wanda Richert.......Peggy Sawyer
Lee Roy Reams.......Billy Lawlor

ART NOTE: A star has fallen off a dressing room door and been replaced with another.

*First of three theatres

No matter if the country is in a Depression, "Julian Marsh is doing a show!" Fresh-off-the-bus newcomer, Peggy, gets her big chance in the chorus, but runs afoul of Dorothy, the show's leading lady (and girlfriend of the producer). When Dorothy breaks her ankle, Julian offers Peggy the role, but she's decided to quit, having had enough of show biz backbiting. Marsh coaxes her back by teaching her to hear "the lullaby of Broadway," and she becomes an instant star.

Go Into Your Dance

As its run of nearly 3,500 performances attests, *42nd Street* is a fine show. It was a throwback, a meticulously crafted tap-dancing piece of nostalgia that came on the heels of a decade of dark, experimental shows and national malaise. But it's more important for what it signified: the final show for two of musical theatre's most influential men, director/choreographer Gower Champion and producer David Merrick.

Champion's big hits, like *Bye Bye Birdie* and *Hello, Dolly!* had all opened in the 1960s; in the '70s he'd had flop after flop. But as a pioneer of cinematic staging techniques and splashy production numbers, he was the ideal choice to bring a classic movie musical to life on stage. Champion pulled out all the stops, drawing on every trick in his (very large) hat and borrowing a few from other famous choreographers of the '30s. Many Warren and Dubin songs that weren't in the movie were added, giving him and the extraordinary dancers (over twenty chorus girls alone!) opportunities galore to shine. No expense was spared, and producer David Merrick footed the $2 million bill.

Merrick had an unmatched record as producer, not just of blockbuster musicals like *Gypsy*, *Oliver!*, and *Hello, Dolly!*, but of prestige plays as well. But he was equally famous for his press gimmicks and petty, cruel treatment of creative and performing talent alike, and *42nd Street* would prove no exception. For starters, Merrick continually postponed the opening, claiming it wasn't ready (it had already had a tryout in DC), and when he finally announced an opening night, he claimed Champion couldn't attend because he was in the hospital with a blood condition. Then, in what some called his most callous stunt ever, Merrick went on stage during curtain call, quieted the ovation, and announced that Champion had died that morning. At his request, the family had not made this public, and he'd locked the show's cast in the theatre for a last-minute "rehearsal" during the afternoon so they wouldn't find out. In front of the audience and the press, the shocked cast began to sob; Jerry Orbach had the curtain brought in to give them privacy. Perhaps, as Merrick claimed, he kept the news secret because Champion would have wanted the cast to have a joyful opening performance; regardless, Merrick got himself, and his final show, the publicity he craved.

MISCELLANEOUS MATTER

- ★ When another Merrick show, *Subways Are for Sleeping*, was struggling at the box office, he found men with the same names as all the major theatre critics, treated them to a preview and dinner, and then took out an ad with glowing quotes using their names. One paper actually ran it; the others smelled a fraud.
- ★ Wanda Richert went from show biz hit to show biz hit: she was a replacement Cassie in *A Chorus Line* and left *42nd Street* to join the cast of *Nine*.
- ★ The show was truly lavish. Costume designer Theoni V. Aldredge created 400 costumes, one set of which were only onstage six minutes and cost over $50,000 (in 1980!). Robin Wagner's set included an electrified backdrop, a life-size Pullman train car, and multiple turntables.

Book and lyrics by Tom Eyen ★ Music by Henry Krieger
Directed by Michael Bennett
Choreographed by Michael Bennett and Michael Peters

Imperial Theatre, December 20, 1981–August 11, 1985

Jennifer Holliday.......Effie Melody White
Sheryl Lee Ralph.......Deena Jones
Cleavant Derricks.......James Thunder Early
Ben Harney.......Curtis Taylor Jr.

ART NOTE: A golden hit record and three 1960s-style gowns for the Dreams.

The sweeping saga of Black girl-group The Dreamettes (later The Dreams), following them from their big break at an amateur talent show to disbanding after becoming legends. Their transition from R&B to mainstream pop causes manager Curtis to replace fierce belter Effie as lead singer (and as his girlfriend) with more conventionally pretty Deena. Effie, devastated, disappears, but later makes a comeback just as Deena dumps Curtis. A final farewell concert brings the original Dreams together one last time.

I Am Changing

When *Dreamgirls* opened, *A Chorus Line* was in the middle of its sixth year on Broadway and still going strong. It had made Michael Bennett a household name; it was impossible to mention one without the other. Though Bennett constantly told people that *Dreamgirls* was "not a Black version of *A Chorus Line*," it had a similarly unusual developmental process: actors worked with the creative team over the course of multiple workshops, contributing ideas and material through exercises and improvisations that the writers then crafted into the final show.

A big part of that process centered around the involvement of a twenty-year-old gospel singer with one short-lived Broadway credit to her name. Houston-born Jennifer Holliday knew little of musical theatre, and had little interest in becoming a Broadway star, even in the next Michael Bennett show; she wanted to make albums. During the long workshop process, when her role of Effie was diminished and written out of act two, she simply left the production, twice (the second was a "fired/quit" kind of situation). But Bennett and the writers knew that they'd never find another actress with the raw emotion and powerhouse voice needed to deliver the act one finale, "And I Am Telling You I'm Not Going," so Bennett reached out to smooth things over, promising her a storyline that continued into the second act. Holliday came back, and a star was born.

"And I Am Telling You I'm Not Going" became one of the towering numbers in Broadway history, a kind of R&B aria for a woman tearing her heart out to get her man to stay. The lyrics are surprisingly free, almost conversational on the page, but set to wailing riffs, they're clearly coming from a woman at the edge. Throughout the show, Eyen and Krieger combine this sort of conversational text with the same type of lush scoring as in the show's major songs—strong grooves, funky percussion, and thick keyboard and string chords—to create sustained musicalized arguments and scenes. They're aided in this by the perfect period orchestrations by Harold Wheeler, which also expertly illustrate the progression from R&B and soul to a more mainstream, "white" pop sound. *Dreamgirls* gave audiences a surprisingly technical glimpse of the artistic and commercial considerations behind the scenes of the music industry, much as *A Chorus Line* had for the dance world.

MISCELLANEOUS MATTER

- ★ Holliday released a single version of "And I Am Telling You" in 1982 that won the Grammy for Best R&B Vocal Performance.
- ★ The story of the Dreams mirrored that of the real-life Supremes: Diana Ross replaced original lead singer Florence Ballard and had a romantic relationship with manager Berry Gordy Jr.
- ★ *American Idol* finalist (and now EGOT winner) Jennifer Hudson won her Oscar for playing Effie in the 2006 film adaptation.

Book by Arthur Kopit ★ Music and lyrics by Maury Yeston
Based on the film *8½* by Federico Fellini
Directed by Tommy Tune ★ Dances by Thommie Walsh

46th Street Theatre, May 9, 1982–February 4, 1984

Raul Julia.......Guido Contini
Karen Akers.......Luisa Contini
Liliane Montevecchi.......Liliane La Fleur
Anita Morris.......Carla

ART NOTE: A tiled arch above a movie camera, with the silhouettes of multiple women watching from the background.

Famed Italian film director Guido Contini's love life is disintegrating around him . . . and he has no ideas for his next film. Floundering, he's overtaken by memories of all the women in his life, past and present, which inspire him to make a movie about Casanova. But filming this story further alienates the women he cares most about and causes him to flirt with suicide. At that moment, his nine-year-old self appears and convinces him it's time to grow up.

Unusual Way

"Brilliantly styled." "Some of the season's most beautiful songs." "Gaudy and overworked." "A gimmick, top to closing." *Nine* was a bold experiment on many levels, and it polarized both audiences and critics. Based on Italian director Federico Fellini's Academy Award–winning film *8½,* the story of an immature film director forced to grow up had captivated Yale music theory professor Maury Yeston ever since adolescence. While working on his adaptation (years later), his book writer at the time slipped a demo cassette of the show under the door of emerging director/choreographer Tommy Tune. Tune had been given his big break a few years earlier by Michael Bennett, who hired him as *Seesaw*'s associate choreographer, while also casting him in a featured role that won him the first of an astonishing ten Tony Awards.

Tune was responsible for many bold choices at the heart of *Nine*. Since much of the story happens in a spa where Guido goes to focus and work, Tune staged the entire show against a set made of white tiles. This not only symbolized Guido's blank headspace and struggling imagination, but also set off William Ivey Long's Italian-fashion-inspired black dresses. And the costumes were almost all dresses, because Tune had the writers eliminate all adult male characters besides Guido when casting was turning up no appropriate actors.

If you just thought, "Wait, they were making huge changes *while* they were casting?", you're on to something. *Nine* had a changing roster of producers in-and-out for years (mostly out), and in 1982 they only had enough money to get to Broadway without any out-of-town tryout. Everything was last-minute (even acquiring the rights to *8½*) in their frantic push to get the show open by the last day of Tony eligibility. As buzz was building, Michael Bennett called his former protégé to (very strongly) encourage him to find a way to go out of town and open in the fall, attempting to eliminate competition for his own *Dreamgirls*. Tune refused, and the resulting Tony battle was one for the ages. *Nine*'s eventual win for best musical was seen as much as a rebuke to *Dreamgirls* producers, the Shuberts (who had just torn down two beloved Broadway theatres to make room for a hotel), as it was support for *Nine*.

MISCELLANEOUS MATTER

- ★ Tommy Tune, at six-foot-six the tallest dancing star in Broadway history, played the high-stepping Ambrose in the *Hello, Dolly!* movie.
- ★ Perhaps the most daring costume in *Nine* was Anita Morris's see-through catsuit of stretchable lace; after drawing a blank on how to costume the character of Guido's oversexed mistress, Carla, this Hail Mary pass was improvised at the last minute, with costume designer Long pinning the fabric directly around Morris's nude body.
- ★ Yeston came up with Liliane's famous "Folies Bergères" number while having lunch in a café with Montevecchi. He wrote it on the tablecloth and took it home with him.

Book by Harvey Fierstein ★ Music and lyrics by Jerry Herman
Based on the play by Jean Poiret
Directed by Arthur Laurents ★ Choreographed by Scott Salmon

Palace Theatre, August 21, 1983–November 15, 1987

Gene Barry.......Georges *George Hearn.......Albin*

ART NOTE: A close-up look as Albin puts a "Little More Mascara" on.

George and Albin—gay couple and (respectively) owner and star drag performer of St. Tropez nightclub La Cage aux Folles—face a crisis when George's son Jean-Michel announces his engagement to Anne, daughter of a conservative, anti-gay politician. When the two families meet, Albin shows up in drag as Jean-Michel's "mother," but when his true identity is revealed, Anne's parents forbid the marriage, at least until a series of farcical complications place them in the gay couple's debt.

I Am What I Am

With drag very much in the mainstream today, and gay characters and relationships common across all media, it's easy to forget that not that long ago, it was considered a huge risk for a musical to even have an openly gay character. It was 1969's *Coco* that featured the first (an unfortunate stereotype); *Applause* came shortly after with a much better-written character (and a trip to a gay bar!). *A Chorus Line* had frank discussions about sexuality, and Paul's heart-wrenching monologue about his father discovering him performing in a drag burlesque show won Sammy Williams a Tony. But *La Cage aux Folles* was a much bigger step for gay representation: a show that centered around a gay couple.

Creators Herman, Laurents, and Fierstein knew they would have to tread lightly; Herman in particular was adamant that they give the audience "a great-looking musical comedy, an old-fashioned piece of entertainment," not a lecture. It helped that one half of the male couple spent a lot of time in a dress—drag was still considered primarily comedic by mainstream audiences. More important, Albin and George were written as a real couple, aging but very much in love, and the fight for their dignity was portrayed with depth and humanity.

Though the subject matter was, for the time, modern, the show itself was nearly as old-fashioned as *42nd Street.* Unlike that hit show, *La Cage aux Folles* had brand-new songs, but written by an old master; Herman hadn't had a hit for fifteen years, and he was terrified. Having seen Broadway musicals get more conceptual and intellectual (and rock/pop-based), and having endured multiple flops in a row, he wondered if there was still a place for his kind of heartfelt entertainment. He found out quickly, when the out-of-town reception in notoriously conservative Boston was ecstatic. *La Cage aux Folles* touched audiences of every background, but it was especially meaningful to gay theatregoers, who saw not just the usual comic-relief character, or a stage full of stereotypes, but an everyday businessman and his husband fighting for their family. The act one finale was a trademark Herman anthem, "I Am What I Am," but with a difference: instead of a group number like "Hello, Dolly!" or "Mame," George Hearn stood alone center stage, proclaiming his right to be who he is. And when, at song's end, he ripped off his wig and marched out through the house, he marched right into Broadway history.

MISCELLANEOUS MATTER

- ★ "The Best of Times" was used by the 1992 Bush campaign and played at the GOP Convention. Herman saw it as a demonstration of a shared humanity; many found it bitterly ironic given the party's opposition to civil rights protections for gays.
- ★ At the first preview in Boston, the overture finished, the curtain came up and the set fell over.
- ★ Playing Anne's mother was Broadway pro Merle Louise, who was in the original companies of four Sondheim shows: *Gypsy*, *Company*, *Sweeney Todd* (as the Beggar Woman), and *Into the Woods.*

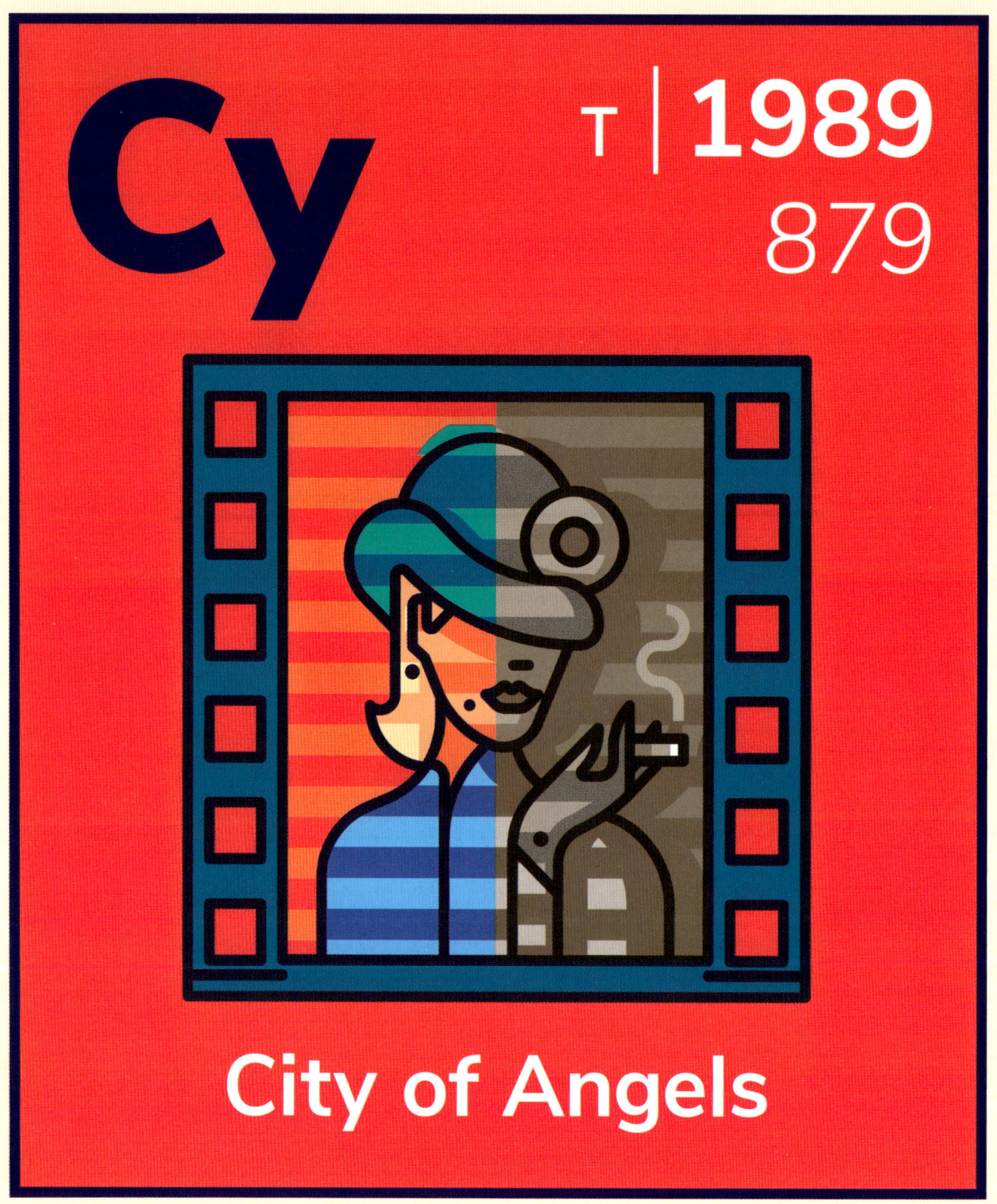

Book by Larry Gelbart ★ Music by Cy Coleman ★ Lyrics by David Zippel
Directed by Michael Blakemore

Virginia Theatre, December 11, 1989–January 19, 1992

Gregg Edelman.......Stine
James Naughton.......Stone
Randy Graff.......Oolie/Donna
Kay McClelland.......Bobbi/Gabby

ART NOTE: One frame from a film negative, half color, half black-and-white, showing a femme fatale sliced by Venetian blind shadows.

Novelist Stine has landed his dream job of adapting one of his hard-boiled detective books into a screenplay. As he writes, the characters in his book/movie come to life on stage, and his real-life personal troubles are mirrored by the book's plot. Characters on both sides of the screen clash, and the film's producer ruins his screenplay; but just as Stine hits rock bottom, his detective, Stone, grabs the typewriter and writes everyone a happy "Hollywood ending."

Double Talk

Jazz artists have taken Broadway show tunes and made them their own since the genre emerged in the 1920s; Gershwin, Porter, Rodgers, and many more Broadway giants found huge success when their tunes ended up on jazz albums. But even sixty years later, an original musical with a truly jazz score had yet to hit big. A few revues like *Ain't Misbehavin'* and *Sophisticated Ladies* had brought jazz standards to Broadway, and *West Side Story* had occasional forays into a kind of academic bop, but songs that could fully translate jazz idioms into musical theatre song forms required the particular talents of one man: Cy Coleman.

Coleman had started out as a successful jazz pianist, performing regularly with his trio and jazz stars like Ella Fitzgerald. Some of his early Broadway scores like *Sweet Charity* and *Little Me* had definite jazz influences but remained mostly within the traditional musical comedy vernacular. By the late 1980s, Coleman wanted to write a true jazz score and raised the idea of a 1940s private eye story with Larry Gelbart, witty librettist of *A Funny Thing Happened on the Way to the Forum*. Gelbart, for his part, was eager to skewer Hollywood after his experience cowriting the blockbuster movie *Tootsie*. With his jazz chops unleashed, and a collaborator fluent in Raymond Chandler–style film noir dialogue, Coleman proceeded to write a lush and complex score that swung for the rafters. The red-hot orchestrations were by famed Count Basie arranger Billy Byers, and a tight-harmony vocal quartet, the Angel City 4, popped up throughout, singing the most demanding vocal charts ever found on Broadway.

The production's greatest theatrical trick: the film characters and their story were designed entirely in black-and-white, while the real-life characters inhabited a full color 1940s Hollywood. James Naughton's hard-boiled detective Stone prowled a world of gray-on-gray Venetian blind shadows; Gregg Edelman's writer Stine tried not to get lost on Technicolor sound stages. The storyline highlighted parallels between these worlds, and when Stone and Stine's love interests joined forces to complain about the men in "What You Don't Know About Women," the split-stage split-screen effect was a stunner. A final treat: the pit featured jazz musicians from Count Basie's, Woody Herman's, and Gerry Mulligan's big bands, and during the exit music as the audience gathered their things, they got to take solos to swing everyone out into the night.

MISCELLANEOUS MATTER

- ★ Oolie's self-deprecating song "You Can Always Count on Me" is very reminiscent of another Coleman song, "Nobody Does It Like Me," from 1973's *Seesaw*. He actually asked Graff at her audition if she knew it (she did); they hadn't written "Count on Me" yet but knew it would be in the same style and wanted to hear her take. Clearly, they liked it.
- ★ The Angel City 4's vocal arrangements were created by Cy Coleman and Yaron Gershovsky, Grammy Award–winning arranger and musical director for the world-famous vocal quartet The Manhattan Transfer.
- ★ In 2009, it was announced there were plans afoot to finally make a movie version of this musical that's all about making a movie; Barry Levinson was to direct, with Larry Gelbart adapting his own script, but the project never reached the screen.

Book by Ken Ludwig ★ Music by George Gershwin ★ Lyrics by Ira Gershwin
Inspired by material by Guy Bolton and John McGowan
Directed by Mike Ockrent ★ Choreographed by Susan Stroman

Shubert Theatre, February 19, 1992–January 7, 1996

Jodi Benson.......Polly Baker
Harry Groener.......Bobby Child
Bruce Adler.......Bela Zangler
Michele Pawk.......Irene Roth

ART NOTE: A Western cactus, sporting the *Follies* headpiece.

Bobby Child, son of a banking family and expected to take over the family business, is bitten by the show-biz bug. When he's instructed to travel to Nevada to foreclose on a rundown theater, he decides instead to stage a show to resuscitate the building and the town. A talented local girl distrusts him, so he disguises himself as a Broadway producer to charm her; despite the resulting confusion, love triumphs and the show becomes a hit.

Our Love Is Here to Stay

Like two other giants of Tin Pan Alley, Cole Porter and Irving Berlin, George and Ira Gershwin may seem underrepresented on the Periodic Table, with only *Porgy and Bess* (an opera) and *Crazy for You*. Although the brothers wrote dozens of songs that have become standards, they wrote in an era (the 1920s and '30s) when musicals were not meant to be lasting works; a six-month run was considered respectable, and only one Gershwin show, *Of Thee I Sing*, ran a full year (and it won a Pulitzer). One of the great tragedies of American culture was George's death at the age of thirty-eight from a brain tumor; we will never know what he might have created had he lived into the Golden Age of integrated musicals that began six years later with *Oklahoma!*

Musical films featuring scores assembled from hit songwriters have long been popular. *Yankee Doodle Dandy* (George M. Cohan), *Easter Parade* (Irving Berlin), *An American in Paris* (the Gershwins), and *Singin' in the Rain* (Arthur Freed) are just a few that capitalized on the popularity of existing songs by creating new stories around them. But on Broadway, building a new story around existing songs was quite rare—coincidentally, one of the only other shows to have tried this trick was also a Gershwin compilation, 1983's *My One and Only*. (While the smash hit of that decade, *42nd Street*, did add additional standards from the Warren and Dubin songbook, these merely fleshed out the score of the original movie, and the plot remained the same.)

Although *Crazy for You* is described as based on the original Gershwin show *Girl Crazy*, and does use half a dozen of its songs, Ken Ludwig essentially jettisoned all of the original book aside from its Western setting and some New York interlopers. The result was a joyous reimagining of beloved songs, especially in the wildly inventive choreography of Susan Stroman, whose use of props was quickly becoming legendary. (In "Slap That Bass," for example, chorus girls each hold a simple piece of rope vertically in front of their bodies and, *voilà*, they've become upright basses played by the chorus boys.) The show's all-American pizzazz was a balm for those who still lamented the "British invasion" of the '80s, and many celebrated its opening in the Shubert Theatre, which had, until two years prior, hosted *A Chorus Line* for its record-breaking run.

MISCELLANEOUS MATTER

★ As an example of just how disposable the plots of those early Broadway shows were, even the original *New York Times* review of *Girl Crazy,* after trying to describe the story, said "That is not all, but you get the idea. What is important is that, with the music, dancing, and some of the comedy, it does not matter more than it should."

★ *Girl Crazy* introduced Ethel Merman singing "I Got Rhythm" and made an instant star of Ginger Rogers. The pit was full of the most famous jazz and big band players of the day (and the future).

★ When *Crazy for You* opened, more audience members recognized Jodi Benson's voice than her face, since she'd been the voice of Ariel in the animated film *The Little Mermaid.*

Book by George C. Wolfe ★ Music by Jelly Roll Morton
Lyrics by Susan Birkenhead ★ Additional music and orchestrations by Luther Henderson
Directed by George C. Wolfe ★ Choreographed by Hope Clarke
Tap choreography by Gregory Hines and Ted L. Levy

Virginia Theatre, April 26, 1992–September 5, 1993

Gregory Hines.......Jelly Roll Morton
Keith David.......Chimney Man
Savion Glover.......Young Jelly
Tonya Pinkins.......Anita

ART NOTE: Morton's hands playing a piano that is literally falling apart under him.

Legendary jazz pianist and bandleader Jelly Roll Morton has just died and woken up in a kind of purgatory. He is ordered by a mysterious "Chimney Man" to reevaluate his claim that he invented jazz, and to reflect on his lifelong rejection of his Black roots in favor of the European Creole side of the family. Once he sees how his own racism hurt him and those he loved, he embraces his full identity and ascends to jazz heaven.

That's How You Jazz

The same season as *Jelly's Last Jam*, two other shows opened featuring material by celebrated popular composers: *Crazy for You* slotted Gershwin standards into a (mostly) new story, while *Five Guys Named Moe* was a revue celebrating jazz musician Louis Jordan. It would be natural to assume that *Jelly's Last Jam* would follow one model or the other, but it was neither and both. Writer/director George C. Wolfe, only thirty-seven, had already made a name for himself creating plays that took a hard look at the Black American experience. His 1986 play, *The Colored Museum*, had skewered Black stereotypes in a series of fantastical skits (in one, two wigs debate Black identity politics). So putting on a fun song-and-dance was not his intention; he wanted to put its title character on trial, as a light-skinned Black Creole who repeatedly denied his Black roots.

It was a tall order for a musical, first because Morton wrote instrumental music (without lyrics), much of it fast and flashy. During the creative process, Luther Henderson (Duke Ellington's protégé and prolific Broadway arranger) adjusted melodies to fit vocal ranges or changed tempos so lyricist Susan Birkenhead could add lyrics; usually he offered her one or two options for each dramatic beat in Wolfe's script they sought to musicalize. "The ideas flew back and forth so fast," said Birkenhead, "that in the end, we couldn't remember who came up with what."

Jelly's Last Jam's other mountain to climb was one that had faced *Pal Joey*: a central character who is simply unlikable. Morton treats people in his life terribly, and only the astonishing talent and charm of Gregory Hines kept audiences on his side. America's leading champion of tap dance, Hines had appeared in two Broadway jazz revues, *Eubie!* (his first Tony nomination) and *Sophisticated Ladies*, and he was also a Billboard charting singer. In *Jelly's Last Jam,* he had the opportunity to showcase his acting chops, and he delivered a tour de force triple-threat performance of blinding charisma and self-hatred. But since Hines was a dancer first, dance was put at the center of the show, serving as a metaphor for improvising at the piano. And cast as Morton's younger self was tap wunderkind Savion Glover, already known as a tap force in his own right.

Both a celebration and a condemnation, *Jelly's Last Jam* was a complex show that never looked down on its subject, or its audience.

MISCELLANEOUS MATTER

★ A section of act two originally dealt with Morton's first wife, but the actress who played her left the show and there was no viable understudy. So, in the middle of the previews, the creators rewrote the story without the character, rehearsing the new version during the day and performing the old version at night until it was ready.

★ When marketing agency Serino Coyne polled audiences as to who they would like to see replace Hines when he left, the number one answer was Michael Jackson. (It ended up being Brian Stokes Mitchell, just beginning a run of Broadway leading roles that would last over a decade.)

★ Savion Glover made his Broadway debut at age eleven in *The Tap Dance Kid* as a replacement. Four years later, he became one of the youngest people ever nominated for a Tony for *Black and Blue*.

Book by Terrence McNally ★ Music and lyrics by David Yazbek
Based on the film directed by Peter Cattaneo, screenplay by Simon Beaufoy
Directed by Jack O'Brien ★ Choreographed by Jerry Mitchell

Eugene O'Neill Theatre, October 26, 2000–September 1, 2002

Patrick Wilson.......Jerry Lukowski
John Ellison Conlee.......Dave Bukatinsky
André De Shields...Noah "Horse" T. Simmons
Jason Danieley.......Malcolm MacGregor

ART NOTE: A moon (get it?) wearing the final stripper-costume security guard hat.

In Buffalo, steel mills are closed, and many men have lost their jobs. Picking up on local wives' "enthusiasm" for a Chippendales-style male strip show, divorced-dad Jerry and out-of-shape Dave decide they can make the bucks they sorely need (and gain back their self-esteem) by staging their own. They recruit a crew of varied ages and sizes, and despite all obstacles—including their own misgivings—they go through with the show, which brings the town together in surprising ways.

The Goods

At the turn of the millennium, the "British invasion" of the 1980s seemed to have run its course; long-term tenants like *Cats*, *Miss Saigon*, and *Les Misérables* felt more and more old-fashioned, and were nearing the ends of their long runs. Happily, a large crop of new American musical-makers was stepping up to fill the void. Jason Robert Brown, Andrew Lippa, Lynn Ahrens and Stephen Flaherty, Michael John LaChiusa, Jeanine Tesori, and Adam Guettel had all recently had exciting productions on and off-Broadway; about to join them was a young writer named David Yazbek who had an unusual set of credentials perfectly suited to pushing musical comedy forward.

Yazbek's first success was as part of the Emmy Award–winning writing team for the David Letterman show, but his love of music and musicals pulled him in a different direction. He was busy writing jingles and TV theme songs when Adam Guettel recommended him to director Jack O'Brien for an adaptation of the hit British indie comedy *The Full Monty*; once on board, Yazbek combined his comedy chops, cultural references, and general irreverence with a pop sensibility to create a score that was at once fresh, witty, and colloquial. Thanks to his deft touch, a bunch of working-class steel workers somehow ended up sounding totally genuine singing their emotions, allowing us to see the fear and tenderness beneath their tough exteriors.

The show was the latest in a string of successful shows for prolific playwright and librettist Terrence McNally. In the late '60s and '70s, McNally had been known for pushing boundaries in the avant-garde theatre, often writing about gay life and characters. In the '80s, he achieved more commercial success with the hit play *Frankie and Johnny in the Clair de Lune* and wrote his first musical, *The Rink,* with Kander and Ebb. He won four Tony Awards (two for plays, two for musicals) in the '90s, each show offering finely wrought characters and surprising relationships overflowing with humor. In translating the British sensibilities of the original *The Full Monty* film to Rust Belt America, McNally maintained all the fine detail that had won film audience's hearts while creating something authentically American.

MISCELLANEOUS MATTER

- ★ The show marked the Broadway debuts of two actresses who went on to become leading lady favorites: Heidi Blickenstaff (*Something Rotten!*) and Kate Baldwin (*Big Fish*).
- ★ Guettel knew of Yazbek because they played together in a band called, simply, Barn.
- ★ Mitchell's only other Broadway choreography credit at the time was for *You're a Good Man, Charlie Brown*; fittingly for *The Full Monty*, he was at least as well known for creating the dances for *Broadway Bares*, a yearly burlesque charity show.

Book by Mel Brooks and Thomas Meehan ★ Music and lyrics by Mel Brooks
Directed and choreographed by Susan Stroman

St. James Theatre, April 19, 2001–April 22, 2007

Matthew Broderick.......Leo Bloom
Nathan Lane.......Max Bialystock
Gary Beach.......Roger De Bris
Cady Huffman.......Ulla

ART NOTE: A shady character absconding from a pretzel-adorned theatre with an armful of money.

A seasoned, down-at-the-heels Broadway producer discovers, with the help of his mousy new accountant, that he raised more money for his last flop than he spent. This sparks an idea for a scam: they'll pair up, raise $2 million, stage a guaranteed one-performance stinker, then pocket the unspent money. Unfortunately, their appalling gay Hitler romp becomes an unexpected smash, revealing their scheme. Ending up as cellmates, they produce a show in jail that becomes a bona fide Broadway hit.

When You Got It, Flaunt It

TV comedy writer Mel Brooks had the above ridiculous idea for a movie in 1967, and somehow it got made, starring Gene Wilder and Zero Mostel (the original Tevye in *Fiddler on the Roof*). It received very mixed reviews, with its central gag—two Jewish producers presenting a terrible show about Hitler—proving simply too tasteless for many critics and audience members. Thirty years later, when music and movie industry heavyweight David Geffen approached Brooks about making it into a musical, tastes had changed (and the wounds of WWII weren't as fresh). Geffen asked Brooks to call Jerry Herman to write the score, but Herman convinced the comic auteur to write it himself—after all, Brooks had written catchy, delightfully silly songs for many of his hit movies.

But who could fill the very large shoes of Mostel and Wilder? Over the years, the film had become a cult hit, and finding the right cast might mean the difference between flop and smash. For the larger-than-life Max Bialystock, no one but Nathan Lane would do. Lane was already a Broadway star, having led the 1990s revivals of *Guys and Dolls* and *A Funny Thing Happened on the Way to the Forum.* And for Leo, Brooks went with Matthew Broderick, who'd tiptoed into musicals (after being a star in non-singing roles since his teens) with a revival of *How to Succeed in Business Without Really Trying* five years earlier.

The inventive choreographer Susan Stroman made the difficult, but ultimately joyful choice to also take on directing duties after her husband, director Michael Ockrent, passed away suddenly just as they were starting work on the show. And she outdid herself, taking the props-heavy style she'd used so effectively in *Crazy for You* and amping it up to ridiculous proportions: elderly investors tap-dancing with walkers, giant pretzels doing kick lines, and a rotating-swastika ode to Golden Age movie director Busby Berkeley. The whole evening—sets, costumes, lights—became a rapturous send-up and homage to classic and more recent Broadway shows (a few of which were running across town), and any danger of real vulgarity was eliminated when wrapped in tinsel and delivered with a wink and a sequin. It seemed like all of New York lost its mind for the giddy absurdity, and the show won a record-breaking twelve Tony Awards, in every category for which it was nominated.

MISCELLANEOUS MATTER

- ★ At the height of its popularity, scalpers and websites were offering tickets for an insane $800 apiece. To "strike a blow at the heart of the scalping operation," the producers offered premium tickets for a then unheard-of $480.
- ★ Brad Oscar, who was nominated for a Tony for playing Franz, the ex-Nazi author of the show, went on to play Bialystock in Vegas for over 4,000 performances.
- ★ One of the show references they wanted to include was to "Rose's Turn" from *Gyspy*, having Max stammer "M-m-m-Max has gotta let go" (instead of "Momma"). But notoriously difficult book writer Arthur Laurents forbade them, so they cut it.

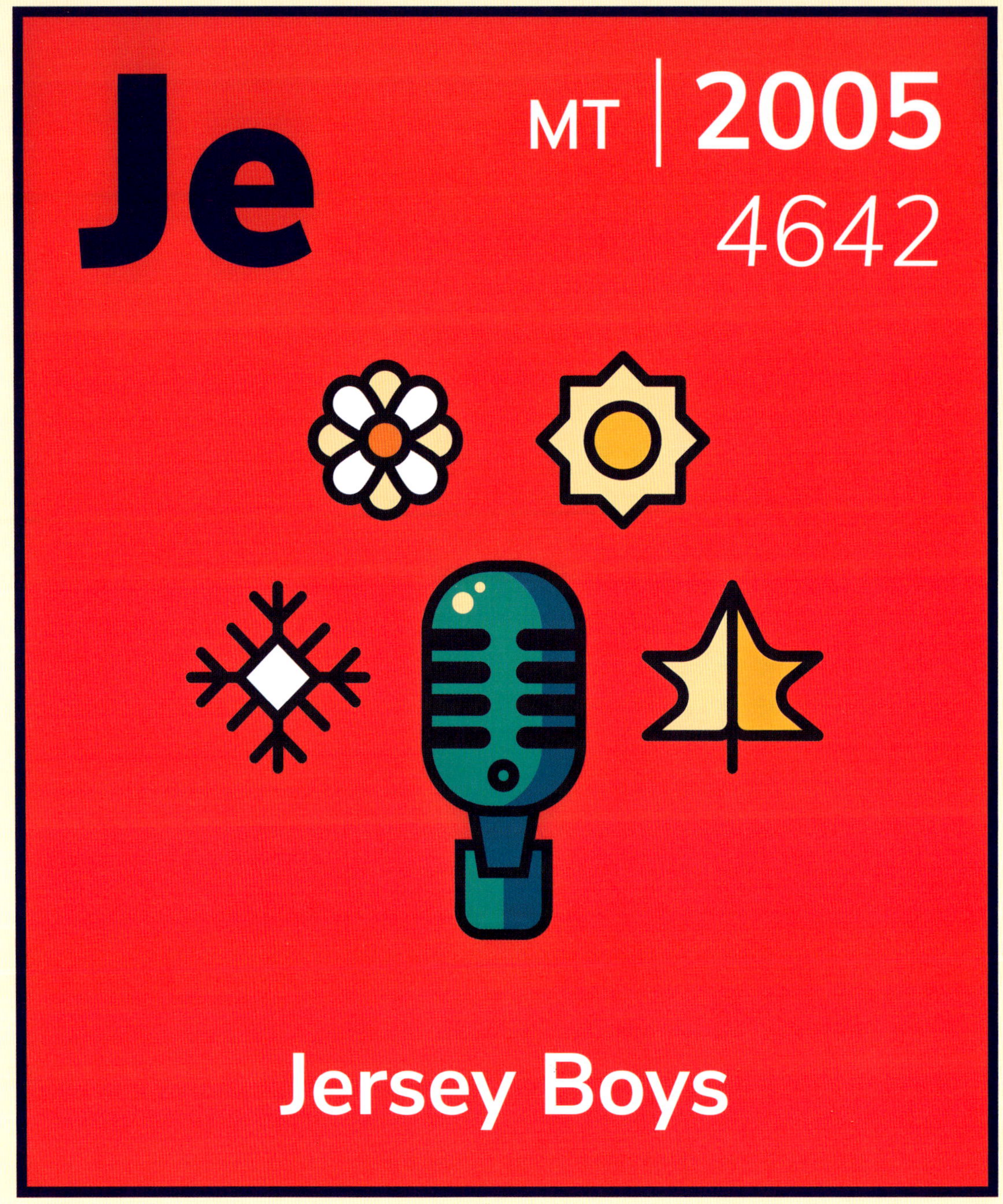

Book by Marshall Brickman and Rick Elice
Music by Bob Gaudio ★ Lyrics by Bob Crewe
Directed by Des McAnuff ★ Choreographed by Sergio Trujillo

August Wilson Theatre, November 6, 2005–January 15, 2017

John Lloyd Young.......Frankie Valli
Christian Hoff.......Tommy DeVito
Daniel Reichard.......Bob Gaudio
J. Robert Spencer.......Nick Massi

ART NOTE: Four "season" icons cluster around a period microphone.

The four members of the 1960s singing sensation the Four Seasons take turns narrating their individual and collective journeys, starting with multiple brushes with the law when they were growing up in New Jersey. Though they never quite agree on all the facts, their rise through the charts is undeniable. The songs they made famous are woven throughout their story as they deal with inner conflicts, confront addiction and gambling debt, and survive personal loss.

Let's Hang On (to What We've Got)

After *Mamma Mia!* became a smash hit, there came such an onslaught of jukebox musicals that people began bemoaning the state of Broadway afresh (a recurring habit among those who love musical theatre). *Lennon*, *Good Vibrations* (the Beach Boys), and *All Shook Up* (Elvis) had all already opened in 2005—to generally bad, even mocking receptions—when *Jersey Boys* put its nickel in the slot. And proceeded to surprise people.

The creative team was superlative. Writers Marshall Brickman, an Oscar-winning screenwriter and veteran of the *Tonight Show*, and Rick Elice, an experienced industry professional with an MFA from Yale Drama, started by interviewing the original members of the Four Seasons, discovering their various checkered pasts and the conflicting memories of exactly what happened along their ride to stardom. Instead of sanitizing that history, the writers leaned into the numerous brushes with the law as well as their differing stories, having each character narrate a section and allowing them to clash with each other. The result gave the evening a grown-up texture that effectively set off the essential sweetness of the original songs. And director Des McAnuff, who had so effectively brought a rock-and-roll sensibility to Broadway with *The Who's Tommy*, re-created that magic with his fluid staging and use of an onstage band.

But the knockout performance of the evening was the Broadway debut of John Lloyd Young, who won a Tony and every other award for his raw and uncanny portrayal of Frankie Valli. He channeled Valli's seemingly inimitable falsetto croon with such passion and accuracy that the group's sound, far from being a pale, synthetic copy of the original, sprung to life as if straight from the Jersey bowling alley gig where the group got its name. Despite the Four Seasons' difficulties and colorful past (or perhaps because of them), the show went on to run for years and gross $2 billion dollars. When it finally closed, it followed the *Avenue Q* model and simply transferred to the off-Broadway New World Stages a few blocks away, where it ran for over three more years.

MISCELLANEOUS MATTER

- ★ Of the thirty-three songs in the show, eleven were ones that made it to the Billboard Top Ten.
- ★ Massi's son, angered at his father's paltry take of the group's revenue over the years, was often found scalping tickets outside the theatre.
- ★ Clint Eastwood directed the 2014 movie adaptation, with John Lloyd Young reprising his performance.
- ★ When the show set up a residency in Las Vegas in 2008, it was at a new theatre at the Palazzo at the Venetian hotel built specially for the production and named (yes, really) the Jersey Boys Theatre.

Book by Douglas McGrath
Music and lyrics by Gerry Goffin, Carole King, Barry Mann, and Cynthia Weil
Directed by Marc Bruni ★ Choreographed by Josh Prince

Stephen Sondheim Theatre, January 12, 2014–October 27, 2019

Jessie Mueller.......Carole King
Jarrod Spector.......Barry Mann
Anika Larsen.......Cynthia Weil
Jake Epstein.......Gerry Goffin

ART NOTE: A radio plays hits "Up on the Roof."

Musically gifted Brooklyn teenager Carole teams up with (and marries!) lyricist Gerry, and the pair becomes successful writing for pop groups of the 1960s. They find kindred spirits in another writing team, Barry and Cynthia, and the two couples begin a friendly competition that results in dozens of hit songs. After both couples hit bumpy water, Carole catches Gerry cheating and leaves him, finding the courage to record her own solo album, which becomes a huge hit.

Natural Woman

The Brill Building at 1619 Broadway in New York City was the center of the music publishing and songwriting business as far back as the 1930s. Scores of writers worked there, and aspiring tunesmiths would bring their songs to sing, hoping to be signed by a major publisher and maybe get their song performed by a star, or even an up-and-coming group. Throughout the '60s, the Jersey Boys themselves (the Four Seasons) and other established groups were operating out of the Brill Building, while just a block away at 1650 Broadway, two producers were looking for the next hot writers—teenagers, if they could find them—to write songs for teenage performers and teenage audiences.

Beautiful is the softer, gentler *Jersey Boys*, a story of young talent making it big and writing the new classics of American pop music. Instead of police records and gambling debts, the conflicts in this female-centered story are more intimate: relationships gone astray, personal betrayals, and rivalries. Carole King was a Jewish girl from Brooklyn who met her songwriting partner, Gerry Goffin, at Queens College and married him at age seventeen. They had their first number one hit the next year, "Will You Love Me Tomorrow" for the Shirelles, a first for a Black girl group, and the string of hits went on from there.

For many audience members, it was a surprise (or a needed reminder) that these two, along with their friendly rivals Cynthia Weil and Barry Mann, were the creative forces behind songs for so many artists, both white and Black, including Aretha Franklin, Elvis Presley, Dolly Parton, the Drifters, and the Pointer Sisters. The sense of artistic community in the show was palpable and refreshing; so many backstage stories are full of hot tempers, jealousies, and egos that to watch a group of artists genuinely get along drew Broadway audiences in night after night. The other major draw: a leading role for Jessie Mueller, who had already turned heads in the 2011 gender-swapped revival of *On a Clear Day You Can See Forever* and the 2012 revival of *Drood*. Quiet, un-showy, but always deeply present and vulnerable, Mueller perfectly inhabited a Brooklyn girl on her journey toward finding her confidence and letting her own voice shine through. Mueller's next Broadway triumph would come in *Waitress*, singing the songs of an heir to Carole King's pop legacy, Sara Bareilles.

MISCELLANEOUS MATTER

- ★ Four days into rehearsals for their out-of-town tryouts in San Francisco, Anika Larsen was told she needed immediate abdominal surgery, with a probable eight-week recovery time. Six days later, she was back in the studio, on her way to a very nice reward: a Tony nomination.
- ★ While she was in high school, Carol Klein (later King) made demo records with her then friend, and future legend, Paul Simon.
- ★ When King, a deeply private woman, first heard the show was being worked on, she sent her daughter to a workshop to kill it, but on being told the show was wonderful, she allowed it to go ahead. When she finally attended a performance, she came in disguise, surprised the cast and audience during the curtain calls, and helped raise over $30,000 for charity that night alone.

THE LEADING LADIES SERIES

STRONG SOURCES OF STAR POWER

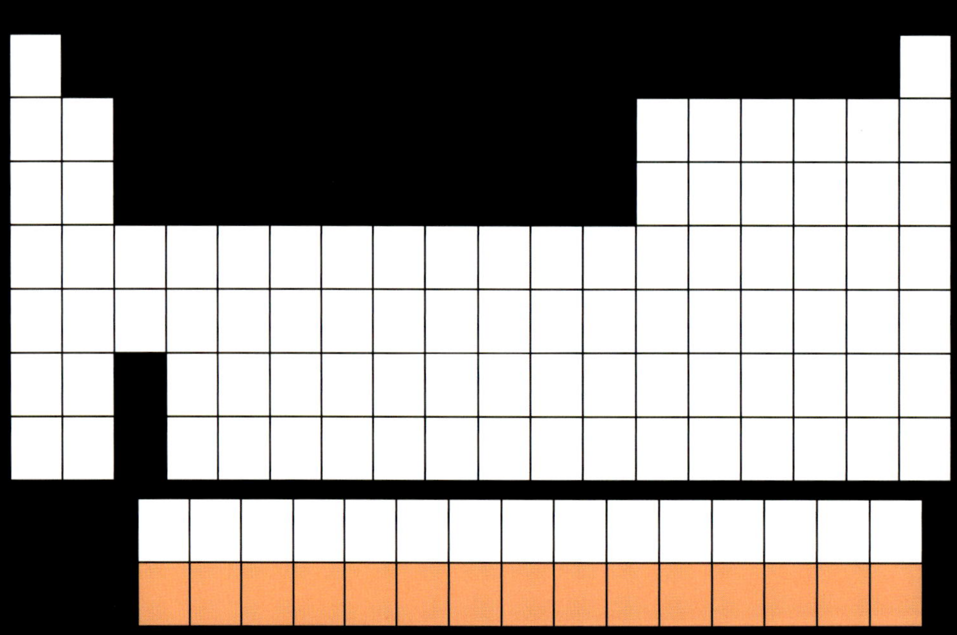

For many people, Leading Lady shows are what they picture when they hear the words *musical theatre*. The titles have become practically synonymous with "Broadway musical": *Gypsy, Evita, Wicked, Chicago, Funny Girl, Annie, Hello, Dolly!* What links all of these shows is that each one either has a larger-than-life female character at its center or was built for a star female performer (usually both). Just like the titles, the list of performers who created these roles includes some of the most legendary names in Broadway history: Ethel Merman, Mary Martin, Carol Channing, Gwen Verdon, Chita Rivera, Barbra Streisand, Angela Lansbury, Patti LuPone.

Not every show that has a central female character is a Leading Lady show. What makes these shows special is that, in each one, the woman in question forges a visceral, personal connection with the audience through song (and sometimes, dance), driving the story with her charm and sheer force of will. Almost every one of them features a climactic number where the star steps center stage—sometimes backed by the entire company—and creates theatrical magic using only the force of her personal charisma.

Clearly, there are male Broadway stars, and numerous leading roles for men, but male leading roles tend not to be as bravura or flashy. Leading men's characters usually don't dominate a story in the same way, more often than not sharing the focus of the show with a romantic interest (*Oklahoma!*, *The Pajama Game*, *She Loves Me*, *Carousel*, *West Side Story*, *Parade*), a buddy or buddies (*On the Town*, *Big River*, *Jersey Boys*, *The Producers*), or an antagonist (*City of Angels*, *Les Misérables*, *Jesus Christ Superstar*). The very few true Leading Men shows (*The Music Man*, *Man of La Mancha*, *How to Succeed in Business . . .*, *Nine*) all feature characters with a larger-than-life flamboyance and a loose relationship with reality that allows for the same type of showstopping moments.

Whatever the reasons for this disparity, Leading Lady shows are certainly among Broadway's most beloved, home to many of its most iconic songs, scenes, and performances, and suitably filling out the Table's bottom row—in the original periodic table, all these elements are radioactive.

Book by Herbert and Dorothy Fields ★ Music and lyrics by Irving Berlin
Directed by Joshua Logan ★ Choreographed by Helen Tamiris

Imperial Theatre, May 16, 1946–February 12, 1949

Ethel Merman.......Annie Oakley *Ray Middleton.......Frank Butler*

ART NOTE: One of Annie's targets, with three bulls-eyes (naturally).

Inspired by the real-life romance of two famous road show sharpshooters, Annie Oakley and Frank Butler, the show follows them from their first meeting—a shoot-off that she wins—to their marriage. As she transforms from simple country girl to international star, his ego can't handle her continuing to eclipse him. And so to land the man she loves, she throws a final shoot-off and intentionally loses, after which he invites her to join forces professionally and romantically.

They Say It's Wonderful

Dorothy Fields was one of the most successful wordsmiths of Broadway and Tin Pan Alley when she pitched a new show to Rodgers and Hammerstein (who'd started producing other writers' work after *Oklahoma!*). It would be based on the life of renowned 19th-century sharpshooter Annie Oakley; Fields and her brother Herb would do the book, she'd do lyrics, and esteemed *Show Boat* composer Jerome Kern the music. What made the idea can't-miss was that Ethel Merman was on board to play Annie. Already a Broadway legend, Merman and her unique and powerful voice had introduced numerous songs, frequently by Cole Porter, that went on to become standards and Billboard chart-toppers.

Rodgers and Hammerstein were in, and everything was a go until Kern died suddenly shortly after work began. Irving Berlin's name immediately came to mind as a perfect replacement—the most all-American composer for this all-American story, and a one-man hit factory for decades. But would Berlin work on a show that wasn't his idea? The tunesmith did have reservations, but not the ones they expected. In the wake of 1943's *Oklahoma!*, musical theatre had changed; songs needed to be deeply rooted in story and character, and Berlin wasn't sure he could write that way. Hammerstein convinced him to try, and in a few short days Berlin came back with what would become four of the best-loved numbers in the show, including the now iconic "There's No Business Like Show Business." The finished score includes some of Berlin's finest and most nuanced writing, while never sacrificing the trademark melodies and, yes, pop song showmanship that had made him a household name since the '20s.

Director Josh Logan brought a cheerful energy to the piece and managed to cajole Merman into making Annie a three-dimensional character . . . even getting her to occasionally play vulnerable. But when she sang, Merman was just Merman, standing center stage and belting out great Berlin tunes (nine of them, not counting reprises). Just as Annie Oakley outshines Frank Butler, Merman dominated costar Middleton; in this vocal battle of the sexes, he was simply outgunned.

MISCELLANEOUS MATTER

★ Texas-born Mary Martin was eager to step into Annie's boots, and she starred in the national tour, winning a special Tony Award for "spreading theatre to the country."

★ Just before rehearsals started, someone noticed that "No Business Like Show Business" had mysteriously vanished from the score; Berlin thought people hadn't liked it when he first presented it, so he'd cut it. It quickly went back in.

★ The MGM movie was supposed to have starred Judy Garland, but her personal demons got in the way after shooting a few scenes, and she was replaced with goofball belter Betty Hutton, who gave the film a totally different flavor.

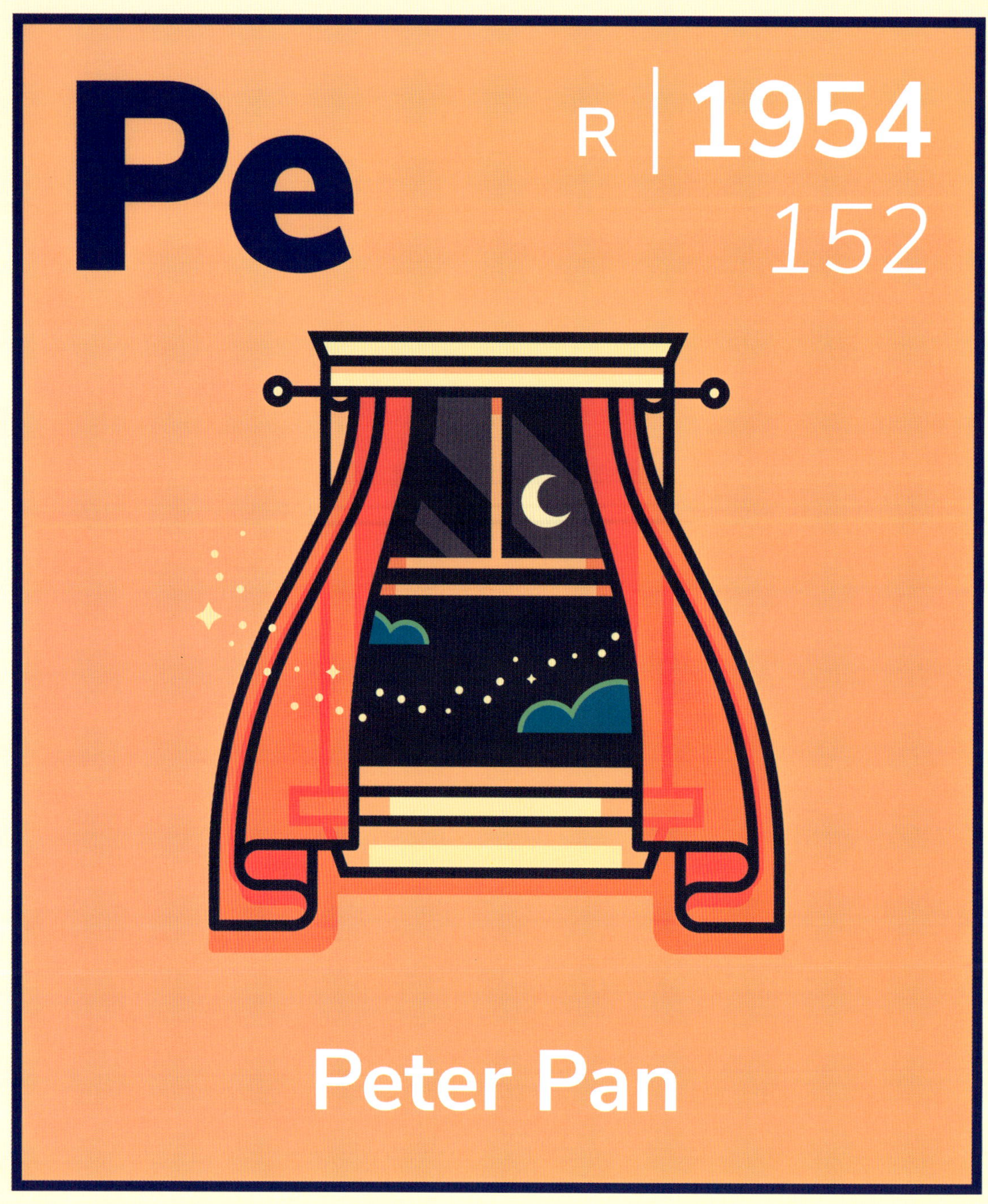

Based on the play by J. M. Barrie
Music by Moose Charlap; additional music by Jule Styne
Lyrics by Carolyn Leigh; additional lyrics by Betty Comden and Adolph Green
Directed and staged by Jerome Robbins

Winter Garden Theatre, October 20, 1954–February 26, 1955

Mary Martin.......Peter Pan
Cyril Ritchard.......Mr. Darling/Captain Hook
Sondra Lee.......Tiger Lily
Joe E. Marks.......Smee

ART NOTE: The open window of the Darling children's bedroom, a trail of fairy dust leading out into the night sky.

The three Darling children are led to magical Neverland by a mysterious flying boy, Peter Pan, and his fairy companion, Tinker Bell. Once there, they meet his crew of Lost Boys, who have vowed never to grow up; the oldest Darling child, Wendy, becomes this ragtag bunch's new "mother." Together, they defeat the nefarious Captain Hook and his band of pirates, but the Darling children eventually return home. Peter visits years later to introduce a now grown-up Wendy's daughter to Neverland.

I Won't Grow Up

The classic J. M. Barrie children's story first reached Broadway in 1905 as a play, and the story was revived five times between then and a 1950 production for which Leonard Bernstein wrote seven songs. But the version of *Peter Pan* that became a true sensation—and was for many children their first introduction to musical theatre—was the musical developed for (and by) *South Pacific* star Mary Martin. After a pre-Broadway run in California, where Martin felt the material wasn't showcasing all her talents, director/choreographer Jerome Robbins (his debut wearing both hats) brought in A-listers Jule Styne and Comden and Green to add to the existing Charlap and Leigh songs, hence the long list of creators. The resulting score expertly walks a line between simple, joyful songs for younger children (like "I've Gotta Crow," which gets everyone cock-a-doodle-doo-ing), villainous ditties for Hook, and heartbreaking ballads like "Never Never Land" that never fail to remind parents that childhood is fleeting.

Though she had been a highly respected star before, it was *Peter Pan* that made Mary Martin *beloved.* Her tomboy exuberance and clear joy in flying (both physically and emotionally) through this charming children's show endeared her to a generation. Her unabashed faith in the show's message—that the magical innocence of youth is something to be treasured even after one grows up—transported theatregoers of all ages. (Peter Pan has almost always been played by female actors, in a tradition that goes back to English *pantomimes*, a type of holiday family entertainment.) The show likewise made a star of Australian character actor Cyril Ritchard, whose Hook dripped with delicious British upper-crustiness and more than a hint of camp.

During tryouts, producer Richard Halliday (Martin's husband) worked out a deal with NBC to include a ninety-minute televised version of the production as part of their 1955 *Producer's Showcase*, a live series shot in color to promote the new color televisions. It was such a hit they filmed it two more times, in 1956 and 1960, bringing its two stars into people's living rooms and winning Martin an Emmy. A glimpse into her fame during this time: she also filmed *Annie Get Your Gun* for the same series in 1957, toured with two one-woman shows (both televised on Easter Sunday, 1959), and starred on Broadway in *The Sound of Music* (while filming the 1960 *Peter Pan*).

MISCELLANEOUS MATTER

- ★ Joe E. Marks also played Smee in Bernstein's *Peter Pan* and went on to originate Pappy Yokum in *Li'l Abner*.
- ★ Mary Martin's daughter Heller Halliday played Liza, the Darling's maid.
- ★ Peter Foy was the inventor responsible for improving 100-year-old theatrical flying rigs so Martin could fly more freely. His company, Flying by Foy, continued to innovate and even helped NASA astronauts prepare for weightlessness during the Gemini and Apollo programs.
- ★ The "part" of Tinker Bell was portrayed by a lighting effect and a celesta (bell piano) in the pit, played by prolific dance arranger and music director Peter Howard (*Chicago, Hello, Dolly!, Annie*).

Book by Arthur Laurents ★ Music by Jule Styne ★ Lyrics by Stephen Sondheim
Based on *Gypsy: A Memoir* by Gypsy Rose Lee
Directed and choreographed by Jerome Robbins

Broadway Theatre and Imperial Theatre, May 21, 1959–March 25, 1961

Ethel Merman.......Rose	*Jack Klugman.......Herbie*
Sandra Church.......Louise	*Lane Bradbury.......June*

ART NOTE: One of Gypsy Rose Lee's trademark gloves, holding a rose (which is just slightly falling apart).

Rose, a ruthlessly ambitious stage mother, pushes her daughter June to be a vaudeville star, while June's more reserved sister Louise plays second fiddle. When June runs away, Rose turns her ferocious energy toward Louise's career, even forcing her to go on one night as a burlesque stripper. To everyone's surprise, the elegant and teasingly modest character Louise comes up with, "Gypsy Rose Lee," becomes an international sensation, and exposes Rose's underlying rage and jealousy at never having been a star herself.

Let Me Entertain You

If you had to choose a perfect Broadway musical, only a few would be in contention, and everyone agrees *Gypsy* would be one of them. The score is a knockout, one dazzling number after another, with indestructible Jule Styne tunes (polished to blinding show biz brass by orchestrators Sid Ramin and Robert Ginzler), and witty, punch-you-in-the-gut lyrics from the young Stephen Sondheim. The character of Rose towers over other leading ladies, at once an obsessed stage mother who will do anything to make one of her children a star, no matter who it hurts, and a damaged woman living through her daughters to find a slice of the fame that should've been hers.

Broadway has always loved a backstage story, but the grittiness and grim desperation of *Gypsy*'s theatrical world, set in the dying days of vaudeville, felt bracing and fresh in 1959. The naive tackiness of the children's numbers and seedy theatres and lodging houses stood in shocking contrast to Rose's notion that somehow her girls would rise above it all to become famous. It's a very unusual show where an audience roots *against* its protagonist—we hope Rose will come to her senses and release her girls from her schemes, which are a toxic combination of blind ambition and denial. The only reason we don't end up hating her is Laurents's nuanced comic scene writing and the irresistible razzle-dazzle of the score.

Rose has been described as the Broadway musical's King Lear, and her famous eleven o'clock breakdown number, "Rose's Turn" is truly Shakespearean in its emotional range. The creators wanted the number to shock the audience with its fury, and originally felt allowing applause at the end ruined the effect, so it didn't really finish. It was Oscar Hammerstein who, after seeing a preview performance, advised that if the audience couldn't express their excitement at Merman's ferocious performance, they'd be too frustrated to listen to the last scene. So Styne added the now familiar big ending. It was only when Laurents directed the 1974 Angela Lansbury revival that a way was found to keep the ovation but make the moment "emotionally true." In this version, after Rose acknowledged the audience's thunderous applause, she kept on bowing even after the clapping died out—revealing we'd been a part of her fantasy, too. This psychological richness is just one reason why *Gypsy* has had five Broadway revivals (and counting).

MISCELLANEOUS MATTER

- ★ Unbelievably, *Gypsy* won zero Tony Awards—even though 1960 was the only year with a tie for best musical. Merman lost to Mary Martin (*Sound of Music*), and Robbins to George Abbott (*Fiorello!*), and those were the two shows that tied for best musical.
- ★ Robbins originally asked Sondheim, with whom he'd worked on *West Side Story*, to write music and lyrics. But Merman had just had a flop called *Happy Hunting*, and she demanded a seasoned pro for the music.
- ★ Merman was devastated to be passed over for the film *Gypsy*. The role went to Rosalind Russell (who had to be dubbed for most of her songs), thanks to some backstage maneuvering by Russell's agent and husband, Frederick Brisson; Merman thereafter referred to him as "The Lizard of Roz."

Book by Michael Stewart ★ Music and Lyrics by Jerry Herman
Suggested by the play *The Matchmaker* by Thornton Wilder
Directed and choreographed by Gower Champion

St. James Theatre, January 16, 1964–December 27, 1970

Carol Channing.......Mrs. Dolly Gallagher Levi
David Burns.......Horace Vandergelder
Eileen Brennan.......Irene Molloy
Charles Nelson Reilly.......Cornelius Hackl

ART NOTE: A cupid's bow worthy of Dolly, with an 1890s elegance, festooned with feathers from her signature red hat.

Dolly Gallagher Levi, widow and all-around "woman who arranges things," has been hired as a matchmaker by curmudgeonly Horace Vandergelder, a "well-known, unmarried, half-a-millionaire" from Yonkers. Deciding it's high time for her to rejoin the human race, she resolves to marry him herself, and so proceeds to shamelessly plot, scheme, and maneuver to bring this about. Along the way, she also manages to find perfect matches for Vandergelder's two clerks and niece.

It Takes a Woman

Hello, Dolly!—perhaps the most iconic example of a Leading Lady show—was originally conceived as an ensemble piece, not a star turn. It was only over the course of its out-of-town tryout that the character of Dolly became the show's indisputable center. Oddly, the source material had undergone the same shift in focus on its way to success (Thornton Wilder's *The Merchant of Yonkers* flopped in 1938, becoming a hit only when he reframed it as *The Matchmaker* in 1951), so it's a little surprising that the creators of the musical made a similar miscalculation.

The show's out-of-town premiere was widely panned by critics (though everyone loved Carol Channing). Undaunted, director/ choreographer Gower Champion and the writers added new scenes and numbers (with some help from uncredited songwriters Bob Merrill and the team of Charles Strouse and Lee Adams), and by the time the show opened on Broadway the critics hailed it as a smash. The show was the first major hit for composer/ lyricist Jerry Herman, launching him into the pantheon of great Broadway songwriters (he would have two other long-running hits, *Mame* and *La Cage aux Folles*), and Gower Champion's unflaggingly inventive staging and extended dance sequences elevated the occasionally corny material at every turn.

Hello, Dolly! went on to win an unprecedented ten Tony Awards, and eventually became the longest-running musical in history (until it was surpassed by *Fiddler on the Roof* a year later). Its longevity was, to a great extent, due to producer David Merrick's then novel strategy of bringing in big-name stars as replacements (Carol Channing was followed by, among others, Ginger Rogers, Betty Grable, and Ethel Merman). And, in 1967, he made headlines again when he recast the entire show with Black performers, led by stars Pearl Bailey and Cab Calloway.

Yet few shows are as indelibly linked with its original star as *Hello, Dolly!* is with Carol Channing, partly because she continued to play the role on Broadway and the West End for over thirty years, but mostly because of her one-of-a-kind combination of comic timing, enormously expressive features, and instantly recognizable voice. Her love for and commitment to the show was the force that delighted audiences for decades, and any subsequent Dolly must play the role in her shadow.

MISCELLANEOUS MATTER

- ★ In the Tony race for Best Actress, Carol Channing beat Barbra Streisand in *Funny Girl*; Barbra, though, got the last laugh when she beat out Carol to play Dolly Levi in the 1969 film version of *Hello, Dolly!*
- ★ The role of Dolly Levi was originally written for, and offered to, Ethel Merman; leery of another long run (she was just coming off *Gypsy*), she turned it down.
- ★ Early drafts of the show carried the title *Dolly: A Damned Exasperating Woman*, after a song of Vandergelder's (eventually cut); when it opened in New York, the opening night tickets still carried the much longer title. The title was changed after Louis Armstrong's recording of the song "Hello, Dolly," released before the show opened, started to climb the charts.

Book by Isobel Lennart ★ Music by Jule Styne ★ Lyrics by Bob Merrill
Directed by Garson Kanin ★ Musical staging by Carol Haney

Winter Garden Theatre*, March 26, 1964–July 1, 1967

Barbra Streisand.......Fanny Brice *Sydney Chaplin.......Nick Arnstein*

ART NOTE: Fanny Brice sporting the *Follies* headpiece and blowing a raspberry.

**First of three theatres*

Loosely based on the life of gutsy and irreverent comedienne Fanny Brice, the show follows her rise from struggling comic to star of the Ziegfeld Follies. Her genius and confidence on stage is in stark contrast to her ineptitude in romantic relationships, and when she lands the sophisticated Nick Arnstein, she does everything she can to keep him. But after her star continues to rise and he lands in jail, they decide they're better off apart.

I'm the Greatest Star

Some shows are smooth sailing from conception to opening night; *Funny Girl* was not one of them. Ray Stark, the producer, was Fanny Brice's son-in-law, and he was determined to create a project based on her colorful life, either a biography or a feature film. By the early 1960s, the plan had changed to creating a stage musical, based on a script by Academy Award nominee Isobel Lennart and coproduced by David Merrick. A succession of stars was considered—Mary Martin, Anne Bancroft, Carol Burnett, Eydie Gormé—and multiple directors were briefly attached, including Jerome Robbins and Bob Fosse. Composer Jule Styne was there from the beginning, and it was he who suggested Barbra Streisand, who was then performing her nightclub act. Her astonishing pipes, comic flair, and Jewish background now make her seem an obvious choice, but before *Funny Girl,* she'd had only one supporting role in a Broadway flop (albeit one that earned her a Tony nomination). And she was only twenty-one.

After several pre-rehearsal hiccups, including Merrick leaving the production, the show made it to Boston for tryouts, which were equally challenging. Streisand clashed with costar Chaplin, and nearly an hour of material needed to be trimmed. Director Kanin wanted to cut the song "People," feeling it was out of character, but Streisand had already recorded it and it was so popular audiences applauded it in the overture. Robbins returned to the project as "Production Supervisor," while a slew of rewrites meant the New York opening was delayed five times. But when *Funny Girl* finally opened, Streisand more than delivered, as everyone (including herself) knew she would. She had already begun cultivating the "odd one out" persona that would take her to super-stardom (she'd dropped the second "a" from her name just to be different) and publicly owned her not-conventionally-pretty looks. "I knew I had to be a star or nothing," she said just before opening night.

Time has not changed the show's reputation as a first-rate score with an unfocused, overly long book that demands a world-class singer/comic. Fanny is in nearly every number, and Styne's powerhouse songs demand incredible range and stamina from a performer. In addition, anyone stepping into Fanny Brice's shoes must deliver comic brilliance as well, a combo that comes once in a generation, at most.

MISCELLANEOUS MATTER

- ★ Future blockbuster songwriter and Streisand music director Marvin Hamlisch made his Broadway debut creating the show's vocal arrangements.
- ★ Fran Stark, Fanny's daughter and Ray's wife, allegedly balked at signing the kooky young Streisand, stating, "That girl will never play my mother!"
- ★ Robbins (while he was initially attached) and Styne wanted Sondheim to pen the lyrics, as he had for *Gypsy.* But when Sondheim heard they were considering non-Jews to play Fanny (see list above) he decided to decline the offer. Besides, by this point he wanted to only write lyrics for his own music, as he'd done for 1962's *A Funny Thing Happened on the Way to the Forum.*

Book by Neil Simon ★ Music by Cy Coleman ★ Lyrics by Dorothy Fields
Based on the screenplay *Nights of Cabiria* by Federico Fellini
Conceived, staged, and choreographed by Bob Fosse

Palace Theatre, January 29. 1966–July 15, 1967

Gwen Verdon.......Charity

John McMartin.......Oscar

ART NOTE: A ticket for one taxi dance, surrounded by groovy 1960s flowers.

Dance hall hostess Charity can't catch a break romantically. Her job requires her to make lonely men feel special on the dance floor, but in real life she gets rudely dumped time and again. When she finally meets a nice tax accountant, she can't face telling him about her job, but he finds out anyway. He says he wants to marry her regardless, then changes his mind and he, too, dumps her, leaving her to carry on "hopefully ever after."

The Rhythm of Life

In 1965, Bob Fosse was going strong, having choreographed six major Broadway shows since 1954's *Pajama Game*. And his wife, triple threat and four-time Tony winner Gwen Verdon, was ready to come back to the stage after a few years off raising their daughter. As he looked for a new project, the Oscar-winning Fellini film *Nights of Cabiria* caught his attention. Although he changed the movie's "hooker with a heart of gold" story to a "taxi dancer with a heart of gold" to conform to Broadway's mainstream tastes, the final product, as created by Fosse, Coleman, and Fields, clearly showed that, in everything but name, the employees of the Fandango Ballroom were "working girls."

While Jule Styne's bump-and-grind music for *Gypsy*'s strippers had kept things fun and sassy, Coleman and Fields's spare, minor-key "Big Spender," which introduced the taxi dancers, was a different story. Its chromatic smears and suggestive silences conveyed a forced, exhausted sexuality, and inspired Fosse to create the fullest realization of what would become his trademark style. The girls lined up behind a bar in "broken doll" poses, twisted exaggerations of feminine sensuality that stared at the audience (and prospective customers) with expressionless masks as if to say, "I'm paid to pretend you're attractive, but I don't have to pretend to like it." It was a nasty way to introduce the world of the dance hall, and it set Charity apart from her coworkers—she was not in the song and could keep her optimism till the final curtain.

Unlike Jerome Robbins, who adapted his choreography to the world of each show he worked on, Fosse settled on this angular style and used it in much of his future work, from the *Cabaret* movie to *Pippin* to *Chicago,* whether or not it was period appropriate. Fosse also didn't shy away from the "show-ness" of a show, using self-conscious staging techniques like having actors walk through sets as they changed around them to remind the audience that they're watching a show in a theatre. Both times that a man dumps Charity by pushing her into a lake, Fosse had Verdon fall into the orchestra pit! Verdon's return to Broadway certainly made a splash; the show was a big hit and a personal triumph for both husband and wife.

MISCELLANEOUS MATTER

★ Fosse did the adaptation and original book, but the king of Broadway comedies (and close friend of Fosse) Neil Simon was brought in to create the book they finally used.

★ Shirley MacLaine played Charity in the 1969 movie; since being discovered in *Pajama Game*, she had built a major film career. Good sport Verdon stuck around to assist Fosse and teach MacLaine her numbers.

★ *Sweet Charity* was the first show to play the renovated Palace Theatre (formerly a vaudeville house). It has been a favorite Broadway theatre ever since, hosting shows and starry concerts like Judy Garland's in 1967, and in a nice coincidence, Shirley MacLaine's in 1976.

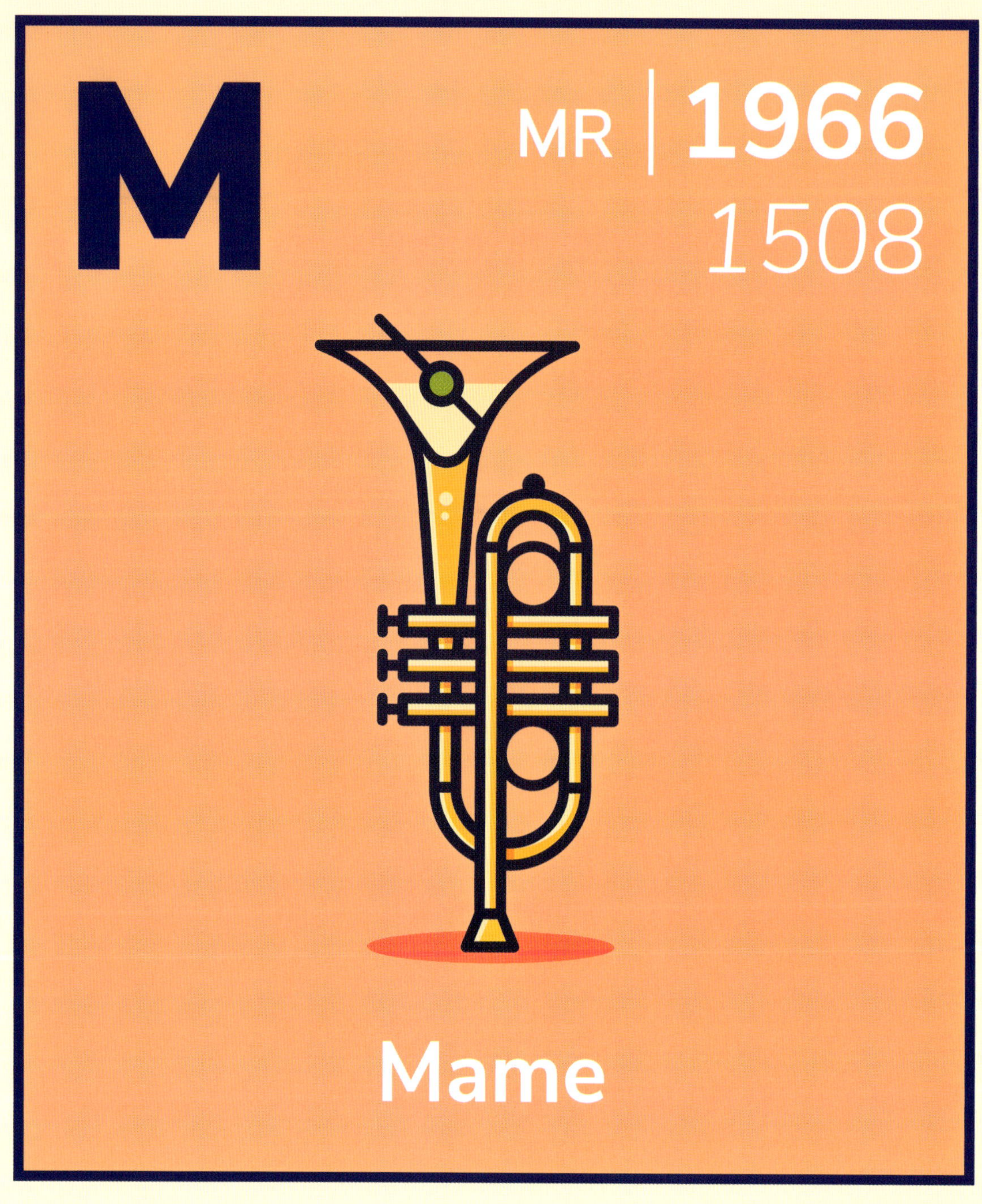

Book by Jerome Lawrence and Robert E. Lee ★ Music and lyrics by Jerry Herman
Based on the novel *Auntie Mame* by Patrick Dennis and the play *Auntie Mame* by Jerome Lawrence and Robert E. Lee
Directed by Gene Saks ★ Dances and musical numbers staged by Onna White

Winter Garden Theatre and Broadway Theatre, May 24, 1966–January 3, 1970

Angela Lansbury.......Mame Dennis
Beatrice Arthur.......Vera Charles
Frankie Michaels.......Young Patrick
Jane Connell.......Agnes Gooch

ART NOTE: The bugle Mame plays and gives to Patrick, in which someone has fixed a martini.

At the height of the Roaring '20s, no one throws more roaring parties than Mame Dennis. When her young, orphaned nephew Patrick arrives unexpectedly, she decides that showing him "all life has to offer" has become her most important responsibility. Their emotional bond grows as Mame careens through theatrical, literary, and matrimonial adventures, and even survives an older Patrick's engagement to a vacuous, small-minded debutante; Mame unashamedly, and with typical élan, breaks the couple up and steers Patrick to someone better.

Open a New Window

Patrick Dennis's account of growing up in the freewheeling, open-minded care of his Auntie Mame was a well-known and hugely popular story in 1966. It had started as a novel, was adapted into a Broadway play that ran nearly two years, then was released as a hit movie shortly after the play closed. The character of Mame, with her over-the-top exuberance and antiestablishment philosophy, was made for musicalization, and Jerry Herman's infectious tunes had everyone yearning to be her nephew.

Angela Lansbury had been a successful, Oscar-nominated character actress in Hollywood for fifteen years before she made the move to Broadway. Her first musical, Sondheim's *Anyone Can Whistle*, was a flop but nevertheless introduced her to Broadway as a singing actress. (It also introduced her to Sondheim and began a collaboration that culminated many years later with *Sweeney Todd.*) Her extensive career in movies and straight plays meant that she approached her musical theatre roles as an actress first and a singer second, setting her apart from many other musical stars of the day. (One of the few other actresses who fits that description competed with Lansbury for the Best Actress in a Musical Tony in 1966: classical actress Julie Harris. Lansbury won.) These acting chops allowed her to shine in one of the most complex songs—both dramatically and musically—in the entire Jerry Herman catalogue: "If He Walked Into My Life." In a heartbreaking moment of sudden self-awareness after Patrick has rebelled against her carefree ways, Mame must look herself in the eye and ask the difficult question: "Could I have been a better mother to him?" Lansbury delivered it with a surprisingly sober strength miles from Mame's usual manic hedonism.

When Warner Brothers released a film version, they passed over Lansbury in favor of TV superstar Lucille Ball. Unfortunately, Ball was really not a singer, and though her slapstick was second to none, her dancing was a different story. The film's one saving grace is that Bea Arthur reprised her claws-out, dry-as-a-martini Broadway performance as Vera. Thankfully, Lansbury's full performance on stage was captured on bootleg video (albeit from the brief 1983 revival). That, and the original cast album, remain monuments to her thrilling Leading Lady performance.

MISCELLANEOUS MATTER

- ★ In an odd mixture of Broadway and Hollywood, veteran songwriters Betty Comden and Adolph Green wrote the screenplay for the movie version of the play but had nothing to do with the musical.
- ★ Lansbury and Arthur's duet, "Bosom Buddies," is perhaps the greatest musicalized catfight in Broadway history, and it became a signature number for the pair.
- ★ Costume designer Robert G. Mackintosh was doing an impressive double duty during rehearsals, creating the show's 275 costumes (twenty-seven for Lansbury alone) while also completing a fashion line for the manufacturer Musette. One eliminated costume (a tiger-patterned coat) ended up being adapted and sold for the line.

Book by Fred Ebb and Bob Fosse ★ Music by John Kander ★ Lyrics by Fred Ebb
Based on the play *Chicago* by Maurine Dallas Watkins
Directed and choreographed by Bob Fosse

46th Street Theatre, June 3, 1975–August 27, 1977

Gwen Verdon.......Roxie Hart
Chita Rivera.......Velma Kelly
Jerry Orbach.......Billy Flynn
Barney Martin.......Amos Hart

ART NOTE: A reporter's camera, hat, and press badge, with a showgirl as the flashbulb.

Dissatisfied housewife Roxie Hart kills her lover but still convinces her pushover husband, Amos, to pay for a high-priced lawyer, Billy Flynn. In prison awaiting trial, Roxie meets former vaudeville-star-turned-murderess Velma Kelly and begins to mimic her type of limelight-stealing antics to gain press and jury sympathy. Velma suggests that, after they're acquitted, they create a duo act, but Roxie is intent on staying solo . . . at least until a new female murderer grabs headlines, eclipsing Roxie's fame.

Razzle Dazzle

If you're thinking *Chicago* actually has two leading ladies, you'd be mistaken—it has three, if you count the woman who started it all, playwright and reporter Maurine Dallas Watkins. A Harvard/Radcliffe playwriting student, she moved to Chicago and joined the staff of the *Chicago Tribune* in 1924, where she covered a couple of high-profile cases involving young women accused of murder (it seems this was something of a '20s trend, an odd side effect of female emancipation in the Jazz Age). The sob-story narratives spun by various media outlets, and the eventual verdicts (usually not guilty) seemed often to have little to do with these women's actual guilt or innocence, and Watkins thought this an ideal subject for a play. Titled simply *Chicago,* it played Broadway in 1926, was made into a silent film by renowned director Cecil B. DeMille, and remade in 1942 as *Roxie Hart*, starring Ginger Rogers.

In the '60s, Bob Fosse, at the urging of his wife, Gwen Verdon, tried repeatedly to get the rights to *Chicago*, but by that time Watkins had soured on the play, feeling that it glorified the morally challenged women and their lifestyle. But upon the playwright's death in 1969, her estate finally granted Fosse the rights, and after completing the movie of *Cabaret*, he brought in that show's writers, Kander and Ebb, to write the new piece.

With Fosse's guidance, they created a score fashioned after a series of vaudeville numbers, neatly driving home the idea of justice and journalism as extensions of the entertainment industry. For example, "We Both Reached for the Gun" is a riff on a vaudeville favorite, the ventriloquist act, with Roxie as the literal puppet of her lawyer as he charms the press. Also during development, *West Side Story* star Chita Rivera was cast as Velma, and the part was greatly increased to showcase her endless talents.

The original production received mixed reviews, with some critics and audiences turned off by its bleak commentary on American culture, and the show was shut out at the Tonys by theatrical juggernaut *A Chorus Line.* But a 1996 staged concert revival as part of New York City's Encores! series was such a smash that it moved to Broadway. The transfer maintained the pared-down concert aesthetic, and with a small running budget and revolving door of stars, has now become the second-longest running show in Broadway history.

MISCELLANEOUS MATTER

★ Fosse had a series of heart attacks during the rehearsal period, delaying the opening; in fact, as late as the Philadelphia tryouts, the show was not completely finished.

★ Walter Kerr's original *New York Times* review was quite bad, but when Liza Minnelli stepped in to replace an ailing Verdon for six weeks as a favor, it was re-reviewed by Clive Barnes, who said it "must be seen by anyone interested in the Broadway musical."

★ In the tour of the original play, a then unknown Clark Gable played Amos Hart, Roxie's milquetoast husband.

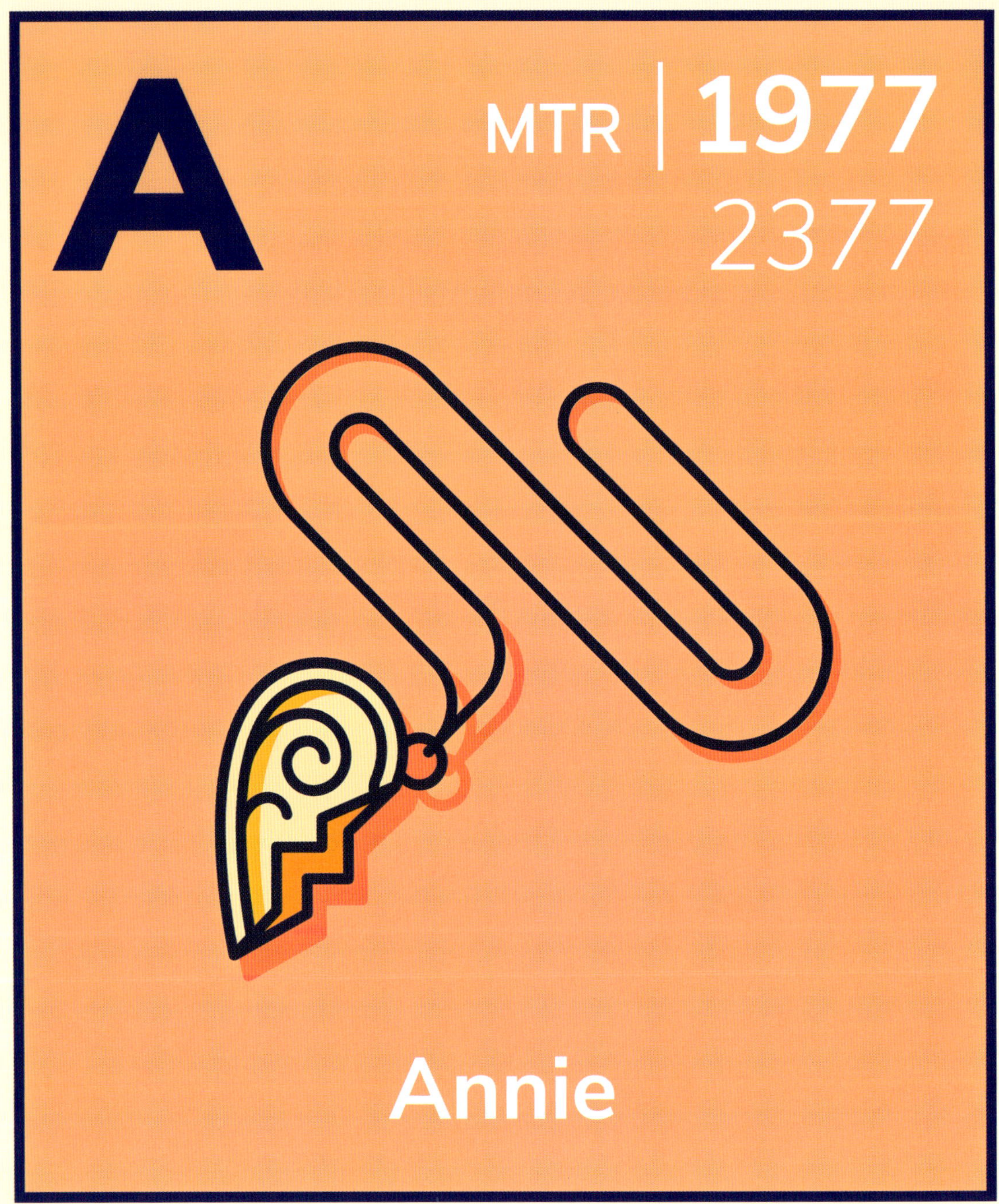

Book by Thomas Meehan ★ Music by Charles Strouse ★ Lyrics by Martin Charnin
Based on the comic strip *Little Orphan Annie* by Harold Gray
Directed by Martin Charnin ★ Choreographed by Peter Gennaro

Alvin Theatre*, April 21, 1977–January 2, 1983

Andrea McArdle.......Annie
Dorothy Loudon.......Miss Hannigan
Reid Shelton.......Oliver "Daddy" Warbucks
Sandy Faison.......Grace Farrell

ART NOTE: The half a locket Annie wears around her neck, hoping her parents will show up with the other half and claim her.

**First of four theatres*

One day during the Great Depression, a plucky orphan runs away, acquires a stray dog as a pet, meets people in a shantytown, is returned to the orphanage by the police, then is chosen to spend the holiday season in the mansion of Oliver Warbucks. The bald billionaire quickly decides to adopt her, and despite a fiendish plot by Miss Hannigan (the horrible woman who runs the orphanage) to derail the adoption, all ends well, just in time for Christmas.

Little Girls

This genial family favorite is notable for having the youngest leading lady in the Leading Ladies Series . . . or does it? The show presents something of a conundrum, since it has always featured two standout female roles: Annie and Miss Hannigan. In the original production, it was Dorothy Loudon as Miss Hannigan who was awarded the Tony Award for Best Actress in a Musical, and in many subsequent revivals, it's Miss Hannigan who has gotten top billing. Over the years, Miss Hannigans have included Jane Lynch, Faith Prince, Katie Finneran, Jane Connell, Betty Hutton, and Nell Carter (for whom Strouse and Charnin added a new song).

But let's be real: the character of *Annie* is the star of the show, regardless of who plays her. It's Annie that audiences cheer for, and it's her hopeful anthem "Tomorrow" they go out humming. Speaking of "Tomorrow," composer Charles Strouse was at first unsure about whether audiences would accept it, since it is stylistically so different (i.e., contemporary-sounding, in 1970s terms, with a soft-rock backbeat) from the rest of the 1930's-inspired score. But audiences have loved the song since the very first performance, and it was one of the few songs from musicals in the 1970s to enter the mainstream consciousness.

In almost every respect, *Annie* was an unlikely hit. Compared to the bold theatrical experimentation of late 1960s and early 1970s successes like *Cabaret*, *Hair*, *Jesus Christ Superstar*, *Company*, *A Chorus Line*, etc., *Annie* was decidedly old-fashioned. In fact, it had a hard time finding producers, since most of the New York theatre community thought it was hopelessly un-hip and uncommercial—*Oliver!* with a girl. It didn't reach the stage until a regional theatre, the Goodspeed Opera House in Connecticut, decided to take a risk and put it on (a risk that would line that theatre's coffers for years to follow).

So, what accounts for *Annie*'s big success? Obviously, there is no definitive answer, but it would seem that the show opened at just the right time, a moment when Americans wearied by Watergate, Vietnam, and the country's economic doldrums were looking for a dose of sunny, morale-boosting optimism. The show was also perfectly cast, full of laughs, and featured a tuneful, memorable score that audiences couldn't help but fall in love with, just like its diminutive leading lady.

MISCELLANEOUS MATTER

★ One week into the show's initial run at Goodspeed Opera House, the creative team decided they needed a feistier, harder-edged Annie. They replaced the lead with Andrea McArdle, who had been playing the orphan named "Toughest." McArdle rocketed to fame when the show reached Broadway, becoming the youngest performer to ever be nominated for a Tony Award for Best Actress in a Musical.

★ Among the replacement Annies on Broadway was future star Sarah Jessica Parker.

★ *Annie* reached the big screen twice: with a traditional (if not very faithful to the stage show) adaptation in 1982, and in an updated, present-day version in 2014, which featured contemporary pop and hip-hop-inspired arrangements of the show's songs, along with three new songs written by other writers.

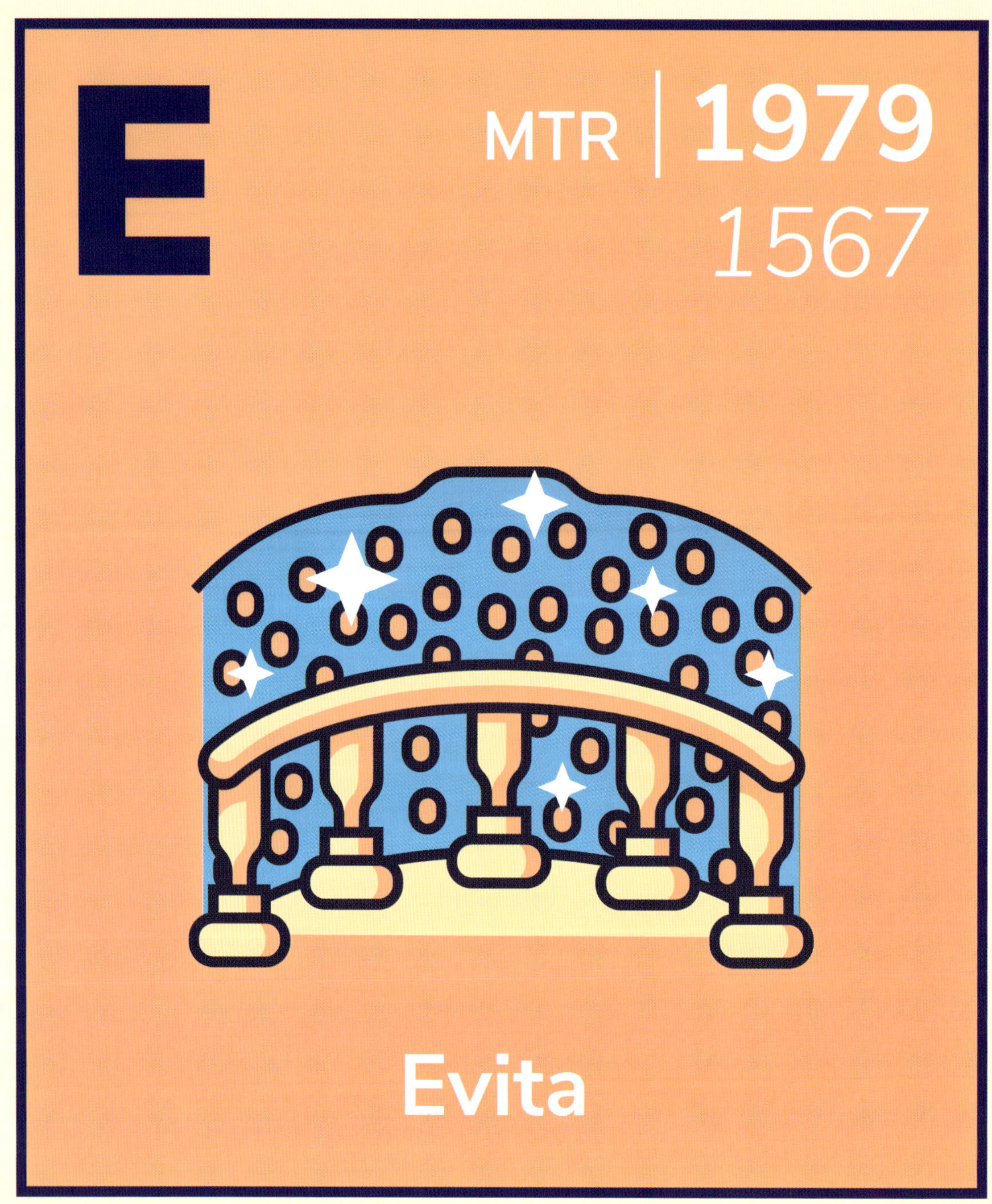

Book and lyrics by Tim Rice ★ Music by Andrew Lloyd Webber
Directed by Harold Prince ★ Choreographed by Larry Fuller

Broadway Theatre, September 25, 1979–June 26, 1983

Patti LuPone.......Eva Perón
Mandy Patinkin.......Che
Bob Gunton.......Perón
Mark Syers.......Magaldi

ART NOTE: Evita's view of the crowd from the balcony of the Casa Rosada.

As beloved Argentinian first lady Eva Perón is publicly mourned, a man known only as "Che" steps forward to offer a more cynical evaluation of her life. The show then flashes back to follow her climb up the social ladder from poor, aspiring actress to glamorous wife of a general who later becomes president. Though Che questions the populist motives (and financial chicanery) behind Eva's charitable works, her early death spares her the repercussions of her polarizing actions.

Oh What a Circus

Like Andrew Lloyd Webber and Tim Rice's breakout hit, *Jesus Christ Superstar, Evita* began as a concept album, a natural step for writers who preferred writing shows with little to no book. Lloyd Webber was a huge fan of Harold Prince's work on *Cabaret,* and he was determined to wait until the director became available before mounting a full production of *Evita*; he particularly wanted Prince's expertise at staging long, complicated musical sequences. The English theatre scene went mad awaiting the next show from these three giants, as well as the results of the national casting call for Eva (Julie Covington, who sang Eva on the album, wasn't interested in playing her on stage). Elaine Paige, who ended up with the plum role, became a sensation in the United Kingdom when the show was a massive hit.

A similar casting circus unfolded when the Broadway transfer was announced, since Prince and the producers wanted an American to play Eva. Everyone from Meryl Streep to Charo was up for it, but in the end, it was thirty-year-old, Juilliard-trained Patti LuPone who left her indelible mark on Broadway history. Prince had some concerns bringing *Evita* to the United States; he feared the story of a fascist's wife who got rich while ostensibly fighting for the poor would not play well here, and though Lloyd Webber and Rice protested their show was critical of Eva, Prince demanded they go further. So they beefed up the character of Che (unofficially the Argentinian Marxist rebel Che Guevara) and his criticism of Eva's hypocrisy, but for some critics it was still not enough. It's hard to listen to a beautiful woman in a beautiful gown singing a beautiful anthem and not feel some kind of pull, and the Cinderella aspect was equally appealing; audiences rooted for Eva, even as Che (and perhaps their own consciences) told them she wasn't what she seemed.

The score is considered by many to be Lloyd Webber's finest, a savvy mashup of Latin rhythms, plaintive ballads, and his trademark Brit pop/rock, plus just enough hints of more "serious" writing to give it gravitas. The legendary difficulty of the role of Eva also cemented the show's place in the Leading Lady firmament; it's one of the rare roles where actresses routinely play only a six-show week, with matinees performed by an alternate, to give the first-stringer time to rest her voice.

MISCELLANEOUS MATTER

- ★ Paramount Studios snapped up the film rights in 1981, but the movie didn't get made until 1996, starring Madonna and Antonio Banderas.
- ★ LuPone was famously unhappy during the run, describing the punishing vocal writing as the work of a misogynist and blasting the producers for treating her as a nobody. Her feud with Lloyd Webber was the stuff of Broadway legend (she was later fired from his *Sunset Boulevard,* and successfully sued him for $1 million), until they finally made up nearly forty years later.
- ★ "Don't Cry for Me Argentina" became an international hit, with 100 versions of the song recorded in Germany alone.

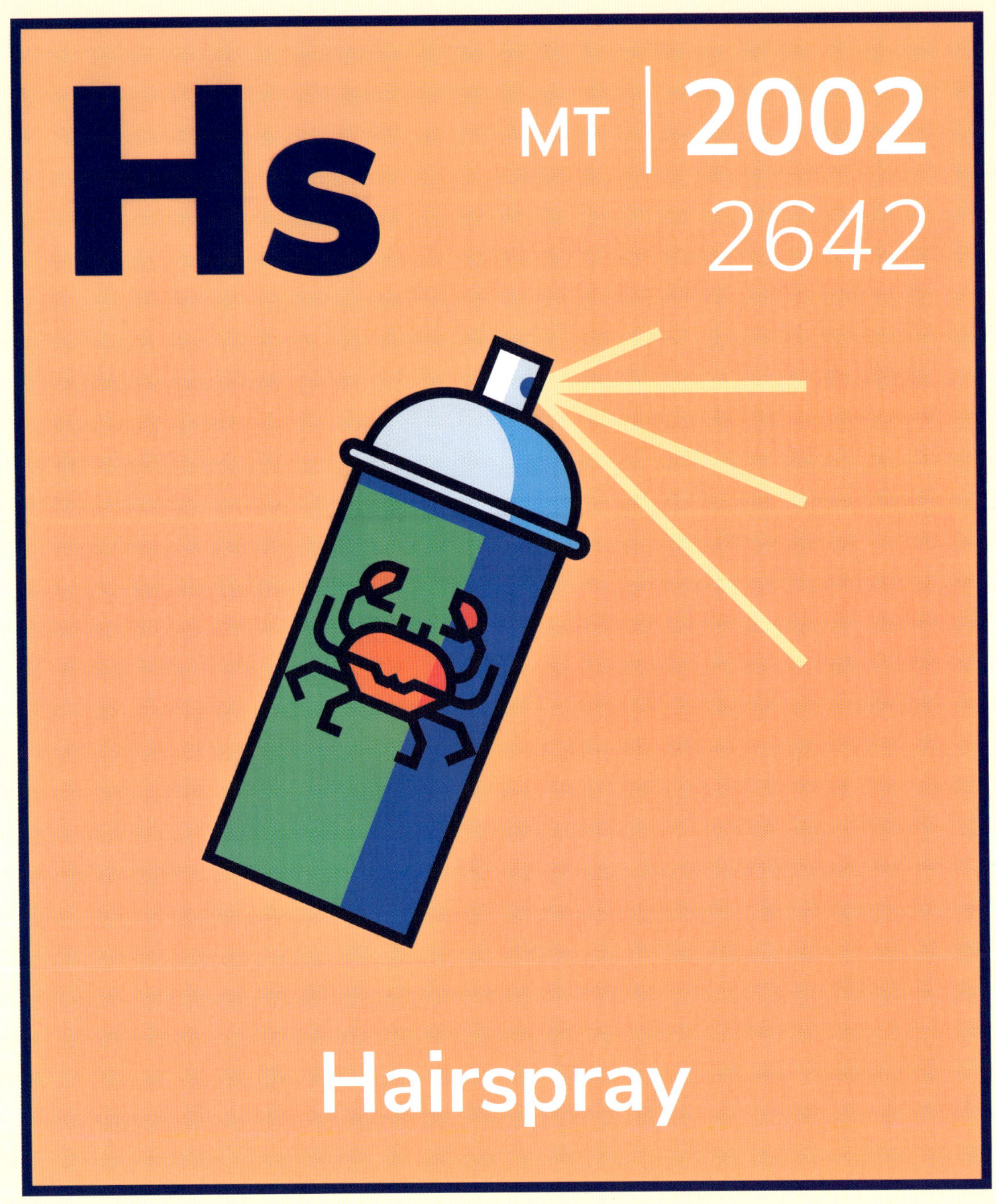

Book by Mark O'Donnell and Thomas Meehan ★ Music by Marc Shaiman
Lyrics by Scott Wittman and Marc Shaiman
Based on the film directed by John Waters
Directed by Jack O'Brien ★ Choreographed by Jerry Mitchell

Neil Simon Theatre, August 15, 2002–January 4, 2009

Marissa Jaret Winokur.......Tracy Turnblad
Harvey Fierstein.......Edna Turnblad
Matthew Morrison.......Link Larkin
Laura Bell Bundy....Amber Von Tussle

ART NOTE: A can of hairspray proudly displaying a Maryland crab.

Tracy, a plus-size teen in 1962 Baltimore, is initially rejected as a dancer for The Corny Collins Show. But after seeing the fresh new moves that she learned from a Black student, Corny himself puts her on the air. Nevertheless, she and her friends protest his program's segregationist policies and are jailed. They escape and storm a live taping of the Miss Teenage Hairspray Competition, effectively integrating the show to public acclaim . . . and earning Tracy a first kiss from heartthrob Link.

Welcome to the '60s

After 9/11, the future of the New York entertainment landscape felt in question, yet at the same time full of promise, with a crop of new writers beginning to achieve success. But what kind of shows would audiences want? Not surprisingly, given the state of the world, the answer was *fun*, as the two biggest hits of the preceding year proved: musical comedy powerhouses *The Producers* and *Mamma Mia!*

John Waters had been a cult favorite film director for decades, creating risqué, campy romps that pushed against the boundaries of conventional respectability. But 1988's *Hairspray* was his bid for mainstream success, and when producer Margo Lion saw it, she immediately contacted him about the rights, lining up veteran TV and film songwriter Marc Shaiman and his partner, Scott Wittman to write the score. This was an inspired choice—*Hairspray* is a spoof of the pop culture of the early '60s, and Shaiman, in particular, had years of experience writing comedy songs for *Saturday Night Live* and world-class comics like Bette Midler and Billy Crystal. He was a musical chameleon who could perfectly channel whatever time period or artist he was tasked with imitating, and the *Hairspray* score felt like someone had switched on the radio in 1962 (albeit to a very silly station). Equally responsible for the spot-on sound was orchestrator Harold Wheeler, who had created the vibrant R&B and pop sounds for *Dreamgirls* and *The Wiz*.

Director O'Brien assembled a top-notch cast, centered around the five-foot-nothing firecracker Winokur. She had been the very first person to audition, but the creative team kept looking, not believing that the perfect Tracy had just walked through the door. She continued to take voice lessons even as she played the role in Seattle, to perfect the '60s timbre and prepare for the grueling Broadway schedule. And playing her mother, Edna, was none other than Tony Award–winning playwright Harvey Fierstein. In many of his films, Waters had cast a drag performer named Divine to play over-the-top female characters (including Edna), and the creators decided to maintain this "tradition" for the musical version. A trailblazing voice for gay artists since his breakout play *Torch Song Trilogy* and book for *La Cage aux Folles*, Fierstein's exaggerated but sympathetic portrayal of Edna introduced a whole new kind of leading lady to Broadway musicals seven years before *RuPaul's Drag Race* would start to make drag queens household names.

MISCELLANEOUS MATTER

- ★ Marc Shaiman received an Oscar nomination for "Blame Canada" from the *South Park* movie (with Trey Parker), a gig he credits for landing him *Hairspray.*
- ★ For one number, the stage's entire proscenium arch was replaced by an enormous pink flip hairdo.
- ★ Tony Award–winning playwright and librettist Fierstein was also an uncredited writer on *Hairspray*, and penned adaptations for Las Vegas and the Hollywood Bowl. Despite these deep connections, the role of Edna for the movie adaptation went to John Travolta.

Book by Winnie Holzman ★ Music and lyrics by Stephen Schwartz
Based on the novel *Wicked: The Life and Times of the Wicked Witch of the West* by Gregory Maguire
Directed by Joe Mantello ★ Musical staging by Wayne Cilento

Gershwin Theatre, October 30, 2003–publication

Kristin Chenoweth.....Glinda
Idina Menzel.....Elphaba
Norbert Leo Butz.......Fiyero
Joel Grey.......The Wonderful Wizard of Oz

ART NOTE: Glinda's magic wand crossing Elphaba's green broom.

The Wizard of Oz witches get a prequel/origin story, starting with their time as college roommates. Glinda the "good" witch torments outcast Elphaba, teaches her to be superficially popular, then kisses up to every corrupt authority figure she meets. Elphaba, realizing Oz is rife with injustice, refuses to play along, earning her a reputation as "wicked." Dorothy arrives, setting off the familiar chain of events, but in the end, the two witches reconcile even as their stories diverge.

Popular

Shows based on existing stories and characters, whether from novels, plays, or movies, have always been popular. Producers like them because they believe ticket buyers familiar with the original property will want to see these beloved characters come to life and sing, and audiences like knowing that what they're shelling out big bucks for will at least resemble something they already like. *Wicked* managed to deliver both familiar characters and an original story, a narrative banquet with something for everyone.

Winnie Holzman's book deviated from Gregory Maguire's novel in significant ways, but still capitalized on the audience's deep knowledge of many of the characters, making character development shortcuts and in-joke references possible (and delightful). And Maguire's genius concept—questioning and eventually turning upside-down which witch is truly wicked—felt as much a revelation as the drawing back of the wizard's curtain in the original.

Wicked's story of two extremely powerful women resonated for many theatregoers, especially teenage girls, and the show has now run so long that those same girls are bringing their daughters to meet Glinda and Elphaba. During the San Francisco tryouts, the story was weighted more toward Glinda, and Chenoweth's bubbly, high-octane characterization was overshadowing the more grounded Menzel. The show was reworked during a three-month hiatus before Broadway rehearsals started, and it's now Elphaba's powerhouse "Defying Gravity" that defines the score. It's one of those songs that not only becomes a hit but changes the way performers sing: "Defying Gravity" forced a generation of music theatre actresses to learn how to negotiate its extreme high belt notes. Both of the show's central roles feature vocal pyrotechnics, and transformed the two actresses who created them, each with major Broadway credits already under their belts, into full-fledged stars.

Given that the story of Elphaba is about a girl ostracized because of the color of her skin, it has been something of a mystery why (as of publication) the only Black actress to play Elphaba as a principal (i.e. not a standby or understudy) has been the West End's Alexia Khadime (Tony nominee Saycon Sengbloh was named a replacement standby in 2005). This is one reason people were excited to see Cynthia Erivo (*The Color Purple*) take on the role in the two-part film adaptation.

MISCELLANEOUS MATTER

- ★ With the success of *Wicked*, Schwartz became the only composer/lyricist to have three Broadway shows run longer than 1,900 performances (with *Pippin* and *The Magic Show*).
- ★ The success of the musical version of his 1995 novel caused author Gregory Maguire to pen a sequel, 2005's *Son of a Witch*, which revolves around Elphaba's son, Liir. Many more *Oz* books followed.
- ★ The first seven notes of "Over the Rainbow" from *The Wizard of Oz* are reconfigured into *Wicked*'s "Unlimited Theme," heard in "The Wizard and I," "For Good," and "Defying Gravity."
- ★ Willemijn Verkaik holds the current record for the longest-running Elphaba, having played it over 2,000 times in Germany, the Netherlands, Broadway, and the West End, and in three languages!

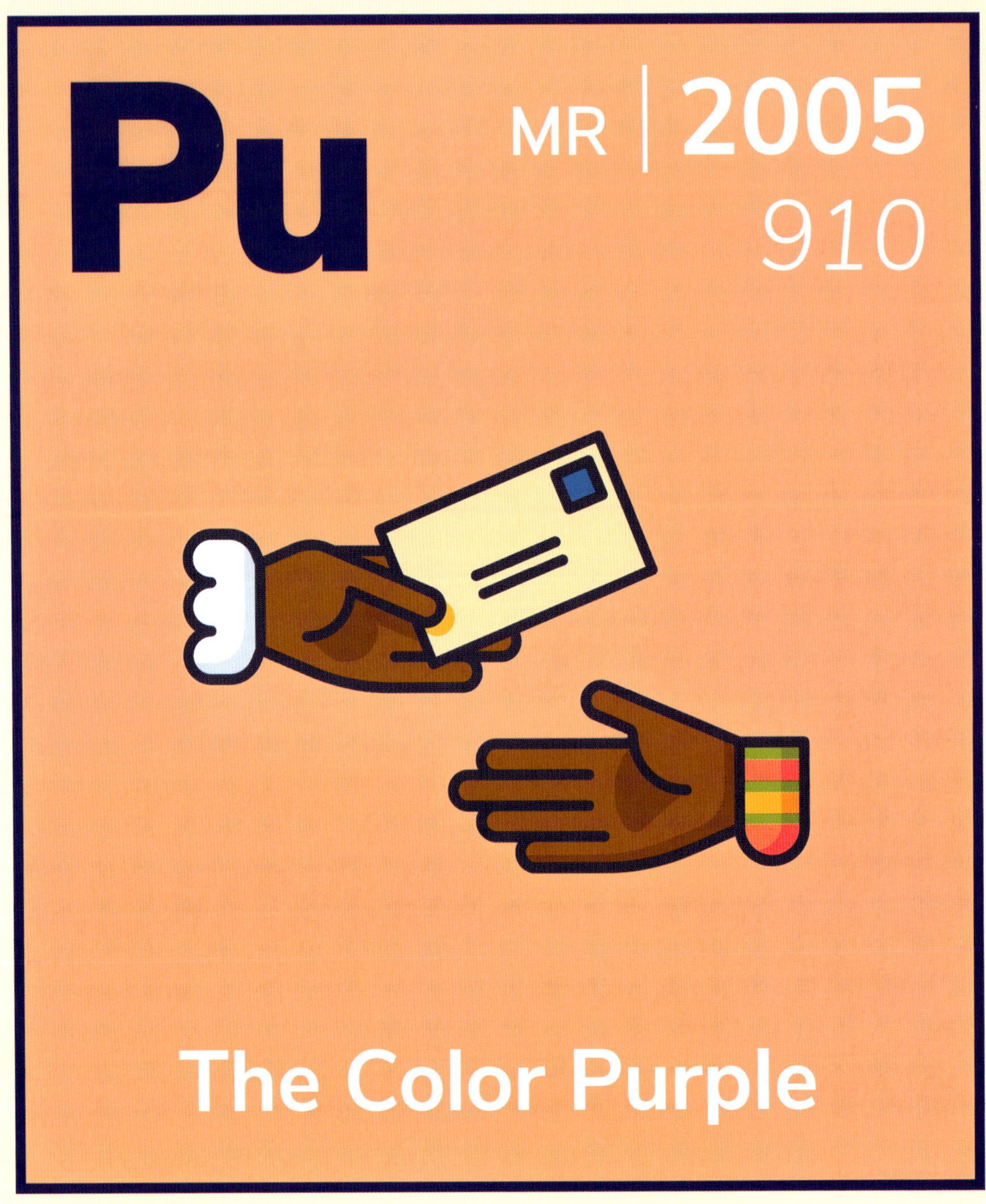

Book by Marsha Norman
Music and lyrics by Brenda Russell, Allee Willis, and Stephen Bray
Based on the novel by Alice Walker
Directed by Gary Griffin ★ Choreographed by Donald Byrd

Broadway Theatre, December 1, 2005–February 24, 2008

LaChanze.......Celie
Kingsley Leggs.......Mister
Elisabeth Withers-Mendes.......Shug Avery
Renée Elise Goldsberry.......Nettie

ART NOTE: Celie delivering a letter to Nettie in Africa, and two sisters' hands wearing American and African designs.

In rural Georgia in 1913, eighteen-year-old Celie leaves her abusive father's home to marry the equally abusive "Mister," who treats her as a servant and forbids contact with her sister, Nettie. Over the next decade, the friendship and love Celie finds in a traveling jazz singer, Shug, and Mister's son and his wife give her the courage to stand up to Mister, cursing him as she leaves. Broken and chastened, he helps reunite Celie with Nettie, who has been living in Africa.

Somebody Gonna Love You

Alice Walker's 1982 novel was a sensation, winning the Pulitzer Prize for fiction, a first for a Black woman. Her frank and deeply human descriptions of difficult subject matter were what made the book so powerful, but have also made it difficult to adapt to other mediums. Stephen Spielberg's acclaimed 1985 film version of *The Color Purple* sparked some backlash for its perceived negative depictions of Black men, and industry uproar when it won none of the eleven Oscars for which it was nominated. Unsurprisingly, the musical adaptation also faced challenges and pushback. The original Broadway production was sharply criticized for rushing through the story and still being too long, as well as minimizing important plotlines that might offend a mainstream audience, like Celie and Shug's romantic relationship. Despite generally poor reviews, the cast was unanimously praised, and LaChanze won a Tony for her incandescent portrayal of Celie.

The 2005 production had a decent run and three national tours, and a London production ran in 2013 at the respected Menier Chocolate Factory. It was this production, directed by John Doyle, that began a new chapter for the show when it eventually transferred to Broadway in 2015. Doyle had made a name for himself directing stripped-down revivals of *Sweeney Todd* and *Company* in which the actors also played instruments instead of having a pit orchestra. He was also known to be liberal about pruning the material as well, but for *The Color Purple*, he and book writer Marsha Norman cut almost nothing from the script. What he did do was pare down production values, essentially creating the whole world out of wooden chairs, thus eliminating the need for scenic transitions. This allowed the story to flow smoothly, and to revolve around Celie, played by the British actress Cynthia Erivo (from the Menier production). This production got rave reviews, won Erivo a Tony, and beat the ecstatically received *She Loves Me* for Best Revival.

The Color Purple is remarkable not only for its story of women banding together in an oppressive, male-dominated community, but for being one of a very few Broadway book musicals (i.e., not revues) with an all-Black (or majority-Black) cast. Its success demonstrated to producers that there was an audience for Black shows of depth, and such shows have become ever so slightly more common in the past decade.

MISCELLANEOUS MATTER

- ★ John Doyle's revival opened less than eight years after the first run ended, making its success even more astounding.
- ★ Pop songwriters Bray, Willis, and Russell spent a year reading about Broadway composing, and watching and rewatching different versions of *Sunday in the Park with George* before working on the score.
- ★ The show marked Goldsberry's first time originating a role on Broadway; she would go on to create the role of Angelica Schuyler in *Hamilton*.

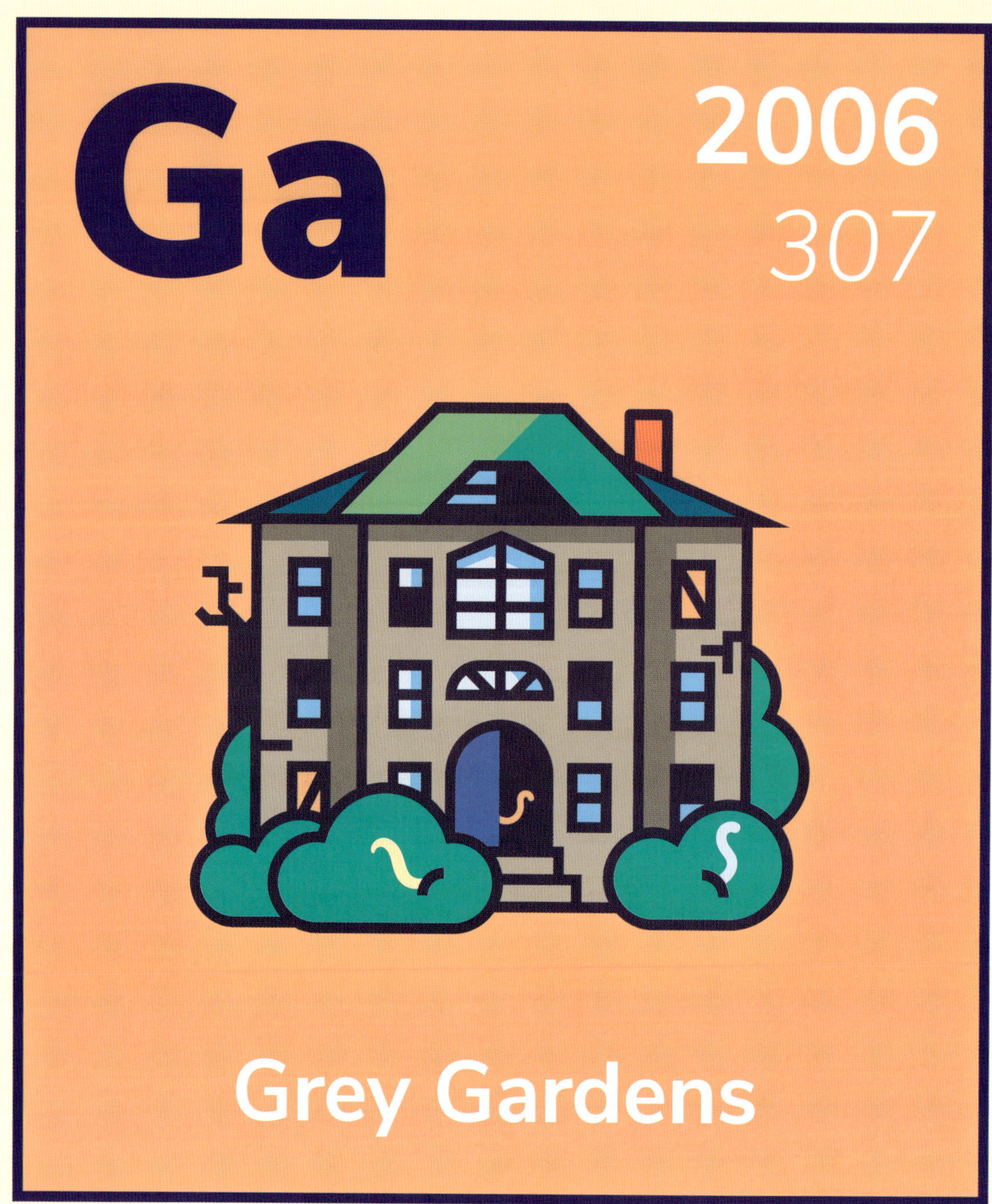

Book by Doug Wright ★ Music by Scott Frankel ★ Lyrics by Michael Korie
Based on the documentary film by Albert and David Maysles
Directed by Michael Greif ★ Musical staging by Jeff Calhoun

Walter Kerr Theatre, November 2, 2006–July 29, 2007

Christine Ebersole.....Edith Bouvier Beale/ "Little" Edie
Mary Louise Wilson.....Edith Bouvier Beale
Erin Davie.....Young "Little" Edie Beale
John McMartin.....J. V. "Major" Bouvier/ Norman Vincent Peale

ART NOTE: The dilapidated mansion, with several feline inhabitants (perhaps escaped from *Cats*).

Act one finds us in the 1940s socialite world of the Bouvier Beale family. Mother Edith gives vocal performances in her salon, embarrassing her debutante daughter, Little Edie, and driving away potential suitors, including her fiancé, Joe Kennedy Jr. Little Edie angrily leaves, but in act two the two women are together again thirty years later, living in the now-dilapidated "Grey Gardens," their Hamptons estate, each blaming the other for their sad fate but knowing they have no one else.

The House We Live In

Though it's defined by its leading lady, *Grey Gardens* could've been in the Groundbreakers or True Stories families. For one thing, it was the first Broadway musical to be based on a specific documentary film. In 1974, respected filmmakers the Maysles brothers were introduced to mother and daughter Edith and "Little Edie" Bouvier Beale, aunt and cousin of Jacqueline Kennedy Onassis, who were living in shocking conditions in a run-down mansion in wealthy East Hampton, on Long Island. They turned their lenses on this eccentric pair, and the resulting film became a cult classic.

Composer Scott Frankel had the idea that these characters could sing, and he and lyricist Michael Korie wanted Pulitzer Prize–winning playwright Doug Wright to write the book, but Wright was wary of tackling the iconic women. Frankel and Korie came up with an ingenious solution that convinced him it was possible: save the film's contents for act two and write an act one centered on the family's early days as minor American royalty. Seeing them hobnobbing with the Kennedys and living the high life would serve as a sobering contrast to their addled act two squalor, and made possible a one-of-a-kind leading lady double casting, with the same actress who plays the mother in act one playing the grown-up daughter in act two. In this showy double role, Christine Ebersole astonished audiences with her transformation from flighty songbird socialite to a spot-on channeling of the grown-up Little Edie, strutting around in homemade "fashion" and sounding exactly like the real-life recluse from the film.

The score also has a virtuoso double identity, a musical embodiment of the battle between present and past, reality and nostalgia. In act one, Mother Edith's salon songs are pure early 20th-century parlor music, sentimental, sweet, and decades out of fashion, but Little Evie's tour de force "Daddy's Girl," a quasi-breakdown in which she begs her fiancé not to leave her over her checkered past, is all angular harmonies and meter changes, foreshadowing her future mental instability. In act two, the music remains adventurous, translating the two women's idiosyncratic speech patterns into off-kilter, defiant show tunes. But the final, devastating word goes to Little Edie, who compares her life to "Another Winter in a Summer Town." While her mother hums along, oblivious in the background, we see a glimmer of recognition at the life that could have been but will never come again.

MISCELLANEOUS MATTER

- ★ During the run, the real Jerry, a handyman at Grey Gardens who appeared in the documentary, was working as a part-time cab driver, and would pick up audience members after the show, ask them what they thought, and, if they liked it, reveal his identity.
- ★ John McMartin was Broadway royalty when he accepted the relatively small parts, having originated the roles of Oscar in *Sweet Charity* and Benjamin Stone in *Follies*. He received his fifth Tony nomination for *Grey Gardens*.
- ★ After the documentary had won her a bit of newfound fame, "Little" Edie decided to put on a cabaret, something she'd dreamed of since she was a teenager. She performed at Reno Sweeney, the famous Greenwich Village cabaret, with a mix of favorites and songs she wrote herself.

Book by Heather Hach ★ Music and lyrics by Laurence O'Keefe and Nell Benjamin
Based on the novel by Amanda Brown and the film by MGM
Directed and choreographed by Jerry Mitchell

Palace Theatre, April 29, 2007–October 19, 2008

Laura Bell Bundy.......Elle Woods
Orfeh.......Paulette
Christian Borle.......Emmett Forrest
Richard H. Blake.....Warner Huntington III

ART NOTE: Bruiser the chihuahua in a fetching blond wig and holding a judge's gavel.

Rejected by her politically ambitious boyfriend Warner as not "serious" enough, UCLA senior Elle crams for the LSATs, aces them, and follows him to Harvard Law School. Her bubbly demeanor and sense of style (pink) make her a target for fellow students and faculty alike, but she impresses a wealthy client by dramatically winning her trial with a deep knowledge of hair care. When Warner finally proposes, she rejects him, then proposes herself to her best friend and confidant, Emmett.

Serious

Much like its ebullient leading lady, *Legally Blonde* was a canny bundle of fun, and much smarter than many expected. But people shouldn't have underestimated its IQ—music and lyrics were by husband-and-wife team Laurence O'Keefe and Nell Benjamin, who met at Harvard and were perfectly suited to skewering their alma mater. The score featured many long, complex musical scenes, with each character expressing themselves in hyper-literate, intricately rhymed stanzas. Add to the mix bubblegum pop grooves with key changes seemingly every ten bars and it made for a manic ride. Jerry Mitchell, directing for the first time, as well as choreographing (he had previously created dances for *The Full Monty*, *Hairspray*, and others), was generally praised for staying true to the feel of the movie. And in the court of public opinion, that can be the trickiest case to win.

The mid-2000s was the high-water mark for peppy, traditional musical comedy movie adaptations. Along with *Legally Blonde*, Broadway audiences could see reimagined versions of *The Wedding Singer*, *Cry-Baby*, *High Fidelity, Sister Act*, *9 to 5*, *Flashdance,* and *Dirty Rotten Scoundrels*, not to mention the animated favorites *Shrek*, *Tarzan*, and *The Little Mermaid.* However, of all these well-produced shows, only *Dirty Rotten Scoundrels* recouped its investment. Familiar stories and characters, though attractive for producers, were seemingly not always enough to guarantee success, and sometimes, the more popular the original film, the more the musical had to compete with fans' memories of its style and indelible performances. After all, two of Broadway's most notorious flops were based on blockbuster properties: 1966's *Breakfast at Tiffany's*, which closed after only four previews, and 2010's *Spider-Man: Turn Off the Dark*, by far the most expensive musical ever staged, which, despite its all-star creative team, lost an astonishing $60 million.

In the end, *Legally Blonde* received a split decision. For many die-hard fans, it was the perfect musical translation of a daffy, guilty pleasure; for others (including most critics), it was a bit too much sugar, without the bite of the original. Nonetheless, the show has lived on to have numerous productions around the country and around the world. When it premiered in London in 2011, it even won the Olivier Award for Best New Musical, a pretty serious accolade for this not-so-ditzy *Blonde*.

MISCELLANEOUS MATTER

- ★ Following the model of the 2007 *Grease* revival, which cast its leads from a reality TV competition, *Legally Blonde* did the same to replace Bundy when her contract ran out. The competition show aired on MTV, which also broadcast a live recording of the show with the original cast.
- ★ Bundy painted her dressing room bright pink and hung an Albert Einstein calendar (she was a long-time fan) to help her slip into character. She also dressed in pink every day during workshops.
- ★ There were five dogs backstage: two who went onstage, their standbys, and one who was cut for not barking on cue but still came to the theatre to hang out, so as not to upset the others. Chico, the original "Bruiser" (Elle's chihuahua), passed away in 2019 and received obits from *People*, CNN, and *Deadline*.

THE ENSEMBLE PIECES

CASTS SHARING NUMEROUS BONDS

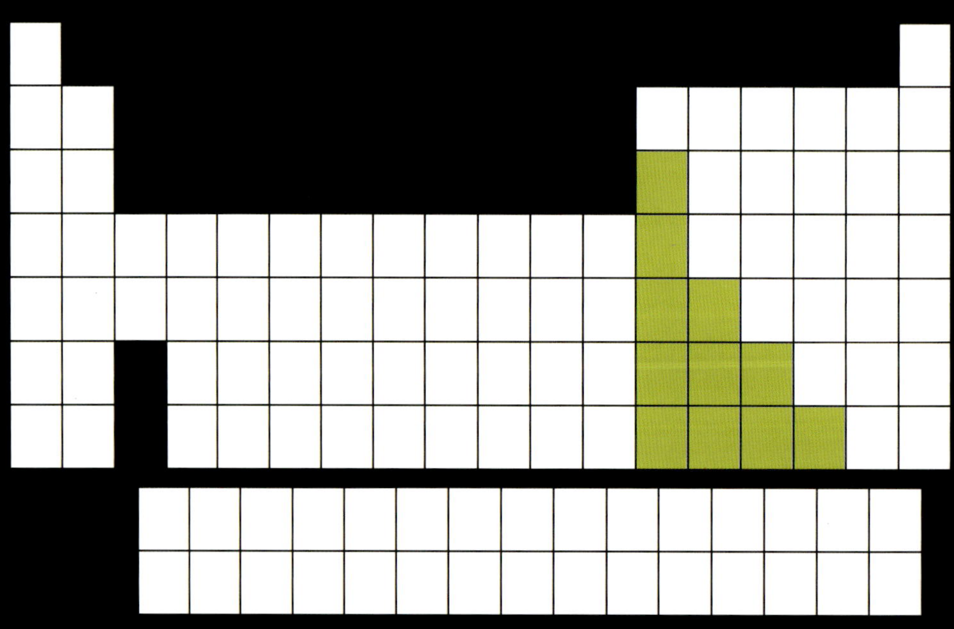

Any actor will tell you that being part of a cast can create the feeling of belonging to a family, at least for the run of the show. But as *Falsettos* star Michael Rupert puts it, in an ensemble show "you're a piece of the puzzle, and when the whole big puzzle is put together, it really means something." Because of this puzzle nature, ensemble shows can be trickier to assemble. In a show with only one or two big leading roles, well-cast performers can carry the whole production. But when everyone's role is the same size, each character often "reacts" with everyone else, and the chemistry between all the actors must be just right.

You'll notice the first show in the family, *Company*, doesn't appear until 1970. That's not only because during the "Golden Age" era of the 1940s through the 1960s, cast sizes were much larger, with generously sized choruses; it's because, for more than twenty-five years, the Rodgers and Hammerstein story formula of main romantic couple/secondary, often comic romantic couple remained dominant (the major exception being *My Fair Lady*). In the early '60s, a few shows started tiptoeing away from it, notably three fairly rare Leading Man shows, *Fiddler on the Roof*, *How to Succeed . . .* , and *Man of La Mancha*. But those shows still had anonymous chorus members; *Company*, by hanging the show on a concept (marriage) rather than a strong linear plot, was able to split with the old story formula entirely and give musical theatre fans something totally fresh and new.

Ensemble shows can take many different forms. They can be meta-theatrical events, like *Godspell* or *Drood*, where performers play actors or storytellers who are putting on a show. *Ain't Misbehavin'* is a revue, and the performers simply play themselves (or heightened versions of themselves) and sing songs in different configurations (solos, duets, trios, etc.). Some ensemble pieces feel like intimate plays, like *Falsettos*, or were based on a classic play (like *Raisin*, adapted from *A Raisin in the Sun*) or a series of playlets (*Company*). Some send up children's shows or Broadway itself like *Avenue Q* or *Drowsy Chaperone,* while others simply chart their own course, weaving together fairy tales like *Into the Woods* or riffing on a fable like *Once on This Island.*

What makes a show an Ensemble Piece is that each person in the show gets extended stage time, allowing audiences to know them with a richness and dimensionality usually reserved, in a more standard Broadway musical, for leading characters.

Book by George Furth ★ Music and lyrics by Stephen Sondheim
Directed by Harold Prince ★ Musical staging by Michael Bennett

Alvin Theatre, April 26, 1970–January 1, 1972

Dean Jones.......Robert
Elaine Stritch.......Joanne
Merle Louise.......Susan
Donna McKechnie.......Kathy

ART NOTE: Someone's engagement ring floating in Joanne's favorite vodka stinger, against a backdrop of Manhattan.

Robert is a perpetually single man finding his way through the sometimes-exhausting world of relationships in late 1960s New York. In a series of vignettes, his married and partnered friends variously counsel, warn, encourage, and fix him up, exposing their own (often jaded) beliefs and misgivings about the institution of marriage. Robert eventually comes to the realization that despite the hassles and sacrifices that come with a relationship, he's ready to give it a try.

Side by Side by Side

When Sondheim gave producer Hal Prince a series of eleven one-act plays by his actor friend George Furth, Prince thought they could be turned into a terrific musical. *Company* still has the bones of that idea, though Furth kept only one and a half of the original one-acts; the musical consists of a series of vignettes with one main character (the commitment-phobic Bobby) dropping in to observe his married friends' lives. The *concept* of marriage becomes the unifying thread instead of a traditional narrative. One can debate what the first "concept musical" was, but *Company* made the term stick.

Sondheim struggled to find the musical form appropriate for this loose collection of characters and skit-like scenes. He landed on a commentary/counterpoint structure, where the songs allow the various couples to share their opinions on the institution of marriage without needing to advance the plot. Of course, this lack of dramatic momentum demands that every song be an outright winner, and boy, did Sondheim deliver. By turns witty, ironic, somehow simultaneously bitter and romantic and composed in a dazzling variety of styles, the score won him his first Tony Award.

Company is notable for being the first of the famed Sondheim-Prince collaborations, as well as Sondheim's first show with the brilliant theatre artist who would join him for many future successes: orchestrator Jonathan Tunick. Tunick was the perfect musical match for Sondheim's complex, genre-straddling score, bringing a big band background and knowledge of Golden Age techniques plus an interest in pop scoring trends. His "cold" timbres, like muted trumpets, bells, and steely synth sounds, and weaving one song's melody into the accompaniment of another, perfectly encapsulated the dizzying, dehumanizing pace of New York City.

Another invaluable collaborator on the show was set designer Boris Aronson, a favorite of Prince (he'd designed the director's two previous shows, *Zorba* and *Cabaret*). Aronson embraced modern technology to create a sterile "urban jungle gym" (with a working elevator!), turning the couples' apartments into transparent cages behind which were projected views of the city. Together with Prince's perpetual-motion staging, the scenery helped achieve the effect Sondheim and Furth were going for: "I want the audience to laugh uproariously for two hours," Sondheim said, "and then go home and not be able to sleep."

MISCELLANEOUS MATTER

- ★ Dean Jones, the original Bobby, was going through a divorce during rehearsals. He was so obviously miserable that Prince told him that after opening he'd release him from his contract as soon as possible. Press releases said he contracted "hepatitis," and Larry Kert, the original Tony from *West Side Story*, who'd been in California selling dogs, stepped in.
- ★ Vivian Blaine, the original Miss Adelaide in *Guys and Dolls,* replaced Elaine Strich for the last two months of the run.
- ★ Bennett was initially reluctant to come on board, but when Prince told him his favorite dancer, Donna McKechnie (*Promises, Promises*), was already cast, he agreed, knowing he'd get at least one real dance number (the song, "Tick Tock," now usually cut).

Book by Robert Nemiroff and Charlotte Zaltzberg
Music by Judd Woldin ★ Lyrics by Robert Brittan
Based on the play *A Raisin in the Sun* by Lorraine Hansberry
Directed and choreographed by Donald McKayle

46th Street Theatre and Lunt-Fontanne Theatre, October 18, 1973–December 7, 1975

Joe Morton.......Walter Lee Younger
Ernestine Jackson.......Ruth Younger
Deborah Allen.......Beneatha Younger
Virginia Capers.......Lena Younger ("Mama")

ART NOTE: The house Mama Younger buys and then is asked to sell back to keep the neighborhood white.

In this musical version of the hit 1959 play A Raisin in the Sun, *the Black Younger family must decide how to invest a $10,000 life insurance policy—buying a liquor store or a family home in a white neighborhood. Over Walter's objections, Mama buys the house but is forced to confront racial realities when a neighborhood representative offers to buy it back to ensure the neighborhood stays white.*

How a Dream Can Fade

Raisin is one of very few Tony Award winners for Best Musical that have not gone on to lasting popularity. Many people have never even heard of this musical version of Lorraine Hansberry's groundbreaking play, *A Raisin in the Sun* (the first Broadway play written by a Black woman, and itself nominated for four Tonys). But *Raisin* ran for 847 performances, longer than any Sondheim show (including *West Side Story* and *Gypsy*), and was considered one of the most important Black musicals of the century. Its ads in the *New York Times* boasted a full page's worth of pull quotes from rave reviews. So where did it go?

Like the play on which it's based, *Raisin* is a true ensemble piece. Director Donald McKayle felt the original play's casting of stars like Sidney Poitier caused it to "suffer," and so the musical's cast had no stand-out names (like several other shows in the Ensemble Pieces category). It opened out of town at the Arena Stage in Washington, DC, a theatre in the round, which added to the ensemble feel since it was hard for one actor to upstage another. The writing is powerful, with many critics feeling the book, by Charlotte Zaltzberg and Hansberry's ex-husband, Robert Nemiroff, actually improved on the original play. The action of the show was expanded from the play's single-room apartment into different locations around Chicago. And the arrangements and orchestrations, by big band pros Al Cohn and Robert M. Freedman, are sophisticated, funky, and as surprising and electrifying today as in 1973.

Which leaves the score itself, which was not singled out in most reviews, and has come under stronger criticism as the years have passed. Songwriters Judd Woldin and Robert Brittan had been writing together for ten years, and though they had not yet had a show produced, Nemiroff sensed their connection with the play and hired them. Their ambitious score ranged from the expansive aria "Sweet Time" to high-octane ensemble numbers like "Runnin' to Meet the Man" that, like *In the Heights*, conjured an entire neighborhood with great detail and affection. But on the whole, perhaps the songs were too integrated into the book, not flashy enough; it foreshadows *Caroline, or Change,* another play-like musical that opened thirty years later. Or perhaps the book was *so* strong that some of the gentler, poetic anthems just made audiences long for the taut, dramatic scenes. In the end, McKayle may have been right—the star of this show was the book, and it was "A Whole Lotta Sunlight" to compete with.

MISCELLANEOUS MATTER

★ The cast included Deborah Allen, who didn't become "Debbie" until she was a replacement in another Ensemble show, *Ain't Misbehavin',* six years later.

★ When Ralph Carter was cast in the sitcom *Good Times, Raisin*'s producers only let him out of his contract if the TV show stated in its credits, "Ralph Carter appears courtesy of the Broadway musical *Raisin*."

★ Even after the show was successful, Woldin kept his job as "saloon pianist" at a Brooklyn steakhouse.

★ Lena Horne and Lou Rawls both recorded songs from the show years before it opened, but none recorded them after.

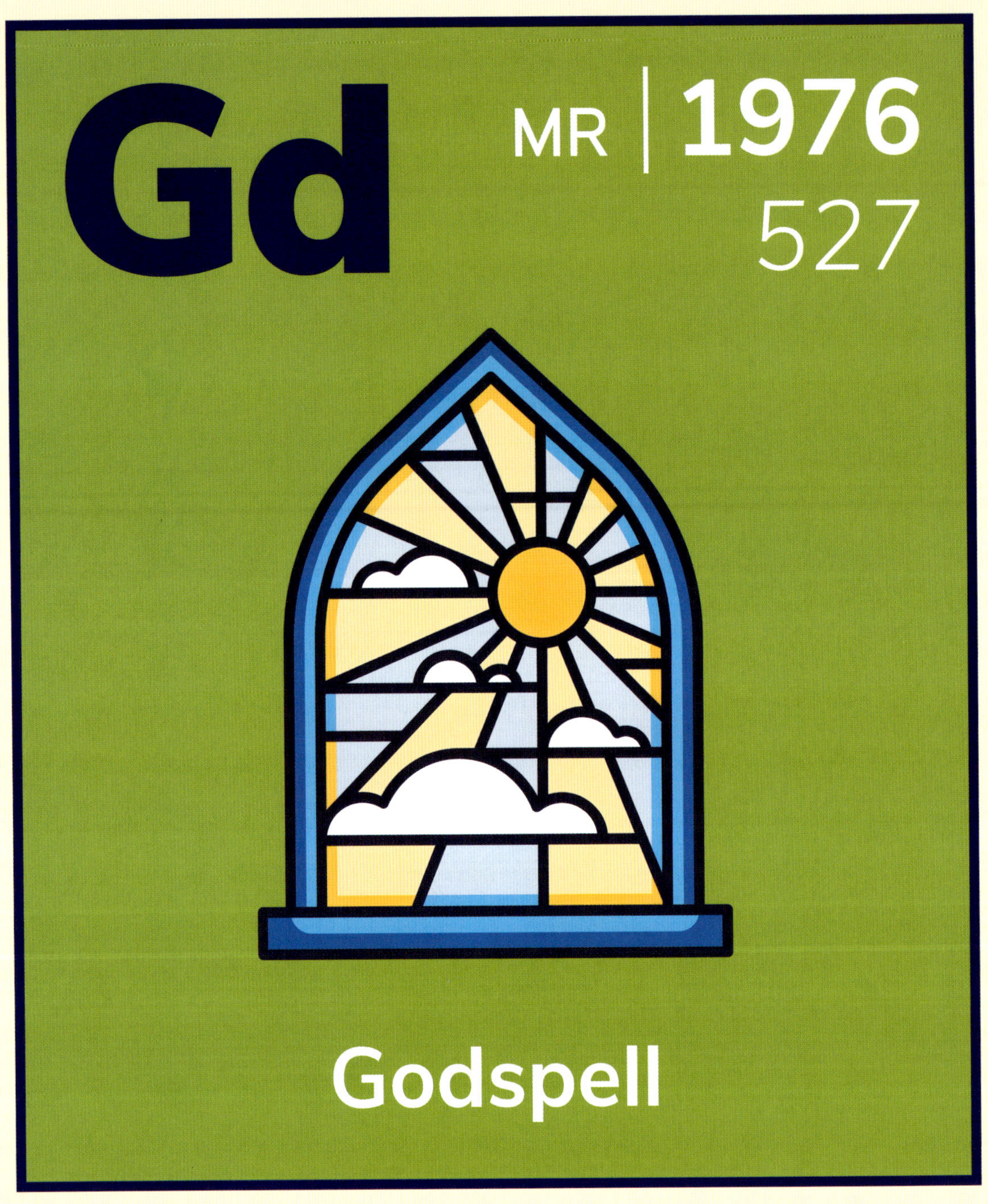

Music and lyrics by Stephen Schwartz
Based upon the Gospel According to St. Matthew
Conceived and directed by John-Michael Tebelak

Broadhurst Theatre*, June 22, 1976–September 4, 1977

Don Scardino.......Jesus

Tom Rolfing.......John the Baptist/Judas

ART NOTE: A folk-style church window showing the "Light of the World."

**First of three theatres*

An ensemble cast of ten portrays Biblical philosophers, apostles, and Jesus Christ in a group reenactment of Jesus's life and several of the Parables. The performers become a community, searching for answers together, even while Jesus's story plays out to its inevitable tragic conclusion.

Day by Day

Godspell was a Carnegie Mellon master's thesis that became a play with music that became an original musical that ran for three months downtown and then five years way uptown (the Upper West Side) before transferring to Broadway, where it ran for over a year. The scale of the little show's success is staggering: at one point it was running in eight different U.S. cities simultaneously, it had eight foreign productions, a movie version was made, and its hit song, "Day By Day," made it to the Billboard pop charts. Such was the improbable story of Stephen Schwartz's first work for the theatre. Schwartz was actually a late addition to *Godspell*, brought on to the project before its move to off-Broadway by John-Michael Tebelak (a fellow Carnegie Mellon alum) to replace the show's original songs. Schwartz's almost completely new score draws on a variety of musical styles from vaudeville to folk to pop, and his unique, eclectic voice attracted many new fans to musical theatre.

The off-Broadway cast was comprised of young, unknown performers (some from the original Carnegie Mellon production) who were not musical theatre regulars; notably, only three of the cast members who made the transfer to the Broadhurst were ever seen on Broadway again. The Toronto production, however, launched the careers of many future TV and stage stars, including Martin Short, Eugene Levy, Andrea Martin, Gilda Radner, and Victor Garber (who joined the off-Broadway cast and went on to play Jesus in the movie). These now well-known actors are all brilliant comedians, and *Godspell*'s tone was decidedly clownish—Jesus's costume consisted of a red nose, a red heart painted on his forehead, and a Superman T-shirt.

Though *Godspell* was a popular hit, many critics found its whimsy grating and its naivete phony. And like its Christian rock predecessor *Jesus Christ Superstar*, the show received criticism from fundamentalist Christians because it didn't portray Jesus's resurrection. Schwartz responded by saying the show was about the formation of a community, not specifically about Jesus; in effect, it's an ensemble show without a star.

Even though the dates listed here are its Broadway dates, it actually opened off-Broadway before Schwartz's other early hit, *Pippin*, which also had its beginnings at Carnegie Mellon. Schwartz credits those four years, in which he wrote a show a year, as teaching him much about how to put on a show.

MISCELLANEOUS MATTER

★ Schwartz had a total of five weeks to write the new songs between the day he saw the show and the day it went into rehearsal off-Broadway.

★ The movie version opened the 1973 Cannes Film Festival as an antidote to the "despair and bewilderment" its director said was a through-line in many of the festival's entries.

★ In 1972, a producer from South Africa petitioned for the rights to present it there, citing the importance of the show's message to the country. Schwartz refused on the grounds that the government's ban on racially integrated casts was the antithesis of "love thy neighbor as thyself" and that a segregated production of *Godspell* would be "the basest sort of hypocrisy."

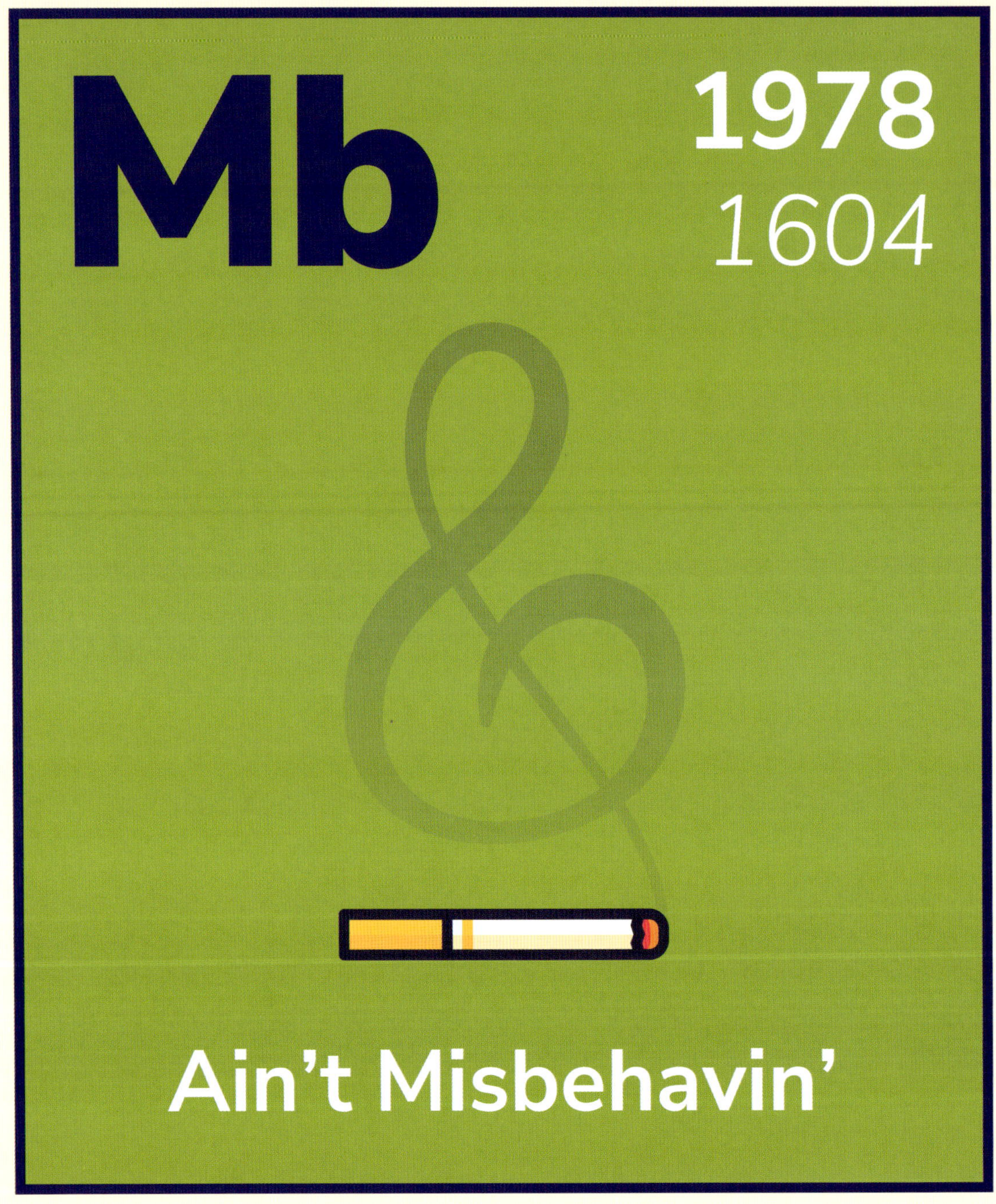

Music by Thomas "Fats" Waller, with Harry Brooks, Jimmy McHugh, and others
Lyrics by Andy Razaf, Ted Koehler, Richard Maltby Jr., and others
Based on an idea by Richard Maltby Jr. and Murray Horwitz
Directed by Richard Maltby Jr. ★ Musical staging by Arthur Faria

Longacre Theatre*, May 9, 1978–February 21, 1982

Starring Nell Carter, André De Shields, Armelia McQueen, Ken Page, and Charlayne Woodard

ART NOTE: A smoky treble clef wafts from one of Waller's trademark cigarettes; the Viper might have smoked something stronger . . .

*First of three theatres

Five actors (using their own names) celebrate the hard-swinging, joyous, and sometimes somber songs of pianist and composer Thomas "Fats" Waller, including the hits "Honeysuckle Rose" and the title song.

The Joint Is Jumpin'

The one-composer revue is a particularly tricky form to get right—many songwriters tend to write songs in a certain style or about similar subjects, without enough variety to sustain an entire evening. However, with the music of Thomas "Fats" Waller, the innovative jazz pianist and composer of more than 400 songs, writer Murray Horwitz knew he'd have more than enough material, and convinced director and lyricist Richard Maltby Jr. to collaborate on creating the show. Waller's high-energy swing, stomp, and stride piano dominated much of the first act, with songs about everything from the hottest music trends to wartime rationing. Act two brought an even wider range of subjects, insult songs like "Your Feet's Too Big" and "Fat and Greasy," and a celebration of a certain kind of misbehavin' called "The Viper's Drag."

But it was the inclusion of more serious numbers that elevated the show from just an entertainment to something more substantial. Nell Carter's "Mean to Me," performed with just a piano, was a mournful and deeply personal surprise. And "Black and Blue," with lyrics by the great Black lyricist and poet Andy Razaf, was a stunning five-minute ensemble number that took on the pain of racial discrimination. Since there were no characters, and no story, the song's powerful message—including lines like "My only sin is my skin"—felt like it was coming from the actors themselves.

The creative team's choices were bold and specific in every department. Choreographer Arthur Faria created intricate staging with a South Asian flair that somehow meshed perfectly with the sleek, stylish arrangements and piano playing of Luther Henderson. And Maltby leaned into the comedy of many of the songs, writing new lyrics for several and adding humorous staging touches like fake "altercations" between cast members. The five stars quickly made names for themselves, especially the laser-voiced Nell Carter, who learned to vary her vocals to match the songs.

The success of *Ain't Misbehavin'* led to Broadway revues celebrating other writers like jazz legends Eubie Blake (*Eubie!*) and Duke Ellington (*Sophisticated Ladies*), Jerry Herman (*Jerry's Girls*), and jazz and pop writers like Louis Jordan (*Five Guys Named Moe*) and Leiber and Stoller (*Smokey Joe's Cafe*). But *Ain't Misbehavin'*s combination of wit, bawdy humor, and real emotion set it above the rest, as acknowledged by its Tony Award for Best Musical.

MISCELLANEOUS MATTER

- ★ Horwitz started his career as a clown for Barnum & Bailey.
- ★ "Black and Blue" and the title song were originally in a 1929 Broadway revue called *Hot Chocolates*, which featured Louis Armstrong in his Broadway debut.
- ★ The role of Effie in *Dreamgirls* was originally written for Nell Carter.
- ★ Carter said her dream was "to be Judy Garland without the tragedy," but she died at age fifty-five, living only eight years longer than Garland.

Book, music, and lyrics by Rupert Holmes
Suggested by the unfinished novel by Charles Dickens
Directed by Wilford Leach ★ Choreographed by Graciela Daniele

Imperial Theatre, December 2, 1985–May 16, 1987

Betty Buckley.......Edwin Drood
Cleo Laine.......The Princess Puffer
Patti Cohenour.......Rosa Bud
Howard McGillin.......John Jasper

ART NOTE: An unfinished novel with a choose-your-own-ending voting card.

In this British music hall show-within-a-show, the cast enacts the story of an unfinished Charles Dickens murder mystery. At its center is young Edwin Drood, a rich orphan engaged to the pure-of-heart Rosa Bud; unfortunately, Rosa is also lusted after by Edwin's opium-addicted uncle Jasper and mysterious Neville Landless (an immigrant from Ceylon). When Edwin disappears, there's no shortage of suspects, so to complete Dickens's story, the audience must vote for who they think the murderer is.

A British Subject

When Gail Merrifield, the Public Theater's director of new play development, attended Rupert Holmes's nightclub act in 1983, she knew only that he was a successful pop songwriter whose songs had been recorded by Dolly Parton, Barry Manilow, and Barbra Streisand. But something in his act made Merrifield believe Holmes had the chops to write a musical. He was immediately interested in this idea and recalled a text he had loved since his childhood in England, Charles Dickens's *The Mystery of Edwin Drood.* Adaptations of works of literature were nothing new, but Holmes faced a unique challenge with *Drood*: Dickens had died before completing the book and revealing the murderer's identity.

Holmes saw this as an opportunity to play up what he loved about live theatre: the fact that it's different every night. He devised a mechanism whereby each audience could vote for who they wanted the murderer to be at that performance (as well as a happy couple to give the show a love story, and the real identity of a shadowy detective). He combined this ingenious device with a show-within-a-show framework, and a British music hall musical vocabulary to add to the evening's fun. The first draft he showed at the Public Theater clocked in at three hours and forty minutes. ("I offered to cut one number," quipped Holmes.) The show that eventually opened at the Public's outdoor Delacorte stage in Central Park ran just under three hours; the version that transferred to Broadway was shorter still.

But what the audience sees on stage at any given performance of *Drood* is far from all the material Holmes created. In order to satisfy the choose-your-own-ending structure, which included six potential murderers, each of whom needed a confession, he penned "an entire third act's worth" of material to cover any eventual outcome. The cast had to learn all six endings, of course, and after the audience voted (the theatre was divided into six groups, and votes tallied by cast members in the aisles), the results were tabulated backstage and the results passed discreetly to the performers onstage.

Rupert Holmes joined a very elite group of creatives who wrote music and lyrics *and* book for a Broadway musical (the list in 1985 included Frank Loesser and Meredith Willson; in the years since, however, it has grown to include Jonathan Larson, Lin-Manuel Miranda, Dave Malloy, Anaïs Mitchell, Michael R. Jackson, and Shaina Taub). Holmes, however, was the only one who also did his own orchestrations!

MISCELLANEOUS MATTER

★ The show officially changed its name to *Drood*, with the subtitle "The Music Hall Musical," *after* it won the Tony, the first show ever to do so.

★ Actors obviously only got to sing their confession if the audience voted for them; in a play to garner votes and more stage time, one actress started very unsubtly stashing a knife up her sleeve in the dinner table scene. She was asked to stop.

★ During the outdoor Delacorte run, Howard McGillin swallowed a bug during the act one finale; happily, only the song and not the actor came to "a premature end."

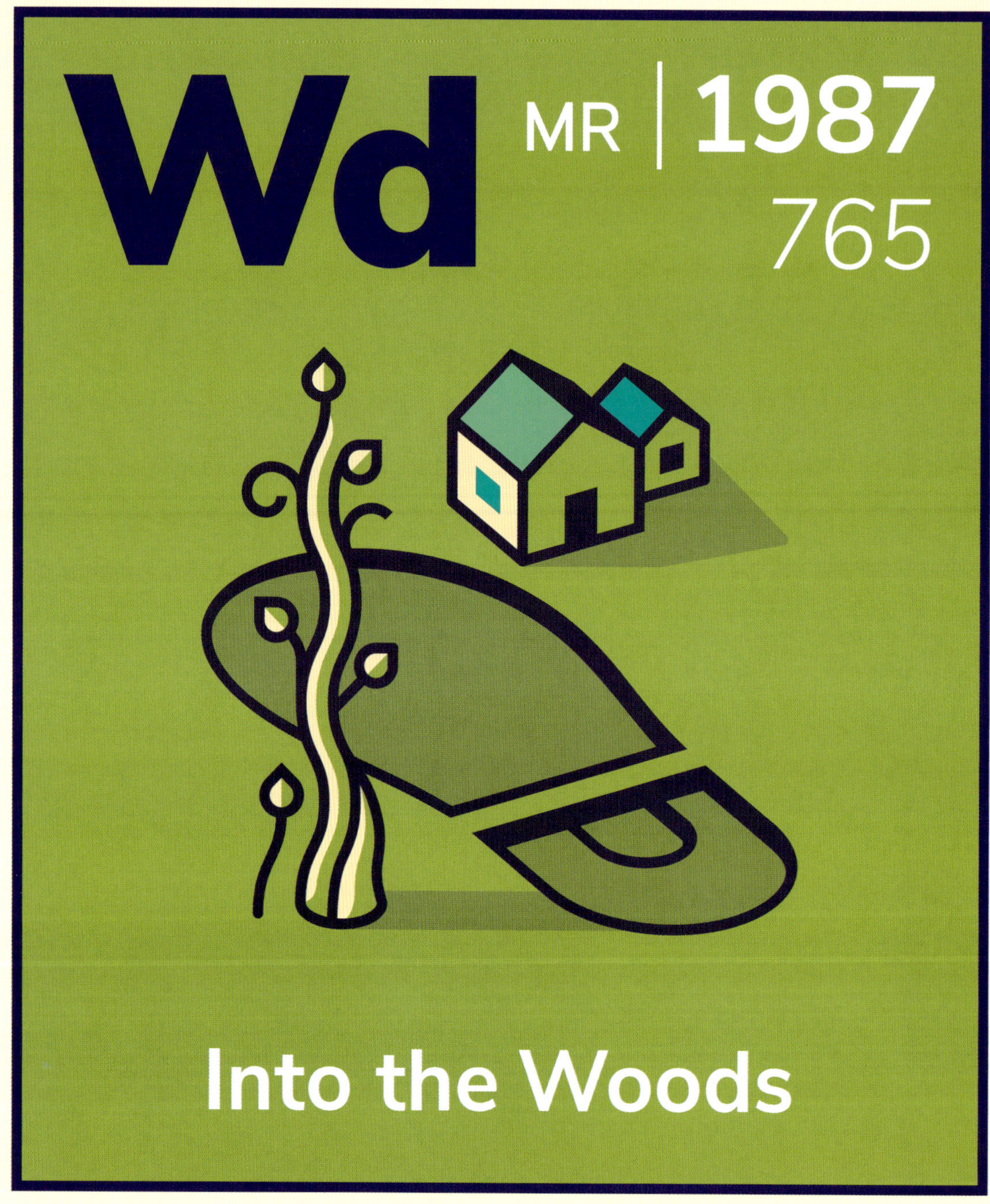

Book by James Lapine ★ Music and lyrics by Stephen Sondheim
Directed by James Lapine ★ Musical staging by Lar Lubovitch

Martin Beck Theatre, November 5, 1987–September 3, 1989

Bernadette Peters.......Witch
Joanna Gleason.......Baker's Wife
Chip Zien.......Baker
Danielle Ferland.......Little Red Riding Hood

ART NOTE: The Giant's footprint, the beanstalk she came down, and the Baker's and Witch's houses.

Characters from classic fairy tales cross paths in a forest: a childless baker and his wife, an old witch and her daughter, Rapunzel, Jack (of beanstalk fame), Cinderella and her family, two princes, and Little Red Riding Hood (and her Wolf). When a giant crashes down the beanstalk meaning to kill Jack, the resulting chaos forces each character to reevaluate their somewhat childish morality and grapple with what happens when you actually get what you wish for.

I Know Things Now

In a 2000 interview with Stephen Sondheim, critic Frank Rich began a question "When you grew up . . ." to which Sondheim shot back, "I never grew up." For those of us who consider Sondheim's shows to be the epitome of grown-up theatre, delving into the disappointment and ambivalence of conflicted and often unhappy characters, this statement is a bit surprising. *Into the Woods* was also a surprise for audiences, who for over twenty years had frequently chafed at the sometimes unpleasant and thorny subjects of Sondheim musicals; by 1987, they'd come to expect and even eagerly anticipate them. Where was the edge? Where were the veiled recriminations and simmering self-doubts? The master of urban disaffection had delivered a show filled with, as he called them, "ditties," sung by fairy-tale characters we all already knew and loved. Many critics predicted *Into the Woods* might become Sondheim's most accessible and successful show, but not everyone was happy about it.

Just as in Sondheim's previous collaboration with director and book writer James Lapine, *Sunday in the Park with George*, the intermission in *Into the Woods* is a great chasm, not in time but in tone. What seems like a clever bumper-car collision of different fairy tales in act one becomes something darker; when the curtain rises again, there's now a vengeful Lady Giant crashing through the woods. Some audiences in 1987, searching for deeper, darker meanings from a Sondheim show, read her as an AIDS crisis analogue; in the 2002 revival, some viewed the Giant as a reference to 9/11. Sondheim insisted no larger meaning was intended.

The transformation of the Witch from old crone to beauty is one of the delights of any production. The role itself underwent a transformation when megastar Bernadette Peters volunteered to join the ensemble cast, immediately changing the audience's expectations of what had been just another ensemble role. (Star role it has remained; for the excellent 2014 movie adaptation, they hired Meryl Streep.) But in the end, the authors maintain her position as merely one more character trying to find her path through the Woods. Her character also allows for some of that trademark Sondheim edge: the most unpleasant character ends up having the truest things to say.

MISCELLANEOUS MATTER

★ During the run, a two-story-tall parade-style balloon of the Giant's booted foot was draped over the side of the Martin Beck Theatre.

★ In one point of the development process, the narrator was the Baker's son, not his father, giving the character an entirely different reason for telling the story.

★ The voice of the Giantess is often pre-recorded by a celebrity; Judi Dench, Glenn Close, and Whoopi Goldberg have all taken their turn terrorizing the Woods' inhabitants.

★ The "Witch's Rap" section of the Prologue is all that remains of an original plan to give each character a different musical style: rap for the Witch, operetta for Cinderella, blues for the Wolf, etc.

Book and lyrics by Lynn Ahrens ★ Music by Stephen Flaherty
Based on the novel *My Love, My Love* by Rosa Guy
Directed and choreographed by Graciela Daniele

Booth Theatre, October 18, 1990–December 1, 1991

LaChanze.......Ti Moune
Jerry Dixon.......Daniel
Eric Riley.......Papa Ge
Kecia Lewis-Evans.......Asaka

ART NOTE: The rich stranger's car that sparks Ti Moune's curiosity.

In this Caribbean retelling of The Little Mermaid, *the gods wager whether love is stronger than death. Papa Ge (Death) allows Ti Moune, a poor girl, to trade her life for a nobleman's who is badly injured in a car crash. They fall in love, and though the nobleman must marry another, Ti Moune refuses Papa Ge's offer to go back on the deal if she kills him, thereby proving love is the stronger force.*

The Human Heart

Once on This Island opened in October of 1990—only the second Broadway musical to open that year, after *Aspects of Love* six months earlier. It's no wonder this vibrant, kinetic, and home-grown musical captured audiences' and critics' hearts. With few exceptions, musicals in the 1980s had grown bigger and bigger; just six months after *Once on This Island* opened, *Miss Saigon* arrived, featuring a helicopter landing on stage and symbolizing for many the triumph of spectacle over substance.

Lynn Ahrens had been writing songs for popular children's TV shows like *Schoolhouse Rock* when she met Flaherty, twelve years her junior. Ahrens happened to pick up a copy of *My Love, My Love* in a bookstore and was charmed by the romantic fable. Two years later, the show opened off-Broadway at Playwrights Horizons on 42nd Street, at the time the preeminent incubator of new musicals. It marked the first time well-known choreographer Graciela Daniele directed a production, and she combined her Argentinian background and ballet training to create an evening of nearly nonstop calypso, African, and European-derived movement that set the small theatre on fire. Ahrens and Flaherty, whose *Lucky Stiff* had played Playwrights the year before, likewise channeled Caribbean rhythms and simpler folk tale language to great effect, earning them Tony nominations for their first Broadway show. It was also the first major Broadway role for LaChanze, who lit up the stage as the yearning Ti Moune.

But it was a return to the most basic, primal storytelling rituals that felt like the freshest breeze coming off this *Island.* The actors, when not portraying the story's characters, were just people telling us the tale, as if around a fire, or as a parent might read a fairy tale to a child. The sets were made from homespun elements like a giant quilt and the hand-painted impressionistic murals of designer Loy Arcenas; minimal changes were made to the design when the show transferred to the larger Booth Theatre, most notably a new proscenium arch of decorated packing crates. This feeling of a communal event is further evoked by the opening and closing numbers, "We Dance" and "Why We Tell the Story," which make palpable the essential human need to create art and share it with each other.

MISCELLANEOUS MATTER

- ★ The West End premiere won the Olivier Award for Best New Musical. Sharon D. Clarke, who was nominated for playing Asaka, was later nominated for a Tony for her star performance in the 2022 revival of *Caroline, or Change.*
- ★ The Tony Award–winning 2018 revival was staged in the round in the aftermath of a hurricane and featured, among other things, a goat in diapers.
- ★ One of Zendaya's earliest roles was as Little Ti Moune in a production at Berkeley Playhouse.
- ★ LaChanze became the first female producer to win two Tonys on the same night in 2023, for the revival of the play *Topdog/Underdog* and the musical *Kimberly Akimbo.*

Book by William Finn and James Lapine ★ Music and lyrics by William Finn
Directed by James Lapine

John Golden Theatre, April 29, 1992–June 27, 1993

Stephen Bogardus.......Whizzer
Michael Rupert.......Marvin
Chip Zien.......Mendel
Barbara Walsh.......Trina

ART NOTE: "Four Jews in a Room Bitching" represented as pieces from "The Chess Game" (Jason is the pawn in the middle).

"Homosexuals, women with children, short insomniacs . . . and the lesbians from next door," in a story of love, death, and chosen families. In brief: Marvin divorced Trina to be with Whizzer. Trina marries Marvin's psychiatrist. Whizzer and Marvin fight. Dr. Charlotte sees worrying signs of a new disease emerging. And adolescent Jason just tries to keep up. When Whizzer falls ill in act two, everyone must come to terms with what it costs to love people more deeply than they intended.

I Never Wanted to Love You

Falsettos followed a long and winding path to Broadway. Its two acts, set only two years apart in 1979 and 1981, began life as two one-act off-Broadway shows written a full nine years apart, and its small size and challenging subject matter had producers wondering what to do with it. The first of those one-acts, *March of the Falsettos* (which itself was a follow-up to yet another one-act, *In Trousers*), received raves for its freshness and topicality in 1981; it addressed gay and straight relationships with humor and a frank and bracingly conversational tone. Finn's third one-act musical about Marvin, 1990's *Falsettoland,* dealt with the tragedy and trauma that had emerged over the intervening years since *March of the Falsettos*, namely the AIDS crisis. When the two pieces were combined, the transition from light to dark gave the combined two-act *Falsettos* its affecting humanity.

The characters in *Falsettos* do not have everything figured out. They can barely keep up with a changing world, and they express themselves with a self-knowing and often frantic irony that was miles away from Golden Age composers like Jerry Herman, whose soignée 1983 *La Cage aux Folles* had likewise dealt with a gay couple. But Finn didn't embrace the in-your-face modern musical energy of contemporary smash hits *Dreamgirls* or *Evita* either, and he sprinted in the opposite direction from the '80s onslaught of European pop operas like *The Phantom of the Opera* and *Les Misérables*. This was a chamber musical with acoustic instruments (the original *March of the Falsettos* wasn't even amplified), about intimate relationships, with all their flaws on parade. Did it even belong on Broadway?

With a show that was not only very gay, but very, very Jewish, and had a leading character die of AIDS, it's not surprising that producers Fran and Barry Weissler burned through $800,000 on advertising to connect with a mainstream audience they believed was out there. They landed on a series of audience testimonies, from Midwest families to nuns to Miss America to Dr. Ruth, each giving their own somewhat hokey thumbs up (or, in the case of a rabbi, a four-star-of-David review). Audiences who gave the show a shot quickly became converts—Michael Rupert remembered routinely seeing stoic faces gradually soften and finally tear up as the intimate moments of this quirky extended family resonated with their own, no matter how different they appeared.

MISCELLANEOUS MATTER

★ It would take more than thirty years for another intimate, gay-centered musical, *Fun Home*, to follow *Falsettos*'s footsteps from off-Broadway to Broadway; *Fun Home* would close just six weeks before a Tony-nominated *Falsettos* revival opened in 2016.

★ When asked if the show was a hit, Fran Weissler replied, "A nervous hit. We never know in the morning whether we'll have an audience that night. There's still no advance. But the people keep coming."

★ Rupert, the original Marvin, played the character on and off for twelve years, ceding the role to Mandy Patinkin in January 1993. In 2007's *Legally Blonde*, Rupert appeared with Christian Borle, who played Marvin in the 2016 revival.

Book by Pete Townshend and Des McAnuff
Based on the album *Tommy* by The Who
Music and lyrics by Pete Townshend
Directed by Des McAnuff ★ Choreographed by Wayne Cilento

St. James Theatre, April 22, 1993–June 17, 1995

Michael Cerveris.......Tommy
Jonathan Dokuchitz.......Captain Walker
Marcia Mitzman.......Mrs. Walker
Paul Kandel.......Uncle Ernie

ART NOTE: Tommy in front of a musical pinball machine.

Young Tommy Walker witnesses his father kill his mother's boyfriend and becomes deaf, blind, and mute. When he demonstrates a surprising talent for pinball, Tommy becomes a minor celebrity; when he suddenly regains his senses, he transforms into a major star. But when his fans try to turn him into a kind of spiritual cult leader, he rejects them and returns to his family, reunifying with his younger selves in the process.

Smash the Mirror

Rock music and Broadway have always had a wary relationship. Rock's beginnings as counter-cultural rebellion have rarely meshed with Broadway's mainstream ambitions: producers pursue material they think will please enough of the general audience to earn investors money. At its heart, Broadway wants to please; rock wants to break things.

Before *The Who's Tommy*, there had been *Hair*, but that show's counter-cultural ambitions didn't lead to an era of real rock shows. While *Jesus Christ Superstar* had some sections that felt like genuine guitar-smashing, the nominal descendants of *Hair*—shows like *Dreamgirls*, *The Wiz*, *Grease*, *Rent*—were musical theatre pieces first, interested in telling stories with intricate lyrics and fully-drawn characters much more than they were primal rock screams. Rock was a condiment, not the meal. So when this staged version of the seminal double concept album *Tommy*, originally released in 1969 by British rock superstars The Who, opened at the St. James in 1993 with a book by the band's lead guitarist, audiences ate it up.

The show played like a fever dream, with wall-to-wall music, intricate, kinetic staging, and urgent and inventive choreography. The guitars were ferocious, the drums were in your face. Shattered projections towered over a mostly dark stage slashed with what looked like glowing guitar strings. It was definitely a new look, and as close to rock as Broadway had ever gotten.

But what about rock purists? They had a more mixed reaction, which at its roots comes down to how rock albums are created. There is a homemade quality about the original *Tommy*—Roger Daltry's lead vocals are heartfelt, with great rock texture, but a long way from the obviously trained tenor of Michael Cerveris. There is also no way to replicate how an audience heard The Who in 1969—twenty-five years later, the sound simply couldn't be as fresh or dangerous. And expert dancers and actors sincerely portraying all the characters in a sumptuous production will never be the same as sitting in front of the stereo in your den as a few guys spin a weird, raw story. The feel of the music was close—perhaps as close as it can ever be—to real rock; the experience, however, was something else, something new, and for many, something wonderful.

MISCELLANEOUS MATTER

- ★ One reason Townshend was open to creating the Broadway version was that when McAnuff first called to discuss it, he had smashed his wrist in a bike accident and his doctor told him he'd never play the piano again with his right hand.
- ★ To make up for rapidly rising ticket prices, the producers offered bonus giveaways like free CDs, T-shirts, and souvenir programs.
- ★ The show set a day-after-opening record for ticket sales, nearly $500,000.
- ★ Trap doors were added to the stage deck to allow for WWII paratroopers to jump through the floor.

Book by Jeff Whitty ★ Music and lyrics by Robert Lopez and Jeff Marx
Directed by Jason Moore ★ Choreographed by Ken Roberson
Puppets conceived and designed by Rick Lyon

John Golden Theatre, July 31, 2003–September 13, 2009

Stephanie D'Abruzzo.....Kate Monster and others
Jordan Gelber.......Brian
Ann Harada.......Christmas Eve
John Tartaglia.......Princeton/Rod

ART NOTE: A human and a "monster" find a moment of connection.

A cast of humans and puppet "monsters" inhabit an apartment building in an outer borough of New York City that more than a little bit resembles TV's Sesame Street. *But unlike that children's TV classic, these characters grapple with adult problems that aren't so easily solved, including racism, homophobia, heartbreak, and finding one's purpose in life. In the end, they simply shrug, because everything, bad and good, is "only for now."*

What Do You Do with a B.A. in English?

Like *Raisin*, the songwriters for *Avenue Q* met in the BMI Lehman Engel Musical Theatre workshop where mostly inexperienced writers go to meet collaborators, try their hands at creating mini-musicals, and receive feedback from industry pros. Marx and Lopez quickly found they had similar senses of humor, and they bonded over their (and many Gen Xer's) love of the Muppets. They decided to write a version of Hamlet for the Muppets called *Kermit, Prince of Denmark*, which though successful at BMI, didn't end up impressing the Henson estate enough to grant them the rights.

So they made use of their experience writing for puppets and puppeteers and wrote an original story centered on the near-universal plight of twenty-somethings straight out of college. Originally imagined as a TV show, when it became clear *Avenue Q* would become a theatre piece instead, they made the decision not to hide the puppeteers; just as Harold Prince had done in *Pacific Overtures*, they leaned on the centuries-old Japanese *bunraku* tradition, where puppeteers are dressed in grays and blacks so that, after a few moments, the audience's eye forgets they're there.

When the show opened at off-Broadway's Vineyard Theatre in the spring of 2003, the combination of irreverent, borderline offensive subject matter coming out of the mouths of adorable puppets made it an immediate hit. Many wondered, however, if its cheerful/cynical Gen X vibe would play on Broadway. However, when the transfer opened, it not only represented a welcome contrast to the numerous serious offerings that season (Adam Guettel's *Light in the Piazza*, Ricky Ian Gordon's *My Life with Albertine*, Jeanine Tesori's *Caroline, or Change*), it achieved a stunning upset by winning the Tony Award for Best Musical over the crowd-pleaser *Wicked.* Equally stunning was its producers' decision not to tour the show, as is traditional and expected, but instead to mount a sit-down production in a newly built 1,200-seat house in Las Vegas. In another production first, when the Broadway production closed, *Avenue Q* was able to successfully return to its off-Broadway roots, setting up shop at New World Stages for a further ten-year run. With this additional proof of its broad and lasting appeal, it's clear that *Avenue Q*, with its cuddly characters, alternatively raunchy and erudite humor, and message of solidarity with young people struggling to define themselves, was more than "only for now."

MISCELLANEOUS MATTER

★ When Brian and Christmas Eve got married, they wore white yarmulkes with a red sun design to honor both characters' heritages (Jewish and Japanese).

★ The show's title is a reference to *123 Avenue B,* which was the original working title for *Sesame Street.* There are real lettered avenues A–Z in Brooklyn, but no Avenue Q; instead, where it should be, is Quentin Road.

★ "Gary Coleman," one of the show's characters, is based on the '80s child TV star of the same name. The actual Coleman wasn't happy about his portrayal, though the writers depicted him as someone who overcame disappointment. When he died during the run, they retained the character as a tribute.

Book by Bob Martin and Don McKellar
Music and lyrics by Lisa Lambert and Greg Morrison
Directed and choreographed by Casey Nicholaw

Marquis Theatre, May 1, 2006–December 30, 2007

Bob Martin.......Man in Chair
Sutton Foster.......Janet Van De Graaff
Beth Leavel.......The Drowsy Chaperone
Danny Burstein.......Aldolpho

ART NOTE: Man in Chair's comfy chair, plus an old-fashioned record player from the 1920s.

A "non-specifically sad" man sits in his apartment, listening to his favorite 1920s musical, and offering us commentary on its cast, characters, and story. As we listen, the show comes to life around him, a silly confection of antique stereotypes, mistaken identities, and hackneyed plot twists. Hints of his own melancholy love life come to light as he interprets the show's lyrics (and glitches in the LP), and at the end, the characters gather around him to lift his spirits.

As We Stumble Along

What wedding present do you get for one of the leading comedy writers in Canada and his comedian fiancée? Why, an original show, of course, one that sends up their favorite 1920s musical comedies. That's what songwriters Lisa Lambert and Greg Morrison and playwright Don Kellar did for their friend Bob Martin, and it was such a hit they moved the piece to the Toronto Fringe, adding a character for the groom himself. Martin's Man in Chair, a self-effacingly depressed musical theatre obsessive, instantly became a classic.

The show took the idea of an ensemble piece to a new level, with a lot of the material created or inspired by the actors themselves in a series of theatre games early in the Los Angeles rehearsal process. In one, cast members were put in the "hot seat" (playing the actors within the show) and peppered with questions from other actors pretending to be members of the press. These improvised moments (as well as stories from the real actors' lives) often made it into Martin's script, leading to a richness of detail that brought the world to life and giving the whole cast a sense of ownership of the piece. Cast members still like to meet with any casts working on a new production to continue this process, encouraging them to create their own character backstories.

Man in Chair remained the center of the show. The character embodied the unabashed love for Broadway musicals that many audience members had begun to question after shows like 2001's *Urinetown* and the previous year's *Spamalot* had made traditional Broadway tropes the butt of their jokes. It also gave the show its surprising heart, because as the evening progresses, we realize the show he's listening to, "The Drowsy Chaperone," is not actually very good. The plot is intentionally flimsy, the songs and characters paper thin, and our heart goes out to him as he realizes that the object of his obsession is second-rate.

After a brief poignant detour into details about Man in Chair's rocky love life, there is a happy ending . . . or at least an uplifting one. As the final curtain descends, and the cast/characters of the show-within-a-show acknowledge Man in Chair and welcome him into their world (and onto a plane), our heart soars. Because wouldn't we all want to live, if just for a moment, inside a classic musical?

MISCELLANEOUS MATTER

- ★ The tag line for the Broadway production was "A musical within a comedy." The authors preferred "You'll swear you've heard it before," which the New York producers didn't understand.
- ★ When the show opened in Melbourne, Oscar-winning Australian actor Geoffrey Rush played Man in Chair; Bob Martin said he was the best he'd ever seen.
- ★ Every cast member leaving the company was subject to a "$40 dare," which they had to perform during their last show to win the money. Foster's dare was to faint at the end of act one, which she did—at the top of a long staircase that she then slid down, one step at a time, as the company held the long last note of the number.

THE ENTERTAINERS

INSTANTANEOUS CATALYSTS FOR FUN

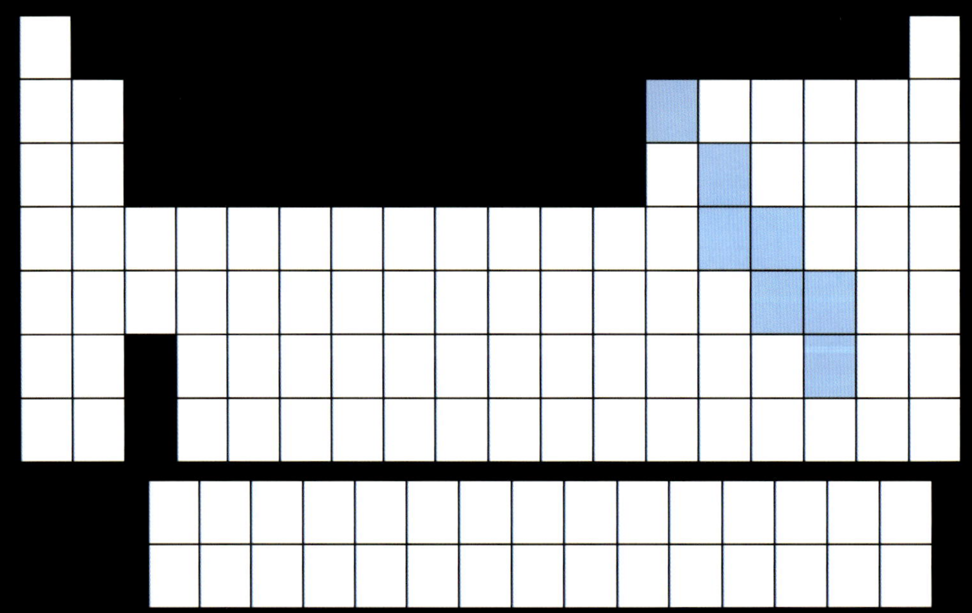

Some shows have social relevance. Some have serious messages about human frailty or smiling through tragedy. Others are bold and innovative, using the basic building blocks of words, music, and movement to create something totally new and unique. And some . . . well, their only aspiration is to be fun and delightful. Silly, even. That's it—no profundities, no moral ambiguities. This type of musical has nothing on its mind except to make an audience laugh, cheer, and maybe tap their toes a little.

The shows in this family are that kind.

"Musical theatre" and "musical comedy" were once basically synonymous. Who wanted a musical if it wasn't a comic delight, full of romance and silliness, a diversion from everyday life and pedestrian woes? The earliest book musicals, the so-called Princess Theatre Shows by the young trio of composer Jerome Kern, lyricist Guy Bolton, and British humorist P. G. Wodehouse, featured drunken socialites, botched engagements, and missing jewels. Through the 1920s and '30s (with the great exception of *Show Boat*), musicals continued to provide mostly light entertainment, show biz capers, and the hijinks of vaudeville stars. With very few exceptions, their ludicrous stories and dated references make them unrevivable.

The Golden Age brought a new sophistication to the form, as writers added deeper psychological insights and social commentary to their shows. These more mature stories expanded the form and for a while pushed shows aside whose only aspiration was to be fun and delightful. But pendulums swing, and soon after *West Side Story* brought full tragedy to musical theatre, unabashedly silly shows started cropping up again, and since the '60s have happily coexisted with more serious ones.

A culture's sense of humor is famously ever evolving, with gags that tickle one generation falling flat for the next, so it's a testament to these creators that these shows still kill. It's also fitting that the first of them is by Princess Theatre alum Guy Bolton, and the last one an homage to the Bard himself, who also knew a thing or two about how to keep a crowd entertained.

Book by Guy Bolton and P. G. Wodehouse
Revised by Howard Lindsay and Russel Crouse
Music and lyrics by Cole Porter
Directed by Howard Lindsay ★ Dances and ensembles by Robert Alton

Alvin Theatre and 46th Street Theatre, November 21, 1934–November 16, 1935

Ethel Merman.......Reno Sweeney
William Gaxton.......Billy Crocker
Victor Moore.......Moonface Martin
Bettina Hall.......Hope Harcourt

ART NOTE: A jubilant party seen through a ship's porthole, with confetti, Champagne bottles, and Gabriel's trumpet.

In this frothy maritime romp, a young Wall Street broker stows away on an ocean liner to pursue an heiress engaged to a British nobleman. Also on the ship are a nightclub-singer-turned-evangelist and a gangster posing as a priest. Over the course of the evening, pretenders are unmasked, plots are hatched and bungled, songs are sung and dances danced, and somehow everyone ends up with the right romantic partner before the ship docks.

I Get a Kick Out of You

There aren't many shows from the 1930s in the Periodic Table, and for good reason: as a whole, they don't date well. The scores, by songwriting greats like George Gershwin, Rodgers and Hart, and Cole Porter can be chock-full of beloved songs, but the plots are generally slapdash affairs that only exist to set up the hit tunes and now seem utterly ridiculous. This was certainly true of *Anything Goes*, which features the classics "I Get a Kick Out of You," "You're the Top," "All Through the Night," and, of course, the title tune, but whose original plot was so disposable that the producer actually did dispose of it.

He had a good reason, though. The original plot of *Anything Goes* revolved around a disaster at sea, but just weeks before the show started rehearsal, the passenger ship *SS Morro Castle* caught fire and more than 100 people were killed, making that story suddenly seem in poor taste and likely to sink at the box office. At that point, the show's original librettists were unavailable, so producer Vinton Freedly asked the show's director Howard Lindsay and production press agent Russel Crouse to concoct a new story that would work with the score Cole Porter had already completed. Not only did the two successfully fulfill their assignment, but their accidental pairing also led to one of Broadway's most durable and successful partnerships—among Lindsay and Crouse's later works were the long-running play *Life with Father* and the book for *The Sound of Music*.

Over the years, each major revival has continued to revise the book to suit the changing tastes and senses of humor of the day, and to interpolate additional Porter classics into the score. Porter's lyrics have been tweaked, too. Sometimes it was his risqué wit that necessitated the change (in the song "Anything Goes," the references to "green pears," "back stairs" and "young bears"—each a kind of lover—were too salacious for some censors), while at other times his penchant for topical references made some once-funny jokes now completely obscure.

What's never changed is the audience response: sheer rapture. *Anything Goes* delivers everything you expect when you hear the words "musical comedy"—some great tap dancing, big laughs, a brassy leading lady, tuneful songs, and (of course) a happy ending. The perfect escape from everyday life.

MISCELLANEOUS MATTER

- ★ Ethel Merman was a favorite of Cole Porter, and he tailored the songs for Reno Sweeney to suit her clarion voice. The role has become a showcase for Broadway belters, with later revivals featuring Patti Lupone, Leslie Uggams, Sutton Foster, and Stephanie J. Block.
- ★ The roles of Billy Crocker and Moonface Martin were originally penned for the well-known comedy team William Gaxton and Victor Moore, with Gaxton's popular disguise-swapping shtick written into the story.
- ★ Though not well-remembered now, choreographer Robert Alton had a long career on Broadway (and in Hollywood), choreographing several other Cole Porter shows, a number of *Ziegfeld Follies*, the controversial hit *Pal Joey*, and the movie versions of *Annie Get Your Gun* and *Show Boat*.

Book by Michael Stewart ★ Music by Charles Strouse ★ Lyrics by Lee Adams
Directed and choreographed by Gower Champion

Martin Beck Theatre*, April 14, 1960–October 7, 1961

Dick Van Dyke.......Albert Peterson
Chita Rivera.......Rose Alvarez
Paul Lynde.......Mr. MacAfee
Susan Watson.......Kim MacAfee

ART NOTE: Birdie's signature hairstyle (which is really all he is), and the traces of "One Last Kiss."

*First of three theatres

Albert's music managing business is in debt, and his biggest star, Conrad Birdie, has just been drafted. His secretary and long-term fiancée Rose cooks up a publicity stunt where Birdie will give a small-town girl one last kiss before shipping out. But when they get to the town, everything goes haywire as Conrad's antics and national press coverage pit kids against parents (and each other) in a hormone-driven frenzy. When Conrad departs, Rose convinces Albert to finally become an English teacher.

We Love You, Conrad!

In January 1956, a Mississippi-born singer named Elvis Presley released his first single for RCA; by September, he was guest starring on all the major TV shows, causing riots at his concerts, and outrage from critics and politicians alike at his pelvic gyrations and "vulgar animalism." By 1958, impersonations and spoofs of his unique style were everywhere, and when he was drafted into the Army, it was a major news event.

Gower Champion was a veteran of a different type of American entertainment. During the 1950s, he and his wife, Marge, appeared as a Fred-and-Ginger-style dancing team in seven classic movie musicals for MGM and Paramount, and were regulars on TV variety shows. But this period would be a decade-long interruption in a Broadway career that had already earned Champion a Tony (for choreographing 1948's *Lend an Ear*). *Bye Bye Birdie* would be his first time directing and choreographing, joining Agnes de Mille, Jerome Robbins, and Bob Fosse in the dual role that was transforming how Broadway shows were created. Decidedly not a fan of rock and roll (he thought it a fad), Champion had no interest in creating another Elvis spoof; he was interested in looking at the effect an Elvis-type star had on everyday Americans, young and old.

He and producer Edward Padula also wanted to create a family-friendly show, with wholesome teeny-boppers instead of the knife-wielding gang members of the recently closed *West Side Story*. The story came together slowly under Champion's precise and demanding eye, led by his unswerving instinct for how to entertain an audience; he also devised scene changes using techniques borrowed from the movies. For example, to show Birdie's train trip from New York City to Sweet Apple, Ohio, the steam from the train's departure in Penn Station masked the ensemble's costume change from businesspeople to small town fans as a sign for the Sweet Apple depot flew in, achieving a cinematic cross-fade effect. This kind of scene change would quickly take over Broadway and allow for a much more fluid and fast-paced evening.

If the finished *Bye Bye Birdie* felt a bit old-fashioned, with musical numbers that were hugely inventive or great fun but really didn't advance the plot, audiences loved it as much as Conrad's fan clubs loved him (without all the shrieking). Though it was the first musical to open that season, it upset heavy-hitter *Camelot*, winning the Tony Award for Best Musical.

MISCELLANEOUS MATTER

- ★ The role of Albert's mother has attracted great character actresses from the beginning. Kay Medford, the original Mae, went on to play Fanny Brice's mother in *Funny Girl*. Film and theatre royalty Maureen Stapleton played the role for the 1963 movie (though she was only six months older than Dick Van Dyke).
- ★ The orchestrations by Robert "Red" Ginzler were a landmark of wit and innovation. His writing for the reed section, which unusually demanded four flutes, was especially notable and gave the show its perfect sparkle and innocence.
- ★ Chita Rivera was a late addition to the cast, and when she joined, Rose's last name was changed from Grant to Alvarez.

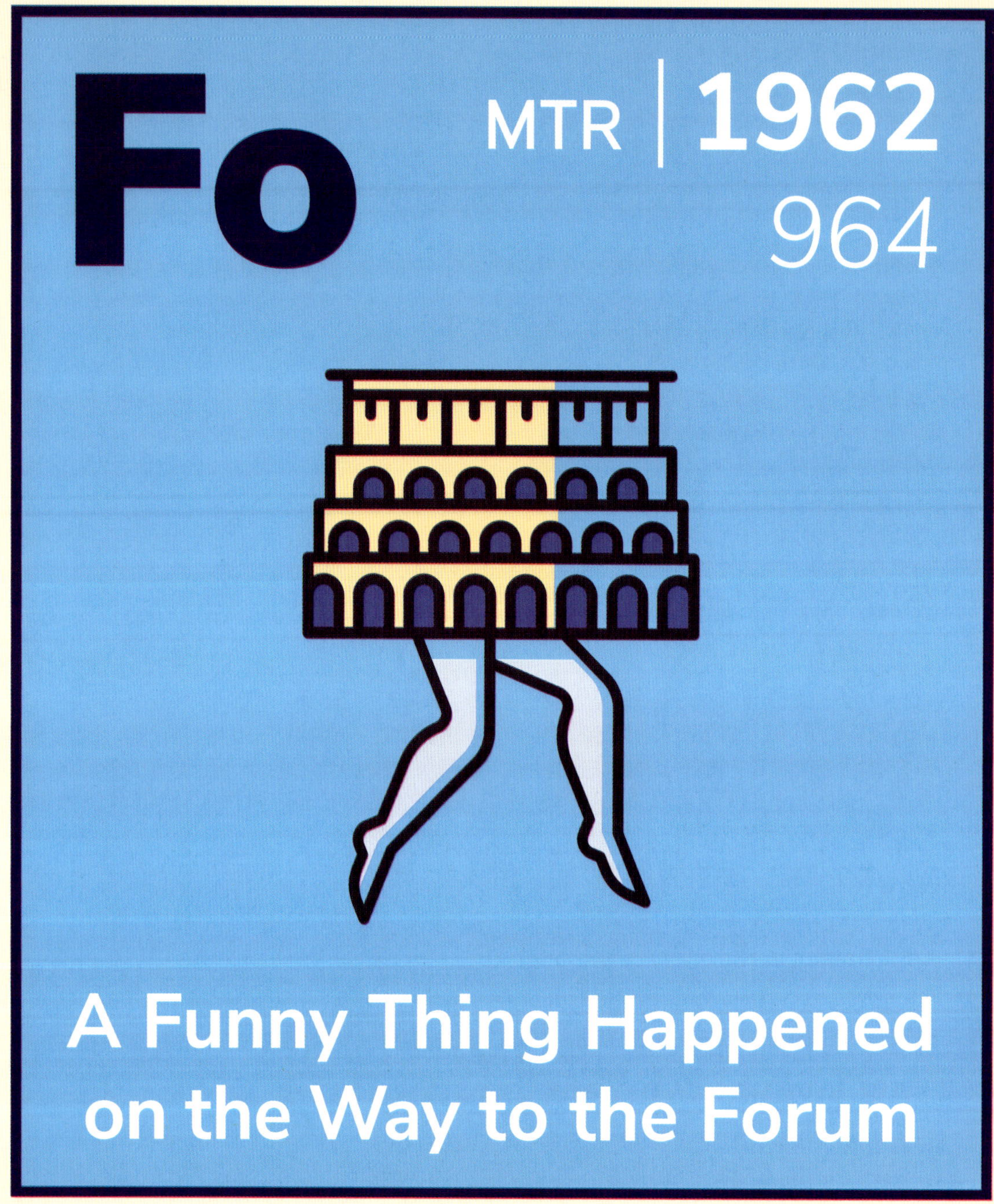

Book by Burt Shevelove and Larry Gelbart
Music and lyrics by Stephen Sondheim
Directed by George Abbott ★ Choreographed by Jack Cole

Alvin Theatre*, May 8, 1962–August 29, 1964

Zero Mostel.......Pseudolus
Jack Gilford.......Hysterium
Ronald Holgate.......Miles Gloriosus
John Carradine.......Marcus Lycus

ART NOTE: The Roman Colosseum scampering about on "Lovely" courtesan legs.

*First of three theatres

Pseudolus, a slave in ancient Rome, will do anything to win his freedom, including trying to hook his master's son up with a courtesan who lives next door (who is unfortunately already promised to a war hero). Countless lies, disguises, and a bottle of mare's sweat later, the entire block is totally tied in knots; only the revelation of two long-lost siblings allows for everyone to end up with the correct romantic partner (or at least a beautiful courtesan).

Impossible

Forum (as it's now generally known) has some of the most obscure source material ever for a musical: the comic plays of Plautus, a hit playwright of ancient Rome. Even more unexpectedly, the show's book writers decided to transform these ancient texts into a lowbrow celebration of baggy-pants slapstick and burlesque innuendo. Shevelove and Gelbart also took a chance on a first-time Broadway composer: Stephen Sondheim. A highly trained musician, Sondheim had previously had to settle for lyrics-only gigs on *West Side Story* and *Gypsy*, in deference to composers Bernstein's and Styne's greater fame and experience. He later claimed this was his most difficult score to write, since the songs needed to serve as necessary breaks from the high-paced hijinks rather than furthering the story or illuminating character (Sondheim's specialties).

Zero Mostel's zany, endlessly inventive performance as Pseudolus immediately made him a musical theatre star (his next role, Tevye in *Fiddler on the Roof*, would make him a legend). Though he hadn't been the producers' first choice, the paunchy, rubber-faced actor was on a professional roll, having won the 1961 Tony Award for Best Actor for the play *Rhinoceros*, in which he transformed into the titular beast in front of the audience without makeup or prosthetics. The performer's onstage agility was even more astonishing in light of the fact that, offstage, Mostel lived in near-constant pain, the result of having his left leg crushed by a city bus in 1960.

The other main key to *Forum*'s success was director/choreographer Jerome Robbins. Though not officially working on the production, he was called in when the show was struggling out of town—the few audience members who showed up simply weren't laughing. Robbins's immediate diagnosis: the show's opening number, the lilting "Love Is in the Air," prepared them for a gentle evening of romantic complications, not a night of belly laughs. Robbins asked Sondheim to write a number that would let audiences know they were in for a comedy, but with one stipulation: "Don't write any jokes, Steve. Leave those to me." In less than a week, Robbins gave the new song, "Comedy Tonight," a frenetic, gag-filled staging, and when it went into the show just before opening night in New York, it had audiences howling. Quite literally, that one song saved the show, turning an almost-certain flop into an enormous hit.

MISCELLANEOUS MATTER

★ Holgate, who created the role of full-of-himself Miles Gloriosus, would later go on to win a Tony for portraying full-of-himself Richard Henry Lee in *1776*.

★ Pseudolus was written for comic Phil Silvers, then offered to radio and TV superstar Milton Berle. Silvers finally got to play the role in the 1972 revival.

★ In the early '60s, long titles were all the rage; the previous season had seen *How to Succeed in Business Without Really Trying* and the next would feature the Arthur Kopit play *Oh Dad, Poor Dad, Mamma's Hung You in the Closet and I'm Feelin' So Sad.*

Book, music, and lyrics by Jim Jacobs and Warren Casey
Directed by Tom Moore ★ Musical numbers and dances staged by Patricia Birch

Eden Theatre*, February 14, 1972–April 13, 1980

Carole Demas.......Sandy Dumbrowski
Barry Bostwick.......Danny Zuko
Adrienne Barbeau.......Betty Rizzo
Timothy Meyers.......Kenickie

ART NOTE: A Rydell High cheerleading megaphone, a greaser high-top, and an ultra-feminine lipstick.

*First of four theatres

Rydell High's senior class of 1959 is buzzing with gossip of summer hookups, the wildest being between "greaser" Danny and straitlaced new student Sandy. For weeks, Danny tries to clean up his act to impress her, ditching his buddies to join the track team, but Sandy defends her nice-girl reputation. However, since she's surrounded by drinking, sex, cigarettes, and rock and roll, in the end Sandy is the one who transforms into a street-tough "Pink Lady," making Danny's dreams come true.

Those Magic Changes

Millions of high schoolers have seen, or been in, a production of *Grease*, and when most people now picture 1950s teenage life, it's the show's wacky, hormone-addled teens in leather jackets or poodle skirts they envision. With its infectious, high-energy tunes and early rock-and-roll grooves—still a novel sound on Broadway in 1972—audiences at the original production left the theatre feeling like they'd attended a nostalgia-fueled theme party. And that party didn't stop for 3,388 performances, allowing *Grease* to dethrone *Fiddler on the Roof* as Broadway's longest running musical.

Oddly enough, an affectionate romp down memory lane is not what creators Jim Jacobs and Warren Casey intended when the show started its life in a blues club on the north side of Chicago. What they wrote was a raunchy, R-rated critique of 1950s culture, a deconstruction of the type of squeaky-clean teen experience Hollywood peddled during that decade. For example, the good girl doesn't follow the cliché and reform the greaser; instead, she grabs a cigarette and hot pants and joins him (in the original script, with an f-bomb). With its unusual cast of urban working-class characters, and plotlines about hot-button '50 issues like teenage pregnancy, the early version of *Grease* in many ways aspired to be a kind of *Hair II.*

Almost as soon as the show transferred from Chicago to New York, however, this tone began to change. The new producers had created an ad campaign that sold the show as a valentine to 1950s culture, disappointing early audiences primed to have a fun night out. So between its disastrous first preview and opening night, the creators deleted the crude jokes and language, turning *Grease* into more of a loving spoof of a Sandra Dee movie—though they did maintain the story's "upside-down" ending.

The 1978 movie continued the transformation, further softening the piece to make it more family-friendly; the film also added new songs that became so popular that subsequent stage productions are almost always forced to include them or risk upsetting audiences. These more recent stage productions often seem not even to know of the show's countercultural roots or notice its portrayal of how rock and roll in the '50s liberated teenagers from their parents' stifling morality. Ironically, a show that tried to criticize and satirize mainstream bubblegum entertainments ended up becoming just that.

MISCELLANEOUS MATTER

★ The list of current and future stars to go through the cast includes Richard Gere, Peter Gallagher, Patrick Swayze, Marilu Henner, Judy Kaye, directors Walter Bobbie and Scott Ellis, and the future film Danny, John Travolta himself (but playing Doody, one of the Burger Palace Boys).

★ *Grease*'s first theatre, the Eden, was off-Broadway but employed Broadway contracts, so it was eligible for the Tonys. It didn't win any, however, the only longest-run record holder not to. Its Broadway revivals have similarly failed to notch a single Tony win.

★ A bizarre fan theory popped up regarding the movie: Sandy drowned over the summer, and the rest of the film is a fantasy that ends with her and Danny flying up to heaven in the car. The authors have, not surprisingly, denied this.

Book by Eric Idle ★ Music by John Du Prez and Eric Idle ★ Lyrics by Eric Idle
Directed by Mike Nichols ★ Choreographed by Casey Nicholaw

Shubert Theatre, March 17, 2005–January 11, 2009

Hank Azaria.......Sir Lancelot (and others)
David Hyde Pierce.......Sir Robin
Tim Curry.......King Arthur
Sara Ramirez.......The Lady of the Lake

ART NOTE: A very frightening killer rabbit who has clearly found his grail.

In an unorthodox retelling of the Camelot legend, King Arthur recruits knights to search for the Holy Grail. Cheered on by the magical Lady of the Lake, they battle a killer rabbit, the vicious Knights Who Say Ni, and French people. Their last task: putting on a Broadway show—in fact, the show we're watching. The Grail is found under an audience member's seat, and the knights either get married or decide to pursue a career in show business.

Find Your Grail

Between 1969 and 1974, there wasn't a more inventive or silly show on TV than the British sketch comedy program *Monty Python's Flying Circus.* The six-man troupe's dedication to formal innovation—they relied heavily on techniques like the cold open, ending sketches with non sequitur interruptions, and surreal animations—and sheer irreverence for all cultural institutions attracted a huge cult following. So just before shooting their final season, they decided it was time to make their first original feature film. Entitled *Monty Python and the Holy Grail*, it featured the six *Python* actors in a Camelot spoof, going on a series of increasingly bizarre adventures and errands to track down the Holy Grail. It, too, became a cult hit, and is often listed in the top ten comedy films of all time.

In the 1990s, *Python* original Eric Idle was growing impatient with the relentless seriousness of Broadway and West End musicals. After the success of the musical version of *The Producers*, he went ahead and started work on a musical of *Grail,* hiring Du Prez and writing several songs. Despite their misgivings, the other *Python* actors enjoyed these first songs and felt they couldn't turn down the money-making possibilities if the show should become a hit. And under the expert direction of veteran Broadway and Hollywood EGOT-winner Mike Nichols, that's exactly what it did.

Interestingly, the random, convention-busting, geeky humor that made the original series stand out, and that had made diehard fans (often geeks themselves) feel uniquely seen in the first place, had in the intervening decades become comedy canon. The specific characters and jokes in *Spamalot* were so famous that an actor could just walk on stage in a certain costume and large parts of the audience would start laughing, knowing the entire scene that would follow. Some worried that *Spamalot* was just continuing the trend of jukebox shows and stage adaptations of movie musicals, recycling already-familiar material instead of creating new stories and songs, but many pointed to the second half—in which the knights' quest is expanded to include producing a Broadway musical—as a complete break from the movie, and the freshest part of the show. It certainly allowed for Sara Ramirez to showcase their impeccable diva chops as an actress whose role isn't what she was promised, winning them one of the show's three Tony Awards.

MISCELLANEOUS MATTER

- ★ The role of Sir Lancelot was tailored to Hank Azaria's singing talents (which is to say the character doesn't sing very much).
- ★ The original *Holy Grail* film was financed in part by some heavyweight British bands and musicians, including Pink Floyd, Led Zeppelin, Genesis, George Harrison . . . and Andrew Lloyd Webber (whom the musical would later parody!).
- ★ In August 2007, two original *Python* stars, Terry Jones and Terry Gilliam, led over 5,000 people in London's Trafalgar square in a "coconut orchestra" rendition of the show's hit song, "Always Look on the Bright Side of Life," smashing the Guinness World Record. (Coconuts are used in the show to simulate the clip-clopping of the knights' horses.)

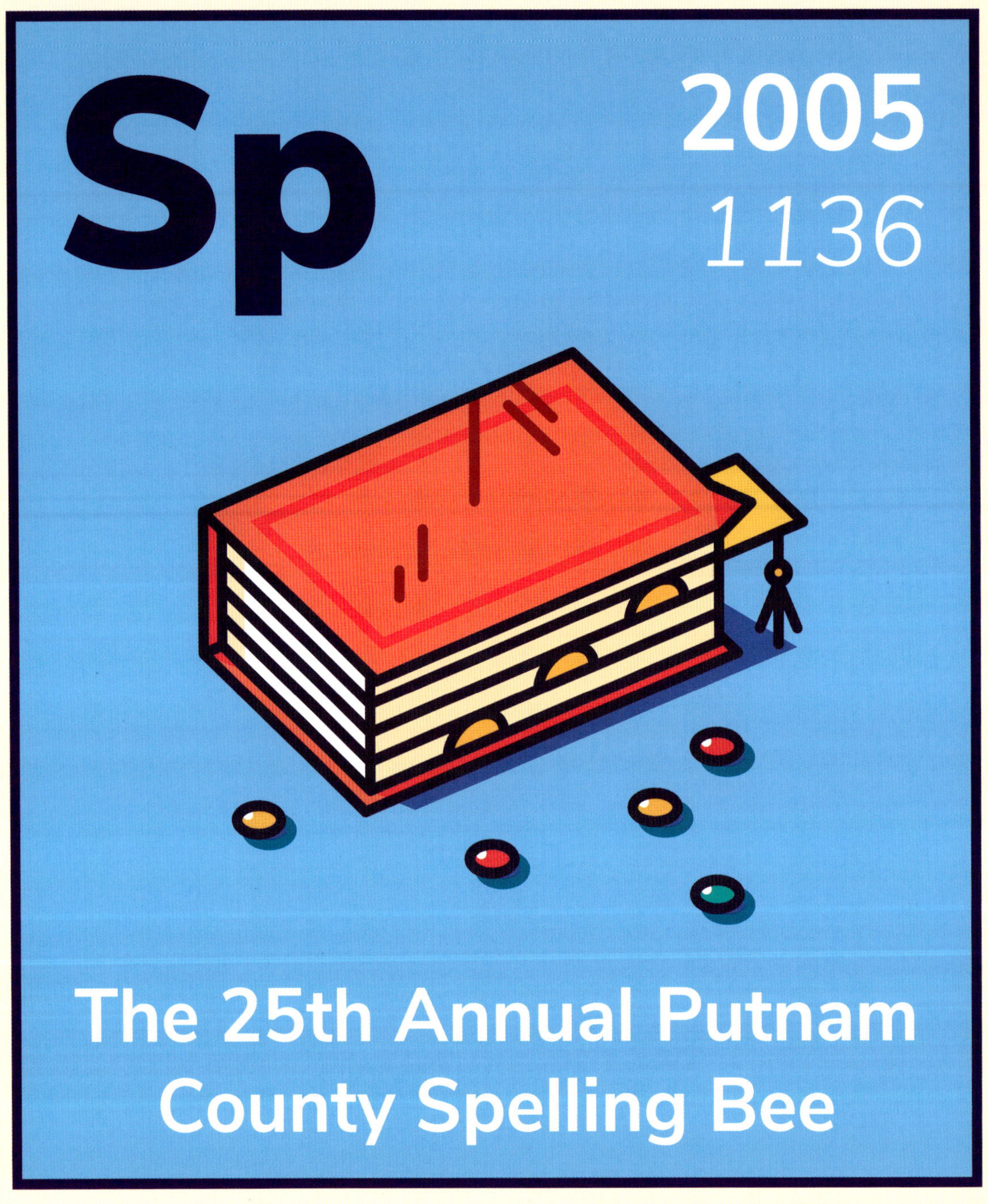

Book by Rachel Sheinkin ★ Music and lyrics by William Finn
Conceived by Rebecca Feldman
Directed by James Lapine ★ Choreographed by Dan Knechtges

Circle in the Square Theatre, May 2, 2005–January 20, 2008

Dan Fogler.......William Barfée
Celia Keenan-Bolger.......Olive Ostrovsky
Jesse Tyler Ferguson.......Leaf Coneybear
Lisa Howard.......Rona Lisa Peretti

ART NOTE: A well-loved dictionary, plus some peanut M&Ms that get tossed around in an unsportsmanlike way.

A motley group of kids (played by adults) compete in a local spelling bee. Distracted by parents (present and absent), hormones, and each other, they battle their competitors—some of whom are audience members—until only Olive and Barfée remain. Barfée has a crush on Olive and considers letting her win, but she convinces him to spell his word correctly. She wins a surprise runner-up award, created to help her pay the entry fee.

My Friend, the Dictionary

The recent popularity of *immersive* theatre—shows where the audience either participates in, moves through, or interacts with the production in some way—has shown that people don't always want to just sit and watch. In the most fully immersive shows, audience members have a function in the story, a role to play in the event as it unfolds (even if just by being there). *Spelling Bee* was one of the first to introduce the joys of this type of show to Broadway, by transforming its audience of theatregoers into attendees at a middle school spelling bee. Those who craved the limelight could even sign up before the show to be actual onstage contestants and were prepped beforehand on what to expect (everything but the words they'd get). The theatre where the show landed after out-of-town workshops and an initial run off-Broadway was particularly suited for this participatory feel. Circle in the Square Theatre is unique among Broadway theatres, as it is set up "in the round," meaning the playing area is in the middle of audience seating. Audience members can therefore see not only the performers but each other's reactions when, for example, a student clearly has the hots for one of them or calls another "mom." And the entire theatre itself was transformed; the lobby was festooned with posters for extracurricular clubs, while the floor of the stage was painted like a basketball court in a junior high "gymnatorium."

Writing a musicalized competition tickled composer/lyricist William Finn, for whom the show would mark a first return to Broadway since 1992's groundbreaking *Falsettos*. His quirkily conversational lyrics and irregular but catchy melodies suited the teenage misfits perfectly—he described the show as "*Survivor* for nerds." He had first seen an early version, then titled *C-R-E-P-U-S-C-U-L-E,* devised by Rebecca Feldman and her improv company The Farm, and recognized in it the potential for a musical. He brought in his former student Rachel Sheinkin to flesh out relationships and give the show more of a musical theatre structure, with the successive rounds of the spelling bee serving as scaffolding. In addition, the creators gave each student their own number and backstory, treating them affectionately and sometimes heartbreakingly as their individual challenges came to light.

MISCELLANEOUS MATTER

★ Actual spelling bee champions would sometimes come and "compete," occasionally getting annoyed when they were given the fake word used to get audience members back to their seats.

★ Though the song "Why We Like Spelling" is on the cast album, it was not in the Broadway production or in the licensed version.

★ Jesse Tyler Ferguson went on to greater fame on TV as Mitchell on *Modern Family,* but he wasn't the only original cast member to leap from stage to screen: Dan Fogler went on to play Luke in *The Walking Dead* and Jacob in the three *Fantastic Beasts* films, and Celia Keenan-Bolger landed a recurring role as Mrs. Bruce on *The Gilded Age.*

Book by Karey Kirkpatrick and John O'Farrell
Music and lyrics by Wayne Kirkpatrick and Karey Kirkpatrick
Directed and choreographed by Casey Nicholaw

St. James Theatre, April 22, 2015–January 1, 2017

Christian Borle.......Shakespeare
Brian d'Arcy James.......Nick Bottom
Heidi Blickenstaff.......Bea
Brad Oscar.......Nostradamus

ART NOTE: Three eggs putting on quite a smelly show.

Nick and Nigel Bottom's theatre company in Renaissance London is in direct competition with the egotistical William Shakespeare's. Hoping to steal the idea for the Bard's next hit, Nick consults a soothsayer, who says it'll be called Omelette *and, bizarrely, will feature actors bursting into song. The brothers furiously write a "musical" about eggs, but when the plot is discovered, they (along with Nigel's love) are banished to America, where they hear of Shakespeare's new hit play,* Hamlet.

It's Eggs!

Something Rotten! could easily have landed in the Show biz series; like *Kiss Me, Kate,* it involves a musicalization of Shakespeare (sort of), and a theatre company trying to get to opening night. But *Something Rotten!* goes so over-the-top and all-in with puns, anachronisms, references, and general silliness that it's more like a show-length version of *Kiss Me, Kate*'s "Brush Up Your Shakespeare," making it definitely an Entertainer at heart.

While the made-up story of "inventing" musicals focused on innovation, the show itself was a throwback. In a season with forward-looking shows like *Hamilton* and *Fun Home, Something Rotten!*'s send-up of musical theatre clichés was clearly a child of the Broadway-skewering *The Producers, Urinetown*, and *The Book of Mormon.* Nashville songwriter Wayne Kirkpatrick and his brother, screenwriter Karey, had been batting the idea for a spoofy Shakespeare musical around since before those shows opened, and finally decided they should maybe write some of their ideas down. They brought in O'Farrell, a British writer who'd worked with Karey on the screenplay of the animated movie *Chicken Run* and started creating a real plot. They pitched this draft to A-list producer Kevin McCollum (*Rent, In the Heights, Avenue Q*) and he brought in Tony-winning director/choreographer Casey Nicholaw (*The Book of Mormon, Aladdin*), who in turn brought in his A-list actors, the top singing comedians in town.

Being surrounded by so much talent felt to the brothers like "a four-year course in the musical," and after much rewriting (only eighteen of the more than forty songs they wrote ended up in the show), there was such good buzz around town that McCollum opted to forego the usual out-of-town tryout and go straight to Broadway, where a theatre had become available due to the surprise flop of the revival of *Side Show*. The parallels with a production of Shakespeare's day weren't lost on the creators—after all, Shakespeare never went out of town, and competition with other companies was fierce even during the Renaissance. The producer's gambit paid off, and the show was a box office hit, if not as well-received by the press or Tony voters. But the creators' smarts won out—the day after they won only one of the seven Tonys for which they were nominated, they released an ad campaign with the word "Loser!" splashed with a rotten tomato. The show ran for another year and a half.

MISCELLANEOUS MATTER

★ The Kirkpatricks (who went on to write the musical *Doubtfire*) joined a very short list of brothers who've written scores for Broadway, which includes Richard M. and Robert B. Sherman (*Chitty Chitty Bang Bang, Over Here)* and George and Ira Gershwin (too many shows to list).

★ Beth Leavel (*The Drowsy Chaperone*) played Bea in the developmental workshops for the show, but when Bea's pregnancy became a plot point, the creators decided they needed a younger actress for the role and hired Blickenstaff.

★ In early drafts, the character of Nostradamus was intended to be the famous Nostradamus (instead of his nephew Thomas,) until the writers discovered the real one died years before Shakespeare became famous.

THE TRUE STORIES

REACTIONS OVER TIME

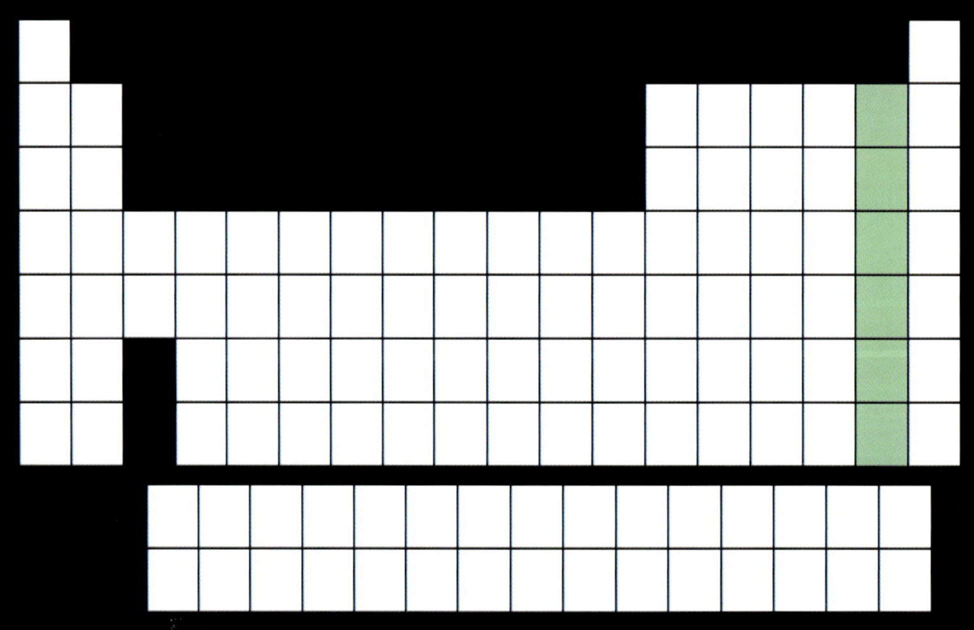

Truth may not always be stranger than fiction, but history is certainly full of wonderful tales—inspiring, harrowing, cautionary, heartwarming, and everything in between. What truth doesn't often do, however, is mold itself naturally into a satisfying form for a theatre piece, with a beginning, middle, and end (ideally with a perfect spot for an intermission). Oh, and is it easy to tell in the space of approximately two and a half hours? Do the characters have the types of personalities where singing might come naturally? What about movement possibilities? And what point of view does the show take? "Just the facts, ma'am" is fine for an article or a TV segment, but a work of theatrical art needs to say something about its world as well as ours.

Savvy musical theatre fans might notice that there *were* musicals based on the stories of actual people prior to *Fiorello!*, the first show in this family. *Annie Get Your Gun* (1946) is the earliest such show on the Table, followed by *The King and I* (1951) and two more in 1959: *Gypsy* and *The Sound of Music*. All took liberties with the actual events in order to wrangle an entertaining evening out of them. Gypsy Rose Lee admitted to making up a lot of the "memoir" the show was based on; years after *the King and I* opened, Anna Leonowens was discovered to have done the same; and the real Maria was a tutor, and to only one von Trapp child, over a decade before WWII started.

Coincidentally, *Fiorello!* also opened in 1959, but what set it apart from the shows discussed above is that it stayed closer to the truth about the famous mayor's rise—it was largely based on a 1955 memoir *Life with Fiorello* by Ernest Cuneo. The rest of the shows in this family are similar in spirit—instead of highly fictionalized or sensationalized stories, these musicals care about historical accuracy. Their source material took a variety of forms: firsthand accounts drawn from interviews, biographies, films, primary source recordings, and oral histories.

Other than an interest in facts, very little connects the musicals in this eclectic category. The settings cover the distant past through the present day, and the scale of the stories range from intimate romances to the origin of nations. They're scored using music from wildly different traditions, everything from musical comedy to hip-hop, Afrobeat, and Celtic folk rock. But each accomplishes the same trick: bringing the past to life in ways that feel immediate and relevant.

Book by Jerome Weidman and George Abbott
Music by Jerry Bock ★ Lyrics by Sheldon Harnick
Directed by George Abbott ★ Choreographed by Peter Gennaro

Broadhurst Theatre and Broadway Theatre, November 23, 1959–October 28, 1961

Tom Bosley.......Fiorello
Pat Stanley.......Dora
Ellen Hanley.......Thea
Patricia Wilson.......Marie

ART NOTE: Fiorello as a Big Apple with his signature hairstyle and hat.

This bio-musical recounts the early life of Fiorello H. LaGuardia (reformist Republican and three-term mayor of New York). In the 1910s, he stands with women strikers, successfully runs for Congress, and fights in WWI. In the '20s, he meets and marries his first wife, fails in his first bid for mayor, and is widowed. By the early '30s, he's decided to marry his long-suffering secretary (who's always carried a torch for him) and finally becomes mayor.

The Name's LaGuardia

Fiorello! not only shared a Tony Award for Best Musical in 1960 (tying with *The Sound of Music,* still the only Best Musical tie ever), it won the Pulitzer Prize for Drama. And yet it's virtually unrevivable. Why? The easy answer is the subject matter is simply too obscure for modern audiences, even if the material itself is strong.

It's not that people don't recognize the name LaGuardia—it decorates numerous institutions in New York, including an airport used by locals and visitors alike—so you might imagine a musical that explained just who this man was and why he's remembered might still be of interest. Unfortunately for the show's longevity, that's not what the creators of this musical set out to do. Because in 1959, with LaGuardia's mayoralty so recent and so well known, they expected everyone in the audience would know that story. So they opted to cover lesser-known events . . . with one major exception, an exception that, in this case, illustrates the larger problem. The show opens with Fiorello narrating the panels of a comic strip into a radio microphone, a reference to the most famous of Mayor LaGuardia's actions: during a 1945 newspaper distribution strike, he read the funnies to New York's children over the airwaves. The musical doesn't bother to provide context for the brief scene, it's just included because the writers figured ticket buyers would all expect it. (See the problem?)

The singular look of the show was created by husband-and-wife design team William and Jean Eckart (responsible for sets, costumes, and lights!). Their work featured stylized, painterly scenery in saturated, nonrealistic colors that gave the show a storybook feel, and the nostalgic parade of costumes they designed nimbly delineated passing decades. The fresh look of the show contributed to its success.

But the main draw was the score; it put the songwriting team Bock and Harnick on the map (five years later they'd write *Fiddler on the Roof*), and it offers rich harmonies, complex musical forms, and lyrics that are both witty and smart—in a song called "Politics and Poker," for example, the political hacks wearily conclude, "If politics seems more predictable that's because usually you can stack the deck." Even if *Fiorello!* is a show of and for its time, its songs, at least, can still speak to ours.

MISCELLANEOUS MATTER

- ★ *Fiorello!* launched the career of actor Tom Bosley, who bore an almost uncanny resemblance to the diminutive, saturnine LaGuardia; this was enough to secure him his first leading role on Broadway at only twenty-two years old.
- ★ In one of the first uses of projected film in a Broadway musical, actual newsreel footage of soldiers returning home from WWI was shown at the end of act one as LaGuardia completed his service.
- ★ *Fiorello!* was the thirty-first Broadway show directed by George Abbott, but the first that earned him a Tony Award for Best Direction of a Musical.

Book by Peter Stone ★ Music and lyrics by Sherman Edwards
Directed by Peter Hunt ★ Musical staging by Onna White

46th Street Theatre*, March 16, 1969–February 13, 1972

William Daniels.......John Adams
Virginia Vestoff.......Abigail Adams
Howard da Silva.......Benjamin Franklin
Betty Buckley.......Martha Jefferson

ART NOTE: A quill pen in the process of drawing the stars from the first flag of the United States.

**First of three theatres*

Delegates to the Second Continental Congress suffer through a sweltering June in fetid, filthy Philadelphia as they debate whether the American colonies should declare themselves independent. The catch? They've agreed that any decision to break from Great Britain needs to be unanimous. Somehow the pro-independence forces—led by the unpopular John Adams, with literary support from Thomas Jefferson—overcome all obstacles, and a new country is born before our eyes.

Cool, Cool Considerate Men

Four decades before *Hamilton,* the idea of having the Founding Fathers break into song and dance struck many people as silly—but that wasn't the only issue *1776* had to grapple with. In storytelling terms, the narrative would seem to have an insurmountable problem: *we all know how this is going to end.* Therefore, the highest praise one can offer the show is that it somehow manages to generate real suspense and tension about whether or not the Declaration will be signed by Congress.

Credit for that must go to book writer Peter Stone. In his *New York Times* review of the original production, Clive Barnes called the book "most gripping," and added "literate, urbane and . . . very amusing." In fact, the show has such a dominant book that it holds the record for the longest scene without music in a musical: a full thirty minutes elapses between songs in Scene 3, a time when some musicians leave the pit for a break.

Stone was a late addition to the writing team; originally the show's composer/lyricist Sherman Edwards had written his own script. Edwards's background was unique among Broadway songwriters. Prior to *1776,* his only musical, he had had some success as a pop songwriter, penning Top Ten hits for Elvis Presley, among others. However, his true passion was history (he'd been a history major turned history teacher), and the idea of creating a musical comedy about the Declaration consumed him. He spent years doing primary research in rare manuscript rooms and historical societies, and creating songs in a vaguely operetta-ish, quasi-18th-century style. (The superb orchestrations by Eddie Sauter would later accentuate and enhance this period-appropriate sound.)

The musical was rejected by producer after skeptical producer, but Edwards persevered until one, Stuart Ostrow, finally saw the piece's potential. To Ostrow, *1776* captured, in its own unique way, the rebellious, anti-establishment mood of the 1960s, even as it also provided a civilized contrast to the turmoil of contemporary politics. His insight was prescient. When brought to life by a stellar company of (nearly all male) singing actors, the story did indeed seem to be the counterprogramming Broadway craved. Up against more contemporary offerings like *Hair* and *Promises, Promises,* this most unlikely of musicals went on to earn critical hosannas, win the Tony Award for Best Musical, and run nearly three years.

MISCELLANEOUS MATTER

- ★ When *1776* was made into a movie, then-president Richard Nixon lobbied his friend Jack Warner, the film's producer, to delete the song "Cool, Cool Considerate Men," a broadside against conservative politics. And Warner did. Only recently has the number been restored for DVD rereleases.
- ★ William Daniels, who delivered an all-too-believable star performance as the "obnoxious and disliked" John Adams, could himself be difficult; he refused to accept his 1969 Tony nomination, piqued because it was for supporting actor rather than best actor.
- ★ The original production's logo (an eaglet waving a U.S. flag emerging from a shell decorated with a U.K. one) actually inspired the song "The Egg," rather than the other way around!

Book by Reg E. Gaines ★ Music by Daryl Waters, Zane Mark, and Ann Duquesnay
Lyrics by Reg E. Gaines, George C. Wolfe, and Ann Duquesnay
Directed by George C. Wolfe ★ Choreographed by Savion Glover

Ambassador Theatre, April 25, 1996–January 10, 1999

Savion Glover.......'da Beat
Ann Duquesnay.......'da Singer
Jeffrey Wright.......'da Voice
Dulé Hill.......The Kid

ART NOTE: A couple of tap shoes and a West African–striped bucket and sticks ready to make some Noise.

Through song and nearly nonstop tap dance, the cast recounts, re-creates, and reexamines the history of Black America and Black tap dancing. From the Great Passage, through the invention of tap by rebellious enslaved Africans stripped of their drums, to the Great Migration north and the incorporation and appropriation of tap by Hollywood, the art of "hoofing" is reclaimed and celebrated.

Shifting Sounds

Though countless dance forms and traditions have been represented on Broadway—from ballet and jazz to modern and hip-hop—in the popular imagination it's tap that's most associated with musicals, especially tap dancing as seen in shows from (or set in) the 1920s to the '40s. Hollywood is greatly responsible for this connection, having showcased the form in countless movie musicals featuring jaw-dropping tap numbers from dancers like Gene Kelly, Fred Astaire, the Nicholas Brothers, Eleanor Powell, and Ann Miller.

But for the small number of up-and-coming young tap dancers in the '80s and '90s, tap had a far deeper meaning and history. As a kid growing up in Newark, New Jersey, Savion Glover felt the connection with that past and dedicated himself to learning the styles of previous generations even as he was establishing his own. He was a replacement lead in the 1983 musical *The Tap Dance Kid*, then appeared as young Jelly Roll Morton in *Jelly's Last Jam* opposite one of his heroes and mentors, Gregory Hines. (Hines described Glover as "probably the best tap dancer that ever lived.") And though *Jelly's Last Jam* was a breakthrough in using tap as a metaphor for musical talent, Glover knew it could do so much more.

Director George C. Wolfe, also from *Jelly's Last Jam,* had a similarly ambitious vision: to paint a sweeping portrait of the history of Blacks in America while showcasing tap as a quintessentially Black art form. The words of champion slam poet Gaines and the songs of Waters, Mark, and Duquesnay gave a lyrical voice to important episodes in Black American history, but it was the choreography that set the theatre afire, translating scenes in settings as varied as a slave ship, a plantation, a factory, and a city street corner into sounds both eloquent and deeply emotional.

Although white oppression was, unsurprisingly, a key theme of the evening, some scorn was reserved for Black dancers, especially in Golden Age Hollywood, who had been content to smile and shuffle for the camera. That kind of dance was not what Glover was about; he referred to his dance as "hoofin'" or "hittin'," and regardless of its target or its volume, it hit audiences hard, winning him the Tony Award for Best Choreography and changing tap into something as current and vital as the hip-hop music that accompanied it.

MISCELLANEOUS MATTER

★ Dulé Hill had been in *The Tap Dance Kid* with Glover when they were both teenagers, along with fellow cast member Jimmy Tate—they were all understudies for the lead role of Willie, played by Alfonso Ribeiro, who went on to TV success in shows like *The Fresh Prince of Bel-Air.* Hill also had a major TV career in shows like *The West Wing* and *Psych.*

★ The show was created during a workshop, beginning with nothing but index cards on a bulletin board. Wolfe sent musicians and actors to different locations in the theatre to brainstorm and riff on different subjects and gradually the show fell into shape.

★ Tony Award–winning actor Jeffrey Wright (*Angels in America*) played multiple characters, with a dozen costume changes, as he narrated the show's journey through time.

Book by Jim Lewis and Bill T. Jones ★ Music and lyrics by Fela Anikulapo-Kuti
Directed and choreographed by Bill T. Jones

Eugene O'Neill Theatre, November 23, 2009–January 2, 2011

Sahr Ngaujah.......Fela Anikulapo-Kuti
Saycon Sengbloh.......Sandra
Lillias White.......Funmilayo

ART NOTE: One of Fela's saxes blowing a map of Africa, with a star for Nigeria.

Composer and performer Fela Kuti's club in Lagos, Nigeria, "The Afrika Shrine," has become a center of resistance against that country's military dictatorship. At a concert, Fela describes the Afrobeat sound he helped create from a mixture of African and American influences and how it made him a success. As he becomes more outspoken in his opposition to the government's abuses, he is the target of a violent raid on his compound and his mother is killed; still he remains defiant.

Originality

By 2008, the jukebox bio-musical was a well-established genre, and producers looking for the next hit were fast acquiring the rights to famous pop songwriters' catalogs. They soon discovered the popularity of the original artist didn't necessarily translate into box office success; the catalogs of Elvis, the Beach Boys, and John Lennon all had the plug pulled on their jukebox musicals after unsuccessful runs. So it was even more surprising when the music of a Nigerian singer-songwriter virtually unheard-of in the United States found an enthusiastic new audience.

Fela Anikulapo-Kuti was an icon in his native country, having risen to fame in the 1970s and '80s. His music was a synthesis of many traditions, a foundation of Ghanaian "highlife" music (a blend of West African rhythms and American jazz instruments), overlaid with funk and soul, James Brown and Frank Sinatra. The genre came to be known as Afrobeat, and Fela's songs were often fifteen to thirty minutes long, much of them instrumental jam sessions. He toured with a large orchestra and played many instruments himself, but he was not just a musician. His politics were at least as important to his public persona as his concerts, and his lyrics, in Nigerian, pidgin English, and Yoruba, had explicitly political content. An outspoken critic of the corrupt Nigerian government, he was arrested over 200 times, becoming a folk hero in his country.

Pioneering choreographer Bill T. Jones (*Spring Awakening*) was also a political artist, and he saw in Fela an opportunity to make a statement with his work. The show was an explosion of beats and horns, accompanied by Antibalas, a Brooklyn band dedicated to preserving Fela's music. Occasionally, video would transport the audience to the Nigerian nightclub that Fela ran. And running *Fela!* was Amsterdam-based American actor Sahr Ngaujah, who dominated the evening with an electric swagger that never waned—he was offstage for only two minutes of the show. His energy and that of the incredible music caught the attention of high-profile musicians and actors like Jay-Z and Will and Jada Pinkett Smith during its off-Broadway run. Although (or perhaps because) they were inexperienced as producers, they believed this improbable subject matter could move mainstream Broadway audiences, and transferred the show, bringing acclaim for all involved. It ran for a respectable thirteen months, but its unexpected and original vision made it one of the most memorable musicals of the decade.

MISCELLANEOUS MATTER

- ★ The show started at 37Arts, the off-Broadway theatre where *In the Heights* first ran in New York.
- ★ Fela changed his middle name from Ransome to Anikulapo after police burned down his compound; it means "he who carries death in his pouch."
- ★ Fela ran for president, and—to circumvent censorship laws—published anti-government pieces in the papers as political advertisements.
- ★ Lilias White earned a Tony nomination for playing Fela's mother; she had previously won the award for Cy Coleman's *The Life.*

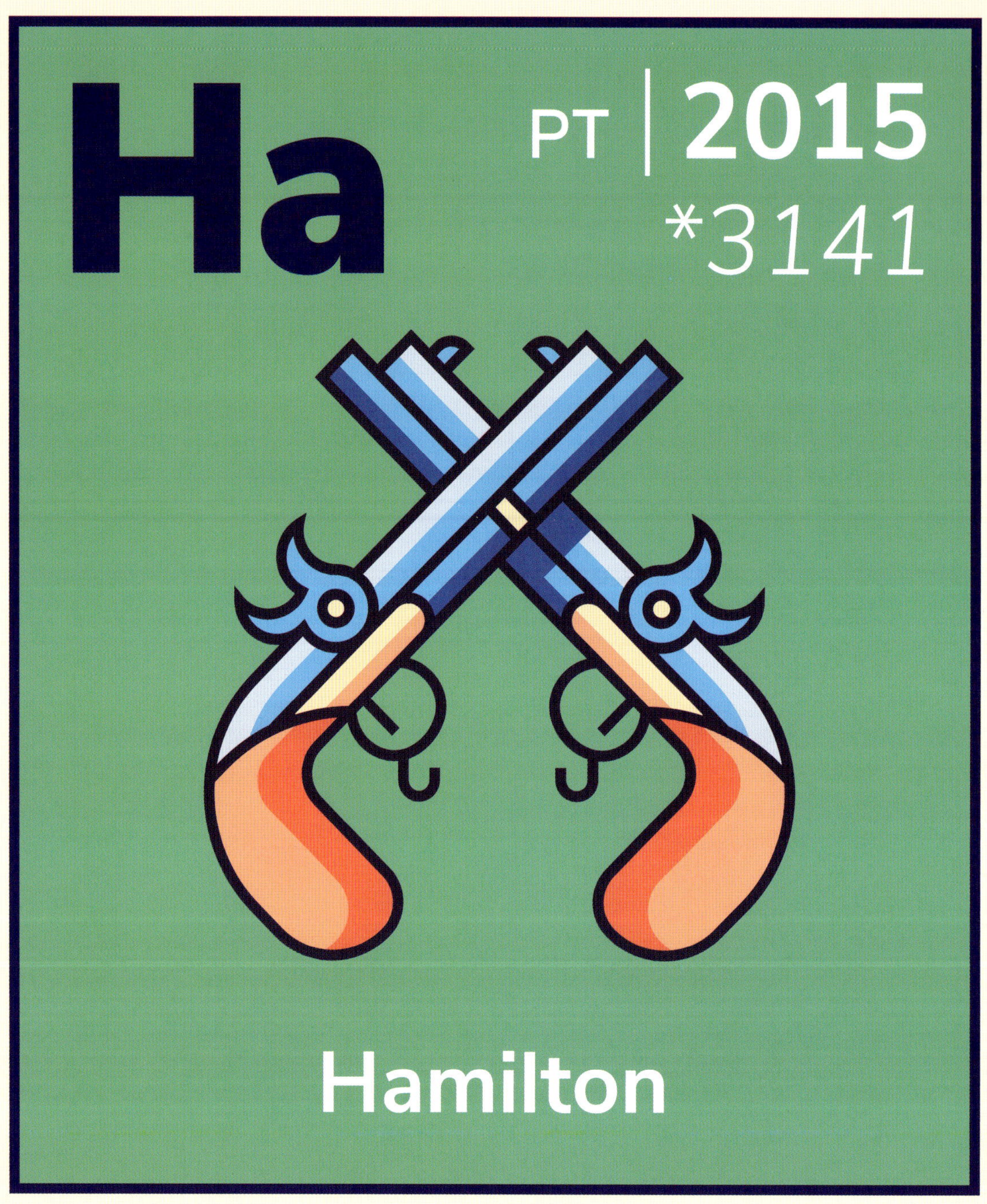

Book, music, and lyrics by Lin-Manuel Miranda
Directed by Thomas Kail ★ Choreographed by Andy Blankenbuehler

Richard Rodgers Theatre, August 6, 2015–publication

Lin-Manuel Miranda.......Alexander Hamilton
Leslie Odom Jr.......Aaron Burr
Phillipa Soo.......Eliza Hamilton
Daveed Diggs.......Marquis de Lafayette/ Thomas Jefferson

ART NOTE: Hamilton and Burr's British Wogdon & Barton dueling pistols.

Alexander Hamilton arrives in the American colonies as an emigrant from the Caribbean and falls in with an ambitious, articulate, and revolutionary crowd. He impresses everyone with his strategic thinking and ends up Washington's aide-de-camp during the war. He marries one of the wealthy Schuyler sisters, Eliza, but after American independence their marriage suffers, and he becomes entangled in bitter political disputes. When rival Aaron Burr kills him in a duel, the cast reflects on the role of historians and storytellers.

History Has Its Eyes on You

Lin-Manuel Miranda's innovations in *In the Heights*, where he brought an authentic hip-hop and Latin American musical vocabulary to Broadway, did not go unnoticed. In 2009, he was invited to perform at the Obama White House, and he brought with him excerpts from a new project he called *The Hamilton Mixtape,* inspired by a bestselling biography by Ron Chernow. Hamilton's birth on the Caribbean island of Nevis reminded Miranda of his own Puerto Rican heritage, and he imagined a show where the Founding Fathers were played by actors of color, a story of America's past that looked like America's present. It was a bold concept that created an unprecedented connection between modern audiences and their history.

While *In the Heights* was traditional musical theatre laced with elements of spoken poetry and hip-hop, *Hamilton* brought Miranda's trademark hyper-literate, intricately rhymed rap to the fore. Vast amounts of exposition and historical detail were delivered with such style that what might have felt dry in any other context was captivating. And *In the Heights* arranger and orchestrator Alex Lacamoire was back, giving every song a straight-from-the-radio sound, and incorporating ensemble vocals to elevate the sonic impact.

Much like its musical theatre predecessor, *1776, Hamilton* transformed a story whose ending we knew into a gripping piece of theatre. It conquered New York and then the country, becoming a once-in-a-generation cultural touchstone. Tickets to *Hamilton*'s run at off-Broadway's Public Theater (which had incubated other groundbreaking shows like *Hair, A Chorus Line,* and *Bring in 'da Noise . . .*) became impossible to score, and the Broadway production sold out for over a year. The cast album hit number one on the Billboard rap chart and debuted at number twelve on the Billboard 200, higher than any musical theatre album since the *West Side Story* film soundtrack in 1962–63. Thanks to Miranda's social media savvy, the show also took off on various platforms, with "Ham-4-Ham" (an impromptu live performance outside the theatre before the nightly ticket lottery) becoming hugely popular.

As public conversations around race have shifted since *Hamilton*'s opening, some have raised issues with parts of the show, including Miranda's decision to largely omit discussions of slavery, criticisms he's called "valid." But the immensity of his achievement, his imagination, and unparalleled craft remain unchallenged, and *Hamilton* will forever be one of the most important musicals in Broadway history.

MISCELLANEOUS MATTER

★ Inspired by their students' passion for the recording, many teachers across the country used the album to introduce concepts in American history, and *Hamilton* gave back, offering reduced-price tickets to students.

★ "Guns and Ships" is one of the fastest patter songs in Broadway history, made even more challenging for Daveed Diggs by the French accent he had to adopt as Lafayette.

★ Miranda's idea for King George's flamboyant song came from a conversation with British actor Hugh Laurie (*House*), who improvised the song's title as a joke about the King's reaction to the Declaration of Independence: "Awww, you'll be back."

Book, music, and lyrics by Irene Sankoff and David Hein
Directed by Christopher Ashley ★ Musical staging by Kelly Devine

Gerald Schoenfeld Theatre, March 12, 2017–October 2, 2022

Ensemble cast, including Jenn Colella, Kendra Kassebaum, Chad Kimball, and Rodney Hicks

ART NOTE: An airplane perched on "the Rock" from the opening number, adorned with a Canadian maple leaf.

On the morning of September 11, 2001, thirty-eight planes heading into the United States were rerouted and forced to land at a small airport in Newfoundland, Canada. Balancing the confusion and fear this engendered in passengers was the kindness shown by the town's citizens, who opened their homes and their hearts to these 7,000 travelers from around the world. Unlikely friendships and even love bloomed during those fraught days, taken up again ten years later at the group's reunion.

On the Edge

A generation-defining tragedy is a nearly impossible subject to tackle. It takes a certain amount of distance, and a "way in," to humanize the enormity of such an event. To succeed as a mainstream musical, it also takes a huge amount of heart. In *Come From Away,* two Canadians brought all of this in spades, added a life-affirming Celtic rock score, and soared all the way to Broadway.

Concentrating on just one tiny corner of that terrible day allowed the creators to delineate the dozens of characters (played by a handful of actors shifting roles) with such finely textured detail that they felt like real people. Of course, that's partly because they were—*Come From Away* was an example of *documentary theatre*, in which material is based not just on secondhand accounts, but on interviews with the people depicted in the story. Playwrights had long used this technique, from the Depression-era Federal Theatre Project's *Living Newspapers* to theatrical examinations of the Holocaust like Peter Weiss's *The Investigation* to Anna Deavere Smith's *Twilight: Los Angeles, 1992* and Moisés Kaufman's *The Laramie Project* (2000). In the early 2000s, an "investigative" theatre company called The Civilians pushed the form closer to musicals, adding witty original songs by Michael Friedman to shows like *Gone Missing* and *(I Am) Nobody's Lunch*, created out of interviews held by the cast members themselves. In *Come From Away,* this approach means that when the "Islanders" and travelers react with a variety of all-too-human emotions to the unthinkable tragedy they are unexpectedly a small part of, they do so in their own words. Which is one of the reasons this show is so powerful and resonated with audiences of all stripes.

Structurally, *Come From Away* departs from traditional Broadway musicals by weaving numerous small stories together in an intricate tapestry, one thread peeking out for a few lines before rejoining the pattern. The score leans heavily on extended musical sequences that involve multiple cast members/characters, rather than a preponderance of solos or duets. Similarly, Ashley and Devine transformed a spare, wooden set and a dozen mismatched chairs into a perpetually shifting array of locations and vehicles. Even in 2017, there was a feeling of "Can this work? Are we allowed to sing about 9/11?" (especially in New York). With this singular and warm-hearted musical, a grateful city discovered just how badly it needed to.

MISCELLANEOUS MATTER

★ On Broadway, the show's set included real trees, and due to the intense artificial lighting, some of them continued to grow and even sprout a few leaves on stage.

★ The song "Screech In" referred to a ceremony Newfoundland natives use to welcome off-Islanders, or those who had "come from away." It gets its name from local Screech rum, and for a time, bottles advertised it as "The official drink of *Come From Away.*"

★ Initially, the show had an intermission, but producers suggested it be cut because none of the people in Gander, Newfoundland were able to take a break over the four days covered in the story.

THE GROUNDBREAKERS

WORKS WITH HIGH DRAMATIC DENSITY

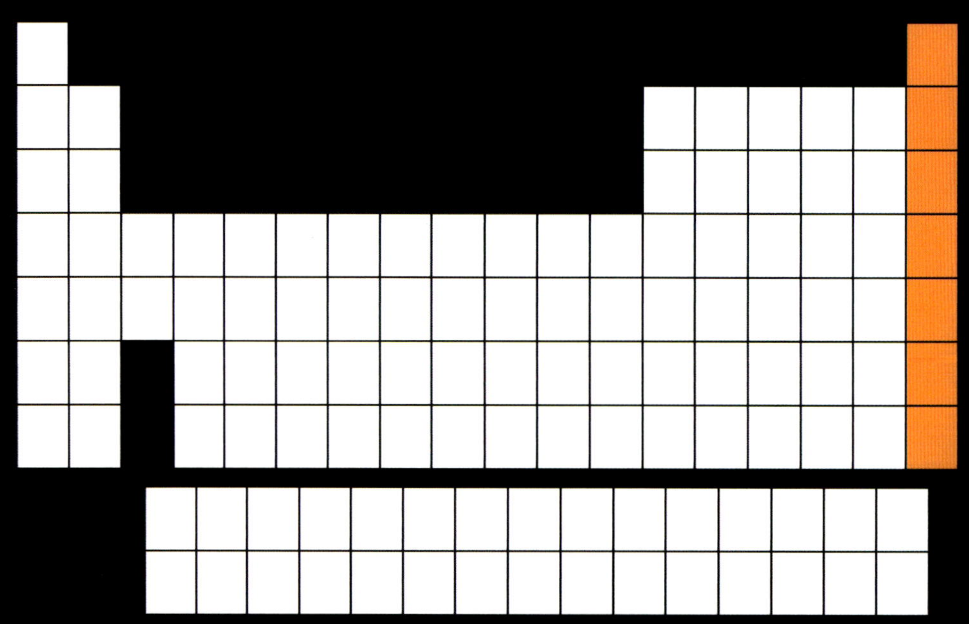

Musicals are singular creations—even the most formulaic musical comedies of Broadway's early years were composed of unique songs, jokes, design choices, and staging. So every time a new show opens, it breaks a little new ground in its own way. But there are certain shows that boldly redefine what a musical is or can be, by tackling subject matter that was previously outside "mainstream" tastes, by creating new musical, choreographic, or staging vocabularies, or by combining traditional and forward-looking techniques into a fresh and unified whole.

A musical's job is not, primarily, to preach, teach, or push an ideology; those that foreground their moral message have generally failed, because what audiences want, and deserve, is first and foremost to be captivated. What the most innovative and influential creators of musicals have learned over the past century is that entertainment can be compatible with ambition. In the right hands, a musical can delve into profound human issues. Musical numbers can electrify even if their content and context is violent or upsetting. Staging that is theatrical, even fantastical, can support realistic characters. And who says a show must be trapped on a stage? The architecture of most Broadway houses has compelled shows to take the proscenium/audience face-off as a given, but visionary directors have found ways to change the audience's perspective by placing them inside the action, making them feel like part of the story.

Sometimes, a groundbreaking show will create ripples, encouraging other artists to continue expanding the genre in the same direction, inspiring them to use the same innovations to tell their own particular stories. But other times, theatrical breakthroughs turn out to be a result of a unique combination of creators; these shows achieve effects that have never been repeated. After all, in chemistry, there's nothing that requires elements to react with each other; the Groundbreakers column in the original periodic table holds the noble gases, elements like neon that stand apart and refuse to combine. But in the right circumstances, they sure do glow.

Book by Oscar Hammerstein II and Joshua Logan
Music by Richard Rodgers ★ Lyrics by Oscar Hammerstein II
Adapted from *Tales of the South Pacific* by James A. Michener
Book and musical numbers staged by Joshua Logan

Majestic Theatre and Broadway Theatre, April 7, 1949–January 16, 1954

Mary Martin.......Nellie Forbush
Ezio Pinza.......Emile de Becque
Juanita Hall.......Bloody Mary
William Tabbert.....Lt. Joseph Cable, U.S.M.C.

ART NOTE: The island Bali Ha'i, its "head sticking out from a low-flying cloud," with an American bomber overhead.

Fate, in the form of WWII, brings together Emile de Becque, a suave widowed French planter, and Nellie Forbush, a spunky army nurse from Little Rock. Though they're well on their way to love at curtain up, their path to a happy ending must surmount the gulf between their ages and backgrounds, and Nellie's initially racist response to Emile's half-Polynesian kids. In a parallel subplot, American Joe Cable falls in love with Tonkinese girl Liat . . . with a less happy ending.

Some Enchanted Evening

Only a handful of times has a Broadway musical succeeded on the scale of *South Pacific*. It's the kind of hit show that somehow, while running in a single theatre in New York City, impacts all American culture. The week after it opened, the show made the cover of national magazines *Newsweek* and *Life*. Branded tie-ins for the original production included sheets and towels, cigarette cases, a "Knucklehead Nellie" doll, and even a home perm kit. The original cast album sold more than a million copies, and was number one on the charts for over sixty weeks; even today, most Americans can hum the opening phrase of "Some Enchanted Evening." The show not only swept the 1950 Tony Awards, it also won the Pulitzer Prize for Drama (its source material, James A. Michener's *Tales of the South Pacific*, had won the Pulitzer Prize for fiction two years earlier).

In addition to being popular, *South Pacific* earns its place as a groundbreaker in two distinct ways. First was its naturalistic staging and use of near-continuous, cinematic-style underscoring (created by Rodgers's longtime arranger, Trude Rittman). Director Joshua Logan eschewed formal choreography, instead working with the performers to design movements real people might improvise. He also created transitions between scenes that kept the dramatic action going even as sets shifted. In fact, Logan deserves equal credit for the show with Rodgers and Hammerstein because, in addition to being director and de facto choreographer, he was also coauthor. Hammerstein stalled after writing dialogue for scene one when he realized he had no idea how military men behave or talk. He then reached out to Logan, a WWII veteran, and the two spent the next ten days together, hashing out the remainder of the script.

The other, more important way that *South Pacific* broke new ground concerns its subject matter. The setting was serious and contemporary—unusual for a musical play in the 1940s—with both of the musical's love stories running aground on the issue of racial prejudice. The song "You've Got to Be Carefully Taught" was a devastating condemnation of how bigotry is spread from generation to generation. Even more shocking, overtly racist attitudes are expressed by the show's heroine, the sunny, spunky, and charming Nellie, an everywoman audiences could, and did, strongly identify with. If even she could struggle with and eventually overcome her biases, couldn't we all?

MISCELLANEOUS MATTER

- ★ In the book *Tales of the South Pacific*, Emile de Becque has eight mixed-race daughters, by four wives (two Javanese, one Tonkinese, and one Polynesian). In the show he has only one daughter and one son.
- ★ Over the years, other notable Nellies have included (in chronological order) Cloris Leachman, Mitzi Gaynor, Florence Henderson, Glenn Close, and Kelli O'Hara.
- ★ *South Pacific* is one of only two Rodgers and Hammerstein shows for which Hammerstein wasn't sole author of the book; the other is *The Sound of Music*, book by Howard Lindsay and Russel Crouse.

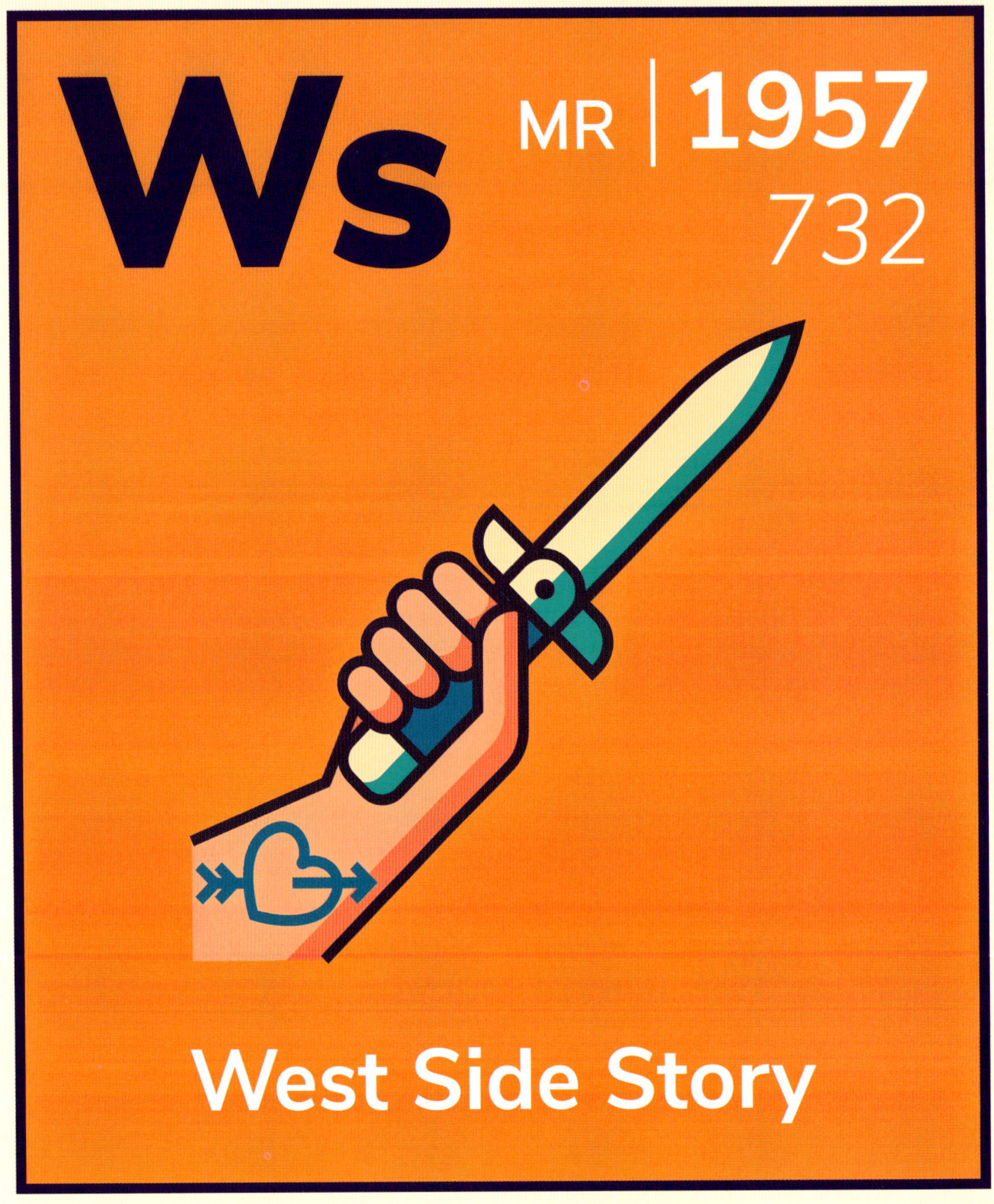

Book by Arthur Laurents ★ Music by Leonard Bernstein
Lyrics by Stephen Sondheim
Directed by Jerome Robbins
Choreographed by Jerome Robbins and Peter Gennaro

Winter Garden Theatre and Broadway Theatre, September 26, 1957–June 27, 1959

Larry Kert.......Tony
Carol Lawrence.......Maria
Chita Rivera.......Anita
Ken Le Roy.......Bernardo

ART NOTE: A hand brandishing a switchblade, with a tattoo representing "One Hand, One Heart."

Two gangs, the white Jets and the Puerto Rican Sharks, fight an ongoing turf war on the streets of New York. When Tony, a Jet, meets Maria, sister of Shark Bernardo, at a dance, it's love at first sight. Later, Tony kills Bernardo in a rumble gone wrong, but Maria stands by him; however, a furious lie by her friend Anita tragically leads to Tony's death. Maria's heartbreak disrupts the cycle of violence, and the gangs come together in Tony's funeral procession.

America

No one wanted to invest in *West Side Story.* Too dark, too violent. Act one ended with two bodies on the stage, and the final curtain came down on another. Who'd want to sit through that after a long day at work? George Abbott, "Mr. Broadway" himself, told Harold Prince not to produce it. Thankfully, Prince ignored his mentor's advice, and he and his partner raised the money—but that was just the first challenge. Jerome Robbins had huge ambitions for the staging and dancing, and demanded eight weeks of rehearsal, double the norm. The virtuosic choreography by Robbins and Gennaro required phenomenal dancers, the book scenes were raw and dramatic, calling for actors of depth and maturity, and the music was uniquely challenging.

West Side Story was Bernstein's third musical about New York City, after *On the Town* and *Wonderful Town*, both musical comedies. With *West Side Story*, he was faced with far different material; challenging, high-stakes emotional territory that allowed him to flex his musical muscles as never before (outside his classical works). Bernstein's first-class training gave him enormous expressive breadth, as well as the structural techniques to craft long instrumental ballets for Robbins. In this score, his signature jazzy, "New York" sound became even sharper, more dissonant, and the Puerto Rican half of the story allowed him to bring in Latin forms and rhythms. His structural vision extended to the entire score, held together with specific key relationships and the use of a single interval, the unstable tritone of "*Ma-ri*-a." Broadway had never heard music this complex, dynamic, or sophisticated.

As if the score wasn't jaw-dropping enough, the way Robbins used dance to convey every emotion from love to violent hatred reinvented what movement could accomplish in a musical. His and Gennaro's physical vocabulary was explosive, portraying young people unable to express themselves verbally, all their emotions instead spilling out in dance. Critics raved and predicted the show would usher in a new era of musical theatre led by Robbins and Bernstein, but their creative chemistry was never to be repeated. Robbins, Sondheim, and Laurents teamed up again for *Gypsy*, another work of genius (if in a more traditional vein), but Bernstein was called away by his symphonic career and wrote only one more show, the quickly forgotten *1600 Pennsylvania Avenue.*

MISCELLANEOUS MATTER

- ★ Comden and Green turned down writing the lyrics; when Laurents ran into the twenty-six-year-old Sondheim at a party, Sondheim expressed interest. He became less interested when he learned he would not be writing music, but figured he might learn something from the genius Bernstein.
- ★ The huge thirty-one-piece orchestra calls for four percussionists playing thirty-five instruments, a big part of the show's violent power.
- ★ To make the 2009 revival more authentically Puerto Rican, Lin-Manuel Miranda translated some of the dialogue and lyrics into Spanish. As the run progressed, due to audience confusion, many of these sections reverted to English.

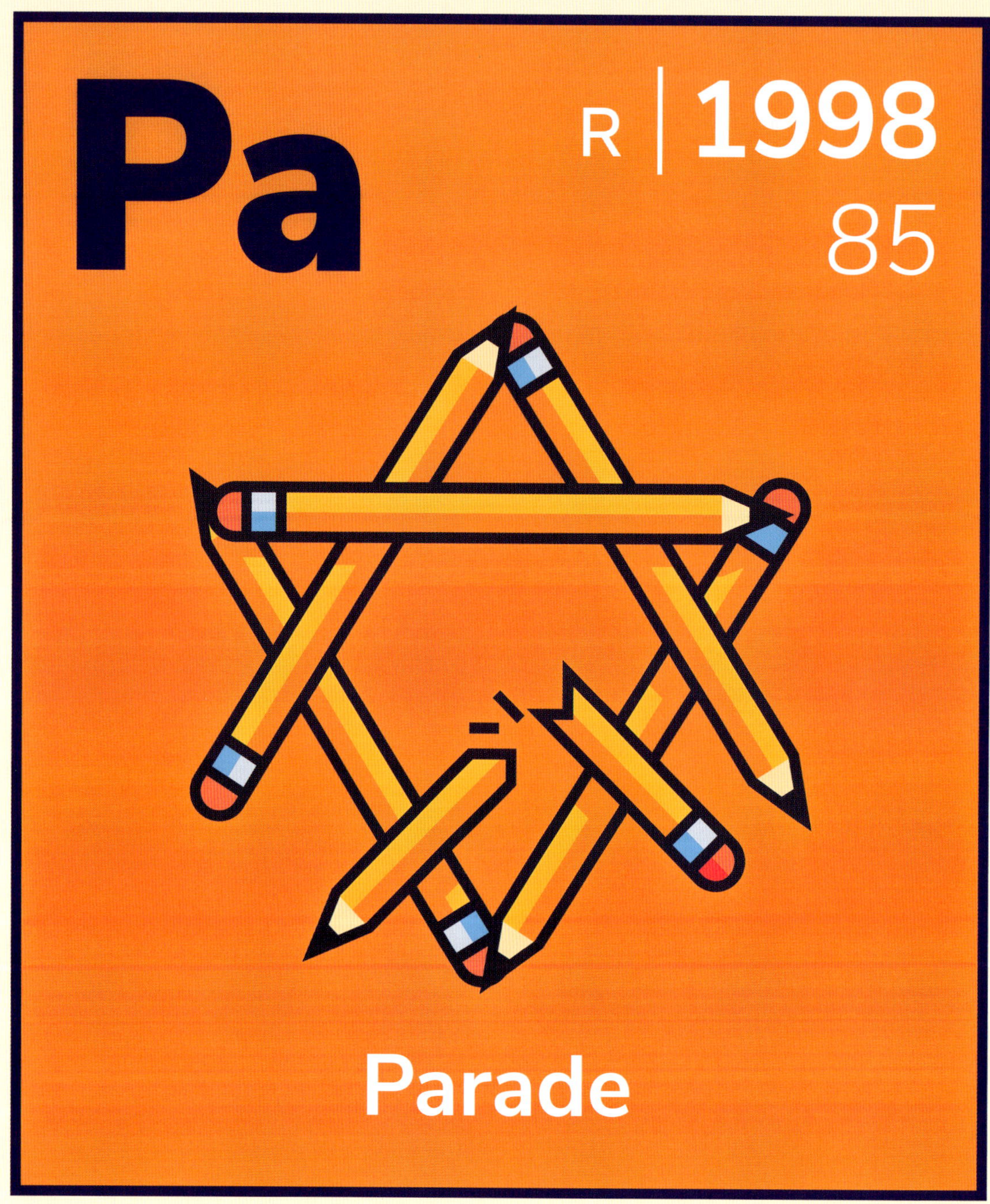

Book by Alfred Uhry ★ Music and lyrics by Jason Robert Brown
Directed by Harold Prince ★ Choreographed by Patricia Birch

Vivian Beaumont Theater, December 17, 1998–February 28, 1999

Brent Carver.......Leo Frank

Carolee Carmello.......Lucille Frank

ART NOTE: The star of David made of pencils from the factory, with one violently snapped in two.

In 1913, Jewish Brooklyn transplant Leo Frank lives in Atlanta with his Southern-born wife, Lucille, where he manages a pencil factory. When a girl who works there is raped and murdered, the town's innate anti-Semitism means suspicion falls on him. Led by the far right-wing media and prosecutor, witnesses are coerced and statements fabricated, and Frank is sentenced to death. Lucille fights for him, but when his sentence is commuted to life in prison, he is kidnapped and lynched.

It's Hard to Speak My Heart

One of the hottest young songwriters, an esteemed Southern playwright, and Broadway's most visionary director tackling a shocking tale of social injustice? The Broadway community in 1998 was ready to be blown away by *Parade*, which opened at the prestigious Lincoln Center's main stage in the middle of a particularly arid season for musicals. Composer/lyricist Jason Robert Brown had met Daisy Prince while working in a piano bar, and together the two had created a popular revue called *Songs for a New World*. Daisy's legendary father, Harold, was impressed, and brought Brown in to work on *Parade* after Sondheim passed on the project. *Parade* had been proposed to Prince by Alfred Uhry, Pulitzer Prize–winning author of *Driving Miss Daisy* and a Georgia native, and the twenty-something songwriter and the sixty-something playwright meshed surprisingly well, crafting a show that felt both new and old, fresh and traditional.

The Tony Award–winning score was universally hailed, a showcase for Brown's multifaceted skills. He created a vibrant collage of period songs, perfectly channeling Sousa marches, ragtime, vaudeville two-steps, and hymns, combining them with his own kind of post-Sondheim dramatic monologues set to roiling ostinatos. It was a unique new synthesis of everything but rock; together with *Rent*, the two scores demonstrated how nearly every kind of popular music, new and old, could be used to tell a story, and pointed the way for songwriters of the next twenty years.

The real challenge was the story, at the heart of which was the prickly character of Leo. He wasn't even an antihero (a hard enough nut to crack, as *Pal Joey* and *Jelly's Last Jam* demonstrated). He was just a sour man—openly scornful of his new community, avoiding conversation, and longing to return to Brooklyn—who happened to become the victim of a terrible injustice. Even Lucille struggled to connect with him until well into the second act, which for many audience members was too late.

Everything was stacked against Leo Frank, both in life and in the musical, with really no one but Lucille on his side. Even the set seemed out to get him, with the giant tree that spelled his doom towering over the stage the entire evening. But though the story and its leading man were very dark, Brown's Broadway debut was a sign of hope for the Broadway musical, maybe even cause for a parade.

MISCELLANEOUS MATTER

- ★ Prince received his last Tony nomination for directing *Parade*; he would direct only two more shows on Broadway, *LoveMusik* and the play *Hollywood Arms*.
- ★ *Parade* reunited Prince with Brent Carver, who won a Tony for originating the role of Molina in *Kiss of the Spider Woman*.
- ★ The revival with Micaela Diamond and *Dear Evan Hansen* star Ben Platt was better received than the original, winning the Tony Award for Best Revival of a Musical.
- ★ Uhry's great-uncle Sigmund Montag once owned the National Pencil Factory.

Book and lyrics by Tony Kushner ★ Music by Jeanine Tesori
Directed by George C. Wolfe ★ Choreographed by Hope Clarke

Eugene O'Neill Theatre, May 2, 2004–August 29, 2004

Tonya Pinkins.......Caroline Thibodeaux
Veanne Cox.......Rose Stopnick Gellman
Anika Noni Rose.......Emmie Thibodeaux
Harrison Chad.......Noah Gellman

ART NOTE: The washing machine from the Gellmans' basement, with money stuck in the door.

In the Jewish Gellman household of Lake Charles, Louisiana, eight-year-old Noah prefers their Black maid, Caroline, to his new stepmother, Rose. He has a bad habit of leaving change in his pockets, and Rose tells Caroline she may keep any money she finds in the wash, after which Noah starts leaving it on purpose. Good intentions curdle into resentments, and the national tensions of the early 1960s are echoed in Caroline's relationship with her employers and her activist daughter.

There Is No God, Noah

In 2004, New York theatre had mostly recovered from 9/11, and musicals were generally delivering what many people needed: big laughs and big entertainment. *The Producers, Urinetown, Avenue Q, Hairspray,* and *Wicked* were all doing well at the box office, as was a goofball 1920s-set comedy, *Thoroughly Modern Millie*, with new music by composer and arranger Jeanine Tesori. But Tesori was at work on another, very different show, that had no interest in simplifying complex issues for entertainment value.

Inspired by events from playwright Tony Kushner's own childhood, *Caroline, or Change* was an uncompromising look at the American South of the early '60s. More of a chamber opera than a musical, it incorporated a wide variety of musical styles from R&B to spirituals to Jewish klezmer and classical chamber music, with a great deal of unrhymed and unmetered text set to spare accompaniment with little traditional melody. Grooves and textures shifted on a dime, and anyone—and *anything*—could sing. Kushner brought the extravagant theatrical creativity he displayed in plays like the seminal *Angels in America*, calling for all manner of objects to burst into song. The opening "Laundry Quintet," for example, is sung by Caroline, the house washing machine, and the radio, played by a three-member girl group. Later, a sad city bus delivers the news of Kennedy's assassination, and the Moon herself offers her opinions.

With such a widely expressive musical and textual palette, the show was able to achieve a challenging complexity in its characters and their relationships. Characters we like say terrible things and make poor choices, idealists are blind to practical realities, and well-meaning people can be bad parents. This was life unvarnished, and the cast portrayed these conflicted people with virtuosity and grace. In the show's huge leading role, Tonya Pinkins was a stoic presence, clinging to dignity even while her own daughter, played by the fierce Anika Noni Rose, condemns her for being a subservient maid. Her refusal to be pitied, and her rejection of most friendships, including that of Harrison Chad's sweet/horrible Noah, was difficult to watch but understandable given her circumstances. Unlike nearly every other show in the musical theatre canon, *Caroline, or Change* denied its audience a heartwarming ending, where characters come together having Learned Something; it knew its audiences were ready for a change.

MISCELLANEOUS MATTER

- ★ The first draft of the libretto was written in all lower-case. "I don't believe in upper-case," said Kushner, "I don't know what that means."
- ★ When Tony Kushner was asked to write a new screenplay for the Steven Spielberg *West Side Story* movie, he brought Tesori in as musical coach and vocal supervisor.
- ★ Tesori has worked with a wide range of playwright collaborators—she often has them read passages of prose or lyrics to her out loud to hear the natural inflection they had in their head.

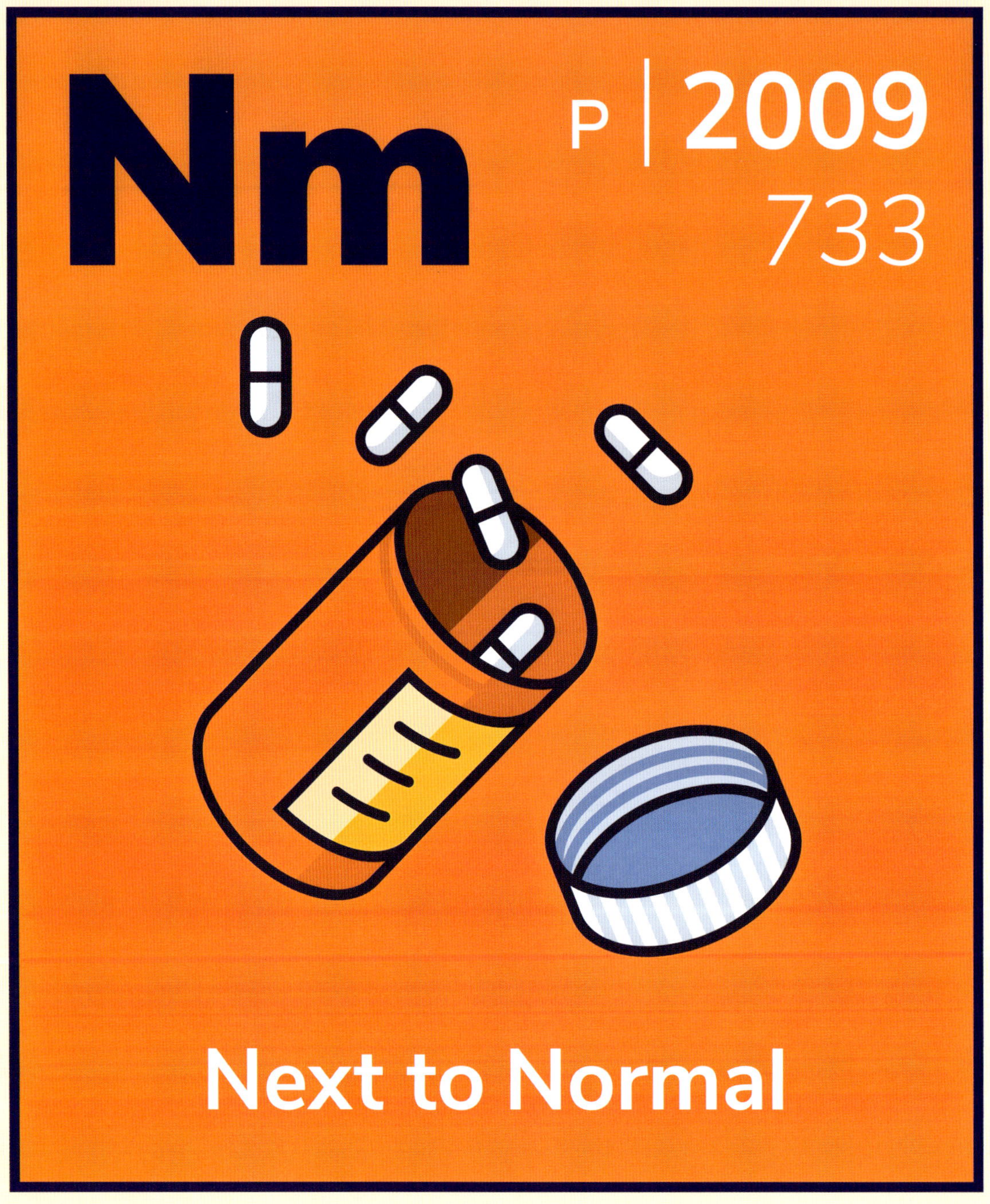

Book and lyrics by Brian Yorkey ★ Music by Tom Kitt
Directed by Michael Greif ★ Musical staging by Sergio Trujillo

Booth Theatre, April 15, 2009–January 16, 2011

Alice Ripley.......Diana
Jennifer Damiano.......Natalie
Aaron Tveit.......Gabe
J. Robert Spencer.......Dan

ART NOTE: A prescription bottle with pills either being thrown away or flying out.

Suburban mom Diana is battling delusional bipolar disorder, and her medications aren't working. Her husband, Dan, is patient but misses the old Diana; teenage daughter Natalie struggles to be perfect while worried she's like her mom. Supportive son Gabe, though, encourages her to flush her pills and rely on him. It's then revealed he's only Diana's hallucination—Gabe died as a baby. As things deteriorate, Diana decides she must leave her family to heal and grieve by herself.

Better Than Before

Next to Normal is an unlikely show that took an unlikely road to Broadway. It began as a ten-minute musical called *Feeling Electric*, based on a *Dateline* segment Yorkey had seen about electroshock therapy, then expanded over the years as he and composer Kitt found they couldn't stop writing songs for it. After out-of-town workshops, and a name change, it had a 2008 off-Broadway production at Second Stage Theatre that got mixed-to-negative reviews. But producer David Stone (*Wicked*) believed in the show, so in a bold move he took it out of town again to Arena Stage in Washington, D.C., where major revisions went in. When the show came back to New York it was much improved, and critics who had formerly criticized or dismissed the piece were now its biggest fans.

One of *Next to Normal*'s strengths had always been its granular, day-to-day depiction of what it's like to have, and to live with, serious mental illness. Not your typical musical theatre fare, but the authors learned that audiences responded to the more universal story of a family trying to stay together under terrible circumstances. The songs deftly rode Diana's highs and lows, and the somehow even worse medicated but emotionless middle. Often described as a rock musical, the music does have the expected driving accompaniments, hard drums, and guitar. But Kitt approached each moment as a dramatist, not just a songwriter, calibrating surprising harmonies to support emotional truths and allowing the score to expand into country, contemporary musical theatre, even classical vocabulary as the scenes demanded. With this broad palette, *Next to Normal* feels like the child of *Rent*'s strong, character-based musical theatre writing.

Fittingly, it was *Rent* director Michael Greif who shaped the show, setting the volatile relationships among the small cast against a black, two-story set, shiny and cold. In one of many devastating moments, Diana stands at the family dinner table with a birthday cake ringed with blazing candles lighting her face. The cake is for her dynamic son, Gabe, whom we've seen sing and converse with her for twenty-five minutes. When Dan has to explain, yet again, that "He's not here," the audience is as shocked at this revelation as Natalie's boyfriend. The show delivered this sort of visceral gut punch multiple times over the course of the evening, making it one of the most emotional musicals of the decade.

MISCELLANEOUS MATTER

- ★ Originally scheduled for the larger Longacre Theatre, Stone had planned to close off the balcony and sacrifice the ticket sales to achieve a more intimate feel. When the 800-seat Booth became available, he grabbed it.
- ★ The song "I Miss the Mountains" was inspired by Yorkey seeing the Rockies out of the Denver airport window, a perfect metaphor for Diana's manic highs.
- ★ *Next to Normal* became the eighth show to win the Pulitzer Prize for Drama, in a controversial decision: the board chose it despite it not being on the jury's three-show short list.

Book and lyrics by Lisa Kron ★ Music by Jeanine Tesori
Based on the graphic novel by Alison Bechdel
Directed by Sam Gold ★ Choreographed by Danny Mefford

Circle in the Square Theatre, April 19, 2015–September 10, 2016

Michael Cerveris.......Bruce
Judy Kuhn.......Helen
Sydney Lucas, Emily Skeggs & Beth Malone.......Alison

ART NOTE: The "Ring of Keys" that Young Alison sees on a woman she is fascinated with.

As forty-something cartoonist Alison works on her autobiographical graphic novel, episodes from her childhood and first year in college come to life. At the center of these memories are her growing realization that she is a lesbian and her difficult relationship with her undertaker father, himself a closeted gay man who takes out his frustrations on his family. Through a shared love of literature, the two eventually make a tentative connection just before the father's death.

Welcome to Our Home on Maple Avenue

Alison Bechdel's 2006 graphic novel/memoir was itself a groundbreaker, pushing both forms. Told non-chronologically, the story was a deeply personal one about a young woman figuring out her sexuality while dealing with shocking revelations about her father, his sexuality, and his past. *Fun Home,* with its unconventional structure, content, and erudite references was one of the first graphic novels to be taken seriously as a work of literature and made many critics' best-of-the-year lists.

But a book is not a show, and playwright Lisa Kron knew she had to reinvent the source material, somehow creating a show *about* creating a book. Keeping the original's feel and structure was vital, and over the five years it took to develop the piece, there were constant revisions and dead ends. The obvious choice of using many of Bechdel's drawings as projections got pared down to only one at the end of the show, but the idea that the audience was watching panels of a graphic novel come to life was suggested by starting narrative sound bites with the word "Caption:". The effect was, like the book, literary and distancing, even as Tesori's music was opening the characters up with loving yet surgical precision.

Despite its challenging subject matter and structure, the off-Broadway production of *Fun Home* came across as surprisingly straightforward. Having three actresses playing the same character at different ages felt so natural it seemed like musicals had been doing it for years. Jumping around in time within one person's memoir simply added richness and suspense. But was it commercial? When the Broadway transfer was announced, people wondered if the first musical with a lesbian central character could find a mainstream audience. Wasn't it too "edgy"? And how could the traditional proscenium staging at the Public Theater be translated to Circle in the Square's theatre-in-the-round format?

The Broadway version turned out to be even more focused and effective in its new space. Gold had panels in the stage floor open at key moments to literally rip the ground out from under characters, and having audiences on all sides put the characters into a kind of glass jar where every gesture and reaction could be observed.

Fun Home became even more of what it always was: a universal story about a troubled family, with children and parents just trying to connect with and understand each other.

MISCELLANEOUS MATTER

★ Bechdel grew up living above her family's funeral business—the "fun" in *Fun Home*—which served her well when constructing a memoir where a death (specifically, her father's ambiguous death) becomes the jumping-off point.

★ Bechdel is credited with creating the Bechdel Test, a way of evaluating how women are represented in film and other media. To pass, a film must have at least two women talk to each other about something other than men.

★ Michael Cerveris, as the dark, obsessive center of *Fun Home*, was equal parts home renovation nerd and sexual predator. Somehow, he and the creators managed to find something understandable in his character's demons, and it won them all Tonys.

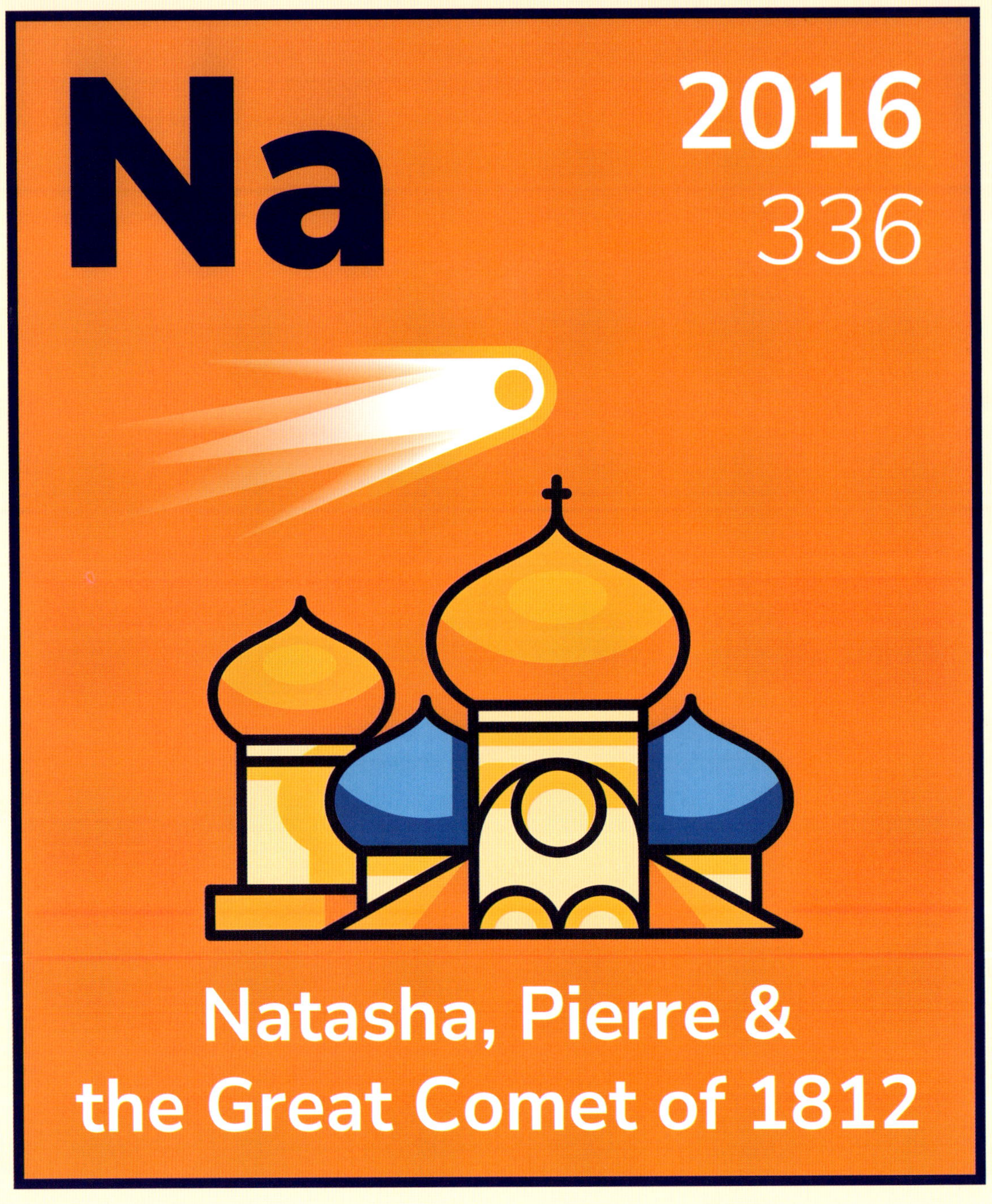

Book, music, and lyrics by Dave Malloy
Adapted from the novel *War and Peace* by Leo Tolstoy
Directed by Rachel Chavkin ★ Choreographed by Sam Pinkleton

Imperial Theatre, November 14, 2016–September 3, 2017

Denée Benton.......Natasha
Josh Groban.......Pierre
Lucas Steele.......Anatole
Brittain Ashford.......Sonya

ART NOTE: The Great Comet streaking across the sky above a traditional Russian onion-domed church.

Moscow, 1812. Andrey is off serving in the war, while at home, his fiancée, Natasha, scandalizes their upper-class circle by having an affair with womanizing Anatole. Unaware that Anatole is married, Natasha calls off her engagement and they plan to elope, but Anatole is shamed by his friend Pierre, who orders him to leave the city. When Andrey returns, he learns of Natasha's betrayal, and Pierre is left to comfort her as they watch the Great Comet streak through the sky.

The Private and Intimate Life of the House

Dave Malloy's interests and influences are as wide-ranging as the sprawling novel he chose as inspiration for his first Broadway show. A college double-major in music composition and English literature, he discovered *War and Peace* while working as a pianist on a cruise ship and saw the opportunity to use his eclectic tastes to bring Tolstoy's deeply thoughtful, deeply human characters to life. Each person would have a distinct musical vocabulary, from Slavic folk to electronica, Björk to Bartók. The text used passages from the original Tolstoy, which melded into more structured lyrics that retained the loose feel of a melancholy poet.

During a trip to Moscow while he was writing the show, Molloy ended up in a café where live musicians encouraged the audience to play along on handmade shakers, which gave him a vision of what *The Great Comet's* atmosphere should be. The show began at a small, narrow New York venue called Ars Nova, and director Chavkin and designer Mimi Lien staged the actors amid the audience, who were seated at café tables set with bottles of vodka and replica shakers. The audience was inextricably situated within the story, among the actors. This intimate, immersive environment was perfect for the show's themes of love and deception, and characters longing to connect. When the show received rave reviews, the question was: how could it be enlarged?

First stop: a 6,000-square-foot tent in the Meatpacking District, where producers added cabaret and circus artists, and offered a seafood and chicken dinner. When that iteration closed, the tent moved to the middle of the Theatre District (scaling back dinner to pierogies), with an eye to ultimately transforming a Broadway house. After a more traditional run in Boston, at long last the Imperial Theatre opened up, and work began constructing staircases and new playing areas throughout the audience to allow actors to move freely through the space and re-create, as much as possible, the intimate feel of the 87-seat Ars Nova. Recording megastar Josh Groban was signed as Pierre in an attempt to attract enough ticket sales to pay for the transfer's $14 million cost. With some of the audience seated on stage, the theatre walls draped with velvet, and a parquet runway extending into the orchestra section, the original drawing room atmosphere was miraculously maintained, a remarkable first for a Broadway musical.

MISCELLANEOUS MATTER

- ★ The show closed suddenly after blowback over the confused casting process when replacing Groban, an unfortunate end to a groundbreaking show.
- ★ Josh Groban continued to spread his theatrical wings, appearing in Lin-Manuel Miranda's *Freestyle Love Supreme* as a "special spontaneous guest performer," then in the title role of the 2023 revival of *Sweeney Todd.*
- ★ When the show closed, the producers opened a pierogi restaurant on the Lower East Side of Manhattan.
- ★ As full of colors as his shows' designs are, Malloy can't see them—he's color-blind.

ALPHABETICAL LIST OF SHOWS

The Classics:
Elemental building blocks

The Hits:
Highly reactive crowd-pleasers

The Broadway Operas:
Lustrous vocal showpieces

The Canon:
Fundamentals of any season

Off-Broadway:
Crucible for innovation

The Show Biz Series:
Stories that glow in a spotlight

The Leading Ladies Series:
Strong sources of star power

The Ensemble Pieces:
Casts sharing numerous bonds

The Entertainers:
Instantaneous catalysts for fun

The True Stories:
Reactions over time

The Groundbreakers:
Works with high dramatic density

★ Ain't Misbehavin' 214

★ Altar Boyz 140

★ And the World Goes 'Round 141

★ Annie 192

★ Annie Get Your Gun 176

★ Anything Goes 232

★ Avenue Q 226

★ Beautiful 172

★ Beauty and the Beast 108

★ Big River 100

★ The Book of Mormon 120

★ Brigadoon 64

★ Bring in 'da Noise, Bring in 'da Funk 252
★ Bye Bye Birdie 234
★ Cabaret 20
★ Camelot 74
★ Candide 46
★ Caroline, or Change 268
★ Carousel 60
★ Cats 38
★ Chicago 190
★ A Chorus Line 150
★ City of Angels 160
★ Closer Than Ever 141
★ The Color Purple 200
★ Come From Away 258
★ Company 208
★ Crazy for You 162
★ Damn Yankees 72
★ Dear Evan Hansen 130
★ Dreamgirls 154
★ The Drowsy Chaperone 228
★ Evita 194
★ Falsettos 222
★ The Fantasticks 136
★ Fela! 254
★ Fiddler on the Roof 36
★ Finian's Rainbow 62
★ Fiorello! 248
★ Follies 148
★ Forever Plaid 141
★ 42nd Street 152
★ The Full Monty 166
★ Fun Home 272
★ Funny Girl 184
★ A Funny Thing Happened on the Way to the Forum 236
★ Godspell 212
★ Grease 238
★ Grey Gardens 202
★ Guys and Dolls 30
★ Gypsy 180
★ Hadestown 132
★ Hair 22
★ Hairspray 196

Alphabetical List of Shows

★ Hamilton 256

★ Hedwig and the Angry Inch 139

★ Hello, Dolly! 182

★ How to Succeed in Business Without Really Trying 76

★ I Love You, You're Perfect, Now Change 139

★ I'm Getting My Act Together and Taking It on the Road 137

★ In the Heights 118

★ Into the Woods 218

★ Jacques Brel Is Alive and Well and Living in Paris 141

★ Jelly's Last Jam 164

★ Jersey Boys 170

★ Jesus Christ Superstar 88

★ The King and I 66

★ Kinky Boots 126

★ Kiss Me, Kate 146

★ Kiss of the Spider Woman 106

★ La Cage aux Folles 158

★ The Last Five Years 140

★ Legally Blonde 204

★ Les Misérables 24

★ The Light in the Piazza 54

★ The Lion King 40

★ A Little Night Music 92

★ Little Shop of Horrors 138

★ Mame 188

★ Mamma Mia! 114

★ Man of La Mancha 84

★ Merrily We Roll Along 96

★ Miss Saigon 102

★ The Most Happy Fella 48

★ The Music Man 32

★ My Fair Lady 18

★ The Mystery of Edwin Drood 216

★ Natasha, Pierre & the Great Comet of 1812 274

★ Newsies 124

★ Next to Normal 270

★ Nine 156

★ Nunsense 138

★ Oklahoma! 16

★ Oliver! 78

★ On the Town 58

★ Once 122

★ Once on This Island 220

★ 110 in the Shade 82

★ The Pajama Game 70

★ Pal Joey 144

★ Parade 266

★ Peter Pan 178

★ The Phantom of the Opera 52

★ Pippin 90

★ Porgy and Bess 44

★ The Producers 168

★ Promises, Promises 86

★ Ragtime 110

★ Raisin 210

★ Rent 26

★ The Secret Garden 104

★ 1776 250

★ She Loves Me 80

★ Show Boat 14

★ Something Rotten! 244

★ The Sound of Music 34

★ South Pacific 262

★ Spamalot 240

★ Spring Awakening 116

★ Sunday in the Park with George 98

★ Sweeney Todd 50

★ Sweet Charity 186

★ The Threepenny Opera 136

★ The 25th Annual Putnam County Spelling Bee 242

★ Urinetown 112

★ Waitress 128

★ West Side Story 264

★ The Who's Tommy 224

★ Wicked 198

★ The Wiz 94

★ Wonderful Town 68

★ You're a Good Man, Charlie Brown 137

INDEX

A

Abbott, George
Damn Yankees, 72
Fiorello!, 181, 248, 249
Funny Thing Happened on the *Way to the Forum, A*, 236
Harold Prince and, 21, 265
Pajama Game, The, 70, 71
Pal Joey, 144
On the Town, 58
Wonderful Town, 68, 69
Actors' Equity Association, 103
Adams, Edith, "Edie," 47, 68, 69
Adams, Lee, 183, 234
Adler, Bruce, 162
Adler, Gary, 140
Adler, Richard, 70, 71, 72, 83
Adrian, Max, 46
Adventures of Huckleberry Finn (Twain), 100
Afrobeat, 255
Ahrens, Lynn, 110, 111, 167, 220, 221
Ainsley, Paul, 88
Ain't Misbehavin', 214–215
Akers, Karen, 156
Alda, Robert, 30
Aldredge, Theoni V., 153
Aleichem, Sholom, 36, 37
Alexander, Cris, 58
Alexander, Jason, 96
Allen, Deborah, "Debbie," 210, 211
Allers, Roger, 40
Altar Boyz, 140
Alton, Robert, 232, 233
Alvarez, Anita, 62
And the World Goes 'Round, 141
Andersson, Benny, 114, 115
Andrews, Julie, 18, 19, 74, 75
Andrews, Maxene, 49
Angelou, Maya, 45
Anna and the King of Siam (Landon), 66
Annie, 192–193
Annie Get Your Gun, 176–177
ANTA in the Village, 85
Anthony, Joseph, 48, 82
Antibalas, 255
Anything Goes, 232–233
Apartment, The (film), 86
Arcenas, Loy, 221
Arden, Michael, 117
Arena Stage, 211, 271
Armstrong, Louis, 215
Aronson, Billy, 26, 37
Aronson, Boris, 21, 209
Ars Nova, 275
Arthur, Beatrice, 36, 37, 136, 188, 189
Ashford, Annaleigh, 126
Ashford, Brittain, 274
Ashley, Christopher, 258, 259
Ashman, Howard, 108, 109, 138
Astaire, Fred, 49
Atkinson, Brooks, 49, 71, 135
Atlantic Theater Company, 117
Auberjonois, René, 100, 101
Auden, W.H., 85
Auntie Mame (Dennis), 188
Avenue Q, 226–227
Avian, Bob, 102, 150
Ayers, Lemuel, 17
Azaria, Hank, 240, 241

B

Bacharach, Burt, 86, 87
Bailey, Pearl, 183
Baldwin, Kate, 167
Bale, Christian, 125
Ball, Lucille, 189
Ballad of Baby Doe, The, 47
Ballard, Florence, 155
Banderas, Antonio, 195
Barbeau, Adrienne, 238
Bareilles, Sara, 128, 129
Barnes, Clive, 93, 191, 251
Barnes, Gregg, 127
Barrie, J.M., 178
Barry, Gene, 158
Bart, Lionel, 78, 79
Barton, Steve, 52
Bassey, Shirley, 79
Battle, Hinton, 102
Battles, John, 58
Baum, L. Frank, 94
Baxley, Barbara, 80
Beach, Gary, 168
Beale, Edie "Little Edie", 203
Beaton, Cecil, 19
Beaufoy, Simon, 166
Beautiful, 172–173
Beauty and the Beast, 41, 108–109
Bechdel, Alison, 272, 273
Bechdel Test, 273
Bell, Marion, 64
Benjamin, Nell, 204, 205
Bennett, Michael
Chorus Line, A, 150, 151
Company, 208, 209
Dreamgirls, 154, 155
Follies, 148, 149
Promises, Promises, 86, 87
Tommy Tune and, 157
Bennett, Robert Russell, 17
Benson, Jodi, 162, 163
Bentley, Jordan, 68
Benton, Denée, 274
Berkman, John, 91
Berle, Milton, 237
Berlin, Irving, 87, 176
Bernstein, Leonard, 43, 57, 237
Candide, 46, 47
Peter Pan, 179
On the Town, 58, 59
West Side Story, 264, 265
Wonderful Town, 68, 69
Big River, 100–101
Bigley, Isabel, 30
Bikel, Theodore, 34
bio-musicals, 255
Birch, Patricia, 92, 238, 266
Birkenhead, Susan, 164, 165
Bishop, Carole "Kelly," 150
Bissell, Richard, 70
Björnson, Maria, 53
Blaine, Vivian, 30, 209
Blake, Richard H., 204
Blakemore, Michael, 160
Blankenbuehler, Andy, 118, 119, 256
Bledsoe, Jules, 14
Blickenstaff, Heidi, 167, 244, 245
Block, Stephanie J., 233
Bloomer Girl, 63
BMI Lehman Engel Musical Theatre Workshop, 227
Bobbie, Walter, 239
Bock, Jerry, 36, 80, 248, 249
Bolger, Ray, 79
Bolin, Shannon, 72
Bolton, Guy, 162, 231, 232
Bond, Christopher, 50
Book of Mormon, The, 120–121
Booth Theatre, 221, 271
Borle, Christian, 204, 223, 244
Bosley, Tom, 108, 109, 248, 249
Bostwick, Barry, 238
Boublil, Alain, 24, 102
Bradbury, Lane, 180
Bramble, Mark, 152

Brantley, Ben, 121
Braxton, Toni, 109
Bray, Stephen, 200, 201
Brecht, Bertolt, 113, 136
Brel, Jacques, 141
Brennan, Eileen, 182
Brickman, Marshall, 170, 171
Brigadoon, 64–65
Brightman, Sarah, 53
Brill Building, 173
Bring in 'da Noise, Bring in 'da Funk, 119, 252–253
Brisson, Frederick, 181
Brittan, Robert, 210, 211
Britten, Benjamin, 55
Britton, Pamela, 64
Broderick, Matthew, 168, 169
Brooks, David, 64
Brooks, Donald, 87
Brooks, Harry, 214
Brooks, Mel, 168, 169
Brown, Amanda, 204
Brown, Anne Wiggins, 44, 45
Brown, Georgia, 78
Brown, Jason Robert, 140, 167, 266, 267
Brown, William F., 94
Bruce, Carol, 145
Bruni, Marc, 172
Brynner, Yul, 66, 67
Bubbles, John W., 44
Buckley, Betty, 38, 216, 250
Bundy, Laura Bell, 196, 204, 205
Burnett, Frances Hodgson, 104
Burns, David, 32, 182
Burns, Ralph, 91
Burrows, Abe, 30, 31, 76, 77
Burstein, Danny, 228
Burton, Richard, 74
Butterell, Jonathan, 54
Butz, Norbert Leo, 140, 198
Bye Bye Birdie, 153, 234–235
Byrd, Donald, 200

C

Cabaret, 13, 20–21, 81, 91, 107, 141, 187, 191, 193, 195, 209
Caird, John, 24, 25
Calhoun, Jeff, 124, 125, 202
Calloway, Cab, 45, 183
Camelot, 74–75, 235
Candide, 43, 46–47
Capers, Virginia, 210
Cariou, Len, 50, 51, 92
Carmelina, 115
Carmello, Carolee, 266
Carnahan, Kirsti, 106
Carney, John, 122, 123
Carney, Reeve, 132
Caroline, or Change, 211, 268–269
Carousel, 45, 57, 60–61, 147, 175
Carradine, John, 236
Carrafa, John, 112, 113
Carter, Nell, 214, 215
Carter, Ralph, 211
Carver, Brent, 106, 266, 267
Casey, Warren, 238, 239
Cassidy, Jack, 80, 81
Cats, 38–39
Cattaneo, Peter, 166
Cerveris, Michael, 224, 225, 272, 273
Chad, Harrison, 268, 269
Champion, Gower, 152, 153, 182, 183, 234, 235
Champion, Marge, 235
Channing, Carol, 69, 182, 183
Chaplin, Sydney, 184, 185
Charlap, Mark (Moose), 178
Charnin, Martin, 192
Chavkin, Rachel, 132, 133, 274, 275
Chenoweth, Kristin, 136, 198
Chernow, Ron, 257
Chess, 115
Chicago, 190–191
Chicago (Watkins), 190
Chodorov, Jerome, 68
Chorus Line, A, 150–151
Church, Sandra, 180
Cilento, Wayne, 198, 224
Circle in the Square Theatre, 243, 273
City of Angels, 160–161
Civilians, The (theatre company), 259
Clark, Victoria, 54, 55
Clarke, Hope, 164, 268
Clarke, Sharon D., 221
Clayburgh, Jill, 90
Clayton, Jan, 60
Close, Glenn, 136, 219, 263
Closer Than Ever, 141
Coe, Peter, 78
Cohan, George M., 33
Cohenour, Patti, 54, 100, 216
Cohn, Al, 211
Cole, Jack, 84, 85, 236
Colella, Jenn, 258
Coleman, Cy, 160, 161, 186
Coleman, Gary, 227
Coleman, Warren, 44
Collins, Dorothy, 148
Collins, Judy, 93
Color Purple, The, 200–201
Colored Museum, The (play), 165
Colvan, Zeke, 14
Comden, Betty
  Mame (film), 189
  Peter Pan, 178, 179
  sketch comedy background, 77
  On the Town, 58, 59
  turning down *West Side Story*, 265
  Wonderful Town, 68, 69
Come From Away, 258–259
Company, 123, 207, 208–209
composer-driven revues, 215
concept musicals, 23, 195, 209
Conlee, John Ellison, 166
Connell, Jane, 188, 193
Convy, Bert, 36, 37
Cook, Barbara, 32, 33, 46, 80
Cooper, Bertram, 77
Coote, Robert, 18, 75
Coppola, Francis Ford, 63
countercultural musicians, 23
Coward, Noël, 67
Cox, Veanne, 268
Crawford, Michael, 52, 53
Craymer, Judy, 115
Crazy for You, 162–163
Crewe, Bob, 170
Crivello, Anthony, 106
Crosby, Bing, 93
Crouse, Russel, 34, 232, 233, 263
Cryer, Gretchen, 137
Cullum, John, 112
Cumming, Alan, 127
Cuneo, Ernest, 247
Curry, Tim, 240

D

Da Costa, Morton, 32
Da Silva, Howard, 16, 250
D'Abruzzo, Stephanie, 226
Daltry, Roger, 225
Damiano, Jennifer, 270
Damn Yankees, 72–73
Daniele, Graciela, 110, 111, 216, 220, 221
Danieley, Jason, 166
Daniels, William, 250, 251
Dante, Nicholas, 150, 151
Darion, Joe, 84, 85
Darling, Jean, 60
David, Hal, 86, 87
David, Keith, 164
Davie, Erin, 202
De Mille, Agnes
  Brigadoon, 64, 65
  Carousel, 60, 61
  director/choreographer dual role, 235
  Oklahoma!, 16, 17
  110 in the Shade, 82
De Shields, André, 94, 95, 132, 166, 214
Deaf West Theatre Company, 101, 117
Deane, Geoff, 126
Dear Evan Hansen, 130–131
Del Aguila, Kevin, 140
Delacorte stage, Central Park, 217

Demas, Carole, 238
Dench, Judi, 39, 219
Dennis, Patrick, 188, 189
DePietro, Joe, 139
Derricks, Cleavant, 154
Devine, Kelly, 258, 259
Diamond, Micaela, 267
Dickens, Charles, 78, 216, 217
Diener, Joan, 84
Diggs, Daveed, 256, 257
Divine, 197
Dixon, Jerry, 220
Dixon, Mort, 152
Doctorow, E.L., 110
documentary theatre, 259
Dokuchitz, Jonathan, 224
Dolan, Judith, 97
Donehue, Vincent J., 34
Dossett, John, 124
Douglass, Stephen, 72, 82, 83
Doyle, John, 51, 123, 201
Drabinsky, Garth, 111
Drake, Alfred, 16, 67, 146
dream ballets, 17
Dreamgirls, 95, 143, 154–155, 225
Dreyfuss, Laura, 130
Drood. See Mystery of Edwin Drood, The
Drowsy Chaperone, The, 228–229
Drury Lane Theatre, 103
Du Prez, John, 240, 241
Dubin, Al, 152
Duncan, Todd, 44
Duquesnay, Ann, 252, 253

E

Eagan, Daisy, 104, 105
Earhart, Amelia, 15
Eastwood, Clint, 171
Eaton, Sally, 22
Ebb, Fred
- *And the World Goes 'Round the Rink,* 167
- *Cabaret*, 20, 21
- *Chicago*, 190, 191
- *Kiss of the Spider Woman*, 106, 107
- revue, 141

Ebersole, Christine, 202, 203
Eckart, William and Jean, 81, 249
Ed Kleban Award, 151
Edelman, Gregg, 160, 161
Eden Theatre, 239
Edwards, Sherman, 250, 251
Egan, Susan, 108, 109
8½ (Fellini), 156, 157
Eisner, Michael, 109
Elice, Rick, 170, 171
Eliot, T.S., 38
Elliman, Yvonne, 88
Ellis, Scott, 239
Epstein, Jake, 172
Erivo, Cynthia, 199, 201
Ernst, Leila, 144
Eugene O'Neill Theatre, 81
Evita, 175, 194–195
Eyen, Tom, 154, 155

F

Fagan, Garth, 40
Faison, George, 94
Faison, Sandy, 192
Faist, Mike, 130
Falk, Willy, 102
Falsettos, 27, 222–223
Fältskog, Agnetha, 89
Fankhauser, Ben, 124
Fantasticks, The, 136
Faria, Arthur, 215
Farm, The (improv company), 243
Fearnley, John, 61
Fela!, 254–255
Feldman, Jack, 124, 125
Feldman, Rebecca, 242, 243
Fellini, Federico, 156, 157, 186, 187
Fenholt, Jeff, 88
Ferber, Edna, 14
Ferguson, Jesse Tyler, 242, 243
Ferland, Danielle, 218
Feuer, Cy, 31
Fiddler on the Roof, 21, 29, 36–37, 207, 249
Field, Ronald, 20
Fields, Dorothy, 176, 177, 186
Fields, Herbert, 176, 177
Fields, Joseph A., 68
Fierstein, Harvey
- *Hairspray*, 196, 197
- *Kinky Boots*, 126, 127
- *La Cage aux Folles*, 158, 159
- *Newsies*, 124, 125

Finian's Rainbow, 62–63
Finn, William, 222, 223, 242
Finneran, Katie, 87, 193
Fiorello!, 181, 247, 248–249
Firth, Tim, 126
Fitzgerald, Christopher, 128, 129
Flaherty, Stephen, 110, 111, 167, 220, 221
Flying by Foy, 179
Fogler, Dan, 242, 243
Follies, 93, 143, 148–149. *See also* Ziegfeld's *Follies*
Ford, Nancy, 137
Forever Plaid, 141
42nd Street, 152–153
Fosse, Bob
- *Chicago*, 190, 191
- *Damn Yankees*, 72, 73
- director/choreographer dual role, 235
- *How to Succeed in Business Without Really Trying*, 76
- *Pajama Game, The*, 70, 71
- *Pippin*, 90, 91
- summer stock actor, 145
- *Sweet Charity*, 186, 187

Foster, John, 112
Foster, Sutton, 228, 233
Foy, Eddie, Jr., 70
Foy, Peter, 179
Frankel, Scott, 202, 203
Fraser, Alison, 104, 105
Freedly, Vinton, 233
Freedman, Robert M., 211
Friedman, Michael, 259
Friedman, Peter, 110
Fryer, Robert, 69
Full Monty, The, 166–167
Fuller, Larry, 50, 96, 194
Fun Home, 223, 272–273
Funny Girl, 184–185
Funny Thing Happened on the Way to the Forum, A, 236–237
Furth, George, 96, 208, 209

G

Gable, Clark, 191
Gad, Josh, 120, 121
Gaines, Reg E., 252, 253
Galati, Frank, 110
Gallagher, John, Jr., 116
Gallagher, Peter, 239
Galvin, Noah, 131
Garber, Victor, 50, 213
Gardner, Ava, 15
Garland, Judy, 177
Gattelli, Christopher, 124
Gaudio, Bob, 170
Gaxton, William, 232, 233
Gaynes, George, 68, 69
Gaynor, Mitzi, 263
Geffen, David, 169
Gehling, Drew, 128
Gelbart, Larry, 160, 161, 236, 237
Gelber, Jordan, 226
Gennaro, Peter, 192, 248, 264, 265
Gere, Richard, 239
Gershovsky, Yaron, 161
Gershwin, George, 44, 45, 77, 87, 162
Gershwin, Ira, 44, 45, 77, 162
Gesner, Clark, 137
Gilbert, Willie, 76
Gilford, Jack, 236
Gilliam, Terry, 241
Gingold, Hermione, 92
Ginzler, Robert "Red," 181, 235
Gleason, Joanna, 218
Glenn, Kimiko, 128
Glover, Savion, 164, 165, 252, 253
Godspell, 91, 212–213

Goffin, Gerry, 172
Goggin, Dan, 138
Gold, Sam, 272, 273
Goldberg, Whoopi, 219
Golden Apple, The, 47, 135
Goldman, James, 148, 149
Goldsberry, Renée Elise, 200, 201
Goldwyn, Samuel, 61
Gonzalez, Mandy, 118
Goodspeed Opera House, 193
Gordon, Ricky Ian, 227
Gordy, Berry, Jr., 155
Gospel According to St. Matthew, 212
Goulet, Robert, 74
Grable, Betty, 183
Graff, Randy, 24, 160
Gray, Amber, 132
Gray, Harold, 192
Grease, 205, 225, 238–239
Green, Adolph
  Mame (film), 189
  Peter Pan, 178, 179
  sketch comedy background, 77
  On the Town, 58, 59
  turning down *West Side Story*, 265
  Wonderful Town, 68, 69
Green Grow the Lilacs (Riggs), 16
Greif, Michael, 26, 130, 131, 202, 270, 271
Grey, Joel, 21, 198
Grey Gardens, 202–203
Griffin, Gary, 200
Griffith, Robert E., 71
Grimes, Tammy, 152
Groban, Josh, 274, 275
Groener, Harry, 38, 162
Groff, Jonathan, 116
Guettel, Adam, 54, 55, 167, 227
Guittard, Laurence, 92
Gunton, Bob, 194
Guthrie, Tyrone, 46, 47
Guy, Rosa, 220
Guys and Dolls, 29, 30–31, 49, 77
Gypsy, 69, 153, 175, 180–181, 237, 247, 265

H

Hach, Heather, 204
Hadestown, 95, 129, 132–133
Hair, 13, 22–23, 225, 251
Hairspray, 196–197
Hall, Bettina, 232
Hall, Juanita, 262
Halliday, Heller, 179
Halliday, Richard, 179
Hamilton, 119, 201, 251, 256–257
Hamilton, Carrie, 27
Hamlisch, Marvin, 150, 151, 185
Hammerstein, Arthur, 15
Hammerstein II, Oscar
  Annie Get Your Gun, 177
  Carousel, 60
  interest in *The Light in the Piazza*, 55
  King and I, The, 66, 67
  Me and Juliet, 147
  offering advice on *Gypsy*, 181
  Oklahoma!, 16, 17
  Show Boat, 14, 15
  Sound of Music, The, 34, 35
  South Pacific, 262, 263
Haney, Carol, 70, 71, 80, 81, 184
Hanley, Ellen, 248
Hansard, Glen, 122, 123
Hansberry, Lorraine, 210
Harada, Ann, 226
Harburg, E.Y. "Yip," 62, 63
Harney, Ben, 154
Harnick, Sheldon, 36, 80, 248, 249
Harper, Ken, 95
Harris, Neil Patrick, 139
Harrison, Rex, 18, 19, 67
Hart, Charles, 52
Hart, Lorenz, 87, 144, 145, 147, 233
Hart, Moss, 18, 19, 74, 75, 96
Hauptman, William, 100
Havoc, June, 144
Hayworth, Rita, 145
Headley, Heather, 40
Hearn, George, 158, 159
Heaviside, Oliver, 39
Hedwig and the Angry Inch, 139
Hein, David, 258
Hellman, Lillian, 46, 47
Hello, Dolly!, 182–183
Henderson, Florence, 263
Henderson, Luther, 164, 165, 214, 215
Henner, Marilu, 239
Henry Miller's Theatre, 113
Herman, Jerry, 99, 158, 159, 169, 182, 183, 188, 189, 215, 223
Heyward, Dorothy, 44, 45
Heyward, DuBose, 44, 45
Hicks, Rodney, 258
Hill, Dulé, 252, 253
Hines, Gregory, 164, 165, 253
Hirson, Roger O., 90
Hoff, Christian, 170
Hoggett, Steven, 122
Holder, Geoffrey, 94, 95
Holgate, Ronald, 236, 237
Holliday, Jennifer, 154, 155
Holm, Celeste, 16
Hollmann, Mark, 112, 113
Holloway, Stanley, 18
Holm, Hanya, 74, 75, 146
Holmes, Rupert, 216, 217
Holzman, Winnie, 198, 199
Hooper, Tom, 25
Horne, Lena, 15, 211
Horton, Robert, 82, 83
Horwitz, Murray, 214, 215
Hould-Ward, Ann, 109
How to Succeed in Business Without Really Trying, 76–77, 113, 237
Howard, Lisa, 242
Howard, Peter, 179
Howard, Sidney, 48
HUAC (House Un-American Activities Committee), 31, 47
Hudes, Quiara Alegría, 118, 119
Hudson, Jennifer, 155
Huffman, Cady, 168
Hugo, Victor, 24
Humphries, Barry, 79
Hunt, Peter, 250
Hutton, Betty, 177, 193
Hytner, Nicholas, 102

I

I Am a Camera (Van Druten), 20, 21
I Love You, You're Perfect, Now Change, 139
Idle, Eric, 240, 241
I'm Getting My Act Together and Taking It on the Road, 137
immersive theatre, 13, 243, 275
Imperial Theatre, 275
In the Heights, 118–119, 255, 257
Into the Woods, 218–219
Irglová, Markéta, 122, 123
Isherwood, Christopher, 20

J

Jackson, Christopher, 118
Jackson, Ernestine, 210
Jackson, Michael, 165
Jacobs, Jim, 238, 239
Jacobson, Irving, 84
Jacques Brel Is Alive and Well and Living in Paris, 141
James, Brian d'Arcy, 244
James, Nikki M., 120
Jay-Z, 255
Jelly's Last Jam, 164–165, 253
Jenkins, Daniel H., 100, 101
Jersey Boys, 143, 170–171, 173, 175
Jesus Christ Superstar, 88–89
John, Elton, 40
Johns, Glynis, 92, 93
Johnson, Catherine, 114, 115
Johnson, Susan, 48
Jones, Bill T., 116, 117, 254, 255
Jones, David, 78, 79
Jones, Dean, 208, 209
Jones, Rachel Bay, 130, 131
Jones, Shirley, 49
Jones, Terry, 241
Jones, Tom, 82, 83, 136

Jordan, Jeremy, 124, 125, 140
Jordan, Louis, 165
Joseph and the Amazing Technicolor Dreamcoat, 89
Julia, Raul, 156

K

Kail, Thomas, 118, 119, 256
Kandel, Paul, 224
Kander, John
  And the World Goes 'Round the Rink, 167
  Cabaret, 20, 21
  Chicago, 190, 191
  Kiss of the Spider Woman, 106, 107
Kanin, Garson, 184, 185
Karnilova, Maria, 36
Kassebaum, Kendra, 258
Kaufman, George S., 30, 96, 97
Kaye, Judy, 52, 114, 239
Kazee, Steve, 122, 123
Keaton, Diane, 23
Keenan-Bolger, Celia, 242, 243
Kellogg, Lynn, 22
Kelly, Gene, 144, 145
Kelton, Pert, 32
Kendrick, Anna, 140
Kern, Jerome, 14, 15, 87, 177, 231
Kerr, Walter, 191
Kert, Larry, 209, 264
Khadime, Alexia, 199
Kidd, Michael, 30, 31, 62, 63
Kiley, Richard, 84, 85
Kimball, Chad, 258
King, Carole, 172, 173
King and I, The, 66–67
Kinky Boots, 126–127
Kirk, Lisa, 69, 146
Kirkpatrick, Karey, 244, 245
Kirkpatrick, Wayne, 244, 245
Kirkwood, James, 150, 151
Kiss Me, Kate, 146
Kiss of the Spider Woman, 106–107
Kitt, Tom, 270, 271
Kleban, Edward, 150, 151
Klugman, Jack, 180
Knechtges, Dan, 242
Koehler, Ted, 214
Kopit, Arthur, 156
Korie, Michael, 202, 203
Korins, David, 131
Kotis, Greg, 112, 113
Kretzmer, Herbert, 24
Krieger, Henry, 154, 155
Kron, Lisa, 272, 273
Krupska, Dania, 48
Kuhn, Judy, 272
Kushner, Tony, 268, 269
Kuti, Fela Anikulapo, 254, 255

L

La Cage aux Folles, 99, 127, 158–159, 223
La Scala opera house, 45
Lacamoire, Alex, 119, 131, 257
Lacey, Franklin, 33
LaChanze, 200, 201, 220, 221
LaChiusa, Michael John, 167
Laine, Cleo, 216
Lambert, Hugh, 76
Lambert, Lisa, 228, 229
Landesman, Heidi, 101, 105
Landesman, Rocco, 101
Landon, Margaret, 66
Lane, Burton, 62, 63, 115
Lane, Nathan, 168, 169
Lang, Harold, 146, 147
Lansbury, Angela, 50, 51, 52, 181, 188, 189
Lapine, James, 98, 99, 218, 219, 222, 242
Larsen, Anika, 172, 173
Larson, Jonathan, 26, 27, 217
Last Five Years, The, 140
László, Miklós, 80
Latarro, Lorin, 128
Latouche, John, 46, 47
Lauper, Cyndi, 126, 127
Laurents, Arthur, 158, 159, 169, 180, 264, 265
Laurie, Hugh, 257
Lawrence, Carol, 264
Lawrence, Gertrude, 66, 67
Lawrence, Jerome, 188
Layton, Joe, 34
Le Roy, Ken, 65, 264
Leach, Wilford, 216
Leachman, Cloris, 263
Leavel, Beth, 228, 245
Lee, Baayork, 151
Lee, Gypsy Rose, 180, 247
Lee, Robert E., 188
Lee, Sondra, 178
Legally Blonde, 204–205
Leggs, Kingsley, 200
Lehman, Ernest, 35
Leigh, Carolyn, 178
Leigh, Mitch, 84, 85
Lennart, Isobel, 184, 185
Leonowens, Anna, 67, 247
Lerner, Alan Jay, 18, 64, 65, 74, 75, 115
Leroux, Gaston, 52
Les Misérables, 24–25, 175
Les Misérables (Hugo), 24
Levene, Sam, 30, 31
Levenson, Steven, 130
Levinson, Barry, 161
Levy, Eugene, 213
Levy, Ted L., 164
Lewis, Jim, 254
Lewis, Robert, 64
Lewis-Evans, Kecia, 220
Lichtefeld, Michael, 104
Lieberson, Goddard, 49
Lien, Mimi, 275
Life with Father, 233
Life with Fiorello (Cuneo), 247
Light in the Piazza, The, 43, 54–55
Liliom (Molnár), 60, 61
Lincoln Center, 267
Lindsay, Howard, 34, 232, 233, 263
Lindsay, Kara, 124, 125
Lion, Margo, 197
Lion King Jr., 29
Lion King, The, 40–41
Lippa, Andrew, 137, 167
Little Night Music, A, 92–93
Little Orphan Annie (Gray), 192
Little Shop of Horrors, 109, 138
Lloyd, Phyllida, 114, 115
Lloyd Webber, Andrew
  Cats, 38, 39
  Evita, 194, 195
  Harold Prince and, 89
  Jesus Christ Superstar, 88, 89
  Phantom of the Opera, The, 52, 53
Loesser, Arthur, 49
Loesser, Frank
  as mentor, 71
  Guys and Dolls, 30, 31
  How to Succeed in Business Without Really Trying, 76, 77
  Most Happy Fella, The, 48, 49
  writer of book, music, and lyrics, 217
Loewe, Frederick "Fritz," 18, 64, 65, 74, 75
Logan, Ella, 62
Logan, Joshua, 176, 177, 262, 263
Long, William Ivey, 157
Longacre Theatre, 271
Lopez, Priscilla, 150
Lopez, Robert, 120, 121, 226, 227
Loud, David, 141
Loudon, Dorothy, 192, 193
Louise, Merle, 159, 208
Lubovitch, Lar, 218
Lucas, Craig, 54, 55
Lucas, Sydney, 272
Ludwig, Ken, 162, 163
Luker, Rebecca, 104, 105
Lund, Art, 48
LuPone, Patti, 25, 194, 195, 233
Lynch, Jane, 193
Lynde, Paul, 234
Lynne, Gillian, 38, 39, 52
Lyon, Rick, 226

M

MacDermot, Galt, 22
Mackintosh, Cameron, 25, 39, 53, 103
Mackintosh, Robert G., 189
MacLaine, Shirley, 71, 187
Maddigan, Tina, 114
Madonna, 195
Maguire, Gregory, 198, 199
Majestic Theatre, 53
Malloy, Dave, 217, 274, 275
Malone, Beth, 272
Maltby, Richard, Jr., 102, 103, 141, 214, 215
Mame, 188–189
Mamma Mia!, 114–115
Mamoulian, Rouben, 16, 17, 44, 45, 60
Man of La Mancha, 84–85, 175
Mann, Barry, 172
Mann, Terrence V., 24, 38, 108, 109
Mantello, Joe, 198
March of the Falsettos, 99
Mark, Zane, 252, 253
Marks, Joe E., 178, 179
Marre, Albert, 84, 85
Marsh, Howard, 14
Marshall, Rob, 107
Martin, Andrea, 213
Martin, Barney, 190
Martin, Bob, 228, 229
Martin, Ernest, 31
Martin, Mary, 34, 35, 177, 178, 179, 262
Martin Beck Theatre, 219
Marx, Jeff, 121, 226, 227
Mason, Karen, 114
Massey, Daniel, 80
Masteroff, Joe, 20, 80, 81
Matchmaker, The (Wilder), 182
Mayer, Michael, 116, 117
Maysles, Albert and David, 202
Mazzie, Marin, 110
McAnuff, Des, 100, 101, 170, 171, 224
McArdle, Andrea, 192, 193
McCarthy, Jeff, 112
McClelland, Kay, 160
McCollum, Kevin, 245
McDonald, Audra, 105, 110, 111
McDowall, Roddy, 74
McGillin, Howard, 216, 217
McGowan, John, 162
McGrath, Douglas, 172
McHugh, Jimmy, 214
McKay, Nellie, 127
McKayle, Donald, 210, 211
McKechnie, Donna, 87, 150, 208, 209
McKellar, Don, 228, 229
McMartin, John, 148, 186, 202, 203
McNally, Terrence, 106, 107, 110, 111, 166, 167
McQueen, Amelia, 214
Mead, Shepherd, 76
Mecchi, Irene, 40
Medford, Kay, 235
Meehan, Thomas, 168, 192, 196
Mefford, Danny, 130, 272
Menier Chocolate Factory, 201
Menken, Alan, 108, 109, 124, 125, 138
Menzel, Idina, 26, 27, 198
Mercer, Johnny, 152
Mercer, Marian, 87
Merman, Ethel
Annie Get Your Gun, 176, 177
Anything Goes, 232, 233
Girl Crazy, 163
Gypsy, 180, 181
Hello, Dolly!, 183
Merrick, David, 79, 83, 87, 153, 185
Merrifield, Gail, 217
Merrill, Bob, 183, 184
Merrily We Roll Along, 96–97
Meyers, Timothy, 238
MGM, 59, 177, 204
Michaels, Frankie, 105, 188
Michele, Lea, 116
Michener, James, 262, 263
Middleton, Ray, 176
Milioti, Cristin, 122, 123
Miller, Patina, 91
Miller, Roger, 100, 101
Mills, Stephanie, 94, 95
Minnelli, Liza, 21, 136, 191
Miranda, Lin-Manuel, 118, 119, 256, 257, 265
Miss Saigon, 57, 102–103, 167, 221
Mitchell, Anaïs, 127, 132, 133
Mitchell, Brian Stokes, 110, 165
Mitchell, Jerry, 126, 166, 167, 196, 204, 205
Mitchell, John Cameron, 139
Mitzman, Marcia, 224
Molnár, Ferenc, 60, 61
Monsoon, Jinkx, 139
Montag, Sigmund, 267
Montevecchi, Liliane, 156
Monty Python and the Holy Grail (film), 241
Monty Python's Flying Circus (comedy program), 241
Moody, Ron, 79
Moore, Jason, 226
Moore, Robert, 86, 87
Moore, Tom, 238
Moore, Victor, 232, 233
Moreno, Rita, 81
Morgan, Helen, 14, 15
Morison, Patricia, 146
Morris, Anita, 156
Morrison, Ann, 96
Morrison, Greg, 228, 229
Morrison, Matthew, 54, 196
Morrow, Doretta, 66
Morse, Robert, 76, 77
Morton, Jelly Roll, 164, 165
Morton, Joe, 210
Moses, Burke, 108, 109
Most Happy Fella, The, 31, 43, 48–49
Mostel, Zero, 36, 37, 169, 236, 237
movie adaptations, 131
Mueller, Jessie, 128, 129, 172, 173
Murphy, Cillian, 123
Music Man, The, 32–33, 175
My Fair Lady, 13, 18–19, 59, 207
My Love, My Love (Guy), 220
My One and Only, 163
My Sister Eileen (play), 68, 69
Mystery of Edwin Drood, The, 216–217

N

Napier, John, 39
Nash, N. Richard, 82, 83
Natasha, Pierre, & The Great Comet of 1812, 274–275
Naughton, James, 160, 161
Nederlander Theatre, 27, 125
Nelson, Gene, 148
Nelson, Jessie, 128
Nemiroff, Robert, 210, 211
Neumann, David, 132
New Amsterdam Theatre, 41
New World Stages, 227
New York Theatre Workshop, 133
Newsies, 124–125
Next to Normal, 270–271
Ngaujah, Sahr, 254, 255
Nicholaw, Casey, 120, 121, 228, 240, 244, 245
Nichols, Mike, 240, 241
Nights of Cabiria (Fellini), 186
Nigrini, Peter, 131
Nine, 156–157
Nixon, Richard, 251
Noblezada, Eva, 132
Norman, Marsha, 104, 105, 200, 201
Novak, Kim, 145
Nunn, Trevor, 24, 25, 38, 39
Nunsense, 138

O

O'Brien, Jack, 166, 167, 196, 197
Ockrent, Mike, 162, 169
Odom, Leslie, Jr., 256
O'Donnell, Mark, 196
Of Thee I Sing, 77
O'Farrell, John, 244, 245

O'Hara, Jill, 86
O'Hara, John, 144
O'Hara, Kelli, 54, 55, 263
O'Horgan, Tom, 22, 88, 89
O'Keefe, Laurence, 204, 205
Oklahoma!, 13, 16–17, 45, 59, 61, 65, 147, 177
Old Possum's Book of Practical Cats (Eliot), 38
Oliver!, 78–79
Oliver Twist (Dickens), 78
Olivo, Karen, 118
O'Malley, Rory, 120
On the Town, 57, 58–59, 69
Once, 122–123
Once and Future King, The (White), 74
Once on This Island, 220–221
110 in the Shade, 82–83
Orbach, Jerry, 86, 136, 152, 153, 190
Oremus, Stephen, 127
Orfeh, 204
Osato, Sono, 59
Oscar, Brad, 169, 244
Ost, Tobin, 125
Ostrow, Stuart, 251

P

Padula, Edward, 235
Page, Ken, 38, 214
Paige, Elaine, 195
Paige, Janis, 70
Pajama Game, The, 70–71, 73
Pal Joey, 144–145, 147, 165, 233, 267
Palace Theatre, 187
Panaro, Hugh, 53
Paper Mill Playhouse, 125
Papp, Joseph, 23, 135, 151
Parade, 140, 175, 266–267
Paramount Studios, 195
Parfumerie (László), 80
Parker, Dorothy, 46
Parker, Sarah Jessica, 193
Parker, Trey, 120, 121
Pascal, Adam, 26, 27
Pasek, Benj, 130, 131
Paterson, Vincent, 106, 107
Patinkin, Mandy, 98, 99, 104, 105, 194, 223
Paul, Justin, 130, 131
Paul VI (pope), 89
Paulus, Diane, 128, 129
Pawk, Michele, 162
Peacock, Michon, 151
Peter Pan, 178–179
Peters, Bernadette, 98, 99, 218, 219
Peters, Michael, 154
Petina, Irra, 46
Phantom of the Opera, The, 43, 52–53
Pierce, David Hyde, 240
Pinkins, Tonya, 164, 268, 269
Pinkleton, Sam, 274
Pinza, Ezio, 262
Pippin, 90–91
Pitre, Louise, 114
Platt, Ben, 130, 267
Playwrights Horizons, 99, 221
Poiret, Jean, 158
Porgy (play), 44
Porgy and Bess, 43, 44–45
Porter, Billy, 126
Porter, Cole, 119, 146, 147, 163, 177, 232, 233
Presley, Elvis, 235
Preston, Robert, 32, 33
Price, Leontyne, 45
Price, Lonny, 96
Prince, Daisy, 267
Prince, Harold
  Andrew Lloyd Webber and, 89
  Cabaret, 20, 21
  Candide, 47
  Company, 208, 209
  Evita, 194, 195
  Follies, 148, 149
  George Abbott and, 265
  Kiss of the Spider Woman, 106
  Little Night Music, A, 92, 93
  Merrily We Roll Along, 96, 97
  Pajama Game, The, 71
  Parade, 266, 267
  Phantom of the Opera, The, 52, 53
  She Loves Me, 80
  Show Boat, 15
  Stephen Sondheim and, 99
  Sweeney Todd: The Demon Barber of Fleet Street, 50, 51
  West Side Story, 265
Prince, Josh, 172
Princess Theatre Shows, 231
Pritchard, Lauren, 116
Prochnik, Bruce, 78
Producers, The, 168–169
Promises, Promises, 86–87
Pryce, Jonathan, 102, 103
Public Theater, 135, 151, 217, 257, 273
Puig, Manuel, 106
Pully, B.S., 31
Pygmalion (Shaw), 18, 19

R

Radner, Gilda, 213
Rado, James, 22
Ragni, Gerome, 22
Ragtime, 110–111
Rainmaker, The (Nash), 82, 83
Raisin, 210–211
Raisin in the Sun, A (Hansberry), 210
Raitt, John, 60, 61, 70, 71
Raize, Jason, 40
Ralph, Sheryl Lee, 154
Ramin, Sid, 181
Ramirez, Sara, 240, 241
Ramos, Anthony, 119
Rando, John, 112
Rannells, Andrew, 120, 121, 139
Rapp, Anthony, 26, 27, 139
Rawls, Lou, 211
Razaf, Andy, 214, 215
Reams, Lee Roy, 73, 152
Redfield, Liza, 33
Reichard, Daniel, 170
Reilly, Charles Nelson, 182
Reiner, Ethel, 47
Rent, 26–27
Revill, Clive, 78
Ribeiro, Alfonso, 253
Rice, Sarah, 50
Rice, Tim
  Beauty and the Beast, 108, 109
  Chess, 115
  Evita, 194
  First shows, 57
  Jesus Christ Superstar, 88, 89
  Lion King, The, 40
Rich, Frank, 219
Richards, Donald, 62
Richardson, Ron, 100, 101
Richert, Wanda, 152, 153
Riggs, Lynn, 16
Riley, Eric, 220
Ripley, Alice, 270
Ritchard, Cyril, 79, 178, 179
Rittman, Trude, 61, 67, 263
Rivera, Chita, 106, 190, 191, 234, 235, 264
Robbins, Jerome
  approach to choreography, 187
  director/choreographer dual role, 235
  Fiddler on the Roof, 36, 37
  Funny Girl, 185
  Funny Thing Happened on the Way to the Forum, A, 237
  Gypsy, 180
  King and I, The, 66, 67
  Pajama Game, The, 70
  Peter Pan, 178, 179
  On the Town, 58, 59
  West Side Story, 264, 265
Roberson, Ken, 226

Roberts, Jimmy, 139
Roberts, Joan, 16
rock musicals, 23, 139, 140, 225
Rodgers, Richard
Annie Get Your Gun, 177
attempt to musicalize *Pygmalion*, 19
Carousel, 57, 60
considered adapting *The Light in the Piazza*, 55
King and I, The, 66, 67
Me and Juliet, 147
Oklahoma!, 16–17
Pal Joey, 144, 145
Rodgers and Hammerstein format as model/inspiration, 65, 121, 127, 207
Sound of Music, The, 34, 35
South Pacific, 262
Rogers, Ginger, 163, 183, 191
Rolfing, Tom, 212
Ropes, Bradford, 152
Rose, Anika Noni, 268, 269
Ross, Diana, 155
Ross, Jerry, 70, 71, 72
Ross, Ted, 94
Roth, Robert Jess, 108
Rounseville, Robert, 46, 84
Royal Shakespeare Company, The, 25
Rubenstein, John, 90
Rubin-Vega, Daphne, 26, 27
Rudin, Scott, 121
Ruffelle, Frances, 24
Runyon, Damon, 30
Rupert, Michael, 207, 223
Rush, Geoffrey, 229
Russell, Brenda, 200, 201
Russell, Rosalind, 68, 69, 181
Ryan, Irene, 90, 91

S

Saddler, Donald, 68
Saidy, Fred, 62
Saks, Gene, 188
Salmon, Scott, 158
Salonga, Lea, 102, 103
Sands, Stark, 126, 127
Sankoff, Irene, 258
Sarnoff, Dorothy, 66
Sater, Steven, 116, 117
satirical musicals, 47, 63, 77, 113, 139
Sauter, Eddie, 251
Scardino, Don, 212
Schmidt, Harvey, 82, 83, 136
Schönberg, Claude-Michel, 24, 102
Schulman, Susan H., 104
Schumacher, Thomas, 41
Schwartz, Stephen, 90, 91, 198, 199, 212, 213
Scott, Bonnie, 76
Scott, Sherie Rene, 140
Sea Cliff Summer Theatre, 145
Second Stage Theatre, 271
Secret Garden, The, 104–105
Seesaw, 157
Segal, Vivienne, 144
Seibert, Wallace, 46
Sengbloh, Saycon, 199, 254
Serino Coyne marketing agency, 165
7½ Cents (Bissell), 70
1776, 250–251
Shaiman, Marc, 196, 197
Shakespeare, William, 145, 146, 245
Sharaff, Irene, 67
Sharman, Jim, 89
Shaw, George Bernard, 18, 19
She Loves Me, 80–81
Sheik, Duncan, 116, 117
Sheinkin, Rachel, 242, 243
Shelly, Adrienne, 128
Shelton, Reid, 192
Sher, Bartlett, 54
Shevelove, Burt, 236, 237
Shire, David, 141
Shor, Miriam, 139
Short, Martin, 213
Show Boat, 13, 14–15
Shubert Theatre, 163
Silvers, Phil, 237
Simon, Lucy, 104, 105
Simon, Neil, 86, 87, 186
Simon, Paul, 173
Simone, Lisa, 27
Sinatra, Frank, 93, 145
1600 Pennsylvania Avenue, 265
Smalls, Charlie, 94, 95
Smith, Alexis, 148
Smith, Oliver, 19, 59, 65, 75
Smith, Will and Jada Pinkett, 255
Sokolow, Anna, 46
Something Rotten!, 244–245
Sondheim, Stephen
Arthur Laurents and, 265
Candide, 47
Company, 208, 209
Follies, 148, 149
Funny Thing Happened on the Way to the Forum, A, 236, 237
Gypsy, 180, 181
Harold Prince and, 99
Into the Woods, 218, 219
Little Night Music, A, 92, 93
Merrily We Roll Along, 96, 97
Sunday in the Park with George, 98, 99
Sweeney Todd: The Demon Barber of Fleet Street, 50
West Side Story, 264
Songs for a New World, 267
Soo, Phillipa, 256
Sorkin, Aaron, 75
Sound of Music, The, 34–35, 233, 263
South Pacific, 262–263
Spamalot, 240–241
Spector, Jarrod, 172
Spencer, Elizabeth, 54
Spencer, J. Robert, 170, 270
Spewack, Bella and Samuel, 146, 147
Spielberg, Stephen, 201
Spring Awakening, 116–117
Stanley, Pat, 248
Stapleton, Maureen, 235
Stark, Fran, 185
Stark, Ray, 185
Steele, Lucas, 274
Stein, Joseph, 36
Stevens, Tony, 151
Stewart, Michael, 152, 182, 234
Stigwood, Robert, 89
Stilgoe, Richard, 52
Stone, David, 271
Stone, Matt, 120, 121
Stone, Peter, 250, 251
Story of the Trapp Family Singers, The (Trapp), 34
Streep, Meryl, 219
Streisand, Barbra, 93, 136, 183, 184, 185
Stritch, Elaine, 208, 209
Stroman, Susan, 141, 162, 163, 168, 169
Strouse, Charles, 183, 192, 193, 234
Styne, Jule
Funny Girl, 184, 185
Gypsy, 180, 181, 187
Pal Joey revival, 145
Peter Pan, 178, 179
Subways Are for Sleeping, 153
Sullivan, Ed, 75
Sullivan, Jo, 48, 136
Sullivan, Lee, 64
Sunday in the Park with George, 98–99, 201, 219
Suskin, Steven, 69
Sutherland, Claudette, 76
Swayze, Patrick, 239
Sweeney Todd: The Demon Barber of Fleet Street, 43, 50–51, 55, 123, 159, 189, 201, 275
Sweet Charity, 73, 161, 186–187, 203
Swenson, Inga, 82, 83
Swerling, Jo, 30
Syers, Mark, 194

T

Tabbert, William, 262
Tales of the South Pacific (Michener), 262, 263
Taming of the Shrew, The (Shakespeare), 146
Tamiris, Helen, 176
Tartaglia, John, 226
Tate, Jimmy, 253
Taylor, Clarice, 94
Taymor, Julie, 40, 41
Tebelak, John-Michael, 212, 213
Terris, Norma, 14
Tesori, Jeanine, 105, 167, 227, 268, 269, 272, 273
They Knew What They Wanted (Howard), 48
37 Arts Theatre, 255
Thompson, Jennifer Laura, 112
Thoroughly Modern Millie, 269
Threepenny Opera, The, 113, 127, 135, 136
Tiffany, John, 122, 123
Till the Clouds Roll By, 15
Tolstoy, Leo, 274, 275
Tommy. *See* Who's Tommy, The
Townshend, Pete, 224
Trapp, Maria Augusta, 34
Trask, Stephen, 139
Travolta, John, 197, 239
Trujillo, Sergio, 170, 270
Tune, Tommy, 156, 157
Tunick, Jonathan, 51, 87, 209
Tveit, Aaron, 270
Twain, Mark, 100
25th Annual Putnam County Spelling Bee, The, 242–243

U

Uggams, Leslie, 233
Uhry, Alfred, 266
Ulvaeus, Björn, 114, 115
Urinetown, 112–113

V

Vallee, Rudy, 76, 77
Van Druten, John, 20, 66
Van Dyke, Dick, 234
Van Laast, Anthony, 114
Vaughan, Sarah, 93
Verdon, Gwen, 53, 72, 73, 186, 187, 190
Vereen, Ben, 88, 90, 91
Verkaik, Willemijn, 199
Vestoff, Virginia, 250
Vickery, John, 40
Vineyard Theatre, 227
Voltaire, *Candide*, 46
Vye, Murvyn, 60

W

Wagner, Robin, 87, 153
Waitress, 128–129
Walker, Alice, 200, 201
Walker, Michael Patrick, 140
Waller, Thomas "Fats," 214, 215
Wallop, Douglass, 72
Walsh, Barbara, 222
Walsh, Enda, 122, 123
Walsh, Thommie, 156
Walston, Ray, 72, 73
Walton, Jim, 96
War and Peace (Tolstoy), 274, 275
Warfield, William, 45
Warner, Jack, 251
Warren, Harry, 152
Warren, Lesley Ann, 82
Warwick, Dionne, 87
Wasserman, Dale, 84, 85
Waters, Daryl, 252, 253
Waters, John, 196, 197
Watkins, Maurine Dallas, 190, 191
Watson, Janet, 100
Watson, Susan, 234
Wayne, David, 62
Wedekind, Frank, 116, 117
Weede, Robert, 48
Weidman, Jerome, 248
Weil, Cynthia, 172
Weill, Kurt, 101, 113, 136
Weinstock, Jack, 76
Weissler, Fran and Barry, 223
Wells, John, 47
West, Matt, 108
West Side Story, 17, 21, 33, 47, 81, 127, 161, 211, 231, 235, 237, 264–265, 269
Wheeler, Harold, 155, 197
Wheeler, Hugh, 47, 50, 51, 92
Where's Charley?, 49
White, Lillias, 254, 255
White, Onna, 32, 188, 250
White, T.H., 74
Whitty, Jeff, 226
Who's Tommy, The, 23, 27, 224–225
Wicked, 198–199
Wicked (Maguire), 198
Wilbur, Richard, 46, 47
Wilder, Gene, 169
Wilder, Thornton, 182
Wilkinson, Colm, 24
Williams, Sammy, 150, 159
Willis, Allee, 200, 201
Willson, Meredith, 32, 33
Wilson, John C., 146
Wilson, Mary Louise, 202
Wilson, Patricia, 248
Wilson, Patrick, 166
Winchell, Walter, 17
Windust, Bretaigne, 62
Winokur, Marissa Jaret, 196, 197
Winter Garden Theatre, 115
Withers-Mendes, Elisabeth, 200
Wittman, Scott, 196, 197
Wiz, The, 94–95
Wizard of Oz, The (film), 63
Wodehouse, P. G., 231, 232
Woldin, Judd, 210, 211
Wolfe, George C., 164, 165, 252, 268
Wonderful Town, 47, 68–69
Woodard, Charlayne, 214
Woolverton, Linda, 108, 109
Wright, Doug, 202, 203
Wright, Jeffrey, 252, 253
Wright, Samuel E., 40

Y

Yazbek, David, 166, 167
Year the Yankees Lost the Pennant, The (Wallop), 72
Yeston, Maury, 156, 157
York Theatre, 51
Yorkey, Brian, 270, 271
Young, John Lloyd, 170, 171
You're a Good Man, Charlie Brown, 137

Z

Zaltzberg, Charlotte, 210, 211
Zendaya, 221
Ziegfeld, Florenz, Jr., 15
Ziegfeld's *Follies*, 15, 41
Zien, Chip, 218, 222
Zippel, David, 160